Putting Knowledge to Work

Putting Knowledge to Work

New Directions for Knowledge-First Epistemology

Edited by
ARTŪRS LOGINS
JACQUES-HENRI VOLLET

OXFORD
UNIVERSITY PRESS

Great Clarendon Street, Oxford, OX2 6DP,
United Kingdom

Oxford University Press is a department of the University of Oxford.
It furthers the University's objective of excellence in research, scholarship,
and education by publishing worldwide. Oxford is a registered trade mark of
Oxford University Press in the UK and in certain other countries

© the several contributors 2024

The moral rights of the authors have been asserted

All rights reserved. No part of this publication may be reproduced, stored in
a retrieval system, or transmitted, in any form or by any means, without the
prior permission in writing of Oxford University Press, or as expressly permitted
by law, by licence or under terms agreed with the appropriate reprographics
rights organization. Enquiries concerning reproduction outside the scope of the
above should be sent to the Rights Department, Oxford University Press, at the
address above

You must not circulate this work in any other form
and you must impose this same condition on any acquirer

Published in the United States of America by Oxford University Press
198 Madison Avenue, New York, NY 10016, United States of America

British Library Cataloguing in Publication Data
Data available

Library of Congress Control Number: 2024930842

ISBN 9780192882370

DOI: 10.1093/9780191976766.001.0001

Printed and bound in the UK by
Clays Ltd, Elcograf S.p.A.

Links to third party websites are provided by Oxford in good faith and
for information only. Oxford disclaims any responsibility for the materials
contained in any third party website referenced in this work.

Contents

Preface	vii
Acknowledgments	ix
List of Contributors	xi

1. Introduction: Taking Knowledge-First Further   1
   Artūrs Logins and Jacques-Henri Vollet

PART 1 HISTORICAL PERSPECTIVES ON KNOWLEDGE-FIRST

2. Where Did It Come From? Where Will It Go?   21
   Timothy Williamson

3. Knowledge as Presence and Presentation: Highlights from the History of Knowledge-First Epistemology   71
   Maria Rosa Antognazza

4. Śrīharṣa on the Indefinability of Knowledge Events   93
   Nilanjan Das

PART 2 KNOWLEDGE AS A MENTAL STATE

5. How the Brain Makes Knowledge First   129
   Robert M. Gordon

6. Factive Mindreading in the Folk Psychology of Action   145
   Carlotta Pavese

7. Natural Curiosity   170
   Jennifer Nagel

8. The Point of Knowledge ... is to Make Good Decisions!   201
   Moritz Schulz

PART 3 KNOWLEDGE AS EXPLANATORILY PRIME

9. Knowledge-First Philosophy of Science   221
   Alexander Bird

10. Wilful Hermeneutical Ignorance to the (Qualified) Rescue of Knowledge-First   237
    Veli Mitova

11. Reasons and Knowledge 260
    Christina H. Dietz and John Hawthorne

12. Knowledge and Prizes 284
    Clayton Littlejohn and Julien Dutant

13. Perceptual Knowledge and the 'Activity' of Belief 308
    Johannes Roessler

Index 331

Preface

Since the publication of Timothy Williamson's groundbreaking book *Knowledge and its Limits* in 2000, the knowledge-first approach has occupied center stage in contemporary epistemology. The essence of the approach is to rethink epistemology by taking knowledge to be prime and fundamental. Epistemologists have discussed extensively the advantages and potential shortcomings of the knowledge-first approach since the publication of Williamson's influential book. One thing, however, has been overlooked in connection to knowledge-first. Despite being an extremely fruitful paradigm in epistemology, where it has generated much new insight and debate, the knowledge-first program has not yet been evaluated with regard to its outward fruitfulness.

The aim of the present volume is to do precisely this. Williamson himself acknowledges that we should judge the knowledge-first approach in the light of its fruitfulness as a research program (cf. Williamson 2013: 6–7). The present volume takes this claim at face value and investigates how interesting and insightful it is to endorse a knowledge-centered approach both within and outside of epistemology. The volume thus has both a broad and a narrow scope. It is about knowledge. But it is also about new and exciting ways of using (the notion of) knowledge in a broader context. After twenty years of fruitful development within traditional epistemology, the time is ripe for exploring knowledge-first implications outside of traditional epistemological debates.

The main audience is epistemologists (including graduate students). This volume will also be useful to philosophers of science, historians of philosophy, philosophers working on value theory (broadly understood), philosophers of emotions and mind, and philosophers of cognitive sciences and perception. Given its scope, the volume will be a useful addition to courses and seminars on applied epistemology as primary or secondary literature.

The idea of preparing a volume on new perspectives for the knowledge-first approach grew out of an insightful conference we had a chance to organize at the University of Geneva for the twentieth anniversary of the publication of *Knowledge and its Limits*, *KAIL at 20* in 2020 (online only). Some of the chapters in this volume are descendants of talks at that conference.

Acknowledgments

We would like to thank all our contributors and all the reviewers for individual chapters. We learned so much from each chapter and the exchanges between authors and reviewers. We would like to extend our deepest condolences to the family of Maria Rosa Antognazza. We would like to thank Howard Hotson for agreeing to include Maria Rosa's minimally updated final version of the paper in the volume, for his assistance in preparing the final version of the paper, and for composing the abstract. Thanks also to Peter Momtchiloff for continuous support during the preparation of the volume and for his encouragement. Thanks to all the people from OUP for the help with the volume, in particular Jamie Mortimer. Thanks to anonymous reviewers for OUP for their insightful comments and suggestions on the volume. Thanks also to Fabrice Teroni, who encouraged us to move on with the volume project and helped us make our idea of the volume concrete. Above all, we would like to thank our families for supporting us all along. The work that led to this publication was supported by Swiss National Science Foundation grants Number 169293 and 186137 and by the Chair of Metaphysics and Philosophy of Knowledge, Collège de France, Paris, France.

List of Contributors

†Maria Rosa Antognazza, King's College London

Alexander Bird, University of Cambridge

Nilanjan Das, University of Toronto

Christina H. Dietz, University of Southern California

Julien Dutant, King's College London

Robert M. Gordon, University of Missouri, St. Louis

John Hawthorne, University of Southern California

Clayton Littlejohn, Australian Catholic University and University of Johannesburg

Artūrs Logins, Université Laval, Québec

Veli Mitova, University of Johannesburg

Jennifer Nagel, University of Toronto

Carlotta Pavese, Cornell University

Johannes Roessler, University of Warwick

Moritz Schulz, Technische Universität Dresden

Jacques-Henri Vollet, Collège de France, Paris

Timothy Williamson, University of Oxford

1

Introduction

Taking Knowledge-First Further

Artūrs Logins and Jacques-Henri Vollet

1. Introduction

It will be extremely difficult, if it is possible at all, for historians of epistemology to describe epistemological debates of the first quarter of the twenty-first century without mentioning the knowledge-first program. Ever since the publication of Timothy Williamson's *Knowledge and its Limits* (Williamson 2000), knowledge-first epistemology—the approach that breaks with the tradition of analyzing knowledge in putatively more fundamental elements (e.g. justified true belief) and proposes instead to appeal to knowledge as prime and fundamental in our theorizing—has been a major player in contemporary epistemology. It is essential for the knowledge-first approach that appeals to knowledge in order to explain other interesting properties and statuses can be shown to be theoretically fruitful.

Most of the debates concerning knowledge-first have been focused on treating well-known epistemological topics by putting knowledge first. For instance, much has been done to show that knowledge can be central to explaining epistemic justification or rationality or that knowledge sets the fundamental norm of belief, assertion, and, in a sense, action. Knowledge has been proposed as fundamental for understanding evidence and evidential probability and even as the basic element in our responses to skeptical challenges. All in all, most of the recent discussions of the knowledge-first approach have remained within more or less traditional topics of epistemology. The lessons of fundamentality of knowledge have been drawn mostly only for other epistemically interesting properties and statuses.

The ambition of the present volume, as we mention in the Preface, is to take the lessons from putting knowledge first even further, namely, to see how far the knowledge-first program can go beyond standard and well-worn topics in epistemology. The aim of the present introduction is to provide a bit more of the background for the volume. In what follows, we first introduce some central elements of the knowledge-first program in epistemology. What is it, and what are its central claims? Then, we situate our volume in the actual context of debates and existing volumes. And finally, we introduce the chapters of the present volume.

2. Knowledge-First Program: A (Very Quick) Overview

The knowledge-first approach in epistemology gained popularity in the 2000s as a fresh alternative to the increasingly sophisticated and sometimes tedious efforts of defining knowledge as a justified true belief of some sort. The idea of defining/analyzing knowledge as justified true belief was put forward by epistemologists of the first half of the twentieth century, arguably, in an effort to block general skepticism about the possibility of knowledge while admitting that knowledge doesn't entail certainty or the impossibility of being wrong (cf. Dutant 2015). However, the tripartite analysis of knowledge as justified true belief ran into trouble due to the tremendously impactful counterexamples from Edmund Gettier (Gettier 1963). Epistemology of the second half of the twentieth century was focused chiefly on responding to Gettier and ever increasingly complex Gettier-style counterexamples. By the end of the century, the effort of Gettierology reached a level of sophistication that raised some doubts about the very project of defining knowledge. Williamson's *Knowledge and its Limits* (2000) and his articles that preceded the book were perceived then as a fresh alternative to the reigning approach in dealing with the Gettier cases. In a way, it incarnated the growing sentiment of the futility of trying to find a fitting analysis of knowledge. To put it simply, Williamson suggested ending the project of analyzing knowledge (and, to put it mildly, lowering our hopes in conceptual analysis in general). For Williamson, knowledge is unanalyzable; it is a *sui generis* state that cannot be explained or defined by an appeal to some more fundamental constituents. This is, as we may call it, the core negative claim of knowledge-first: knowledge cannot be analyzed/defined in more fundamental terms.

However, it is important to note that knowledge-first is not merely a negative project. It also has two positive core claims. The first positive claim is that, despite the impossibility of analyzing/defining knowledge, it can nonetheless be characterized and described in some theoretically insightful ways. For instance, it can be characterized as the most general factive mental state. The second positive claim is that appeals to knowledge can be used to explain other interesting states, properties, and statuses.

In order to present the positive claims, in particular the claim that knowledge can be used as a fundamental element in our epistemological theorizing, it will be useful to present another crucial element of the knowledge-first program as defended by Williamson. Namely, we should mention that central to much of Williamson's theorizing is the rejection of luminosity and the anti-luminosity argument. To say that luminosity fails is to say, roughly, that for any non-trivial condition C, one cannot always know that one is in C whenever one is in C. Applied to knowledge, the claim is that one cannot always know that one knows whenever one knows. This claim can be understood as rejecting a popular KK principle from epistemic logic (cf. Hintikka 1962), according to which whenever one knows that p, one knows that one knows that p (schematically: Kp → KKp). (Note also that, according to Williamson, anti-luminosity applies also to other conditions, not only to knowledge). The rejection of luminosity (or the KK failure) relies on the influential and much-discussed anti-luminosity argument developed in detail in Williamson (2000, ch. 4). Very roughly, the argument relies on the assumption that knowledge is safe—that is, when one knows that p, one couldn't be easily wrong about p and that in situations of gradual small changes, say, in a situation where one goes from experiencing cold to not experiencing cold, combining the luminosity principle with a principle of margin for error (roughly, that if one knows that O obtains at case 1, O obtains also at the close case 2) leads to a contradiction. For Williamson, the margin-for-error principle follows from the general safety principle. According to the anti-luminosity argument, then, to avoid the contradiction, we have to give up the luminosity principle. Very roughly, we get the gist of the argument when we think of a situation where, in the morning, we are clearly cold and know that we are cold, and we imagine that at noon, the temperature has warmed up, and we are clearly not cold. The idea, then, is that there will be a moment during the gradual warming up where our discriminatory powers will not be powerful enough to distinguish the experience of cold from that of not being cold (but at that moment, we will be either cold or not). And since knowledge entails not being easily wrong, we will have to admit that there will be a moment when we will not be in a position to know whether we are cold or not. For further discussion and a more detailed presentation, see Berker 2008 and Srinivasan 2013, among others. Note that the argument doesn't rely only on this specific case; it is rather an illustration of the general idea that safety and in particular its instance in the margin-for-error cases clash inevitably with the idea that we are always in a position to know that a non-trivial condition obtains whenever it obtains.

We can now return to the two positive core claims of knowledge-first. The first was that, according to proponents of knowledge-first, knowledge could be positively characterized, where characterizing is distinct from analyzing or defining and is more akin to a demonstrative showing of the sort of thing we are talking about. According to Williamson, knowledge can be positively characterized as "the most general factive mental stative propositional attitude" (Williamson 2000, 39; see also Williamson 2011 and Nagel 2013). A factive state is such a state that necessarily and for all propositions p, if one has it toward p, then p is true (Williamson 2000, 39). The idea, then, is that knowledge just is (=is characterized as) the state (a stative propositional attitude) one is in whenever one is in a factive mental stative propositional attitude, for example when one remembers that p when one sees that p, and so on. It is important to note that the relevant factive states (of which knowledge is the most general one) are picked out by what Williamson calls Factive Mental State Operators (FMSOs) (Williamson 2000, 34). FMSOs are (i) factive, (ii) states (rather than processes) denoting, (iii) propositional attitudes denoting, and (iv) semantically unanalyzable (Williamson 2000, 34–7). Specifying these conditions allows one not to count believing truly as a state denoted by an FMSO, since 'believing truly' can be further analyzed into 'believes' and 'truly'.

To say that knowledge is the most general factive mental stative propositional attitude is to say that knowledge is a mental state. Hardcore knowledge-firsters take this characterization of knowledge at face value and endorse the claim that knowledge is a *genuine* or *purely mental* state as opposed to, say, a state that is reducible to further mental and non-mental combinations (see Williamson 2000, chs 1–3; Nagel 2013, 2017; Logins 2021; another alternative would be to avoid discussing the mentality of knowledge altogether and insist that knowledge is, say, a social kind; cf. Craig 1990). To characterize knowledge as a genuine mental state then brings up new avenues for knowledge-firsters to theorize about knowledge and its roles or functions in our cognitive and overall mental economy. According to a common assumption in the philosophy of mind, if a state is a genuine mental state (a pure mental state), then it has to be indispensable in, say, action explanation (cf. Noonan 1993, 283–308). More generally, the idea is that if knowledge is a mental state, it has to contribute in an indispensable way in explaining our mental lives, as, for example, in explaining some action. Proponents of knowledge-first have taken up the challenge and proposed concrete instances where knowledge cannot be dispensed with in a good explanation of action or other mental states. For instance, in a famous passage from *Knowledge and its Limits* (62–64), Williamson argues that there are possible cases where only appeals to knowledge can explain some action. One case he imagines is that of a persistent ransacking of a house by a burglar. The persistent action is best explained by the fact that the burglar knows rather than merely believes that there is a diamond in the house. Knowledge makes a difference in explaining why he is not giving up. Knowledge-first skeptics have found the proposal and the case unconvincing and have proposed a number of objections (see Molyneux 2007; McGlynn 2014, 2017; Kipper 2018; see Logins 2021 for a response to some objections). Knowledge-firsters have argued that the objections are misguided and that further empirically informed research supports the indispensability of knowledge in our explanations of action and of the mental more generally (cf. Nagel 2013, 2017; Logins 2021; see also Turri 2017). It would seem that the debate is still on, and the increase of empirical and theoretical studies on mindreading and (folk) action explanation is helping to move the debate on.

The second positive knowledge-first core claim is where most of elaborations of it as well as objections to it have been concentrated. Namely, it is the claim that, roughly, knowledge is the unexplained explainer: We can appeal to knowledge in our explanations of other interesting and important properties, states, statuses, aspects, etc. So, for instance, according to proponents of knowledge-first, evidence can be explained in terms of knowledge, since all of one's evidence is one's knowledge, and all of one's knowledge is evidence one has (E = K). Defenses of (E = K) can be found in Hyman 2006 and Williamson 2000 (and in a sense, in Unger 1975, assuming that reasons to believe are evidence). Once one agrees that evidence is explained in terms of knowledge, one can also use this to propose a knowledge-based approach to evidential probability (see Williamson 2000, ch. 10). Of course, the claim that evidence is defined by appeal to knowledge has received an important number of objections. See Logins 2016, 2017 for an overview and further references. We can also note that assuming the general failure of luminosity allows proponents of knowledge-first to maintain that one is not always in a position to know what evidence one has. This has interesting repercussions with respect to debates on both skepticism and justification, to which we turn now.

The anti-luminosity argument and the idea that knowledge is fundamental are key elements in the knowledge-first approach to general skepticism (see Williamson 2000, ch. 8). The anti-luminosity argument allows one to block the skeptical argument for the general conclusion that we don't know that the external world exists, since that relies on the idea that, to know something, we have to be able to rule out competing alternatives. According to this assumption, for me to know that, say, it is sunny outside, I have to be able to rule out the alternative that it is raining outside. Radical skeptics about the possibility of knowledge about the external world then appeal to this assumption and the idea that massive and radical deception à la Descartes might actually be the case, and we might not even notice it. A radical scenario of massive deception involves us not noticing that we are deceived about the external world. But that means, then, that in order to know that the external world exists, we have to rule out the radical deception scenario, or, in other words, we have to rule out and know that it is not the case that we don't know that the external world exists. Crucially, skeptics argue we are not able to rule out such an alternative. How could we? We couldn't even notice we are being deceived if we were radically deceived. Thus, skeptics argue we don't know that the external world exists (see Stroud 1984). Rejecting Luminosity allows knowledge-firsters to block this skeptical argument by rejecting the assumption that, to know that the external world exists, we have to rule out and know that it is not the case that we are radically deceived on a well-motivated and independent basis. In other words, given the KK failure, proponents of knowledge-first can reject the claim that, to know that p (the external world exists), we must K not-not-Kp, which just amounts to KKp (see Weisberg 2021 for an overview of the argument). We don't always know that we know that p when we know that p, so it cannot be a reasonable requirement for knowing that p. If it is not the case that, to know that p, we have to know that we know that p, we can then reject the claim that, to know that the external world exists, we must know that we are not in a radical deception scenario (that is, that we know that it is not the case that we don't know that the external world exists). We might just know that the external world exists. Knowing is explanatorily fundamental according to knowledge-firsters, and at some point we may just stop engaging with further skeptical scruples:

> This is the usual case with philosophical treatments of skepticism: they are better at prevention than at cure. If a refutation of skepticism is supposed to reason one out of the hole, then skepticism is irrefutable.
>
> (Williamson 2000, 27)

Another place where knowledge has been said to play an insightful explanatory role is the debate concerning epistemic justification. In short, according to the proponents of the knowledge-first approach, the conditions for justified belief can be specified in terms of knowledge. The debate has been so intense on this front that, unfortunately, we cannot elaborate on it here (see Silva 2020 for a recent overview of the debate). Let us present, roughly, two trends within the knowledge-first tradition of thinking about justified belief: the demanding and the more relaxed knowledge-first views (or, alternatively, the radical and the moderate). On the demanding view, only when one knows that p, one has a justified belief that p (Sutton 2007; Williamson 2011). A way to spell this idea out is to maintain that to have a justified belief is to comply with the fundamental knowledge norm of belief (Williamson 2011, forthcoming). We present some more details of this in the next paragraph. On the more relaxed approach, one is not required to know that p to have a justified belief that p. However, even on the more relaxed approach, it is still knowledge that plays a crucial role in justification of a belief. One way of spelling this idea out is to endorse the E=K principle about evidence and then adopt a broadly evidentialist view of justification, according to which, roughly, to be justified in believing that p is to have sufficient evidence for p. A view close to this is suggested in Williamson (2000, 208); see also Dutant (forthcoming). Another popular way to spell the more relaxed view out is to insist that to be justified in believing that p just is to be in a state that is indistinguishable from one's own perspective from the state of knowing (see Bird 2007). More versions of the relaxed view have been proposed in the literature by, for instance, combining the knowledge-first approach with the idea that reasons also play a role in justification (see reasons-first knowledge-first views, for instance, in Lord 2018) or with the idea that dispositions play a role in determining justification (see Lasonen-Aarnio 2010, 2021; Williamson forthcoming) or with the idea that virtues, skills, or competences play a role in justification (Miracchi 2015, forthcoming; Kelp 2016, 2017, 2018) or with the idea that justified beliefs can be understood as fulfilling a knowledge-centered function (see Simion 2019). Still other relaxed or mixed knowledge-first approaches to explaining epistemic justification exist and most of them have received a good deal of discussion and objections in the recent literature (see Silva 2020 for an overview).

As mentioned in the paragraph above, one way of elaborating the demanding or radical knowledge-first view of epistemic justification is to suggest that belief is governed by a fundamental knowledge norm that specifies its correctness/appropriateness conditions and that a justified belief just is a belief that complies with the norm that says, roughly, that one ought not to believe that p unless one knows/is in a position to know that p (see Williamson 2011, 2014, forthcoming; Sutton 2005, 2007; Littlejohn 2017). This approach to explaining justified belief by appeal to a fundamental knowledge norm of belief can be seen as being a part of the 'normative knowledge-first package,' that is, of the knowledge norms (for a recent overview of various knowledge norms, see Benton 2014). The knowledge norm of belief comes, for some knowledge-firsters, together with the knowledge norm of assertion and the knowledge norm of action (and some have suggested even further knowledge norms, e.g. the knowledge-norm of blame; cf. Kelp 2020. Some have questioned the very idea that all these norms should be seen as having a common element, though; see McKenna 2016). According to the knowledge norm of assertion, one ought not to assert that p unless one knows that p (Williamson 2000, ch. 11; see Benton 2014 for further references). The idea is that the knowledge norm of assertion and other knowledge norms are constitutive; they set the internal standard for the very speech act of assertion (or the attitude of belief) in the spirit of the constitutive norms as discussed by Searle (1969). The knowledge norm of action specifies when it is reasonable to act (when one has a reason to act) by requiring knowledge (rather than, say, a mere belief) of the relevant propositions on which one is supposed to act (see Hawthorne & Stanley 2008). Of course, all of the knowledge norms have also received a number of criticisms and objections (for a non-exhaustive list, see Benton 2014). But the debate continues, and discussing the relevant knowledge norms has been a way of elaborating the general idea that knowledge is normatively significant. Note also that some of the more recent debates on knowledge norms contain discussions of a more fine-grained normative picture. For instance, opponents of the idea that knowledge is the norm of belief and that a justified belief is just a belief that complies with the knowledge norm of belief have found this normative picture too demanding. Certainly, according to critics, someone who is, unbeknownst to themselves, in a radically deceived situation and forms a false belief about the external world is doing OK justification-wise (see Silva 2020 for references). Knowledge-first proponents have replied by distinguishing justification from the more general condition of being blameless. Surely, knowledge-firsters respond, the victim of the deception is not blameworthy; they are just OK because they are excused in believing the way they do. But to be excused (and blameless by excuse) is not the same as being positively justified in believing (Littlejohn 2009, 2012, forthcoming; Williamson forthcoming). Critics are not impressed, though. For them, there is just nothing to be excused for in the cases of radical deception (Gerken 2011; see Silva 2020 for further references). The discussion continues (see, e.g., Vollet 2022 for a recent defense of the excuse maneuver). One recent tendency among knowledge-first proponents or knowledge-first sympathizers seems to be to move toward more disposition-centered accounts of normativity and justification in the case of belief (Lasonen-Aarnio 2021; Kelp 2018; Hughes 2021). Williamson himself has proposed recently (Williamson, 2017) distinguishing the rationality of someone who conforms their beliefs to their evidence (content rationality) and the rationality of someone who is generally disposed to conform their beliefs to the evidence (disposition rationality). At any rate, elaborating on knowledge norms and further normative distinctions and aspects is another place where much debate on knowledge-first has taken place and where knowledge-firsters have seen another fruitful application of knowledge in explaining other important properties and statuses.

Overall, we can see that the knowledge-first debates until now have mostly concentrated on the traditionally central questions in epistemology, for example evidence, skepticism, self-knowledge (luminosity), justification, and epistemic norms. Less has been done to explore how far knowledge-first ideas can be taken outside the well-worn topics of contemporary epistemology. Yet it is certainly an aspect that we need to consider in our overall assessment of the knowledge-first program: how fruitful it is in breaking new ground. The new insights it brings should be considered when deciding whether to take the knowledge-first leap.

3. Context, Existing Volumes, and What Is in the Present Volume

As we have seen, the knowledge-first program is characterized by three theses: the negative thesis that knowledge cannot be reductively analyzed into more fundamental constituents and the two positive theses that knowledge is the most general factive mental state and that it can be used in illuminating explanations of other important epistemological notions (such as evidence, reason, justification, and belief). Prominent discussions of these three theses have so far mainly taken place in the context of classical philosophical problems and in response to Williamson's version of the knowledge-first program (as stated in particular in *Knowledge and its Limits*).

A first important volume, edited by P. Greenough and D. Pritchard (2009), presents the first reactions of leading epistemologists to Williamson's proposal in *Knowledge and its Limits* (as well as Williamson's responses). It considers whether knowledge can be analyzed (Q. Cassam; R. Neta), whether and in what sense it is a factive mental state (E. Fricker; F. Jackson; M. Steup; E. Sosa; N. Tennant), and, finally, how putting knowledge first fares in illuminating traditional epistemological issues, including that of evidence and epistemic probability (A. Brueckner; A. Goldman; J. Hawthorne & M. Lasonen-Aarnio; M. Kaplan), skepticism (S. Schiffer), assertion (S. Goldberg; J. Kvanvig), and truth (C. Travis).

A second noteworthy collection of essays, edited by J. A. Carter, E. Gordon, and B. W. Jarvis (2017), provides enlightening discussions of fundamental issues of the knowledge-first program and some ways of expanding it to questions mostly located in classical epistemology and philosophy of mind. The first thesis of the knowledge-first program is discussed in relation to its methodological implications (M. Gerken; Jenkins Ichikawa & C. S. I. Jenkins). The second is approached from the perspective of its psychological bases and consequences (A. McGlynn; M. Smith). The third is explored, first, by considering possible extensions of the knowledge-first methodology to other structurally similar traditional problems, such as that of perception (H. Logue) and action (T. Williamson); second, by evaluating the role of knowledge in relation to the most-discussed epistemological notions of reason (C. Littlejohn), assertion (J. Schechter), justification (A. Meylan), inquiry (J. Turri), and virtue (C. Kelp). The chapters on anti-individualism (D. Pritchard & J. Kallestrup) and legal epistemology (M. Blome-Tillmann) pave the way for an examination of the knowledge-first program in relation to more recent trends in research in epistemology.

Finally, McGlynn (2014) is the first monograph (and the only one so far) providing an overall critical discussion of the knowledge-first program focusing on Williamson's main theses.

The knowledge-first program has been extremely fruitful so far. It has inspired several major books in epistemology, revitalizing the main epistemological theories already on the market and providing new lines of research. For example, Hawthorne (2004) and Stanley (2005) explore and defend knowledge-first variants of pragmatic encroachment in epistemology; Kelp (2018) proposes a knowledge-first approach in the context of virtue epistemology and DeRose (2009) and Ichikawa (2017 in the context of epistemic contextualism. Several books use knowledge-first approaches to understand the notions of justification and what it is to have a reason (Sutton 2007; Littlejohn 2012; and Lord 2018). More recently, Simion (2021) and Kelp & Simion (2021) adopted a knowledge-first perspective to defend functionalist accounts of speech acts (such as assertion). The present overview is hardly an exhaustive list (see Benton 2014 and Silva 2020 for further references).

It is clear that the knowledge-first program is ongoing and extremely lively in classical analytic epistemology (see also the recent topical collection edited by Kelp & Simion 2023). Still, since the publication of *Knowledge and its Limits*, analytic philosophy has gradually gained new territories. It has shown more and more interest in the history of philosophy, philosophy of emotion, artificial intelligence, and social issues, among others. Analytic epistemology has been playing an important role in that development (think, for example, of current debates on the notion of epistemic injustice initiated by Fricker 2007)). It is not a wholly implausible conjecture that the knowledge-first program has contributed to that evolution. Reciprocally, recent developments in analytic philosophy and, more particularly, in epistemology have also influenced the evolution of the knowledge-first program. While exploring the details of this fruitful interaction is far beyond the topic of the present collection, the chapters offered here constitute important steps in that direction. They represent noteworthy attempts to push the knowledge-first program beyond the classical issues in epistemology and to evaluate its prospects from fresh perspectives.

The volume has three parts. Part 1 adopts a historical perspective on the idea that knowledge is first. In Chapter 2, "Where Did It Come From? Where Will It Go?," Timothy Williamson both revisits and puts forward some new perspectives for the knowledge-first program as it was elaborated in his seminal *Knowledge and its Limits* (Williamson 2000, abbreviated as "KAIL"). The chapter is autobiographical and offers personal reflections on how exactly the ideas of KAIL came together in the philosophical context of the late twentieth century. The chapter also gives an overview of the history prior to KAIL, particularly in connection to Oxford realism. In explaining the main philosophical ingredients and motivations of KAIL, Williamson focuses in particular on his earlier work on indiscriminability, knowledge–action connection, philosophy of mind (in particular, externalism about content and attitudes), and assertability. In discussing the new perspectives and the future of knowledge-first ideas, Williamson focuses in particular on the role of knowledge in mindreading (especially the "shared world" approach to mindreading), the role of knowledge in action, models of knowledge, and epistemic norms (especially in connection to anti-luminosity and externalist norms). This chapter is a must-read for anyone interested in the intellectual development of Williamson's knowledge-first program as well as in further paths this program is likely to be taking.

In Chapter 3, "Knowledge as Presence and Presentation: Highlights from the History of Knowledge-First Epistemology," Maria Rosa Antognazza revisits aspects of the Western history of knowledge-first and focuses in particular on what appears to be a robust version of a knowledge-first approach. Antognazza looks into details of theories of cognition from three authors of the early twentieth century who were interested in the new field of scientific psychology and conceived of knowledge as presentation of reality to mind. Knowledge on this view is more fundamental, and belief comes only later in our cognitive journey. Theories of cognition of similar outlook can also be found in authors of the late Middle Ages. Antognazza focuses here in particular on three authors: Duns Scotus, Auriel, and Ockham. For them, knowledge is a cognitive contact of mind with reality. Belief is a cognition that has its own function, but knowledge is more fundamental and prime. The focus on these two periods is justified as an exemplification of the idea that the general knowledge-first approach on which our cognition starts with knowledge and that other sorts of cognition can be explained by appeal to knowledge seems to be a robust view that appears in different intellectual traditions, and we might think that this very fact illustrates that this view captures fundamentals about our cognition.

Recently, there has been an increasing interest among mainstream epistemologists in non-Western epistemological traditions. In particular, there has been an increase in interest in Sanskrit epistemology. Arguably, part of this recent interest in mainstream epistemology has been driven by realizing that cases similar to Gettier cases have been discussed by Sanskrit epistemologists of South Asia since at least the twelfth century CE. Some have also observed knowledge-first themes in Sanskrit epistemology, for example the idea that knowledge cannot be defined. In his historically well-informed and thoroughly resourced chapter (Chapter 4), "Śrīharṣa on the Indefinability of Knowledge-Events," Nilanjan Das revisits the twelfth-century epistemologist Śrīharṣa and his arguments against proponents of the Nyāya approach. Śrīharṣa, according to Das, argues against Nyāya epistemologist proposals to define knowledge events (the focus is on knowledge events, which can be distinguished from knowledge more generally). In arguing for the indefinability of the knowledge event, Śrīharṣa mobilizes Gettier-style counterexamples. Das moves the historical debate forward by maintaining a more nuanced picture with respect to the question of whether Śrīharṣa can be seen as a proponent of the knowledge-first view. While Śrīharṣa argues for the indefinability of knowledge events, he stops short of accepting another core thesis of knowledge-first epistemology, namely, the thesis that knowledge is a unified kind of mental state. According to Das, Śrīharṣa puts forward a much more skeptical position, according to which we cannot conclude that there is a unified mental-kind knowledge event that is tracked by our knowledge-event ascriptions.

The chapters of the Part 2 examine new ways in which the characterization of knowledge as (the most general) factive mental state can be useful for advancing debates on psychology and philosophy of action, mind, and decision.

In Chapter 5, "How the Brain Makes Knowledge First," Robert M. Gordon gives an overview of an increasingly popular and exciting research line in cognition, namely inverse planning, which exploits the idea of the predictive mind, namely that in planning our behavior and explaining the behavior of others our brain predicts and then adjusts or corrects its predictions given whether the expected outcome is confirmed or not, rather than planning from intention to behavior. This way of understanding mentalizing (attributing mental states to others) fits well, according to Gordon, with the "shared world" explanation approach. The empirically supported observation that knowledge attributions are more basic (compared with belief attributions) is only natural, given the shared world approach and predictive planning. Gordon concludes his contribution by extending the shared world and predictive model to a possible explanation not only of behavior (and planning) but also of factive emotions and the difference between factive and other emotions.

It has recently been argued on the basis of experimental data that others' behaviors are primarily understood and predicted thanks to a factive mindreading capacity. In Chapter 6, "Factive Mindreading in the Folk Psychology of Action," Carlotta Pavese questions the role that this capacity could play with respect to skilled and intentional actions ascriptions. She reviews the main experimental studies and shows that, overall, the data lend support to the hypothesis that ascriptions of know-how and propositional knowledge underlie ascriptions of skilled and intentional actions.

In Chapter 7, "Natural Curiosity," Jennifer Nagel explores an empirically up-to-date knowledge-centered explanation of the phenomenon of natural curiosity: the intriguing observation that human and nonhuman animals are curious. The phenomenon is intriguing, since curiosity in humans and animals seems to be best understood as a desire for knowledge for its own sake. Countless experiments indicate that humans and nonhuman animals don't desire merely to know information relevant to the pursuit of their needs or practical aims; they engage in curious behavior on countless apparently useless topics. What explains this curious natural phenomenon is the main question that Nagel aims to answer. In approaching this question, she first reviews the large and rich empirical literature on natural curiosity in nonhuman animals and humans. She then considers a recent alternative, a non-knowledge-centered account of curiosity proposed by Peter Carruthers. In this view, curiosity is not a desire for knowledge (at least not in the strong sense that Nagel defends), since it is a view that downplays the metacognitive aspect. Nagel suggests that even in the more recent version of the view, where a model with less metacognition is accepted, the view still appears to leave something important out. Nagel then reviews a large literature on Reinforcement Learning in artificial-intelligence agents and demonstrates how the differences between curious and incurious agents can be modeled precisely. This modeling helps to understand better the importance of curiosity (as the desire for knowledge, for its own sake) in humans and animals. The key to understanding it is that curiosity allows agents like us in complex environments to be better prepared for long-term tasks by providing ready-to-use tools to motivate us into exploratory behavior. Having these tools is advantageous in a complex environment where the relevant rewards connected to food and reproduction are only sparsely available.

In Chapter 8, "The Point of Knowledge... is to Make Good Decisions!," Moritz Schulz investigates the function of our folk concept of knowledge. He locates the point of tracing knowledge in the fact that knowledge enables good decision-making by providing optimal information for fallible agents. He also argues that the point of ascribing knowledge has to do with the monitoring of our social practice of assertion. This practice has the function of sharing knowledge, and that is effectively done if assertions are governed by a knowledge norm.

Finally, Part 3 is devoted to extensions of the knowledge-first program to fields of research inside and beyond epistemology strictly understood. In Chapter 9,

"Knowledge-First Philosophy of Science," Alexander Bird argues that a functionalist and knowledge-first epistemological perspective on science and scientific evidence allows new solutions to traditional problems, such as that of scientific progress and of the confirmation and refutation of theories by evidence. On Bird's view (realist and anti-realist) empiricism and the ensuing Duhem–Quine thesis should be rejected. One can think of scientific progress as an accumulation of scientific knowledge based on evidence, where evidence includes knowledge produced by scientific theories.

In Chapter 10, "Wilful Hermeneutical Ignorance to the (Qualified) Rescue of Knowledge-First," Veli Mitova considers the ethical fruitfulness of the knowledge-first approach. It is only by embracing an externalist account of epistemic justification that we can explain why willful hermeneutical ignorance (i.e., deliberate ignorance of the epistemic resources of the oppressed) is unjust and typically blameworthy. Such cases of epistemic injustice merely lend qualified support to knowledge-first approaches, though. For they equally support other kinds of externalism, such as non-perspectival objectivism. In addition, hybrid approaches may seem better fitted to getting these cases completely right.

In Chapter 11, "Reasons and Knowledge," Christina Dietz and John Hawthorne defend the knowledge-based picture of reasons (according to which motivating and possessed normative reasons require knowledge) against recent attacks arising from linguistic data and theoretical considerations about the connection between reasons and rationality. They also respond to doubts concerning the factivity of emotions, reasons, and evidence, and they highlight the limits of alternative approaches.

In Chapter 12, "Knowledge and Prizes," Clayton Littlejohn and Julien Dutant revisit a well-known topic, the topic of rational belief. However, their proposal brings the discussion into a new perspective by exploring both the value of knowing as our fundamental epistemic prize and the expectationist framework in thinking about the rationality of belief, the framework that captures rationality in terms of expected value. Rationality, then, is tied to our pursuit of the knowledge prize. The starting point of their discussion is an observation that two intuitively plausible and popular ways of thinking about rational belief, the veritistic strength-centered view (a view similar to the Lockean view) and the explanationist view, lead to problematic results, despite also appearing to get something right about rational beliefs. The former ties rationality of belief to high evidential probability, while the latter appeals to the explanatory relation that has to hold between evidence and rational belief. The former view runs into trouble in lottery (and similar) cases where high probability doesn't seem to be enough to make a belief rational. The latter has problems with metacoherence constraints and has difficulty explaining the preface-paradoxical cases. The authors' solution is to adopt the expectationist knowledge-centered framework, where rational belief has a high expected epistemic value. This way of thinking helps to avoid the problems of the alternatives. Since it is certain that one cannot know lottery propositions, the expected epistemic value is not sufficient for rational belief in lottery propositions, and since one can expect to know propositions in a book that contains an error, the preface cases can also be handled without running into troubles with metacoherence principles. The chapter ends with a more general discussion on prizes and the value of knowledge that appears to stem from the fact that knowledge provides us with contact with reality. This contact with reality that knowledge provides is valuable beyond beliefs. Knowledge matters for our choices, for example for other attitudes and meaningful projects in our lives, projects that realize some further goods. In elaborating their new expectationist knowledge-centered (gnostic) theory of rational belief, Littlejohn and Dutant bring new perspectives on the old debate. In a sense, they put the old debate on rational belief into a more unified expectationist way of thinking about rationality in general (as tied to the expected epistemic value framework). And they break new ground in foundational issues on epistemic value, where theorizing about the prize of knowledge is the key. In short, this is a fruitful new way of appealing to knowledge in elaborating an expectationist view where values depend on the prizes we pursue.

We are answerable for our beliefs. But does that imply that there is something like rational agency or self-determination with respect to them? In Chapter 13, "Perceptual Knowledge and the 'Activity' of Belief," Johannes Roessler emphasizes that we can vindicate perceptual beliefs by referring to our perceptual knowledge. Arguing for a primitivist view of perceptual knowledge, where the explanatory connection between perception and knowledge is basic and irreducible, Roessler maintains that answerability ought to be distinguished from the demand for reasons. The upshot is that there are various ways in which the mind can be said to be "active" or "passive," which crucially need to be disentangled.

Bibliography

Benton, Matthew A. (2014). "Knowledge Norms." In James Fieser & Bradley Dowden (eds.), *Internet Encyclopedia of Philosophy*, https://iep.utm.edu/kn-norms/, accessed February 6, 2024.

Berker, Selim (2008). "Luminosity Regained." *Philosophers' Imprint* 8: 1–22.

Bird, Alexander (2007). "Justified Judging." *Philosophy and Phenomenological Research* 74(1): 81–110.

Carter, J. Adam, Gordon, Emma C., & Jarvis, Benjamin W. (eds.) (2017). *Knowledge First: Approaches in Epistemology and Mind*. Oxford: Oxford University Press.

Craig, Edward (1990). *Knowledge and the state of nature: an essay in conceptual synthesis*. New York: Oxford University Press.

DeRose, Keith (2009). *The Case for Contextualism: Knowledge, Skepticism, and Context*, Vol. 1. Oxford, GB: Oxford University Press.

Dutant, Julien (2015). "The legend of the justified true belief analysis". *Philosophical Perspectives* 29 (1): 95–145.

Dutant, Julien (forthcoming). "Knowledge-First Evidentialism about Rationality." In Fabian Dorsch & Julien Dutant (eds.), *The New Evil Demon Problem*. Oxford: Oxford University Press.

Fricker, Miranda (2007). *Epistemic Injustice: Power and the Ethics of Knowing*. New York: Oxford University Press.

Gerken, Mikkel (2011). "Warrant and Action." *Synthese* 178(3): 529–47.

Gettier, Edmund L. (1963). "Is Justified True Belief Knowledge?" *Analysis* 23(6): 121–3.

Pritchard, Duncan & Greenough, Patrick (eds.) (2009). *Williamson on Knowledge*. Oxford, GB: Oxford: Oxford University Press.

Hawthorne, John (2004). *Knowledge and lotteries*. New York: Oxford University Press.

Hawthorne, John & Stanley, Jason (2008). "Knowledge and Action." *Journal of Philosophy* 105(10): 571–90.

Hintikka, Jaakko (1962). *Knowledge and Belief*. Ithaca, NY: Cornell University Press.

Hughes, Nick (2021). "Epistemology without Guidance." *Philosophical Studies* 179(1): 163–96.

Hyman, John (2006). "Knowledge and Evidence." *Mind* 115(460): 891–916.

Ichikawa, Jonathan Jenkins (2017). *Contextualising Knowledge: Epistemology and Semantics*. Oxford: Oxford University Press.

Kelp, Christoph (2016). "Justified Belief: Knowledge First-Style." *Philosophy and Phenomenological Research* 91(1): 79–100.

Kelp, Christoph (2017). "Knowledge-First Virtue Epistemology." In J. Adam Carter, Emma C. Gordon, & Benjamin W. Jarvis (eds.), *Knowledge First: Approaches in Epistemology and Mind*. Oxford: Oxford University Press, 223–45.

Kelp, Christoph (2018). *Good Thinking: A Knowledge First Virtue Epistemology*. London: Routledge.

Kelp, Christoph (2020). "The Knowledge Norm Of Blaming." *Analysis* 80(2): 256–61.

Kelp, Christoph & Simion, Mona (2021). *Sharing Knowledge: A Functionalist Account of Assertion*. New York: Cambridge University Press.

Kelp, Christoph and Simion, Mona (eds.) (2023). *Knowledge-First Epistemology*, Special Issue, *Synthese*.

Kipper, Jens (2018). Acting on true belief. *Philosophical Studies* 175(9): 2221–37.

Lasonen-Aarnio, Maria (2010). "Unreasonable Knowledge." *Philosophical Perspectives* 24(1): 1–21.

Lasonen-Aarnio, Maria (2021). "Dispositional Evaluations and Defeat." In Jessica Brown & Mona Simion (eds.), *Reasons, Justification, and Defeat*. Oxford: Oxford University Press, 91–115.

Littlejohn, Clayton (2009). "The Externalist's Demon." *Canadian Journal of Philosophy* 39(3): 399–434.

Littlejohn, Clayton (2012). *Justification and the Truth-Connection*. New York: Cambridge University Press.

Littlejohn, Clayton (2017). "How and Why Knowledge Is First." In J. Adam Carter, Emma C. Gordon, & Benjamin W. Jarvis (eds.), *Knowledge First: Approaches in Epistemology and Mind*. Oxford: Oxford University Press. 19–45.

Littlejohn, Clayton (forthcoming). "A Plea for Epistemic Excuses." In Fabian Dorsch & Julien Dutant (eds.), *The New Evil Demon Problem*. Oxford: Oxford University Press.

Logins, Artūrs (2016). "Necessary truths, evidence, and knowledge." *Filosofia Unisinos* 17 (3): 302–307.

Logins, Artūrs (2017). "Common Sense and Evidence: Some Neglected Arguments in Favour of E = K." *Theoria* 83(2): 120–37.

Logins, Artūrs (2021). "Persistent Burglars and Knocks on Doors: Causal Indispensability of Knowing Vindicated." *European Journal of Philosophy* 30(4): 1335–57.

Lord, Errol (2018). *The Importance of Being Rational*. Oxford: Oxford University Press.

McGlynn, Aidan (2014). *Knowledge First?*. New York: Palgrave Macmillian.

McGlynn, Aidan (2017). "Mindreading Knowledge." In J. Adam Carter, Emma C. Gordon, & Benjamin W. Jarvis (eds.), *Knowledge First: Approaches in Epistemology and Mind*. Oxford: Oxford University Press, 72–94.

McKenna, Robin (2016). "Clifford and the Common Epistemic Norm." *American Philosophical Quarterly* 53(3): 245–58.

Miracchi, Lisa (2015). "Competence to Know." *Philosophical Studies* 172(1): 29–56.

Miracchi, Lisa (forthcoming). "Competent Perspectives and the New Evil Demon Problem." In Julien Dutant (ed.), *The New Evil Demon: New Essays on Knowledge, Justification and Rationality*. Oxford: Oxford University Press.

Molyneux, Bernard (2007). "Primeness, internalism and explanatory generality." *Philosophical Studies* 135(2): 255–77.

Nagel, Jennifer (2013). "Knowledge as a Mental State." *Oxford Studies in Epistemology* 4: 275–310.

Nagel, Jennifer (2017). "Factive and nonfactive mental state attribution." *Mind and Language* 32(5): 525–44.

Searle, J. R. (1969). *Speech Acts: An Essay in the Philosophy of Language*. Cambridge: Cambridge University Press.

Silva, Paul (2020). "Knowledge-First Theories of Justification." In James Fieser & Bradley Dowden (eds.), *Internet Encyclopedia of Philosophy*, https://iep.utm.edu/kft-just/, accessed February 8, 2024.

Simion, Mona (2019). "Knowledge-First Functionalism." *Philosophical Issues* 29(1): 254–67.

Simion, Mona (2021). *Shifty Speech and Independent Thought: Epistemic Normativity in Context*. Oxford University Press.

Srinivasan, Amia (2013). "Are We Luminous?" *Philosophy and Phenomenological Research* 90(2): 294–319.

Stanley, Jason (2005). *Knowledge and practical interests*. New York: Oxford University Press.

Stroud, Barry (1984). *The Significance of Philosophical Scepticism*. New York: Oxford University Press.

Sutton, Jonathan (2005). "Stick to what you know". *Noûs* 39(3): 359–96.

Sutton, Jonathan (2007). *Without Justification*. MIT Press.

Turri, John (2017). "Knowledge Attributions and Behavioral Predictions." *Cognitive Science*: 2253–61.

Unger, Peter K. (1975). *Ignorance: A Case for Scepticism*. Oxford [Eng.]: Oxford University Press.

Vollet, Jacques-Henri (2022). "Epistemic Excuses and the Feeling of Certainty." *Analysis* 4: 663–72.

Weisberg, Jonathan (2021). "Formal Epistemology." In Edward N. Zalta (ed.), *The Stanford Encyclopedia of Philosophy*. Spring 2021 edition, https://plato.stanford.edu/archives/spr2021/entries/formal-epistemology/, accessed February 7, 2024.

Williamson, Timothy. (2000). *Knowledge and its Limits*. Oxford: Oxford University Press.

Williamson, Timothy. (2011). "Knowledge first epistemology". In S. Bernecker & D. Pritchard (Eds.), The Routledge companion to epistemology (pp. 208–218). London, England: Routledge.

Williamson, Timothy (forthcoming). Justifications, Excuses, and Sceptical Scenarios. In Fabian Dorsch & Julien Dutant (eds.), *The New Evil Demon*. Oxford: Oxford University Press.

Artūrs Logins and Jacques-Henri Vollet, *Introduction: Taking Knowledge-First Further* In: *Putting Knowledge to Work: New Directions for Knowledge-First Epistemology*. Edited by: Artūrs Logins and Jacques-Henri Vollet, Oxford University Press. © Artūrs Logins and Jacques-Henri Vollet 2024. DOI: 10.1093/9780191976766.003.0001

PART 1
HISTORICAL PERSPECTIVES ON KNOWLEDGE-FIRST

2
Where Did It Come From? Where Will It Go?

Timothy Williamson

Many lines of thought combined into *Knowledge and its Limits* (KAIL), and many spread out from it—not only in my own head. In this informal account, looking back, I will comment briefly on the historical antecedents for a knowledge-first approach in epistemology and, autobiographically, on how I came to take such an approach. Looking forward, I will sketch promising new ways in which the approach is being extended and deepened. To give the big picture, I will use rather schematic formulations and skip over many details and nuances. I make no attempt to survey the massive body of literature relevant to each topic; the chapter is long enough as it is.

Thematically, the chapter is organized into eleven sections:

1. Looking Back: Some History
2. Looking Back: Indiscriminability
3. Looking Back: Knowledge and Action
4. Looking Back: Contents and Attitudes
5. Looking Back: Assertability
6. Looking Back: 'Knowledge First'
7. Before and After
8. Looking Forward: Mind Reading
9. Looking Forward: Knowledge and Action
10. Looking Forward: Models of Knowledge
11. Looking Forward: Epistemic Norms

The structure is non-linear: topically, the backward-looking sections converge on a point, from which the forward-looking sections spread out.

1. Looking Back: Some History

Some people find the knowledge-first approach wildly counter-intuitive. Others find it the merest common sense. The divergence was encapsulated for me when

I gave a talk at the University of New Mexico in 1994 based on material which later became 'Is Knowing a State of Mind?' (Williamson 1995) and then grew into the first two chapters of KAIL. In the discussion period, with reference to my claim that 'knowledge' is unanalysable, one professor exclaimed, 'If I thought you were right, I would give up philosophy!' Also present was a professor from the English literature department, who had come out of loyalty to my father, having known me as the teenage son of his old doctoral supervisor at Oxford. When we talked afterwards, I could see that he was wondering what all the fuss was about, and why it was worth giving a paper answering so easy a question—of course knowing was a mental state; what else would it be? I felt more sympathy with the scholar of English literature than with the philosopher. That knowing is a mental state and the knowledge-first approach more generally are common sense, though that by itself does not prove their correctness. Those who find them counter-intuitive have internalized a specific epistemological tradition which prioritizes appearance over reality and the proximal over the distal.

The situation has been obscured by the legend that the justified true belief (JTB) analysis of knowledge was standard in Western epistemology from Plato to Gettier. If so, a belief-first approach would have been dominant for well over two thousand years. But that history is wrong. Although Plato toyed with a justified true belief analysis, he did not endorse it, and the popularity of the belief-first approach is a far more recent phenomenon (Dutant 2015). The JTB analysis is pointlessly redundant if justification itself already entails truth. The 'fallibilist' idea that truth-entailing justifications are too much to ask may be associated with the collapse of old certainties—for example, that space is Euclidean—under pressure from modern science. Such episodes are salutary but do not warrant the panic-stricken moral that no truth-entailing propositional attitude—such as knowledge—is epistemologically fundamental, any more than cases of reference failure—for example, with the word 'phlogiston'—show that the relation of reference is not semantically fundamental. That philosophers and scientists were once certain of knowing that space was Euclidean, even though it was not, just shows that humans can make mistakes in applying the distinction between knowledge and ignorance, not that they cannot have truth-entailing knowledge.

The general knowledge-first approach is not at all original with me, though, of course, I hope to have taken it further. I suspect that cognitive relations more like knowing than like believing have tended to be central to epistemology whenever and wherever it has been practised. Often, those knowledge-like relations are modelled on the relation of seeing (an object). Even epistemologists who prioritize appearance over reality typically do so on the assumption that we have some sort of immediate awareness of appearances which we lack of the rest of reality. Such immediate awareness is, in effect, knowledge turned inwards and implausibly idealized.

The natural human way of thinking about matters epistemological is, I suggest, knowledge-first (see also Nagel 2014 and forthcoming, and below). For instance, I have been delighted to learn, much classical Indian epistemology takes a knowledge-first approach (for one case, see Vaidya 2022; Williamson 2023c; see also Chapter 4 by Nilanjan Das in the present volume). In a wider epistemological perspective, KAIL is no aberration.

Closer to home, there is a long tradition of Oxonian realism, going back at least to John Cook Wilson, my predecessor as Wykeham Professor of Logic at Oxford from 1889 to 1915. Here is a clear articulation of his knowledge-centred conception of the mind, from his posthumously published work *Statement and Inference* (Cook Wilson 1926: i, 38; 1967: 19–20):

> The unity of the activities of consciousness, called forms of thinking, is not a universal which, as a specific form of the genus activity of consciousness, would cover the whole nature of each of them, a species of which thinking would be the name and of which they would be sub-species, but lies in the relation of the forms of thinking which are not knowing to the form which is knowing.

He also explicitly rejected the demand for a definition of knowledge (Cook Wilson 1926: i, 39; 1967: 20).

Cook Wilson was the dominant Oxford philosopher of his time. Although his contemporary, the idealist F. H. Bradley, now has more name recognition, Bradley was an isolated and reclusive figure. It was Cook Wilson who set the tone—a realist tone exemplified by the then popular anti-Kantian slogan 'Knowledge makes no difference to the known' (on early Oxford realism, see Marion 2000). It was a healthy attitude to start from, though doubtless too crude; doesn't the knowledge that one is thinking make a difference to the known, one's own thought?

By the time I studied mathematics and philosophy as an undergraduate at Oxford (1973–6), Cook Wilson was almost forgotten. However, the relevant section of *Statement and Inference* was included in a then standard book of readings on knowledge and belief (Phillips Griffiths 1967), where I read the Cook Wilson excerpt in 1974. I cannot pretend to have been much impressed. It seemed both eccentric and dogmatic. Nor was what I subsequently learned about Cook Wilson encouraging. He bitterly opposed various forms of progress, despising non-Euclidean geometry and non-Aristotelian logic, then represented in Oxford by Lewis Carroll, aka the mathematician Charles Lutwidge Dodgson. Cook Wilson also treated the difference between knowing and not knowing, quite implausibly, as always in principle accessible to the thinker, in stark contrast with KAIL. He affirmed a strong form of the 'positive introspection' thesis that whenever one knows, one knows that one knows: 'The consciousness that the knowing process is a knowing process must be contained within the knowing process itself'

(Cook Wilson 1926: i, 107). He did not quite endorse the 'negative introspection' thesis that whenever one doesn't know, one knows that one doesn't know, since in cases of error, he says, someone 'doesn't know and is unaware that he doesn't know' (1926: i, 106). However, he goes on to describe those as cases of partly 'unawakened consciousness' (1926: i, 110–11) involving 'a certain passivity and helplessness' (1926: i, 113). Presumably, when consciousness is fully 'awakened', negative introspection holds. Cook Wilson never influenced me directly.

Cook Wilson's legacy was mainly indirect. One of his pupils was H. A. Prichard, White's Professor of Moral Philosophy at Oxford from 1928 to 1937. In his work on epistemology, Prichard overtly followed Cook Wilson; KAIL notes my disagreement with his claims that one is always in a position to know whether one knows or merely believes and that knowing entails not believing (Prichard 1950: 86–8). As students at Oxford, both J. L. Austin and Wilfrid Sellars were impressed by Prichard's lectures (Berlin 1973; Sellars 1975). Their realist emphasis on the priority of the predicate 'is F' to the predicate 'seems F' may show Prichard's influence, and through him Cook Wilson's. Austin is also likely to have read *Statement and Inference* itself; it was a major work of Oxford philosophy published shortly before he began his studies. One might connect Austin's emphasis in *Sense and Sensibilia* (Austin 1962) on the inappropriateness of talk of evidence in straightforward cases of perceptual knowledge with Cook Wilson's attitude that 'In knowing, we can have nothing to do with the so-called "greater strength" of the evidence on which the opinion is grounded; simply because we know that this "greater strength" of evidence of A's being B is compatible with A's not being B after all' (Cook Wilson 1926: i, 100). Methodologically, Austin's claim 'our common stock of words embodies all the distinctions men have found worth drawing, and the connexions they have found worth marking, in the lifetimes of many generations' (Austin 1956–7: 8) is reminiscent of Cook Wilson's 'Distinctions current in language can never be safely neglected' (Cook Wilson 1926: i, 46; 1967: 26).

For several decades after Austin's early death in 1960, the most distinctive manifestation in Oxford of its realist tradition was disjunctivism about perceptual appearances, on which (to put it schematically) 'O looks F' divides into something like a disjunction of the 'good' disjunct 'O is visibly F', which entails 'O is F', and the 'bad' disjunct 'O merely looks F', which entails 'O is not visibly F' (Hinton 1967, 1973; Snowdon 1980–1, 1990; McDowell 1982; Martin 2004; Byrne and Logue 2009). When I returned to Oxford in 1988, after eight years as a lecturer at Trinity College Dublin, disjunctive theories of perception had for years formed one of the main topics of debate amongst Oxford philosophers. However, the theory of perception was not one of my special interests, though I had a general interest in epistemology. The disjunctivist who did most to generalize the view in epistemology was McDowell (1982, 1995), but I had always found his Wittgensteinian quietism and gnomic style intellectually alien. He had no direct influence on me, though in retrospect I could see significant similarities in epistemological outlook. Anyway, the possibility of a general disjunctivism about belief was clear; I recall raising it in conversation with my colleague Mike Martin in 1988: 'believes p' would divide into the disjunction of the good disjunct 'S knows p', which entails that p is true, and the bad disjunct 'S merely believes p', which entails 'S does not know p'. Cook Wilson already held a sort of disjunctivism about cognitive attitudes: 'Beyond then the bare abstraction of conscious activity, there is no general character or quality of which the essential natures of both knowledge and opinion are differentiations, or of which we could say in ordinary language that each was a kind' (1926: i, 100).

KAIL provides a sympathetic critique of disjunctivism about belief (Williamson 2000: 44–8). I objected that the disjunctive form is just a misleading artefact, because the equivalence of 'S believes p' and 'Either S knows p or S believes p without knowing p' is merely a trivial consequence of the accepted entailment from 'S knows p' to 'S believes p'. The bad disjunct 'S believes p without knowing p' is gerrymandered and unnatural. As I made clear, the objection speaks more to the letter than the spirit of disjunctivism. What matters most is the insight that 'S knows p' cannot be understood as the conjunction of 'S believes p' with other factors, all of them somehow prior to 'S knows p' itself. Thus, disjunctivism about belief is better reworked as anti-conjunctivism about knowledge.

Analogous points apply to disjunctive theories of perception. The disjunctive form is again just a misleading artefact, because the equivalence of 'O looks F' and 'Either O is visibly F or O looks F without being visibly F' is merely a trivial consequence of the entailment from 'S is visibly F' to 'S looks F'. The bad disjunct 'O looks F without being visibly F' is gerrymandered and unnatural. Again, the objection speaks more to the letter than the spirit of disjunctivism. What matters most is the insight that 'O is visibly F' cannot be understood as the conjunction of 'O looks F' with other factors, all of them somehow prior to 'O is visibly F' itself. Thus, disjunctivism about perceptual appearances is better reworked as anti-conjunctivism about perception.

For both belief and perceptual appearances, disjunctive theories can take subtler forms, but variants of the same objection still apply.

Already when I was a student, philosophers' search for 'conceptual analyses' corresponding to key terms of natural language such as 'know', 'cause', and 'mean' struck me as a degenerating research programme. There was the familiar depressing pattern of a proposed analysis, a counterexample, and the insertion of another epicycle to give a new proposed analysis. Nor did it feel as though successive analyses were approximating the true analysis more and more closely, if the true analysis was supposed to make explicit our implicit understanding of the term. If such ramshackle definitions were implemented psychologically by something like complicated lexical entries for the defined terms in our heads, they would render those terms virtually unusable, a point that today's aspiring conceptual engineers would do well to remember. With every added epicycle, the proposed definition seemed to get *further* from psychological reality, not closer to it. Of course, one could give up the demand for psychological reality and require only metaphysically necessary and sufficient conditions, presumably with some stipulation to avoid circularity. But it was still quite unclear why one should expect words like 'know', 'cause', and 'mean' to *have* analyses even in that less ambitious sense. Thus, from early on, I did not expect knowledge (the state, the concept, or the word) to be analysable. But since unanalysability would be such a common case, that by itself did not make knowledge primary in epistemological theorizing. It did not exclude the internalist view that what matters most in epistemology is a non-factive standard of justification. Other developments were needed too.

2. Looking Back: Indiscriminability

From the late 1980s onwards, I started to notice ways in which knowledge, rather than non-factive justification, is exactly what is needed for various philosophical purposes.

I had a consciousness-raising moment at a conference in Cambridge (England) to celebrate the fiftieth volume of the journal *Analysis*, in 1990. Jonathan Bennett gave a paper arguing for the failure of all extant attempts to explain why belief is involuntary (published as Bennett 1990). In the subsequent question-and-answer period, I idly suggested that one could try first explaining why *knowledge* is involuntary, which might be easier, since you cannot come to know at will a given proposition to be true. Perhaps one could then use a connection between belief and knowledge to extend the explanation from knowledge to belief. Bennett's response was that he had been philosophizing all his career without employing the concept of knowledge, and he advised me to do the same. The thought instantly struck me: 'That's where you make your big mistake.' Nevertheless, I respected his methodological self-awareness, though not his epistemological judgement. I realized too that many other philosophers were, in effect, following the same policy as Bennett, perhaps with less self-awareness.

A clue to the importance of knowledge had already come to me through my work on the cognitive relation of *indiscriminability*. To explain its relevance, I must first digress, to fill in some background. As a first-year undergraduate, I was intrigued by the challenge of finding a criterion of identity or abstraction principle for qualities and quantities as perceived by an observer (I no longer see the issues in such reductive terms). In the writings of Bertrand Russell and A. J. Ayer, I read that identity in a given perceived respect (for a given subject under given conditions) cannot be defined as indiscriminability in that respect, because identity in any respect is transitive, while indiscriminability in a respect is typically non-transitive, as many sorites series bear witness. For instance, imagine a long series of rods ordered by length, where each rod is indiscriminable in length from those next to it (by the naked eye under given conditions) but the first rod is easily discriminable in length from the last. We cannot stipulate that, under those conditions, two rods are identical in *perceived* length just in case they are indiscriminable in (real) length. For then each rod is identical in perceived length to those next to it (by the stipulation), so the first rod is identical in length from the last (by the transitivity of identity, not indiscriminability), which is not so (again by the stipulation). Somehow, the associated logical issues gripped me. As an undergraduate, I proved a connection with the Axiom of Choice and wrote up a paper, which I submitted to *The Journal of Philosophy*. It received a revise-and-resubmit—quite reasonably, the editors wanted more on the philosophical significance of my technical results. In my ignorance, I misinterpreted the letter as a rejection with a patronizing pat on the head and angrily put the paper aside. A decade later, long after learning what the letter really meant, I got round to rewriting my paper and cashed in the revise-and-resubmit (Williamson 1986).

My renewed work on indiscriminability set me thinking more deeply about its nature, in ways which led to my first book, *Identity and Discrimination* (Williamson 1990). To continue the example, let the (real) length of x be $l(x)$. To discriminate x and y in length is to recognize that x and y differ in length, in other words, to come to know that $l(x) \neq l(y)$. Thus, x and y are discriminable in length just in case, given the available information, it is epistemically necessary that $l(x) \neq l(y)$. Consequently, x and y are *in*discriminable in length just in case, given the available information, it is *not* epistemically necessary that $l(x) \neq l(y)$, or equivalently (by the duality of necessity and possibility) it is epistemically *possible* that $l(x) = l(y)$, which we can write as $\Diamond[l(x) = l(y)]$. That line of thought generalizes to any respect: indiscriminability in a respect is the epistemic possibility of identity in that respect.

This account nicely predicts the logical properties of indiscriminability, given the familiar logical properties of identity and of epistemic possibility, as follows.

Indiscriminability in a respect is reflexive on whatever the respect applies to: x is indiscriminable in length from itself because $l(x) = l(x)$ is a logical truth on the domain (since identity is reflexive), so $\Diamond[l(x) = l(x)]$ is also a logical truth on that domain (if α is a logical truth, so is $\Diamond\alpha$).

Indiscriminability in a respect is also symmetric: if x is indiscriminable in length from y then y is indiscriminable in length from x, for $l(x) = l(y)$ is logically equivalent to $l(y) = l(x)$ (since identity is symmetric), so $\Diamond[l(x) = l(y)]$ is logically equivalent to $\Diamond[l(y) = l(x)]$ (if α is logically equivalent to β, then $\Diamond\alpha$ is logically equivalent to $\Diamond\beta$).

But indiscriminability in a respect is *not* in general transitive, even though identity is transitive. For if x is indiscriminable in length from y, and y from z, then we have $\Diamond[l(x) = l(y)]$ and $\Diamond[l(y) = l(z)]$, but $\Diamond[l(x) = l(z)]$ does *not* follow, even though $l(x) = l(y)$ and $l(y) = l(z)$ together entail $l(x) = l(z)$ (since identity is transitive). The epistemic possibilities in which $l(x) = l(y)$ may not overlap the epistemic possibilities in which $l(y) = l(z)$: crucially, expressions of the form '$l(v)$' are non-rigid designators; they designate different lengths in different epistemic possibilities, to capture the ignorance of length.

As yet, we have not exploited the specifically *epistemic* nature of the possibility expressed by ◊, compatibility with what is known. We could have made the same arguments while using ◊ to express rational *doxastic* possibility, compatibility with what is rationally believed. We need the 'rational' for reflexivity, so that the logical truth of α implies the logical truth of ◊α, for if what is believed is inconsistent, *nothing* is compatible with it.

But indiscriminability has a further logical feature, a kind of strengthened reflexivity: if things are identical in a respect, they are indiscriminable in that respect. If things are identical in length, you cannot discriminate them in length—though you may be under the illusion that you can. Thus, $l(x) = l(y)$ implies $◊[l(x) = l(y)]$. That works for epistemic possibility: if α is true, α is compatible with what is known, since only truths are known, and all truths are mutually compatible. But it does not work for rational doxastic possibility understood so that consistent false beliefs can be rational: if one rationally but falsely believes $l(x) ≠ l(y)$, $l(x) = l(y)$ is true, while $◊[l(x) = l(y)]$ is false on the rational doxastic reading of ◊, since what is rationally believed contradicts $l(x) = l(y)$. Thus, to capture the full logic of indiscriminability, one must invoke specifically *epistemic* possibility; rational *doxastic* possibility will not do, because the relevant body of information must contain only truths.

Identity and Discrimination discusses these formal matters in greater depth and detail (Williamson 1990: 10–42). When I wrote it, the need for knowledge rather than mere rational belief in understanding indiscriminability struck me as significant, because discrimination is so cognitively fundamental. If what is needed there is knowledge, that is some indication that it comes first. Of course, one could add in the truth requirement by hand, interpreting ◊ as rational *true* belief, but I already regarded such gerrymandering as an alarm signal warning of a degenerating research programme.

In analysing the logic of indiscriminability, I used a framework of Kripke models for modal logic, with the modalities interpreted epistemically in the tradition of Hintikka (1962). For simplicity, I excluded quantifiers from the object language, but included atomic formulas of the form $l(x) = l(y)$. To interpret the modality, the model has an *accessibility* relation. Informally, a world x is accessible from w, or epistemically possible at w, if and only if, for all one knows in w, one is in x. Then $◊p$ is true at a world w (p is epistemically possible at w) if and only if p is true at some world accessible from w. Dually, $□p$ is true at w (p is epistemically necessary at w) if and only if p is true at every world accessible from w. Informally, epistemic necessity is identified with knowledge: $□p$ is true at w if and only if one knows p at w.

Even if the object language lacks atomic formulas of the form l(x) = l(y), we can understand the models in terms of indiscriminability more directly by regarding accessibility as itself a relation of indiscriminability between worlds. Thus, the non-transitivity of indiscriminability becomes the non-transitivity of accessibility. As is familiar, the non-transitivity of accessibility in this framework corresponds to the invalidity of the formula $\Box p \supset \Box\Box p$, which is the 'KK' or 'positive introspection' principle that if one knows p, one knows that one knows p. Thus, one may know p without knowing that one knows p, a central theme in KAIL.

KAIL's cover alludes to the non-transitivity of accessibility. It shows Nicolas Poussin's *Landscape with a Man Killed by a Snake*, a painting I have loved since I first saw it as a student in the National Gallery, London. On one common interpretation, it illustrates different levels of cognition: the man who sees the snake-entwined corpse, the woman who sees only the man who sees it, the boatmen in the background who have no idea what is going on. It thus shows the non-transitivity of seeing: the woman sees the man; the man sees the corpse, which she does not see. Seeing is often used as a metaphor for accessibility: a world w 'sees' a world x when x is accessible from w. Metaphorically, therefore, the painting illustrates the non-transitivity of epistemic accessibility.

Admittedly, the argument from the non-transitivity of indiscriminability to the non-transitivity of accessibility oversimplifies the situation. If it worked, the symmetry of indiscriminability would similarly imply the symmetry of accessibility. As is also familiar, the symmetry of accessibility in this framework corresponds to the validity of the formula $\neg p \supset \Box \neg \Box p$: if p is false, one knows that one does not know p. But that principle is notoriously counterexample-prone. In some sceptical scenarios, it is false that one has hands, but one is in no position to know that one does not know that one has hands, because, for all one knows, everything is normal and one knows that one has hands. Thus, although the normal good case is accessible from the sceptical bad case, the bad case is not accessible from the good case. In the good case, one knows that one is not in the bad case. In the bad case, one does not know that one is not in the good case.

The reason for this mismatch between indiscriminability and accessibility is that accessibility involves an asymmetry between two ways in which a world can be presented to a thinker. When 'x is accessible from w' is unpacked as 'for all one knows in w, one is in x', it is envisaged that the world w is presented to one 'by acquaintance' as the world one is in, or 'the actual world', whereas the world x is presented to one 'by description' in some way. The good case is accessible from the bad case because, when one is in the bad case, one does not know 'The case I am in is not the good case'. The bad case is inaccessible from the good case because, when one is in the good case, one knows (or is in a position to know) 'The case I am in is not the bad case'. One knows more in the good case than in the bad case. Since the modes of presentation are not held fixed, the argument from the symmetry of indiscriminability to the symmetry of accessibility does not go through.

For similar reasons, the non-transitivity of accessibility cannot simply be subsumed under the non-transitivity of indiscriminability. In saying that world x is accessible from world w, we envisage x as presented 'by description', whereas in saying that world y is accessible from x, we envisage x as presented 'by acquaintance'. Thus, the mode of presentation of x is not held fixed. Consequently, arguing from the non-transitivity of indiscriminability to the failure of the KK principle is not straightforward. Indeed, *Identity and Discrimination* uses models where indiscriminability is non-transitive but epistemic accessibility is transitive. Nevertheless, one can find cases where non-transitive indiscriminability makes epistemic accessibility non-transitive too. My article 'Inexact Knowledge' (Williamson 1992) does it, in effect, by recycling the non-transitivity of the perceptual indiscriminability of quantities as the non-transitivity of the epistemic accessibility of worlds. The trick was not to argue directly in terms of indiscriminability but to use limits on powers of discrimination to motivate a margin for error principle for knowledge and then apply that. The argument shows that one can know p without even being in a position to know that one knows p, so that not even the watering down with the qualifier 'in a position to' saves the KK principle. In that respect, my version of the knowledge-first approach is very different from those of Cook Wilson and Prichard.

Later, I noticed that the argument of 'Inexact Knowledge' can be generalized to a very wide range of conditions C, with the conclusion that C can hold even though one is not in a position to know that C holds. The generalization appeared in my article 'Cognitive Homelessness' (Williamson 1996a) and later as the anti-luminosity argument in KAIL. The generalized argument plays a key role in my epistemological externalism. Internalism is often motivated by appeal to an access constraint on norms of rationality and the like: rational agents should always be in a position to know whether they are complying with a norm. Externalist norms—such as a knowledge norm on assertion or on knowledge—typically violate that constraint. For instance, one is not always in a position to know whether one has kept a promise. By applying the anti-luminosity considerations, I could argue that *no* non-trivial norm meets the internalist constraint, which makes externalism 'the only game in town'.

3. Looking Back: Knowledge and Action

The knowledge-first approach was not just a development in epistemology. It also grew out of developments in the philosophy of mind and action.

In late twentieth-century analytic philosophy, the dominant framework for understanding intentional action was neo-Humean belief-desire psychology.

Rational agents did things because they believed that doing so would get them what they wanted. The formal version of the view was *decision theory*, which graded the beliefs into credences (represented by subjective probabilities of states of the world) and the desires into preferences (represented by subjective utilities of states of the world). Why pair belief and desire? An attractive answer was that they represented opposite *directions of fit*: the point of belief was to fit mind to world; the point of desire was to fit world to mind. A potential warning sign was that the contrast in direction of fit came from Elizabeth Anscombe, who was, of course, far from being a neo-Humean herself (Anscombe 1957).

Once one considers the relation between knowledge and belief in the context of belief-desire psychology, another question naturally presents itself: what stands to desire as knowledge stands to belief? In direction of fit, knowledge and belief are on the same side. Belief *should* be fitted to the world: when the belief *does* fit the world (truth), not by merely happening to match it but because all went well in the process upstream from the belief, there is knowledge. Analogously, if X stands to desire as knowledge stands to belief, X must have the same direction of fit as desire. Desire *should* fit the world to it: when the world *does* fit the desire (satisfaction), not by merely happening to match it but because all goes well in the process downstream from the desire, there is action—intentionally realizing the desire. On this view, *action* is what stands to desire as knowledge stands to belief.

That analogy strongly encouraged my incipient knowledge-first tendencies from about 1990 on. Just as it would be perverse to sideline action in the philosophy of action, it would be perverse to sideline knowledge in the theory of knowledge. That was not a pedantic insistence on reading the phrases 'philosophy of action' and 'theory of knowledge' literally. Rather, the point was that one cannot properly understand desiring things, intending to bring them about, and trying to bring them about except in relation to the good case of intentionally bringing them about. Similarly, one cannot properly understand states like believing except in relation to the good case of knowing. Since the centrality of action to the philosophy of action was more widely accepted, I could use it as an entering wedge for the centrality of knowledge to epistemology.

4. Looking Back: Contents and Attitudes

Belief-desire psychology was typically treated as the core of a more general propositional attitude psychology. Such intentional states and acts varied on two dimensions: the content (believing p versus believing q) and the attitude to that content (believing p versus desiring p). Comparison of the two dimensions gave further support to the knowledge-first approach. I will explain some more background before discussing the connection with knowledge.

The 1970s saw the beginnings of a major intellectual switch from *content internalism* to *content externalism*. According to content internalism, the content of a thinker's propositional attitude at a time supervenes on what is internal to that thinker at that time: no difference in the attitude without an internal difference. Content externalism is the negation of content internalism; it denies supervenience. 'Internal' there could be understood in various ways: physically, in terms of brain states or bodily states, or phenomenally, in terms of qualia or the like. Such variations do not matter for present purposes; we can use the terms 'internal' and 'external' schematically.

Content externalism was originally driven by developments in the philosophy of language concerning the semantics of natural kind terms and singular terms. The reference of such words does not supervene on what is internal to the speaker. In Hilary Putnam's famous example, the reference of 'water' as used in a given community depends on the chemical constitution of the samples to which the community has applied the word, even if the community has no inkling of the chemistry (Putnam 1973). Even pre-scientific speakers can understand that something may *apparently* belong to a natural kind without *really* belonging. Initially, Putnam took the moral of his example to be just that meaning is not in the head, while still treating psychology as in the head, so that psychology does not determine meaning. However, Tyler Burge soon pointed out that similar arguments show that propositional attitude psychology is also not in the head, a conclusion Putnam accepted (Burge 1979).

To vary the example: the term 'tiger' in English refers to members of a species T. We say 'There are tigers', speaking truly. We thereby express our belief that there are tigers, and our belief is true, for the belief that there are tigers is true if and only if there are tigers, and there are indeed tigers. Imagine a counterfactual possibility where the species T never evolved, so there are no tigers, but people just like us use a natural kind term just like 'tiger' to refer to members of another species T* with which they interact. Superficially, members of T are indistinguishable from members of T*, but they share no common evolutionary ancestry and, owing to subtle genetic differences, would be incapable of interbreeding. Those people say something just like 'There are tigers', speaking truly. However, they do not express a belief that there are tigers, for they lack that belief. In their circumstances, a belief that there are tigers would be *false*, since by hypothesis there are no tigers; but those people are no more in error than we are. In saying 'There are tigers', they express a true belief which stands to T* just as our true belief that there are tigers stands to T, but what they believe is not what we believe. Those people differ from us in the content of their beliefs, but not internally. Thus, content does not supervene on what is internal to the thinker.

One can make analogous arguments with perceptual demonstratives in place of natural kind terms. My counterfactual counterpart and I are exactly alike internally. I see a wasp; he sees an exactly similar wasp. My wasp never lived in his circumstances; his wasp never lived in mine. I say 'This wasp is alive', speaking truly. I thereby express my belief that this wasp is alive, and my belief is true, for the belief that this wasp is alive is true if and only if this wasp is alive, and this wasp is indeed alive. Counterfactually, my counterpart says 'This wasp is alive', speaking truly. However, he does not express the belief that this wasp is alive, for he lacks that belief. In his circumstances, a belief that this wasp is alive would be *false*, since by hypothesis this wasp is not alive; but he is no more in error than I am. In saying 'This wasp is alive', he expresses a true belief which stands to his wasp just as my true belief that this wasp is alive stands to my wasp, but what he believes is not what I believe. He differs from me in the content of his beliefs, but not internally. The conclusion is the same as before: content does not supervene on what is internal to the thinker.

In Oxford, content externalism became an increasingly prominent theme from the 1970s on. In the hands of John McDowell (1977) and Gareth Evans (1982), it took a quite distinctive form. Whereas Putnam and Burge focused on kind terms, Evans and McDowell focused on singular terms, especially perceptual demonstratives like 'this wasp'. Unlike Putnam and Burge, they concentrated on the contrast between the good case where reference succeeds and the bad case where it fails, for example, when the thinker is hallucinating, with no internal difference between the good and bad cases. They argued that in cases of reference failure there is no content, so the external difference is between content and no content, rather than between two internally indistinguishable contents. They framed the issues in neo-Fregean terms, positing 'object-involving' senses, rather than highlighting the failure of supervenience as such. Nevertheless, for present purposes, the similarities are more significant than the differences. One can easily rework the tiger and wasp examples with hallucination instead of another reference in the bad case.

Of course, content internalists did not give up without a struggle. Initially, their resistance tended to involve denying the descriptions of the cases. These denials typically depended on misunderstanding how attitude ascriptions work in natural language, and even on confusing use and mention. They forgot that normally when one uses indirect speech to ascribe a propositional attitude to another, the words in the content clause still mean what the speaker means by them, not what the other does. Later internalist resistance often took the more sophisticated form of conceding that the cases show that attitude ascriptions in natural language work in an externalist way, with 'broad' contents, while arguing on those very grounds that such ascriptions do not cut at the underlying psychological joints. Furthermore, according to such internalists, the attitudes which *do* cut at the underlying psychological joints have 'narrow' contents, and appropriate ascriptions of them work in an internalist way. On this internalist picture, the core of the mental is purely internal, while attitude ascriptions in natural language are hybrids of the internal and the external.

The motivations for content internalism are various—some causal, some epistemic. As a rough generalization, content internalists who self-describe as naturalists tend to have a causal motivation, while content internalists who self-describe as anti-naturalists tend to have an epistemic motivation.

On the causal side, the main fear is that content externalism will imply some kind of magical action at a distance. Beliefs, desires, and other attitudes have causes (for instance, in perception) and effects (for instance, on action), but many reductionists view all the genuine causal work as entirely mediated by underlying brain states and so best characterized in internalist terms, making distinctively externalist aspects of content causally irrelevant. They conclude that any causally relevant attitudes must have narrow contents.

On the epistemic side, the main fear is that content externalism will undermine one's privileged access to one's own present mental states. Many anti-reductionists hold that, as a rational subject, one has special non-observational conscious access to one's present beliefs, desires, and other attitudes of a kind which no one has to the attitudes of anyone else. Since one has no such special access to distinctively externalist aspects of content, they conclude that any attitudes epistemically accessible in the special way must have narrow contents.

The trouble is that although content internalists (of both types) need narrow content, they have no idea how to get it. Of course, they can start with two agents in exactly the same total internal state and say that they share all their narrow contents. But what is hopelessly unclear is what it takes for two agents who are *not* in exactly the same total internal state to share a narrow content. You and I both believe that there are tigers. We share that broad content, individuated externally in terms of the natural kind: tigers. Yet our total internal states will differ in all sorts of ways. What does it take for someone to share the narrow content supposedly underlying your belief that there are tigers? Indeed, since one's total internal state is changing all the time, what does it take for one to retain that narrow content for five minutes? In brief, how are narrow contents to be abstracted from the flux of the internal? There are no pre-theoretic 'intuitive' answers to those questions, for narrow contents are just theoretical posits, promissory notes which have never been redeemed. By contrast, we have at least some understanding of how broad contents work, because we are continually attributing attitudes to them to each other.

Anyway, the causal and epistemic motivations for content internalism are far from convincing. Normally, behaviour to be causally explained is specified in general and external terms. Why did she flip the wasp out of the window? Why did Napoleon invade Russia? Good explanations may invoke mental states specified in similarly general and external terms. She believed that the wasp could sting her. He believed that Russia was militarily vulnerable. Attitudes to narrow contents may be much less explanatory. As for privileged access, content externalism does not preclude it. I know that I believe that this wasp is alive; my second-order knowledge reuses the same perceptual demonstration as my first-order belief. In any case, privileged access has its limits. It is often hard to know what one believes or desires.

Although I have been writing in the present tense, that account of content internalism's troubles would already have elicited my assent in the early 1990s; such a negative assessment of content internalism was then already widespread, though, of course, far from universal. Indeed, content internalism's lack of progress over the intervening decades supports the negative verdict. There was ample time to find a solution to its problems, if one existed.

When I considered why epistemologists and philosophers of mind might resist the classification of knowing as a mental state, I realized that their objections would be like those to content externalism. They were often the very same objections, for what was supposed to play the causal role or to be accessible in the special way was the whole intentional state, which comprised both a content and an attitude to that content. Just as externalism about the content could generate externalism about the state, so could externalism about the attitude; the individuation of the whole state is worldly. Just as examples in favour of content externalism hold the attitude fixed while varying the content externally but not internally, so examples in favour of attitude externalism hold the content fixed while varying the attitude, again externally but not internally. Factive attitudes such as knowing-that, seeing-that, and remembering-that are blatantly externalist. For instance, you are in exactly the same total internal state in the good case and the bad case. In the good case, you know that it is raining. In the bad case, you still believe that it is raining, but you do not know that it is raining, for it is not raining. Consequently, the same general strategies could be used against the causal and epistemic objections to attitude externalism as had been successful against the causal and epistemic objections to content externalism. The details varied from contents to attitudes, but it was clear what to look for. I worked the analogy very hard in defending the claim that knowing is a mental state.

None of this means that content externalism entails attitude externalism or vice versa. Neither the conjunction of content externalism with attitude internalism nor the conjunction of content internalism with attitude externalism is logically inconsistent. But those mixed views have no natural motivation. The natural motivating view both for content internalism and for attitude internalism is a general internalism about the mental, which rules out both mixed views. Conversely, once content externalism has ruled out general internalism, it makes sense to go for attitude externalism too, to complete a unified picture. I regarded content externalism as the first wave of the externalist revolution and my attitude externalism as the second wave. Admittedly, leaders of the first wave were often unwilling to go along with the second wave—for them, it was an externalism too far. That is a common pattern in revolutions.

5. Looking Back: Assertability

When I was an undergraduate and then doctoral student at Oxford (1973–80), the most influential senior figure in the philosophy of logic and language at Oxford was Michael Dummett. He supervised me for the final year of my doctoral studies, just after taking up the Wykeham Chair of Logic. In stark contrast to his distant predecessor Cook Wilson, he tended towards anti-realism. He was sympathetic to a theory of meaning on which the meaning of a declarative sentence is given by the condition for it to be *assertable*, rather than by the condition for it to be true. He intended this as a generalization to all language of the intuitionistic treatment of mathematical language, on which the meaning of a mathematical sentence is given by the condition for something to be a proof of it. The idea was that realist truth conditions problematically transcend speakers' *use* of the language, whereas assertability conditions are immanent in use. By contrast, Gareth Evans, John McDowell, Christopher Peacocke, and others then at Oxford, under the influence of Donald Davidson, preferred a realist theory of meaning in terms of truth conditions. Consequently, assertability conditions were much discussed by Oxford philosophers at the time.

Dummett never presented a full assertability-conditional theory of meaning for a non-trivial fragment of non-mathematical language. Unfortunately, his discussions tended to remain programmatic, apart from occasional intriguing suggestions. However, an assertability-conditional theory of meaning was supposed to be more or less compositional: the meaning of a complex sentence is determined by the meanings of its constituents and the way in which they are put together. For example, the natural assertability-conditional semantic clause for disjunction is this: 'A or B' is assertable when and only when either 'A' is assertable or 'B' is assertable. Dummett was well aware that one can legitimately assert that the number of people in the stadium is odd or even without having counted them to find out which. He handled such cases by reading 'assertable' in the semantic clause as '*canonically* assertable' and ruling that one is entitled to assert a sentence when one knows a procedure for making its canonical assertability condition obtain. Such a theory of meaning is liable to invalidate the law of excluded middle, for it makes 'A or not A' assertable only if either 'A' is assertable or 'Not A' is assertable. Thus, if one knows no procedure for making either 'A' assertable or 'Not A' assertable, one is not entitled to assert even 'A or not A'. For example, 'A' might be 'The number of black holes in the past, present, and future of the universe is even'. For a committed proponent of classical logic, as I had been ever since I found out what classical logic is, such results were good evidence that something had gone wrong with the semantic theory.

Anyway, Dummett never gave a plausible account of canonical assertability conditions even for simple non-mathematical sentences. There are many ways of knowing that Jo is at home; any of them entitles one to assert 'Jo is at home', and English privileges no subset of them as the 'canonical' ones. What unifies those ways is that they are all ways of knowing *that Jo is at home*. Such a line of thought indicated that truth conditions were explanatorily prior to assertability conditions.

My interest in the relation between assertion and knowledge was further piqued by reading Michael Slote's suggestive article 'Assertion and Belief' (Slote 1979). He was my Head of Department at Trinity College Dublin when I started my first full-time university job there in 1980. His article appeared in a volume of conference proceedings so obscure that I would probably never have seen it otherwise.

Reflection on indiscriminability and margins for error later made it clear to me that not even assertability conditions can be as epistemically transparent as Dummett took them to be. In any sense in which truth conditions transcend use, so do assertability conditions. Thus, his arguments for a theory of meaning in terms of the latter rather than the former must fail. Whatever norm governs assertion, one is not always in a position to know whether one is complying with it. Hence, although one is not always in a position to know whether one knows, that does not constitute a good objection to a knowledge norm of assertion. I was free to make a full-blooded case for the knowledge norm (Williamson 1996b).

6. Looking Back: 'Knowledge First'

Several other lines of research went into KAIL. For instance, in 1990–4 the economist Hyun Song Shin and I overlapped as Fellows of University College Oxford. We were both working on epistemic logic and wrote two papers on it together (Shin and Williamson 1994, 1996). He introduced me to the rich literature by theoretical economists on epistemic logic, whose influence can be identified at several points in KAIL.

Since my first published article (Williamson 1982), I had from time to time used a framework of bimodal logic, with both alethic modal operators and epistemic operators, to investigate limits to knowability in response to the so-called paradox of knowability, the proof that if all truths are knowable (as Dummettian anti-realists asserted), then all truths are known (as Dummettian anti-realists were reluctant to assert). The proof was first published by Frederic Fitch, who attributed it to the anonymous referee for an earlier paper he had submitted in 1945 but never published (Fitch 1963). The anonymous referee later turned out to be Alonzo Church (Salerno 2009). My attention was drawn to the result by work of Bill Hart and Colin McGinn (Hart 1979; Hart and McGinn 1976). My original interest was just to show that the full proof did not go through in intuitionistic logic, the preferred logic for Dummettian anti-realists, and to work out how intuitionists might treat the issues it raised. I found it an interesting intellectual exercise, even though my sympathies were all on the side of realism and classical logic. However, Dorothy Edgington proposed an alternative knowability principle for anti-realists that did not collapse into the claim that all truths are known even in the setting of classical logic (Edgington 1985). I argued that Edgington's alternative did not work in the way she needed it to (Williamson 1987a, 1987b; see further Edgington 2010 and Williamson 2021a). I continued to investigate knowability more generally in various classical settings (Williamson 1993).

By the time I came to write KAIL, Dummettian anti-realism no longer felt like a live option. I pointed out essential problems for his conception of assertability, but only in passing. My interest was rather in the ubiquitous way in which our inherently limited powers of discrimination enable knowledge in many cases while disabling it in slightly different cases. Since I regarded classical logic as under no serious threat, I excluded my work on knowability in a non-classical setting from the book. I included only classical arguments for the existence of unknowable truths. Together with the anti-luminosity arguments, they are the limits of knowledge to which the book's title alludes—though, of course, there may be others.

Even in the mid-1990s, I was still not clear how the different papers I was writing fitted together, because I had come at them from different angles, with different interests. I did not write any of them as a mere application of a knowledge-first programme. Still, the role of knowledge in all of them was hard to miss, and the equation $E = K$ of one's total evidence with one's total knowledge was an easy extension (Williamson 1997). Combining that equation with epistemic logic and a prior probability distribution gave a treatment of evidential probability as probability conditional on what one knows (Williamson 1998). It was obviously time to pull all this work, and a bit more, together in a book.

While finishing KAIL, I worried that readers might not see how to fit my position into their mental geography of possible epistemological theories. I was very conscious that my second book, *Vagueness* (Williamson 1994), had had a vastly greater impact than my first, *Identity and Discrimination*, in part because *Vagueness* had a much simpler and clearer take-home message: vagueness is ignorance. Up close, KAIL seemed far more intricate in structure than *Vagueness*. Stepping back, however, the unifying theme was obvious. I gritted my teeth, and put the slogan 'knowledge first' into the first sentence of the Preface. Even readers who got only that far would have some idea what the book was about.

7. Before and After

When KAIL was published in 2000, I feared that epistemologists were too set in their ways of thinking to grasp, let alone adopt, the knowledge-first approach. Some reactions were indeed just as I had predicted, by authors who clearly had no idea how much of their accustomed framework I was rejecting—otherwise they would presumably not have taken it for granted without comment in their objections (some of the essays in Greenough and Pritchard 2009 are examples). I also knew that many epistemologists lacked the formal background in logic and mathematics to be comfortable with the more technical parts of the book.

Nevertheless, KAIL had far more impact than I expected. I was pleasantly surprised at how many epistemologists, especially younger ones, were willing and able to engage seriously with the knowledge-first approach. Epistemology was clearly ready for a change, even though old habits die hard. Some of that readiness came from a more general dissatisfaction with the model of philosophy as 'conceptual analysis' exemplified by the post-Gettier tradition of attempts to analyse 'the concept of knowledge'. One intended methodological moral of KAIL was that logical rigour in philosophy does not depend on conceptual analysis. It is better achieved by formal model-building and explicit theoretical hypotheses which make no claim to be 'analytic truths' or 'conceptual connections'.

KAIL's impact was much greater than the combined impacts of the separate articles out of which it was largely composed. Although analytic philosophy is often observed to be an outlier of the humanities in its publication patterns and closer to the social sciences, with far more emphasis on articles in ranked journals and far less on monographs, books still play a key role. KAIL displayed the various components as working parts of a single theory, and the response showed that many people were looking for such a unified approach to epistemology.

Some developments and applications of KAIL took me by surprise. For instance, I was approached for a meeting in Oxford to discuss KAIL by a Christian missionary writing a doctoral dissertation based on his work in central Africa. He had initially tried to apply the literature on formal models of dialogue to analyse his conversations with non-Christians but had found it quite unhelpful. Instead, the knowledge norm of assertion turned out to give him the traction he needed. As a straightforward atheist, I had not had such applications in mind when working on assertion. Still, I could hardly object. Part of my case for taking assertability to require knowledge rather than the dialectical ability to supply reasoned justification was that the latter gives too much weight to skill in smooth-talking confabulation—a professional skill of philosophers, which they are correspondingly liable to overvalue. But the knowledge norm has also found application to cases where dialogue manifestly does have a highly formal, dialectical structure. In jurisprudence, Michael Blome-Tillmann has argued persuasively that courts' reluctance to admit strong but merely statistical evidence of individual involvement in wrongdoing is best explained by the hypothesis that the operative norm of evidence is implicitly interpreted as a knowledge norm (Blome-Tillmann 2017).

A dimension of generality that I did anticipate in KAIL is the range of potential knowers. I recognized that young children, non-human animals, and perhaps robots with AI can know truths. I deliberately left it open that social entities such as 'science' can possess knowledge, literally and non-derivatively (for social epistemology friendly to a knowledge-first approach, see Bird 2010 and forthcoming; Carter, Kelp, and Simion forthcoming; and Kelp and Simion 2021).

I will discuss in more detail some current developments of the knowledge-first approach in my work and that of others. The survey is by no means intended to be exhaustive. For example, space does not permit me to discuss the close links between knowing and having and acting for *reasons* (Hyman 2015; Hawthorne and Magidor 2018), or refinements of a *safety* constraint on knowledge (Williamson 2009), or the knowledge-first treatment of evidence (Williamson 2024a, forthcoming (a)), or the complications raised by the semantics of attitude ascriptions—including knowledge ascriptions—in cases of coreference (Williamson 2021b, 2024b).

8. Looking Forward: Mindreading

In KAIL, the case for knowing as a core mental state is based mainly on general philosophical considerations about externalism, causal explanation, self-knowledge, the logical form of attitude ascriptions, and so on. One footnote cites a discussion by the psychologist Josef Perner (1993) of evidence that children understand knowledge and ignorance *before* they understand belief and error, and so do not understand knowledge in terms of belief. I found that encouraging but did not build on it. However, as Jennifer Nagel later noted (Nagel 2013), psychologists routinely classify knowing as a mental state. That is not just a terminological point; it draws substance from how they treat the attribution of knowledge as just as central and basic an application of the human mindreading capacity as the attribution of beliefs or desires (see also Nagel 2017). In effect, the human cognitive system thrives on treating knowledge as a mental state.

There is increasingly strong evidence that the capacity to distinguish knowledge from ignorance is cognitively more basic than the capacity to distinguish true belief from error (for an introduction to the recent literature, see Phillips et al. 2020 and associated discussion). Humans attribute knowledge and ignorance before they can attribute true belief and error, and they tend to do it faster and more automatically. Non-human primates attribute knowledge and ignorance to each other, but not true belief or error. Indeed, that combination may extend much more widely across the animal kingdom. The best available explanations of much animal behaviour interpret them as making such distinctions. Reductive attempts to re-explain the behaviour in terms of mere reflexes become ever more ad hoc when faced with the complexity and flexibility of the behaviour. Claims to have found belief attribution at much earlier stages have not proven robust (see Nagel forthcoming, ch. 5, for discussion).

What very young children and non-human primates attribute is clearly knowledge-like, not some doxastic ersatz such as true belief. It is even sensitive to Gettier cases. For example, here is the experimenters' summary of two experiments with rhesus macaques (Horschler, Santos, and MacLean 2019):

> In Experiment 1, monkeys watched an agent observe a piece of fruit (the target object) being hidden in one of two boxes. While the agent's view was occluded, either the fruit moved out of its box and directly back into it, or the box containing the fruit opened and immediately closed. We found that monkeys looked significantly longer when the agent reached incorrectly rather than correctly after the box's movement, but not after the fruit's movement. This result suggests that monkeys did not expect the agent to know the fruit's location when it briefly and arbitrarily moved while the agent could not see it, but did expect the agent to know the fruit's location when only the box moved while the agent could not see it. In Experiment 2, we replicated and extended both findings with a larger sample, a different target object, and opposite directions of motion in the test trials.

In the background is a generic presumption of persistence: the default is that if the fruit is somewhere, it continues to be there, and that if the agent knows that it is there, the agent continues to know that it is there. In effect, when the monkeys see the agent see the fruit put there, they treat the agent as coming to know that it is there. They continue to treat the agent as knowing that it is there when the agent's view is temporarily occluded but the fruit remains there. Thus, they are surprised if the agent reaches for the wrong box, presumably in order to get the fruit. But when the fruit is removed from the box, the monkeys cease to treat the agent as knowing that the fruit is there, since they can see that it isn't. When the fruit is directly put back into the box, they do not treat the agent as again coming to know that the fruit is there, since they can see that the agent did not see it being put back. Thus, they are not surprised if the agent reaches for the wrong box. Had the monkeys been thinking in doxastic terms, they would have treated the agent in both conditions as believing throughout that the fruit is there (this is simply a point about belief; it does not depend on the assumption that knowledge entails belief). Thus, there would be no difference in surprise between the two conditions if the agent reaches for the wrong box. Indeed, the belief that the fruit is there is true in the final stage of both conditions, and even justified, given the presumption of persistence. Since the monkeys reasonably treat the agent as not knowing that the fruit is there after it has been removed and replaced, that is, in effect, a Gettier case, although, of course, they do not think of it as a case of justified true belief.

The experimenters themselves interpret the monkeys as attributing only an 'awareness relation' rather than knowledge to the agent. However, their distinction between knowledge and awareness is unclear and seems to depend on an unnecessarily doxastic conception of knowledge. The results of the experiments make just as good sense on the assumption that the monkeys are distinguishing between knowledge and ignorance (see Nagel forthcoming, chs 4 and 5, for more discussion, including of similar results for young children).

Many philosophers have found the idea that attributing knowledge is easier than attributing belief 'counter-intuitive'. They assume that attributing knowledge *must* be harder and require more sophistication than attributing belief. Sometimes, the assumption comes from a vision of attributing knowledge as attributing some post-Gettier multi-clause *analysans* of knowledge in terms of belief, truth, and one or more other factors, which would, of course, be much harder and require much more sophistication than attributing belief alone. But even philosophers who do not envisage knowledge as having such an analysis often seem to assume that attributing knowledge must require *more* than attributing belief, simply because knowledge itself requires *more* than belief. After all, even in KAIL, knowledge entails belief, while belief does not entail knowledge. At a more general level, a similar thought may influence many internalists: broad mental states must be harder to identify than narrow mental states because identifying broad states requires monitoring *both* the internal *and* the external, whereas monitoring narrow states only requires monitoring the internal.

Such preconceptions are not surprising for *self*-attributions of mental states. But if, as is likely, mindreading capacities evolved through *social* life, their primary role is in attributing mental states to *others*. For that task, states purely internal to the other may be harder to determine than states involving the mutually observable environment. A simple initial case is the *absence* of factive states. Just from knowing that you didn't eat the banana, you can conclude that I don't know that you ate the banana—but you may still wonder whether I *believe* that you ate the banana.

Of course, attributions of positive mental states are more interesting. A good place to start is with *seeing an object*. When you see an apple and I see it too, typically each of us can also see that the other sees it. We can check open eyes, direction of gaze, potential occlusions. That will not satisfy sceptics about other minds, but their sceptical scenarios were scarce in our evolutionary history. Similarly, when two people walking together both hear a loud noise, typically each of them also knows that the other heard it. On the negative side, one may know that the alpha male can't see the apple, because a bush is in the way, or that he is too far away to hear one's breathing. Such knowledge about what others do or don't perceive plays a large role in communication, for example in the use of perceptual demonstratives. When young children interact with other children or adults, mutual gaze at an object is often crucial to communication.

The internal analogue of object-seeing is as-if object-seeing, being in a mental state internally the same as (really) seeing an object. Attributing as-if object-seeing is much more laborious. When I see that you see the apple, I can reason that since every mental state is internally the same as itself, you also as-if see an apple, but that is an artificial intellectual exercise. To consider cases where really seeing and as-if seeing come apart, we can suppose that dreaming that one sees an object involves as-if seeing an object without really doing so. If you see me when I'm asleep gently snoring with my eyes shut, you know that I am not really seeing an apple, but you cannot tell whether I am as-if seeing an apple.

Although object-seeing is not itself a propositional attitude, it is closely related to propositional attitudes. One can see an apple without seeing *that* it is an apple, because it has an unusual shape or one thinks it might be a wax replica or one has been brought up in ignorance of apples. Still, normally, when one sees an apple, one also sees that it is an apple. Conversely, when one doesn't see an apple, one also doesn't see that it is an apple. Thus, it is unsurprisingly typical that when we see an apple together, each of us is in a position to know that the other sees that it is an apple. Seeing-that, 'fact-seeing', *is* a propositional attitude.

Psychologically, perhaps we model seeing that P on seeing an object, treating the state of affairs that P like an object. Just as you can't (really) see what isn't there, you can't (really) see what isn't the case. On this analogy, we treat the non-obtaining of the state of affairs that P like the absence of an object. Just as an object *o* must be there for you to see *o*, it must be that P for you to see that P. Moreover, both object-seeing and seeing-that normally require a suitable causal connection to what is seen: a merely accidental match of your visual image to something external, E, does not constitute seeing E.

In KAIL, I argue that seeing that P is a specific form of knowing that P. Thus, when we see the apple together, typically each of us is in a position to know that the other knows that it is an apple. There would be little point in my judging merely that you *believe* that it is an apple, for why should I make that judgement if I doubt that you see that it is an apple?

Psychologically, seeing-that seems to be treated as a paradigm of knowing-that. 'See' is often used in an extended sense for a wide range of cases of knowing or recognizing (coming to know): 'I see your point'; 'I don't see how that follows'. What drives the generalization from literal seeing and other forms of sense perception to knowing? A crucial factor is *memory*. When you turn away, you no longer *see* that there are apples on the tree, but you still *remember* that there are (or at least were), and many of the effects on action are similar—you may still go to the tree when hungry. Remembering that P is another form of knowing that P. Having seen the agent see the fruit put somewhere, the rhesus macaques continue attributing knowledge that it is there to the agent even when they can see that the agent can no longer see the fruit. A large part of the excess of knowledge over sense perception is simply what remains when sense perception ceases.

In light of these considerations, knowledge attribution looks rather easier and more natural than philosophers' preoccupations can make it seem. We should not be surprised that the level of cognitive sophistication required for attributing knowledge turns out to be *lower* than the level of cognitive sophistication required for attributing belief—just as it can take less to recognize whether someone knows that P than to recognize whether they have an attitude internally similar to knowing that P.

Knowing also takes primacy when we learn from others about the world (Phillips et al. 2020). If you want to know whether P, but are not in a position to perceive whether P, it matters to you whether *I* know whether P. If I do, you can learn from me (whether I happen to have a *belief* as to whether P is not the issue). Imagine us facing each other. You can see things behind my back that I can't see; I can see things behind your back that you can't see. We may wish to share our knowledge: one of us sees signs of a predator and sounds the alarm. Or we may wish *not* to share our knowledge: one of us sees some delicious food and tries not to react, hoping to eat it once the other has gone. The other can benefit by spotting telltale signs that the first has spotted something. In such cases, to focus on the other's internal states is to miss the point.

A converging line of argument comes from considerations of cognitive efficiency, as Robert Gordon has observed (Gordon 2000, 2021; see also his Chapter 5 in the present volume). Creatures with minds put huge effort into learning about their environment and what is happening in it, and keeping their information up to date—it can literally be a matter of life and death. If they are capable of mindreading, they use it to keep informed of similar cognitive states and processes in others. Imagine that whenever they represent something, they must also separately represent how each of the others represent it (for instance, whether they believe, disbelieve, suspend judgement, or have some degree of a credence). That is a massive multiplication of effort. Indeed, it threatens to be infinite: I represent X, you represent how I represent X, I represent how you represent how I represent X, you represent how I represent how you represent how I represent X, and so on. For example, each creature maintains something like a map of its environment. But it also needs to track how each of the others maps the environment, so for each of the others it maintains another map of the environment, representing the other's map. That already threatens to be computationally infeasible, even before we start worrying about the infinite regress of maps of maps.

A much more efficient method would be to maintain just one map, but to try to mark the location of the other knowers on it. That already captures something of their different perspectives on the world. For example, it encodes information about what you can see but others can't, because their view is obstructed by an intervening obstacle. Similarly, it also encodes information about places they can see but you can't. Of course, that is only a start. The rhesus macaques already go further by tracking which present states of affairs another can still view through memory though no longer through sight. The child who can attribute false beliefs is doing something much more complex. Still, the underlying principle may be the same: in mindreading, the default is to treat the other as knowing; the work goes into tracking deviations from that. In Gordon's terms, the default is 'the shared world'. (Harvey Lederman, crediting Taylor Carman for the observation, pointed me to a passage in Merleau-Ponty 1945: 407–8 about the cognitive attitude of young children where he seems to endorse a similar idea.) By contrast, on the mistaken but widespread alternative, the default is to treat the other as a *tabula rasa*, so that attributing any positive mental state requires work.

Watering down the default from knowledge to true belief would make no sense. By default, everything lies open to everyone's view; in those circumstances, there is knowledge, not just true belief.

To make knowledge the default is not to assume that most agents know most truths. Even when that assumption is restricted to simple truths about the environment, it is surely false: think of all the truths about what insects are under what stones, and so on. In practice, mindreading is typically used for matters of actual or potential interest to the agents concerned. The point is that, on such matters, it is typically easier to work down from an initial hypothesis of total knowledge than to work up from an initial hypothesis of total ignorance.

The shared world default may well have been ecologically valid in the conditions under which mindreading evolved: small groups of conspecifics in a local environment, interactions between a predator and prey, and so on. One might worry, though, how much sense it makes in the modern world of highly complex, diverse societies. But that worry may underestimate the epistemic diversity already present under those evolutionary conditions. Even in a small group of hunter-gatherers, there are obvious epistemic asymmetries between adults and children. Children know that they know less than adults, and adults know that they know more than children. Mindreading in both directions guides how children learn from adults. Within a group, differences in life history, recent experience, skills, and abilities can all make for significant differences in knowledge and belief. When one group of hunter-gatherers encountered a new group, perhaps with alien customs, how each group mindread the strangers in those sensitive circumstances could make the difference between things going very well and things going very badly—crudely, between sex and death. Human history is not a simple narrative of increasing diversity; notoriously, imperialism and globalization work in the opposite direction. Even in the modern world, people of very different cultures and mindsets do manage to communicate using a robust capacity for mindreading that evolved under radically different conditions. For that to happen, the shared world is a more effective default than the *tabula rasa*.

The shared world default may also help solve a long-standing problem in game theory and theoretical economics. Many results depend on the hypothesis that various background conditions such as rationality are *common knowledge* amongst the relevant agents, so everyone knows that everyone is rational, everyone knows that everyone knows that everyone is rational, everyone knows that everyone knows that everyone knows that everyone is rational, and so on ad infinitum. Demanding such common knowledge of normal humans seems unrealistic. One might expect that, in practice, a finite approximation to common knowledge would do instead, but that is not always so. Some apparently realistic forms of coordinated action can be achieved under common knowledge but not under 'almost common knowledge' (Rubinstein 1989). Moreover, even a few iterations of 'everyone knows' can be unachievable for epistemological reasons explained in KAIL, since each iteration requires a further margin for error (see also Hawthorne and Magidor 2009, 2010; for a different approach to the problem, see Lederman 2018a, 2018b). Yet an announcement over a loudspeaker can surely *seem* to create common knowledge amongst the people in a room. What is going on?

The knowledge default is implicitly a *common* knowledge default. For substituting 'everyone knows that P' for 'P' in the default schema 'If P, everyone knows that P' gives 'If everyone knows that P, everyone knows that everyone knows that P', and so on, which gives arbitrarily many iterations of 'everyone knows that'. Of course, such a default does not mean that there really is common knowledge. It just means that when nothing inhibits the default, everyone acts as if everything were common knowledge. But that may suffice for coordination to be achieved. It may even be achieved, just as it often seems, with no iteration of epistemic operators, indeed with no epistemic operators at all: the phenomenology is just that of a world open to view. Since the coordination is the predictable result of deeply rooted forms of human thinking, it may even be safe enough for those involved to know in advance that they will coordinate. Naturally, all this needs to be worked out in much more detail. But it promises to be a far more psychologically realistic picture of the cognitive processes underlying apparent common knowledge than any elaborate reconstruction in epistemic logic.

Gordon (2021) connects his arguments about the shared world and cognitive efficiency to the predictive coding model of perception; Daniel Munro (forthcoming) makes a similar connection, arguing that the predictive mind hypothesis is best developed in knowledge-first terms. Incidentally, Gordon (1969, 1987) took a knowledge-first approach to factive emotions long before KAIL.

The distinction between knowledge and ignorance is fundamental to the mindreading capacity of humans and other animals, and so to 'folk epistemology'. By itself, that does not establish that the distinction is also fundamental to epistemology of some more scientific kind, which might in principle use a very different taxonomy of epistemic states. However, the case for psychological fundamentality does hint in that direction. For it does not present the fundamentality as a mere quirk of evolutionary history. Rather, the knowledge–ignorance distinction has primacy because it is cognitively efficient to think in such terms: the distinction is more interpersonally accessible than the 'internal' alternatives, better adapted to sharing information about the world, and much less costly to encode.

Those considerations would apply to a vast range of other possible finite thinkers of quite unfamiliar forms. Thus, the envisaged 'scientific' alternative to knowledge-first epistemology would mostly be understanding these actual and possible thinkers in terms quite alien to those in which they most fundamentally understood themselves and others, where that understanding is itself part of the subject matter of epistemology. That still does not make the alternative scientific enterprise hopeless, but it starts off at a disadvantage.

The crunch comes when a theorist presents a specific alternative to the knowledge-first approach—for example, an informal, ungraded belief-first approach or a formal, graded credence-first variant. One key question is how alternative the proposed alternative really succeeds in being. For the theorist is also a human animal whose default is the shared world, an implicitly knowledge-first way of thinking which can easily slip in under the theorist's radar.

For example, I argued in KAIL that subjective Bayesianism constituted a serious epistemology only by helping itself to a category of 'evidence' for the subject to update on. When such updating is described as 'learning', the mask slips and the tacit reliance on a knowledge-first way of thinking reveals itself, for learning is coming to *know*.

A similar example is the literature on the 'washing-out of priors', with theorems to the effect that, under various conditions, when different prior probabilities are successively updated on new evidence, the results converge in the limit, so that the idiosyncrasies of the priors do not matter (in the infinite limit). The results concern cases where the priors are all updated on the *same* evidence; otherwise, there is no reason for convergence. The only natural rationale for the assumption of common evidence is the picture that the evidence comprises facts open to view for all subjects: in effect, a shared world.

A more recent and bizarre case is the large debate on *disagreement*: when one finds oneself differing from one's epistemic peer who assigns a different credence to the same proposition on the same evidence, should one remain steadfast or conciliate by splitting the difference? In effect, on the standard modelling of such situations in the literature, the agents' relevant evidence is exhausted by their levels of credence in the proposition at issue and their epistemic peerhood (in some sense). Their original evidence, on which their current credence was based, is treated as having no further relevance—even when it is mathematically inconsistent with the proposition at issue or with its negation (as in the popular example of disagreement in adding up a restaurant bill). Yet someone else's degree of credence and whether they are one's epistemic peer are typically much harder to know than the fact at issue (what the total bill is). The model treats an arbitrary slice of the world—credences and peerhood—as shared and open to view, the rest as hidden (contrast Hawthorne and Srinivasan 2013).

Many internalist epistemologies play variations on the same theme, treating just one's internal world—the bubble of consciousness—as open to one's view, making what KAIL calls one's 'cognitive home'. In addition to the anti-luminosity argument, serious work on introspection hardly supports attributing such epistemic privilege to an internal world (Carruthers 2011; Schwitzgebel 2008). Obviously, internalists do not treat what is open to one's view as a *shared* world, since it is not open to another's view, but they still seem to be relying on the cognitively efficient folk technique of modelling one's knowledge of some facts simply by modelling those facts themselves, here with a restriction to 'internal' facts.

None of those epistemological strategies succeeds in fully eliminating the folk epistemological knowledge default. Instead, they restrict it to a privileged class of facts. In the process, they lose much of its flexibility by no longer treating it as a mere default: they bake the privilege into the structure of the theory. In that way, they are more naive than folk epistemology, because they cannot handle ignorance of the privileged facts.

In the limit, there are accounts on which *no* propositions play the role of evidence. KAIL considers such an account: an extreme form of subjective Bayesianism that permits all updates by Jeffrey conditionalization. Such views reduce epistemic normativity to purely formal probabilistic coherence. They find no epistemic fault with the wildest conspiracy theories and the most bigoted prejudices, no matter how out of touch with reality, as long as they conform to standard axioms of the probability calculus and a lax mathematical constraint on updating. For any random finite nonempty set of n possible worlds, they permit one to give probability $1/n$ to each of those worlds and probability 0 to every other world, irrespective of one's sense experience and memories. Epistemology would hardly be worth bothering with, if that were the best it could do.

The track record of attempts to start epistemological theorizing somewhere quite independent of knowledge-first folk epistemology is discouraging. It is also worth noting that folk epistemology is continually tested in practice by our use of it to assess our own epistemic position and that of others and to guide our inquiries. It is surely far from perfect, but it more or less works. By contrast, most epistemological theories are never applied in practice: it is not even obvious how they could be. They are tested against our pre-theoretic verdicts on a few benchmark thought experiments—but those verdicts are themselves likely to be products of folk epistemology.

None of this means that we cannot go beyond folk epistemology. For example, the theory of probability—understood not as something like *plausibility* but as mathematically constrained in effect by something like the standard Kolmogorov axioms—is presumably no part of folk epistemology; that explains why it did not develop until the seventeenth century. Clearly, probability theory has been extensively applied in scientific practice and has amply proved its worth. But that does not vindicate subjective Bayesian epistemology as an alternative to folk epistemology, since its specifically subjective aspect has not been under test: the prior probability distributions in use have been selected by scientists as reasonable for the case at hand in ways implicitly constrained by their background knowledge. Many unreasonable but probabilistically coherent priors would yield quite unreasonable results in practice. As in KAIL, evidential probability theory is an enhancement of folk epistemology, not an alternative to it, just as microscopes and telescopes enhance sense perception rather than enabling scientists to do without it.

Evidently, the research programme on what might be called the psychological reality of knowledge-first epistemology—in both humans and other animals—is in its early stages. We have the barest outline of the picture, but most of the details remain to be filled in: just how are obstacles to knowledge tracked and registered, and just how are false beliefs finally acknowledged? Epistemologists will have much to learn from future developments in the cognitive psychology of humans and other animals, and will have something of their own to contribute to the joint inquiry. For example, it took epistemologists to recognize the significance of Gettier cases. More generally, the epistemic significance of the relations to the world that cognitive systems have the function of implementing is best understood in a setting informed by systematic epistemological theory. But epistemology can only make that contribution properly if it abandons internalist preconceptions.

The knowledge-first approach to mindreading also casts new light on the role of *charity* in interpretation. For Quine and Davidson, a key constraint on interpreting others is, as far as possible, to make what they assent to come out *true*. That applies to both their thought and their talk and is treated as *constitutive*, not just *instrumental*: what it is for an interpretation to be correct is in part for it to be charitable in that sense. Charity is not meant to be merely an effective means to an independently defined end. In *The Philosophy of Philosophy* (Williamson 2007), I argued that Quine and Davidson's principle of charity, by maximizing *true belief*, inherited the problems of epistemology when it concentrates on true belief, a psychologically unnatural category. If an interpretation maximizes true belief by attributing many beliefs that just happen to be true, though the subject is in no position to know their truth, that should not make the interpretation correct, as I illustrated in detail. I argued that a better principle of charity maximizes *knowledge* rather than true belief.

What the arguments in *The Philosophy of Philosophy* do not fully bring out is the *centrality* of knowledge attribution to mindreading. One might get the impression that knowledge maximization acted merely as a tiebreaker, deciding between already given candidate interpretations. But once we understand mindreading as working down from a completely knowing subject, not up from a completely blank slate, it is clear that, without attributing knowledge, interpretation cannot even get started.

9. Looking Forward: Knowledge and Action

One aspect of KAIL never fully satisfied me: the analogy between knowledge and (intentional) action as developed in KAIL's Introduction and recalled above. I worked there with the formula: knowledge stands to belief as action stands to desire. Belief and desire were contrasted as having opposite directions of fit. When all goes well with fitting world to mind, there is action. When all goes well with fitting mind to world, there is knowledge. However, when I tried to work out the details, things never went quite as smoothly as I had hoped. In particular, the formula presented action as more closely related to desire than to belief. But, even from the perspective of belief-desire psychology, belief and desire were more or less symmetrically related to action, equally necessary inputs to decision-making.

I gradually realized that in starting with the question 'What stands to desire as knowledge stands to belief?', I had already conceded too much to belief-desire psychology. I needed to start from a better place, taking the knowledge-action pair as given, and ask: what stands to action as belief stands to knowledge? The natural answer to that question is not desire but *intention*. Consider the global process centred on decision-making, including the origins of the input premises to practical reasoning, the practical reasoning itself, and the results of the output conclusion, and compare it with the local process of the reasoning itself, narrowly understood. When all goes well in the global process, knowledge is the input to the practical reasoning and action is the output. When something goes wrong on the input side, there may be mere belief rather than knowledge, but still playing the same local role as knowledge, of input to the reasoning. When something goes wrong on the output side, there may be mere intention rather than action, but still playing the same local role as action, of output from the reasoning. When the defect is only partial on the input side, the agent may still *reasonably* believe that P, short of knowing that P. When the defect is only partial on the output side, the agent may still *try* to do A, short of intentionally doing A. Richard Holton (2014) had already drawn a related comparison of belief and intention. One can make up one's mind *that P*; one can make up one's mind *to φ*.

Just as there was a degenerating research programme of trying to analyse 'S knows that P' in terms of 'S believes that P', '(it is true that) P', and other factors not presupposing the category of knowledge, so there was a degenerating research programme of trying to analyse 'S intentionally φs' in terms of 'S intends to φ', 'S φs', and other factors not presupposing the category of intentional action. The two research programmes faced analogous obstacles in counterexamples to necessity or sufficiency and in implicit circularity. For instance, just as a causal link from its being true that P to S's believing that P is not the missing ingredient, nor is a causal link from S's intending to φ to S's φing. Both proposals face the problem of deviant causal chains and other difficulties (Williamson 2017a, 2018).

Just as the distinction between S's knowing that P and S's not knowing that P is easier to track by observing S than the distinction between S's believing that P and S's not believing that P (see Section 8), so the distinction between S's intentionally φing and S's not intentionally φing is easier to track by observing S than the distinction between S's intending to φ and S's not intending to φ. Just as we should expect attributions of knowledge to precede attributions of belief, so we should expect attributions of action to precede attributions of intention.

This reworking of the analogy between knowledge and action raises an obvious question: where does desire fit into the new picture? Since desire belongs on the input side, which, when all goes well, is the knowledge side, the natural answer to the question is that desire is a form of belief. For belief is what constitutes knowledge when all goes well. Thus, one arrives at the ultra-controversial view of desire as belief.

Of course, if desires consist in beliefs, it does not follow that the desire that P consists in the belief *that P*. Rather, the desire that P consists in the belief that Φ(P), for some suitable operator Φ. For instance, the desire that P might consist in the belief that it would be good if P, more exactly, in the belief that if P it would be good that P, in a not specifically moral sense of 'good' ('if P' is needed because 'it is good that P' implies 'P').

Such unpacking already defuses the objection that desires cannot be beliefs because inconsistent beliefs are always irrational, while inconsistent desires are sometimes rational. For example, suppose that two of your friends, Mary and John, are among the hundreds of candidates for the same job. Quite rationally, you may both want Mary to get the job and want John to get the job, even though you know that they cannot both get it. For the first desire may consist in the belief that if John got the job, it would be good that he got it, while the second consists in the belief that if Mary got the job, it would be good that she got it. Those two beliefs may be true together, for both outcomes may be good: perhaps Mary and John are equally good candidates and better than all the rest. You desire one outcome and desire another, knowing that the two outcomes are mutually incompatible, but what you believe about the first outcome and what you believe about the second are mutually compatible. If all desires consist in beliefs, and it is irrational to believe incompatibles, it just does not follow that it is irrational to desire incompatibles, because *what* you believe when you desire is not what you desire. Of course, you still have *an* attitude—desire—to incompatible propositions, but that is not in itself irrational. When I wonder whether a pear is ripe, I also wonder whether it is *not* ripe, without thereby contradicting myself. When the glass is half-full, I rationally take the attitude of rejection to both the proposition that it is empty and the proposition that it is full, despite their mutual incompatibility.

In the setting of knowledge-first epistemology, assimilating desire to belief involves subjecting desire to a knowledge norm. On the view developed in KAIL, if you believe that P without knowing that P, your believing is defective. Thus, if you desire that P, and your desire consists in the belief that it would be good if P, but you do not know that it would be good if P, then your desiring is defective. Some philosophers will deny that desire is subject to any such norm. They may contrast belief and desire in just that respect: belief is subject to an epistemic norm, but desire is not. That view often goes with the claim that desire has no function: desire is simply a matter of individual preference. From an evolutionary perspective, that claim is quite implausible. Desires serve an obvious evolutionary function: to motivate creatures to get things that are good for them, either individually or collectively: food, drink, sex, warmth, safety, and the like. Iris, the flowering plant, is poisonous for sheep, but they often want to eat it when they see it. In a natural sense, their desire for it is *mistaken*. In effect, their desire consists in a false belief that it would be good to eat. Similarly, if they want to eat a plant which in fact has the same appearance as iris but is good for them, in an area with an abundance of iris, their desire for it is not mistaken but is still epistemically defective. They believe that it would be good to eat, and their belief is true, but fails to constitute knowledge.

Using the word 'good' to articulate a sheep's propositional attitudes may sound like over-intellectualization. But it is not strange to characterize dumb animals as treating some options as *better* than others, and 'better' is just the comparative of 'good'. What such general evaluative terms express here need not be an intrinsically motivating quality, but simply a common measure for weighing different goods (food, drink, sex, warmth, safety, and the like) against each other, which even dumb animals have to do—and sometimes get wrong.

Presumably, for evolutionary reasons, animals normally are motivated to pursue their own individual or collective good, at least under evolutionary normal conditions, but not out of any metaphysical or conceptual necessity. As we know from the human case, one can believe and even know that it would be good to eat (in a sense of 'good' suitably related to evolutionary fitness), yet still not desire to eat. Thus, when the desire to eat does consist in a belief that it would be good to eat, which motivates one to eat, that is no automatic consequence of believing that it would be good to eat, but an effect dependent on contingent circumstances. If a belief that $\Phi(P)$ *can* constitute a desire that P, it does not follow that a belief that $\Phi(P)$ *must* constitute a desire that P. The belief that doing X would annoy their parents motivates some teenagers to do X, other teenagers to avoid doing X, and leaves still others indifferent. In short, desires play the general functional role of belief—one acts on them—but they also play a more specific functional role of their own, by helping characterize the end state of action in practical terms (this more specific functional role may help explain how children manage to attribute desires—'I want it!'—comparatively early).

If desire has its own functional role, what is gained by assimilating it to belief? One advantage emerges when we try to understand the agent's practical reasoning from a first-personal perspective. We seek an argument in the first person present tense that, as far as possible, favours the action taken, attempted, or at least intended. Even for unreflective agents incapable of articulating their reasons themselves, such an argument should capture something of what they were up to from their perspective. For the argument to favour a specific course of action, it will need *premises*. But they must be premises that the agent in effect assumes or endorses; in brief, the agent should *believe* the premises. Since the role of desire in practical reasoning is to provide some of the inputs, it must in effect contribute believed premises in which the desires consist. Thus, assimilating desire to belief helps us understand the agent's practical reasoning from the agent's point of view.

By applying the knowledge norm of belief to agents' beliefs in the premises of their practical reasoning, we can then assess the epistemic standing of their starting point. This is close to a connection between knowledge and action for which John Hawthorne and Jason Stanley have argued independently (Hawthorne and Stanley 2008).

Perhaps the 'practical reasoning' is sometimes as simple as 'Playing loud music will annoy my parents, so I'll play loud music', with no mediating conception of the wider good to be served by annoying the parents. The recalcitrant teenager may even *know* the truth of the premise. In the unlikely event that there is really no more to it than that, we may just have to settle on the verdict that the premise is in an epistemically fine position, but the argument is a non sequitur.

The challenge to articulate the agent's reason for action in first-personal terms poses a significant difficulty for standard decision theory, which works on the agent's credences (subjective probabilities) and preferences (subjective utilities)—the graded analogues of beliefs and desires. The problem may not be obvious at first sight, since the decision theorist can present the usual calculation of the subjectively expected utilities of the various options as a formal representation of the agent's implicit practical reasoning. The trouble is that, in doing so, they represent the agent as reasoning *about* her own mental states.

For example, when a mother searches for her baby, the decision-theoretic calculation has a premise like 'The mother greatly prefers her baby being found to her baby being lost'. Thus, when put into the first person, it represents the mother as implicitly reasoning from a premise like 'I greatly prefer my baby being found to my baby being lost'. But that is quite implausible, even though there is no suggestion that the mother says such words to herself. For the mother's thoughts are much less likely to be on her own preferences than on her baby's needs. The decision-theoretic representation misrepresents the mother as self-absorbedly reasoning as though it were all about her.

Decision theorists can, of course, represent the mother's altruism by giving more weight to the baby's welfare than to the mother's in the latter's ranking of possibilities. That is not in doubt. The point is rather that when the decision-theoretic calculation is treated as something the mother could in principle endorse as giving her reason for action, her reason is represented as consisting in facts about her own subjective psychological states. She is depicted as pathologically self-regarding, as treating the reasons for action as all about her. That gets her psychology hopelessly wrong.

The point applies just as much to the agent's credences as to her preferences. The decision-theoretic calculation has premises such as 'The mother has a much higher credence in her baby being upstairs than in her baby being downstairs'. Thus, when put into the first person, it represents the mother as implicitly reasoning from a premise like 'I have a much higher credence in my baby being upstairs than in my baby being downstairs'. But that too is quite implausible, even though there is no suggestion that the mother says such words to herself. For the mother's thoughts are much less likely to be on her own doxastic states than on where her baby is objectively likely to be. She is trying to be true to the world, not true to herself. Here too the decision-theoretic representation depicts the mother as self-absorbedly reasoning as though it were all about her.

The problem is exacerbated when, as often, decision theory is proposed as a normative theory about the decision-making of ideally rational agents. For, if anyone can articulate their reason for action in the first person, it is an ideally rational agent. But, as just observed, an agent whose reason for action is articulated in the first person as the subjective decision-theoretic calculation is thereby revealed to be pathologically self-regarding, which would be an unfortunate consequence of ideal rationality.

None of this is to deny the value of calculating the expected utility of various options when appropriate. For that value does not depend on interpreting the probabilities and utilities as merely subjective. One can rationally estimate the genuine costs and benefits of different outcomes and their probabilities on one's evidence, and calculate the expected utility of various options accordingly. But the premises of the calculation will be true or false, depending on how the world is; they will not be a mere expression of one's own subjective psychological state.

The 'shared world' approach to mindreading helps with attributing desires as beliefs. For example, when something is good to eat or drink, the default is for that to be out in the shared world, observable to others too. As usual, the default can be overridden in many ways. When a task is hard (for me), I must not automatically treat it as hard (for you); likewise, when something is good (for me), I must not automatically treat it as good (for you). Some adjustments are needed for mindreading other members of the same species, since we may be competing for scarce resources; larger adjustments are needed for mindreading members of a species on the other side of a predator–prey distinction. Nevertheless, such adjustments are a fair price to pay for not having to start by treating others as blank slates with respect to desire.

The analogy between knowledge and action can take one a long way. I will briefly sketch some further connections between knowledge-first epistemology and the philosophy of action.

When I was completing KAIL, I was also working on a paper with Jason Stanley arguing for the *intellectualist* view that knowing-how is a special case of knowing-that, thereby rejecting the cliché that knowing that and knowing how are mutually exclusive, one theoretical and one practical (as though theory and practice were mutually exclusive). Our article 'Knowing How' appeared the following year (Stanley and Williamson 2001; see also Stanley 2011). Roughly, to know how to φ is to know, of some way w, that w is a way for one to φ. At least in paradigmatic cases of knowing how, one has the knowledge under a *practical mode of presentation* of w, under which w is ready for one to implement. That was to be expected from obvious analogies between 'how' (in what way?) and comparable interrogative words such as 'why' and 'wherefore' (for what reason?), 'when' (at what time?), 'where' (in what place?), 'whence' (from what place?), 'whither' (to what place?) 'who' and 'whom' (what person?), 'whose' (of what person?), 'whether' (yes or no?), 'which' (of given alternatives?), and 'what' itself. If 'how' had been spelt and pronounced 'whow', there might have been less fuss.

Considerations of semantic compositionality, combined with the semantics of indirect questions, strongly favour intellectualism: at least the literal reading of 'S knows how to φ' is intellectualist. Of course, 'S knows how to φ' might also have an idiomatic meaning too, but then it would be ambiguous and so should pass standard tests for ambiguity, a point most anti-intellectualists ignore.

Critics have noted that in some languages one asks the equivalent of 'Can she swim?' when in English one might ask 'Does she know how to swim?', but that hardly shows the questions to be synonymous. After all, it is usually a matter of indifference whether one asks 'Can she speak English?' or 'Does she speak English?', even though the questions are not semantically equivalent—perhaps she can speak English but refuses to do so.

Although both KAIL and 'Knowing How' are centrally about knowledge, the two projects were pursued independently. There was no reason to fear that they might lead to inconsistent conclusions. Gradually, more connections between them have emerged, not least through the work of Carlotta Pavese. In an important series of papers, she has developed a knowledge-first conception of action as radically informed and controlled by knowledge (Pavese 2015, 2016, 2017, 2019, 2020a, 2020b, 2021, and Chapter 6 of the present volume). Stanley and I have argued for a related view of *skill* (contrast *strength*) as a disposition to have the knowledge required for controlling action (Stanley and Williamson 2017). Thus, action is not merely the *analogue* of knowledge on the output side; it is itself deeply knowledgeable. More recently, I have explored how desire as belief, a knowledge norm for belief, an action norm for intention, and intellectualism about knowing how combine to transform a traditional belief-desire account of means-end reasoning step by step into a knowledge-first account of the role of knowing how in action (Williamson 2023a).

Perhaps this unification of knowledge and action can be taken still further. In particular, *intentionally bringing it about* that P might be understood as a kind of *active knowing* that it will be that P (maker's knowledge). That also suggests an assimilation of *intending to bring it about* that P to a kind of *believing* that it will be that P.

Some deny that 'S intentionally brings it about that P' is sufficient for 'S knows that it will be the case that P' on the grounds that luck can play too large a role for knowing without playing too large a role for intentionally bringing it about, though it is unclear whether such claims are robust. Even if there is no entailment, perhaps all central cases of intentionally bringing it about that P are cases of knowing that it will be that P, which would already be a significant result. In this area, as in most others, much remains to be understood.

10. Looking Forward: Models of Knowledge

KAIL makes extensive use of a model-building methodology, in the tradition of epistemic logic. Even very simple models can cast light on epistemic structure. For instance, in assessing sceptical arguments, we can understand the non-symmetry of the accessibility relation by considering a model with just two worlds, corresponding to the good case and the bad case (the sceptical scenario).

By itself, the framework of Kripke models is neutral towards the knowledge-first approach. We can do epistemic logic, requiring accessibility to be reflexive (since knowledge entails truth), but equally we can do doxastic logic, not requiring accessibility to be reflexive (since belief does not entail truth)—though we might still require it to be *serial*, so every world sees at least one world (if inconsistent belief is excluded). However, when one surveys applications of the framework in computer science and economics, one typically finds the models explicitly described in terms of knowledge, not of mere belief. Usually, the models are multi-agent, with one accessibility relation per agent, which is required to be an equivalence relation, so it induces a partition of the worlds in the model into mutually exclusive, jointly exhaustive cells. The agent cannot discriminate between any worlds in the same cell, but can discriminate between any worlds in different cells. For each agent, accessibility is reflexive, since any world is in the same cell as itself. Thus, the models are genuinely epistemic rather than doxastic. This is surely not the result of any prior theoretical commitment to a knowledge-first approach on the part of computer scientists or economists. They are just using the simplest non-trivial multi-agent models within the overall framework, which strikingly turn out to be of knowledge rather than just belief.

Partitional models also endow agents with perfect introspection, both positive and negative: they always know whether they know a given proposition. That is often a defensible idealization: in studying communicative obstacles to inter-agent epistemic transparency (common knowledge), it makes sense to stipulate away obstacles to intra-agent epistemic transparency, in order to isolate the phenomena of interest. Unfortunately, that idealization has tended to harden into an ideological dogma, resulting in a kind of self-imposed epistemological naivety in non-philosophical formal epistemologists, who have never properly confronted the sceptical consequences of their assumptions, if treated as more than temporarily useful model-building idealizations.

The arguments in KAIL against positive introspection, the KK principle, were inspired by devising models of agents with limited powers of discrimination. Subsequently, I extended the arguments to reach stronger conclusions. For example, imagine someone with normal but not perfect vision looking at an unmarked clock. On that basis, how much can she know about where the hand is pointing? If one models the situation, including a probability distribution, in the simplest, most natural way, one can prove that, for some proposition p in the model (as it were, the proposition that it is pointing between 3.05 and 3.15), the agent knows p, even though it is almost certain on her evidence that she does *not* know p. Many variations can be played on this theme (Williamson 2011, 2014). Thus, KK does not just fail in the model; it fails as drastically as it could.

Of course, a single type of model is never conclusive by itself. With enough ad hoc gerrymandering, one can almost always remodel a given phenomenon so as to avoid the feature one dislikes. That applies in particular to the phenomenon of the agent's knowledge of the unmarked clock and the feature of KK failure. In response, rather than simply pointing out ad hoc aspects of particular alternative models, it is more satisfying to prove that any model of the given phenomenon which lacks the controversial feature will have a specified ad hoc feature. In the case of the unmarked clock, that can be done. For the relevant space of possibilities has natural rotational symmetry, induced by the rotational symmetry of the clock face itself, without the hand; in any given possibility, the hand breaks the symmetry, because it has a specific position, but there is still symmetry in the overall range of prior possibilities. One can prove that, in any epistemic model of the case with rotational symmetry, if the agent learns *something* but not *everything* about the hand's position by looking at the clock, then KK fails for some proposition (Williamson 2021c). Thus, to reconcile the case with KK without being hopelessly unrealistic, the model must be ad hoc by breaking the symmetry. In that sense, the counterexample to KK is *robust*.

The model-building methodology can play a further role in making epistemological conclusions more robust. For it is not far-fetched to worry that the standard procedure of analytic epistemology relies on a kind of *naive falsificationism*. Universally general theories in epistemology make predictions about hypothetical scenarios; by doing the relevant thought experiment, we either verify or falsify the prediction. If it is falsified, so is the epistemological theory, since we have a counterexample to the generalization. Thus, the refuted theory can be dismissed. One trouble with the naive falsificationist methodology in natural science is that scientists are not infallible in designing, conducting, and interpreting experiments in real life. For example, they may neglect an interfering factor. That is why experiments need to be repeatable, preferably by different people, under different conditions, by a different method. Not every apparent falsification is genuine. In analytic epistemology, universal generalizations are often treated as refuted by a single thought experiment. The danger is that we dismiss a true theory on the basis of a mistaken verdict on one thought experiment. The mistake will not be merely idiosyncratic, since the epistemological community dismisses a theory only when it reaches consensus on the theory. But the negative verdict in the thought experiment might result from our reliance on a natural but imperfectly reliable *heuristic*, such as an easy, quick and dirty way of judging whether knowledge is present in a given case. Sometimes, we have no pre-theoretic way to second-guess our heuristic; what indicates its merely heuristic status is that its outputs can be mutually inconsistent (for philosophers' and linguists' reliance on such heuristics, see Williamson 2020b, 2021b). An output of such a heuristic may well secure interpersonal assent, even when false.

This worry about reliance on thought experiments may remind readers of the 'negative program' in experimental philosophy, initiated by the work of Jonathan Weinberg, Shaun Nichols, and Stephen Stich (2001). Some early results seemed to indicate that received verdicts on standard thought experiments in analytic epistemology vary with subjects' ethnicity or gender and so are unreliable. A salient case in point was the verdict that the protagonist of a Gettier case lacks knowledge. Proponents of the negative program drew the moral that philosophers should stop relying on 'philosophical intuitions', though they never satisfactorily explained what counts as a 'philosophical intuition' (there is nothing peculiarly philosophical about the judgement that someone doesn't know something). Might the old justified true belief analysis of knowledge be right after all? However, most of the early results proved misleading: they were not repeated when experiments were redone more carefully. In particular, the negative verdict on Gettier cases turned out to be more like a cross-cultural human universal, prompting experimental philosophers to postulate a universal 'folk epistemology' (Machery et al. 2017). I have criticized the negative program elsewhere, and will not repeat those arguments here (Williamson 2021d; see also Nagel 2012). Still, it did highlight the risks involved in treating a single thought experiment as a conclusive counterexample (see Alexander and Weinberg 2014 on 'error fragility'). Indeed, even if the negative verdict on Gettier cases is a human universal, that does not automatically mean that it is *true*. For it may be the output of a humanly universal fallible heuristic. Brian Weatherson has suggested that the word 'know' could refer to justified true belief by virtue of the latter's being the most 'natural' property to approximately fit the use of 'know', despite our reaction to Gettier cases (Weatherson 2003).

Since real-life cases are just as relevant to epistemology as are counterfactual thought experiments, I will write simply of 'examples', to cover both.

The point is not that judgements on examples are *especially* fallible, but simply that they *are* fallible. The same applies to perceptual judgements. We cannot do science if we never rely on sense perception, but we still have to control for perceptual error. Similarly, we have to control for error in judgements on examples. This is where model-building can help. We can use it as an independent test of conclusions reached through examples. For instance, one can model the JTB analysis of knowledge as justified true belief, to explore its consequences in a formal setting. Contrary to the impression of it as a beautiful theory tragically and unjustly slain by counterexamples, one can show that it reduces the known to awkward disjunctions, where one disjunct secures truth while the other secures justified belief, and that it has various consequences inimical to the views of those who treat justification as epistemologically fundamental (Williamson 2013a, 2013b, 2015). Naturalness works *against* the JTB analysis, not for it. Similarly, one can assess the slogan 'evidence of evidence is evidence' by exploring its unfortunate consequences on various interpretations in a formal setting (Williamson 2019).

In general, we can make our conclusions more robust by testing them with different methodologies. The idea is not that formal models supersede examples, any more than examples supersede formal models. It is just that hypotheses confirmed by *both* examples *and* formal models are better confirmed than those confirmed in only one of the two ways.

Obviously, much work in epistemology is resolutely informal, and its authors might well reject the challenge to model it formally as inappropriate. In doing so, however, they give up the chance to test and develop their hypotheses in one of the most rigorous and fruitful ways available. Nor is it clear *why* the challenge of formal modelling is supposed to be inappropriate. After all, the task is not to formalize the epistemological theory itself, but just to show exactly how it works in a mathematically precise, simple but not quite trivial case. If theorists cannot manage even that much, one may suspect that something is amiss with their theory.

Formal model-building in epistemology is, of course, not confined to the knowledge-first approach. It has a much longer history in the Bayesian tradition. A welcome recent development is the increasing interaction between formal and informal epistemology: when pursued in mutual isolation, both sides suffer. In particular, subjective Bayesian epistemology confined itself to a purely formal standard of rationality, on which a consistent Nazi whose credences satisfy the Kolmogorov axioms and who updates only by conditionalizing on Nazi-vetted propositions counts as perfectly rational. Epistemology can do better than that. One place to start is with the observation that the Nazi grossly violates the knowledge norm of belief. One advantage of the knowledge-first approach is that it formally models both knowledge and belief.

11. Looking Forward: Epistemic Norms

Epistemic justification is often treated, more or less definitionally, as what it takes to comply with the basic epistemic norm for belief, whatever that is. On a knowledge-first view, the norm is knowledge. Thus, a belief is justified if and only if it constitutes knowledge (I leave tacit the gloss 'epistemically' on 'justified'). Consequently, only true beliefs are justified.

Alas, another constraint is often treated as more or less definitional too: that beliefs are equally justified in corresponding good and bad cases. Thus, since my belief that I have hands is justified in the actual good case, it is also justified in a corresponding bad case, a sceptical scenario where I lack hands. Consequently, not only true beliefs are justified.

To treat *both* identity with the basic epistemic norm for belief *and* equality across the good and bad cases as simultaneously definitional is cheating. For it sneaks in the contentious internalist assumption that compliance with the basic epistemic norm for belief is equal across the good and bad cases, as if it were a matter of stipulation (Williamson forthcoming (c)).

KAIL treats justification as *graded*, and measured by probability on the evidence. Thus, a false belief may be justified to some degree. Still, only knowledge is *fully* justified. I became more forthright on that point after KAIL was published (Williamson forthcoming (c); see also Srinivasan 2020 on externalism about justification).

Of course, a question remains: *why* are so many epistemologists so tempted to judge that beliefs are as justified in the bad case as in the good case? A natural answer is that beliefs in the two cases are envisaged as resulting from the very same cognitive dispositions. In general, dispositions are typically more durable than their manifestations. If you are put in circumstances where it is harder for you to exercise your skills effectively, it does not follow that you have become less skilful. Were we to suspect that the agent changed cognitive dispositions in being switched between the good and bad cases, we might well be much less tempted to judge that the level of justification remained constant over the switch. But we must not confuse judging the believer with judging the belief.

An analogy: someone borrows a book, promising to return it. But the book gets stolen, so she cannot return it. She did her best, but she failed to keep her promise. So she violated the norm of promise-keeping on that occasion (promising to φ is not merely promising to do your best to φ). However, she does have an excellent *excuse* for having violated the norm of promise-keeping. Similarly, imagine that it is illegal for a commoner to touch the royal sceptre. You are a law-abiding commoner. A troublemaker throws the sceptre in your face, making you touch it. You did your best, but you broke the law. However, you do have an excellent *excuse* for having broken the law. Likewise, although the brain in a vat does its best, it violates the knowledge norm of belief, and even a truth norm, by believing that it has hands. However, it does have an excellent *excuse* for violating the knowledge norm of belief.

We cannot hope to do justice to such examples if we approach them with a radically impoverished normative vocabulary, consisting only of 'justified' and 'unjustified'. We need at least the category of excuses for cases of fully or partly blameless norm violation. When I have applied it, I have sometimes been interpreted as doing so on the basis of an *analysis* of excusability into necessary and sufficient conditions. That is a misinterpretation. We need the category of excuses to handle the gap between the inflexible simplicity of many norms and the unpredictable, messy, human complexity of real-life cases. Any attempt to codify excusability in terms of necessary and sufficient conditions misses exactly that point.

Still, we can identify some salient types of excuse. Given a primary norm N on acts, there is a secondary norm on agents: to be disposed to comply with N. Thus, the brain in a vat's beliefs violate the knowledge norm, but the brain may still comply with the corresponding secondary norm by being disposed to form beliefs that constitute knowledge (if we treat its envatment as abnormal), even though its attempts to exercise that disposition misfire in its unfortunate circumstances. There is even a tertiary norm, on acts again: to act as someone disposed to comply with N would. That an act complies with the tertiary norm is typically a good excuse for its failure to comply with the primary norm.

Maria Lasonen-Aarnio (2010, 2014, 2021) has used the distinction between a primary 'occurrent' norm and a corresponding secondary 'dispositional' norm in a converse way to argue against the alleged phenomenon of knowledge defeat by misleading counter-evidence. Ignoring counter-evidence is a bad cognitive disposition; its normal effect is to block opportunities for agents to learn from their mistakes. However, agents occasionally benefit from their bad habits and achieve undeserved success. Those who ignore counter-evidence are sometimes lucky enough to be retaining genuine knowledge. They comply with the primary norm of belief but violate the secondary norm—the opposite of the brain in the vat.

Unfortunately, epistemologists often fail to distinguish between primary and tertiary norms of belief. That failure is especially prevalent in discussions of rational belief, partly because we apply the term 'rational' to both acts and agents (Williamson 2017b). For generality, we may suppose just that the primary rational norm (on beliefs) is to *accord with* one's evidence, where 'accord with' is schematic. The knowledge norm is one way of implementing that schema, but not the only one. Thus, the secondary norm (on believers) is to be disposed to form beliefs that accord with one's evidence; that is what it is to be a rational believer. The tertiary norm (on beliefs) is to believe what a rational believer would believe in the circumstances. Epistemologists often confuse the primary and tertiary norms by treating 'Does it accord with one's evidence?' and 'Would a rational believer believe it?' as interchangeable tests for the rationality of a belief. But the primary and tertiary norms are equivalent only if the beliefs that accord with one's evidence are exactly the beliefs a rational believer would have. That equivalence is far from trivial. For example, if the primary norm is implemented by the knowledge norm, then, as typically envisaged, the brain in a vat's beliefs violate the primary norm (they are not knowledge) but comply with the tertiary norm (they are what a rational believer in the relevant sense would believe in the circumstances); thus, the equivalence fails.

More generally, suppose that there can be *illusions of evidence*, where something seems to be evidence but isn't or seems not to be evidence but is. Then, the disposition to form beliefs that accord with one's evidence can misfire, because it generates beliefs that accord with one's *apparent* evidence but not with one's *real* evidence. Such beliefs violate the primary norm but comply with the tertiary norm. Consequently, epistemologists who treat the primary and tertiary norms of rational belief as interchangeable in effect assume that there are no illusions of evidence, in other words, that evidence is *transparent*.

Similarly, if either the presence or the absence of evidence is non-luminous in the sense of KAIL, one would not expect the primary and tertiary norms of rational belief to be equivalent. Thus, epistemologists who treat the two norms as interchangeable in effect assume that both the presence and the absence of evidence are luminous.

Given the anti-luminosity argument and similar considerations, the primary and tertiary norms of rational belief are *not* equivalent (see Srinivasan 2013 for a reply to the objections in Berker 2008 to the anti-luminosity argument). Thus, conflating the two norms amounts to assuming a false internalist principle.

These considerations are quite general. For any non-trivial norm, complying with it, being disposed to comply with it, and doing as someone disposed to comply with it would do are pairwise non-equivalent. Moreover, as in KAIL, complying with it, being in a position to know that one is complying with it, and not being in a position to know that one is not complying with it are pairwise non-equivalent too. Thus, any non-trivial norm is surrounded by a cloud of closely related but non-equivalent norms, each of which seems to have its own distinctive force. For example, although the dispositional norm derives from the occurrent norm, we may be more concerned with agents' dispositions to infringe than with their actual infringements. Similarly, we may be more concerned with agents' knowledge of their standing with respect to the primary norm than with that standing itself. *None* of these norms provides the agent with fully operational guidance (Williamson 2008; Srinivasan 2015; Hughes 2018).

In such circumstances, when we start out not knowing which norm is primary, the normative landscape is very hard to map. Undifferentiated pre-theoretical reactions to individual cases are a recipe for confusion, since one has no way of holding the operative norm constant, especially when the judgements are supposed to be 'all things considered'. We are pulled in opposite directions by variant norms, which can create something like epistemic dilemmas (Hughes 2019, forthcoming (a), forthcoming (b)).

We do better to proceed abductively rather than inductively, first conjecturing a single primary norm—the simpler and more perspicuous the better—and then trying to explain the relevant normative phenomena on that basis, invoking its derivative norms as necessary.

For belief, truth and knowledge are the two most salient candidates for the primary norm (KAIL argues that a knowledge norm explains more than a truth norm). By contrast, if one starts only with a norm of internal coherence or reflective equilibrium, it is quite unclear how to explain what is wrong with the belief system of a Nazi who consistently sees the world in Nazi terms (Williamson 2023b). Internalist attempts to refute the possibility of such a person are far from convincing. As we saw, subjective Bayesianism faces the same problem.

To make the explanatory starting point maximally perspicuous, we should formulate the primary norm simply in terms of a condition for compliance, not in terms of a condition for permissibility. The reason is that, semantically, deontic modals such as 'permissible' depend on a domain of contextually relevant possible worlds; variations in that parameter are extraneous to the underlying norm but easily cause confusion. For example, they have led to many needless complications in the debate on a truth norm for belief (Williamson 2020a).

What *kind* of norm is an epistemic norm for belief? Much of the literature focuses on reflective, responsible, rational persons—perhaps professional philosophers as they might like to be. Moralizing talk of epistemic 'virtues' and 'vices' encourages that impression. Once we appreciate how widespread knowledge and belief are amongst non-human animals, we should be wary of such over-intellectualization.

A broadly functional starting point is more promising. But we should not confine ourselves to norms on individual beliefs, for one could in principle comply with such norms by just suspending all belief (if that were psychologically possible). Instead, we should consider norms on whole cognitive systems (Williamson forthcoming (b)). After all, why does an animal have a cognitive system in the first place? The natural, evolutionarily plausible answer is: to provide it with knowledge to act on. That function is not served by suspending belief. Nor is it served by non-knowledgeable beliefs; they are *defective*: something went wrong. Only knowledge will do.

There is no obvious internalist alternative to providing knowledge as the function of a cognitive system. Why bother with such a system if its goal is merely to achieve internal coherence or reflective equilibrium? Although Mona Simion (2019) tries to locate a non-factive standard for justified belief on a knowledge-first functionalist approach, the term 'justification' seems out of place in such a setting.

What function would be analogous to that of providing knowledge for a cognitive system with probabilistic credences rather than outright beliefs? Sarah Moss (2018) proposes that such an analogue is available if the contents of attitudes are reconfigured in probabilistic terms, but it is not clear that such radical complications are well motivated (Williamson forthcoming (d)).

An evolutionary perspective is useful, because it reminds us what a cognitive system is *for*. If it tempts us into an overspecific biological reductionism, we can correct that tendency by considering the generality to which epistemology aspires over many kinds of cognition and many kinds of cognizer. At that level, the category of knowledge is as natural as the category of nutrition.

Acknowledgements

Thanks for very helpful comments on drafts of this chapter to Robert Gordon, Daniel Kodsi, Harvey Lederman, Jennifer Nagel, participants in a class at Yale given with Jason Stanley, the editors of this volume, and an anonymous referee for it.

References

Alexander, J., and Weinberg, J. (2014). 'The "Unreliability" of Epistemic Intuitions', in E. Machery and E. O'Neill (eds.), *Current Controversies in Experimental Philosophy* (London: Routledge): 128–45.

Anscombe, G. E. M. (1957). *Intention* (Oxford: Blackwell).

Austin, J. L. (1956-7). 'A Plea for Excuses', *Proceedings of the Aristotelian Society* 57: 1–30.

Austin, J. L. (1962). *Sense and Sensibilia*, ed. G. J. Warnock. (Oxford: Oxford University Press).

Bennett, J. (1990). 'Why Is Belief Involuntary?', *Analysis* 50: 87–107.

Berker, S. (2008). 'Luminosity Regained', *Philosophers' Imprint* 8/2: 1–22.

Berlin, I. (1973). 'Austin and the Early Beginnings of Oxford Philosophy', in I. Berlin et al. (eds.), *Essays on J. L. Austin* (Oxford: Clarendon Press): 1–16.

Bird, A. (2010). 'Social Knowing: The Social Sense of "Scientific Knowledge"', *Philosophical Perspectives* 24: 23–56.

Bird, A. (forthcoming). *Knowing Science* (Oxford: Oxford University Press).

Blome-Tillmann, M. (2017). '"More Likely than Not": Knowledge First and the Role of Statistical Evidence in Courts of Law', in J. A. Carter, E. C. Gordon, and B. W. Jarvis (eds.), *Knowledge First: Approaches in Epistemology and Mind* (Oxford: Oxford University Press): 278–92.

Burge, T. (1979). 'Individualism and the Mental', *Midwest Studies in Philosophy* 4: 73–121.

REFERENCES

Byrne, A., and Logue, H. (2009). *Disjunctivism: Contemporary Readings* (Cambridge, MA: MIT Press).

Carruthers, P. (2011). *The Opacity of Mind: An Integrative Theory of Self-Knowledge* (Oxford: Oxford University Press).

Carter, J. A., Kelp, C., and Simion, M. (forthcoming). 'On Behalf of Knowledge-First Collective Epistemology', in P. Silva and L. Oliveira (eds.), *Doxastic and Propositional Warrant* (London: Routledge).

Cook Wilson, J. C. (1926). *Statement and Inference*, ed. A. S. L. Farquharson, 2 vols (Oxford: Clarendon Press).

Cook Wilson, J. C. (1967). 'The Relation of Knowing to Thinking', in A. Phillips Griffiths (ed.), *Knowledge and Belief* (Oxford: Oxford University Press): 16–27. Reprint of Cook Wilson (1926), i: 34–47.

Dutant, J. (2015). 'The Legend of the Justified True Belief Analysis', *Philosophical Perspectives* 1: 95–145.

Edgington, D. (1985). 'The Paradox of Knowability', *Mind* 94: 557–68.

Edgington, D. (2010). 'Possible Knowledge of Unknown Truths', *Synthese* 173: 41–52.

Evans, G. (1982). *The Varieties of Reference*, ed. J. McDowell (Oxford: Clarendon Press).

Fitch, F. (1963). 'A Logical Analysis of Some Value Concepts', *Journal of Symbolic Logic* 28: 135–42.

Gordon, R. (1969). 'Emotions and Knowledge', *Journal of Philosophy* 66: 408–13.

Gordon, R. (1987). *The Structure of Emotions* (Cambridge: Cambridge University Press).

Gordon, R. (2000). 'Sellars's Ryleans Revisited', *Protosociology* 14: 102–14.

Gordon, R. (2021). 'Simulation, Predictive Coding, and the Shared World', in M. Gilead and K. Ochsner (eds.), *The Neural Basis of Mentalizing* (Cham: Springer).

Greenough, P., and Pritchard, D. (eds.) (2009). *Williamson on Knowledge* (Oxford: Oxford University Press).

Hart, W. (1979). 'The Epistemology of Abstract Objects: Access and Inference', *Proceedings of the Aristotelian Society*, sup. 53: 152–65.

Hart, W., and McGinn, C. (1976). 'Knowledge and Necessity', *Journal of Philosophical Logic* 5: 205–8.

Hawthorne, J., and Magidor, O. (2009). 'Assertion, Context, and Epistemic Accessibility', *Mind* 118: 377–97.

Hawthorne, J., and Magidor, O. (2010). 'Assertion and Epistemic Opacity', *Mind* 119: 1087–105.

Hawthorne, J., and Magidor, O. (2018). 'Reflections on the Ideology of Reasons', in D. Star (ed.), *The Oxford Handbook of Reasons and Normativity* (Oxford: Oxford University Press): 113–40.

Hawthorne, J., and Srinivasan, A. (2013). 'Disagreement without Transparency: Some Bleak Thoughts', in D. Christensen and J. Lackey (eds.), *The Epistemology of Disagreement: New Essays* (Oxford: Oxford University Press): 9–30.

Hawthorne, J., and Stanley, J. (2008). 'Knowledge and Action', *Journal of Philosophy* 105: 571–90.

Hintikka, J. (1962). *Knowledge and Belief* (Ithaca, NY: Cornell University Press).

Hinton, J. M. (1967). 'Visual Experiences', *Mind* 76: 217–27.

Hinton, J. M. (1973). *Experiences* (Oxford: Oxford University Press).

Holton, R. (2014). 'Intention as a Model for Belief', in M. Vargas and G. Yaffe (eds.), *Rational and Social Agency: Essays on the Philosophy of Michael Bratman* (Oxford: Oxford University Press): 12–37.

Horschler, D., Santos, L., and MacLean, E. (2019). 'Do Non-Human Primates Really Represent Others' Ignorance? A Test of the Awareness Relations Hypothesis', *Cognition* 190: 72–80.

Hughes, N. (2018). 'Luminosity Failure, Normative Guidance and the Principle "Ought-Implies-Can"', *Utilitas* 30: 439–57.

Hughes, N. (2019). 'Dilemmic Epistemology', *Synthese* 196: 4059–90.

Hughes, N. (ed.) (forthcoming (a)). *Epistemic Dilemmas* (Oxford: Oxford University Press).

Hughes, N. (forthcoming (b)). 'Epistemology without Guidance'. *Philosophical Studies*.

Hyman, J. (2015). *Action, Knowledge, and Will* (Oxford: Oxford University Press).

Kelp, C., and Simion, M. (2021). *Sharing Knowledge: A Functionalist Account of Assertion* (Cambridge: Cambridge University Press).

Lasonen-Aarnio, M. (2010). 'Unreasonable Knowledge', *Philosophical Perspectives* 24: 1–21.

Lasonen-Aarnio, M. (2014). 'Higher-Order Evidence and the Limits of Defeat', *Philosophy and Phenomenological Research* 88: 314–45.

Lasonen-Aarnio, M. (2021). 'Dispositional Evaluations and Defeat', in J. Brown and M. Simion (eds.), *Reasons, Justification, and Defeat* (Oxford: Oxford University Press): 93–115.

Lederman, H. (2018a). 'Two Paradoxes of Common Knowledge: Coordinated Attack and Electronic Mail', *Noûs* 52: 921–45.

Lederman, H. (2018b). 'Uncommon Knowledge', *Mind* 127: 1069–105.

McDowell, J. (1977). 'On the Sense and Reference of a Proper Name', *Mind* 86: 159–85.

McDowell, J. (1982). 'Criteria, Defeasibility, and Knowledge', *Proceedings of the British Academy* 68: 455–79.

McDowell, J. (1995). 'Knowledge and the Internal', *Philosophy and Phenomenological Research* 55: 877–93.

Machery, E., Stich, S., Rose, D., Chatterjee, A., Karasawa, K., Struchiner, N., Sirker, S., Usui, N., and Hashimoto, T. (2017). 'Gettier across Cultures', *Noûs* 51: 645–64.

Marion, M. (2000). 'Oxford Realism: Knowledge and Perception', Parts I and II, *British Journal for the History of Philosophy* 8: 299–338 and 485–519.

Martin, M. (2004). 'The Limits of Self-Awareness', *Philosophical Studies* 120: 37–89.

Merleau-Ponty, M. (1945). *Phénoménologie de la perception*. (Paris: Gallimard.)

Moss, S. (2018). *Probabilistic Knowledge*. Oxford University Press.

Munro, D. (forthcoming). 'Perceiving as Knowing in the Predictive Mind', *Philosophical Studies*.

Nagel, J. (2012). 'Intuitions and Experiments: A Defense of the Case Method in Epistemology', *Philosophy and Phenomenological Research* 85: 495–527.

Nagel, J. (2013). 'Knowledge as a Mental State', *Oxford Studies in Epistemology* 4: 275–310.

Nagel, J. (2014). *Knowledge: A Very Short Introduction* (Oxford: Oxford University Press).

Nagel, J. (2017). 'Factive and Nonfactive Mental State Attribution', *Mind and Language* 32: 525–44.

Nagel, J. (forthcoming). *Recognizing Knowledge: Intuitive and Reflective Epistemology*.

Pavese, C. (2015). 'Practical Senses', *Philosophers' Imprint* 15: 1–25.

Pavese, C. (2016). 'Skill in Epistemology', Parts I and II, *Philosophy Compass* 11: 642–60.

Pavese, C. (2017). 'Know-How and Gradability', *Philosophical Review* 126: 345–83.

Pavese, C. (2019). 'The Psychological Reality of Practical Representation', *Philosophical Psychology* 32: 785–822.

Pavese, C. (2020a). 'Practical Representation', in E. Fridland and C. Pavese (eds.), *The Routledge Handbook of Philosophy of Skill and Expertise* (Abingdon: Routledge): 226–44.

Pavese, C. (2020b). 'Probabilistic Knowledge in Action', *Analysis* 80: 342–56.

Pavese, C. (2021). 'Knowledge, Action, and Defeasibility', in J. Brown and M. Simion (eds.), *Reasons, Justification, and Defeat* (Oxford: Oxford University Press): 177–200.

Perner, J. (1993). *Understanding the Representational Mind* (Cambridge, MA: MIT Press).

Phillips, J., Buckwalter, W., Cushman, F., Friedman, O., Martin, A., Turri, J., Santos, L., and Knobe, J. (2020). 'Knowledge before Belief', *Behavioral and Brain Sciences* 44: e140.

Phillips Griffiths, A. (ed.) (1967). *Knowledge and Belief* (Oxford: Oxford University Press).

Prichard, H. (1950). *Knowledge and Perception* (Oxford: Oxford University Press).

Putnam, H. (1973). 'Meaning and Reference', *Journal of Philosophy* 70: 699–711.

Rubinstein, A. (1989). 'The Electronic Mail Game: Strategic Behavior under "Almost Common Knowledge"', *American Economic Review* 79: 385–91.

Salerno, J. (2009). 'Knowability Noir 1945–1963', in J. Salerno (ed.), *New Essays on the Knowability Paradox* (Oxford: Oxford University Press): 29–48.

Schwitzgebel, E. (2008). 'The Unreliability of Naïve Introspection', *Philosophical Review* 117: 245–73.

Sellars, W. (1975). 'Autobiographical Reflections (February 1973)', in H.-N. Castañeda (ed.), *Action, Knowledge, and Reality: Studies in Honor of Wilfrid Sellars*, (Indianapolis, IN: Bobbs-Merrill): 277–93.

Shin, H., and Williamson, T. (1994). 'Representing the Knowledge of Turing Machines', *Theory and Decision* 37: 125–46.

Shin, H., and Williamson, T. (1996). 'How Much Common Belief Is Necessary for a Convention?', *Games and Economic Behavior* 13: 252–68.

Simion, M. (2019). 'Knowledge-First Functionalism', *Philosophical Issues* 29: 254–67.

Slote, M. (1979). 'Assertion and Belief', in J. Dancy (ed.), *Papers on Language and Logic* (Keele: Keele University Library): 177–90

Snowdon, P. (1980-1). 'Perception, Vision and Causation', *Proceedings of the Aristotelian Society* 81: 175–92.

Snowdon, P. (1990). 'The Objects of Perceptual Experience', *Proceedings of the Aristotelian Society*, sup. 64: 121–50.

Srinivasan, A. (2013). 'Are We Luminous?', *Philosophy and Phenomenological Research* 90: 294–319.

Srinivasan, A. (2015). 'Normativity without Cartesian Privilege', *Philosophical Issues* 25: 273–99.

Srinivasan, A. (2020). 'Radical Externalism', *Philosophical Review* 129: 395–431.

Stanley, J. (2011). *Know How*. (Oxford: Oxford University Press).

Stanley, J., and Williamson, T. (2001). 'Knowing How', *Journal of Philosophy* 98: 411–44.

Stanley, J., and Williamson, T. (2017). 'Skill', *Noûs* 51: 713–26.

Vaidya, A. (2022). 'Elements of Knowledge-First Epistemology in Gaṅgeśa', *Oxford Studies in Epistemology* 7: 336–64.

Weatherson, B. (2003). 'What Good Are Counterexamples?', *Philosophical Studies* 115: 1–31.

Weinberg, J., Nichols, S., and Stich, S. (2001). 'Normativity and Epistemic Intuitions', *Philosophical Topics* 29: 429–60.

Williamson, T. (1982). 'Intuitionism Disproved?', *Analysis* 42: 203–7.

Williamson, T. (1986). 'Criteria of Identity and the Axiom of Choice', *Journal of Philosophy* 83: 380–94.

Williamson, T. (1987a). 'On Knowledge and the Unknowable', *Analysis* 47: 154–8.

Williamson, T. (1987b). 'On the Paradox of Knowability', *Mind* 96: 256–61.

Williamson, T. (1990). *Identity and Discrimination* (Oxford: Blackwell; 2nd edn, 2013).

Williamson, T. (1992). 'Inexact Knowledge', *Mind* 101: 217–42.

Williamson, T. (1993). 'Verificationism and Non-Distributive Knowledge', *Australasian Journal of Philosophy* 71: 78–86.

Williamson, T. (1994). *Vagueness* (London: Routledge).

Williamson, T. (1995). 'Is Knowing a State Of Mind?', *Mind* 104: 533–65.

Williamson, T. (1996a). 'Cognitive Homelessness', *Journal of Philosophy* 93: 554–73.

Williamson, T. (1996b). 'Knowing and Asserting', *Philosophical Review* 105: 489–23.

Williamson, T. (1997). 'Knowledge as Evidence', *Mind* 106: 717–41.

Williamson, T. (1998). 'Conditionalizing on Knowledge', *British Journal for the Philosophy of Science* 49: 89–121.

Williamson, T. (2000). *Knowledge and its Limits* (Oxford: Oxford University Press).

Williamson, T. (2007). *The Philosophy of Philosophy* (Oxford: Wiley-Blackwell).

Williamson, T. (2008). 'Why Epistemology Can't Be Operationalized', in Q. Smith (ed.), *Epistemology: New Essays* (Oxford: Oxford University Press): 277–300.

Williamson, T. (2009). 'Probability and Danger', *Amherst Lecture in Philosophy* 4: 1–35.

Williamson, T. (2011). 'Improbable Knowing', in T. Dougherty (ed.), *Evidentialism and its Discontents* (Oxford: Oxford University Press): 147–64.

Williamson, T. (2013a). 'Gettier Cases in Epistemic Logic' *Inquiry* 56: 1–14.

Williamson, T. (2013b). 'Response to Cohen, Comesaña, Goodman, Nagel, and Weatherson on Gettier Cases in Epistemic Logic', *Inquiry* 56: 77–96.

Williamson, T. (2014). 'Very Improbable Knowing', *Erkenntnis* 79: 971–99.

Williamson, T. (2015). 'A Note on Gettier Cases in Epistemic Logic', *Philosophical Studies* 172: 129–40.

Williamson, T. (2017a). 'Acting on Knowledge', in J. A. Carter, E. C. Gordon, and B. W. Jarvis (eds.), *Knowledge First: Approaches in Epistemology and Mind* (Oxford: Oxford University Press): 163–81.

Williamson, T. (2017b). 'Ambiguous Rationality', *Episteme* 14: 263–74.

Williamson, T. (2018). 'Knowledge, Action, and the Factive Turn', in V. Mitova (ed.), *The Factive Turn in Epistemology* (Cambridge: Cambridge University Press): 125–41.

Williamson, T. (2019). 'Evidence of Evidence in Epistemic Logic', in M. Skipper and A. Steglich-Petersen (eds.), *Higher-Order Evidence: New Essays* (Oxford: Oxford University Press). 265–97.

Williamson, T. (2020a). 'Non-Modal Normativity and Norms of Belief', *Acta Philosophica Fennica* 90: 101–25.

Williamson, T. (2020b). *Suppose and Tell: The Semantics and Pragmatics of Conditionals* (Oxford: Oxford University Press).

Williamson, T. (2021a). 'Edgington on Possible Knowledge of Unknown Truth', in L. Walters and J. Hawthorne (eds.), *Conditionals, Paradox, and Probability: Themes from the Philosophy of Dorothy Edgington* (Oxford: Oxford University Press): 195–211.

Williamson, T. (2021b). 'Epistemological Consequences of Frege Puzzles', *Philosophical Topics* 49: 287–319.

Williamson, T. (2021c). 'The KK Principle and Rotational Symmetry', *Analytic Philosophy* 62: 107–24.

Williamson, T. (2021d). *The Philosophy of Philosophy* (enlarged edn, Oxford: Wiley-Blackwell).

Williamson, T. (2023a). 'Acting on Knowledge-How', *Synthese* 200/6: 479. doi: 10.1007/s11229-022-03677-z.

Williamson, T. (2023b). 'Boghossian, Müller-Lyer, the Parrot, and the Nazi', in L. Oliveira (ed.), *Externalism about Knowledge* (Oxford: Oxford University Press): 377–96.

Williamson, T. (2023c). 'Vaidya on Nyāya and Knowledge-First Epistemology', *Oxford Studies in Epistemology* 7: 365–75.

Williamson, T. (2024a). 'E = K, but What about R?', in M. Lasonen-Aarnio and C. Littlejohn (eds.), *The Routledge Handbook of the Philosophy of Evidence* (Abingdon: Routledge): 30–9.

Williamson, T. (2024b). *Overfitting and Heuristics in Philosophy*. New York: Oxford University Press.

Williamson, T. (forthcoming (a)). 'Dunn on Inferential Evidence', *The Monist*.

Williamson, T. (forthcoming (b)). 'Epistemological Ambivalence', in N. Hughes (ed.), *Epistemic Dilemmas* (Oxford: Oxford University Press).

Williamson, T. (forthcoming (c)). 'Justifications, Excuses, and Sceptical Scenarios', in J. Dutant and F. Dorsch (eds.), *The New Evil Demon: New Essays on Knowledge, Justification and Rationality* (Oxford: Oxford University Press).

Williamson, T. (forthcoming (d)). 'Knowledge, Credence, and Strength of Belief', in A. K. Flowerree and B. Reed (eds.), *Expansive Epistemology: Norms, Action, and the Social World* (London: Routledge).

3
Knowledge as Presence and Presentation
Highlights from the History of Knowledge-First Epistemology

Maria Rosa Antognazza

1. Introduction

By knowledge-first epistemology I mean theories of cognition according to which knowing is a mental state which has ontological priority as well as cognitive primacy over other cognitive modes, notably believing. Knowing is not a species of believing which meets certain criteria but the most primitive mode of cognition upon which any successful cognition (that is, any cognition which successfully tracks what is the case) is ultimately built.

Elsewhere I have argued that this kind of position is not only well attested but also prevalent in long periods of Western philosophical thought.[1] Furthermore, I have made the case for a historically prominent version of this family of views according to which knowing and believing are two mutually exclusive mental states: either one is in a mental state of knowing or one is in a mental state of believing. Therefore, on this account, knowing does not entail believing. Whereas knowing, at its most fundamental, is a cognitive contact between mind and reality which has priority over other cognitive modes, believing is a different mental state with its own crucial and distinctive role in our cognition, namely that of aiming at truth where and when knowledge is out of our cognitive reach. Therefore, in this framework, belief typically aims at truth, not at knowledge.[2]

In this chapter I will highlight some striking but less widely known accounts of knowledge as the primitive contact with reality from which human cognition starts. In particular, these accounts foreground a conception of knowledge as direct presence, 'presentiality' and/or presentation of objective reality to a cognitive subject. I will begin with what is closer to us, namely with conceptions of knowledge offered in the early twentieth century by three philosophers who are nowadays little known but whose pieces originally appeared in highly visible places: Helen Wodehouse (1880–1964), Charles Albert Dubray (1875–1962), and

[1] See Antognazza 2015; Ayers and Antognazza 2019, 2020, 2024.
[2] Antognazza 2020, 2024.

Francis Aveling (1875–1941). It is significant that, while coming from different backgrounds, Wodehouse, Dubray, and Aveling share a major interest in the pioneering scientific psychology of the late nineteenth and early twentieth century. I will then turn to what is, in many ways, very distant from us, namely the theories of cognition of three thinkers of the late Middle Ages: John Duns Scotus (*c.*1266–1308), Peter Auriol (*c.*1280–1322), and William of Ockham (*c.*1287–1347). My aim is *not* to suggest specific influences of these medieval thinkers on the twentieth-century philosophers. Rather, I merely aim to highlight some instances of a conception of knowledge as presence and presentation which resurfaces in widely separated historical periods and in very different intellectual contexts. In my view, this very fact indicates that this conception of knowledge is tracking something in the structure of human cognition which runs deeper than culturally and historically conditioned ideas.

2. Knowledge as Presentation and as a Primitive Fact of Consciousness

2.1. Knowledge as Presentation

'Knowledge as Presentation' is the title of a paper by Helen Wodehouse published in *Mind* in 1909.[3] Wodehouse takes as her starting point a 'text' to which (she claims) 'most English psychologists at any rate seem to have no objection'.[4] The text is 'Knowledge consists of the presentation of reality in consciousness.'[5]

To start with, it is remarkable that a conception of knowledge as 'presentation of reality in consciousness' is not offered by Wodehouse as a ground-breaking new account she will set out to defend but as a widely accepted view of the pioneering scientific psychology of her time, the philosophical significance of which

---

[3] See also Wodehouse (1910), where the theory of knowledge is tackled 'from the point of view of a philosophical psychology' (p. ix). Helen Marion Wodehouse read first mathematics and then moral sciences at Cambridge University, before gaining a Teacher's Higher Diploma (1903), an MA (1904), and a DPhil (1906) from Birmingham University. After serving as a lecturer in philosophy at Birmingham, she became the first woman professor at the University of Bristol as Professor of Education (1919). In 1931 she returned to Cambridge as Mistress of her former college, Girton. In the introduction to Wodehouse (1910), she acknowledges James Ward (1843–1925), Alexius Meinong (1853–1920), and G. F. Stout (1860–1944) as the leading thinkers to whom she felt most indebted, although she is also forcefully critical of aspects of their work with which she disagrees (see, for instance, Wodehouse 1910: 18 and 57).

[4] Experimental psychology is widely regarded as having emerged in the later part of the nineteenth century at the University of Leipzig, where Wilhelm Maximilian Wundt (1832–1920) founded the first laboratory for research in psychology (1879). It rapidly established itself in a number of countries, including Germany, Austria, France, Russia, and the USA. In Britain, a Psychological Society was founded in 1901 at University College London. In 1906 it changed its name to the British Psychological Society and continues to serve to this day as a main learned and professional body in the field of psychology.

[5] Wodehouse 1909: 391.

she will endeavour to unpack. But there is more. She tackles her task head-on by suggesting that 'modern philosophers' generally agree that '*reality* is presented', unless (due to 'sheer habit') they inattentively 'slip back into ways of speaking which are inconsistent' with this view. Furthermore, she claims, some form of direct realism commends itself: if 'what is presented to us is always reality, we must assume no shifting world of intermediaries between us and the real'.[6]

One may well be taken aback. What about F. H. Bradley and the so-called British Idealists? Did not Bradley's *Appearance and Reality* (1893) appear in London roughly a decade before Wodehouse's article in *Mind* (1909)?[7] And did he not take the view that reality does not consist of objects existing independently of each other but of ideas and experience? It seems to me that Wodehouse's statement should be interpreted as compatible with different ontologies. The point is that whatever is presenting itself to us is always some kind of reality. The issue of its precise nature (Is it an independent material object? Is it ideas and experience?) is a *further* metaphysical question.[8] Whatever the nature of the presented reality, I understand Wodehouse to be saying, it does not make sense to postulate intermediate entities between us and the real. In short, 'the primary fact is the presentation of reality'[9]—that is, I take it, knowledge is a primitive and most fundamental direct cognitive contact with a world which is presenting itself to the mind, whatever the precise ontological nature of this world may then turn out to be.

On the other hand, although Wodehouse's claim that 'what is presented to us is always reality' is arguably compatible with different ontologies, as far as I can see, Wodehouse herself is no idealist.[10] Not only does she appear unsympathetic towards 'the subjective idealism which describes the object as a mere experience of the percipient'.[11] In her book of 1910, *The Presentation of Reality*, she also construes 'to have a presentation' as 'to come up consciously against the real world' or as a 'direct meeting with something real'.[12] 'In apprehending,' she explains, 'I do nothing to my object. I simply keep my eyes open and see.' This description, she adds, guards us 'against more than one mode of expression which seems to be dangerous. One such mode is found in the statement of many idealists that in knowledge we construct reality.'[13] By contrast, for her:

---

[6] Wodehouse 1909: 391. See also Wodehouse 1910: 60.
[7] Bradley 1893 (2nd edn 1897). Wodehouse 1909 cites Bradley 1883 on p. 399; Wodehouse 1910 engages with both Bradley 1883 and 1893.
[8] Cf. Wodehouse 1910: x: 'I shall try to describe the process of knowing reality, but shall always endeavour to put aside if possible the question of the nature and origin of reality.'
[9] Wodehouse 1909: 391.
[10] I disagree here with Mary Warnock, who states in her entry on Wodehouse in the *Oxford Dictionary of National Biography*, without justification, that 'Philosophically Helen Wodehouse remained an idealist' (Warnock 2004). I cannot find idealism in the position defended by Wodehouse in her key pieces of 1909 and 1910.
[11] Wodehouse 1909: 392, n. 1.   [12] Wodehouse 1910: 4.   [13] Wodehouse 1910: 7.

> the objects of thought...are real objects, not constructed by us but given to us; they are materials and circumstances; they are 'hard' facts, which we 'face'; in them we meet with the solid objective work. We construct nothing; the effort required is only that of focussing and guiding our sight.[14]

In brief, Wodehouse is speaking of knowledge as presentation of an objective reality which impinges on us. We grasp it, first of all, through the senses, although thought too 'brings us into contact with reality'.[15]

'An idea', Wodehouse goes on to say, 'is not a thing but a process or event', namely 'the event of presentation'. Its 'meaning' is just 'the reality which is being presented' and 'the phrase "idea of a thing" becomes a general name for the presentation of that thing in thought-consciousness'.[16] Interestingly, the view that ideas are not things but activities (or, as Wodehouse conceives of them, 'processes' or 'the event of presentation') is defended also in the heyday of 'the way of ideas', that is, the early modern period. Early modern philosophy is not infrequently charged with the infamous doctrine that ideas are spooky mental things one carries around in one's head as intermediaries between mind and world—a doctrine which is more a caricature of the 'way of ideas' by its detractors than the genuine view of leading early modern thinkers. At any rate, prominent philosophers such as Antoine Arnauld and Baruch Spinoza do not think of ideas as mental things but as mental acts. In his *Des vrais et des fausses idées* (1843 [1683]), Arnauld argues that 'idea' should be understood as the mental act of apprehending something (that is, '*la perception*') and not as a 'representative being' (*être représentatif*) mediating between mind and things. Taken in the latter sense, Arnauld warns, ideas are 'superfluous entities'.[17] For his part, Spinoza makes clear in the *Ethics* that an idea is not an inert entity like an image or a copy deposited in the mind ('something mute like a picture on a tablet') but 'a mode of thinking, namely the act of intellection itself'—that is to say, ideas are mental acts by which things are grasped.[18] And in the *Emendation of the Intellect*, he explains that certainty is simply our awareness of things themselves (in the Scholastic vocabulary he uses, our perceiving 'the formal essence [essentiam formalem]').[19]

---

[14] Wodehouse 1910: 76. See also 1910: 76: 'the founded object which we apprehend was not produced by the apprehension but founded in reality'.

[15] Wodehouse 1910: 72 and 69.

[16] Wodehouse 1910: 72. See also Wodehouse 1910: 17–18:

> the whole difficulty comes...from thinking that the contents of consciousness must be things that people carry about in their heads. It is so hard to be content with their having eyes in their heads.... There are not such things as ideas.... All that happens is that *I see things*.

[17] Cf. Arnauld 1843 [1683]: 365–80. I offer a more detailed discussion of Arnauld on ideas in Antognazza 2024: 138–41. Unless otherwise stated, translations are my own.

[18] Spinoza, *Ethica*, part II, prop. 43, scholium. See also Spinoza, *Ethica*, part II, prop. 49, scholium.

[19] Spinoza, *De Intellectus Emendatione*, ii, 15.

But let us return to Wodehouse. Next, she focuses on the claim that 'knowledge *consists* in presentation'. 'All we do is to see,'[20] Wodehouse stresses once again, and in so doing she places herself in a long and illustrious tradition (starting with Plato and resurfacing in the history of philosophy in a variety of forms) according to which knowing comes with seeing.[21] That is, in the more recent words of Michael Ayers, 'at least central or basic cases of knowledge involve conscious apprehension, whether literal seeing or otherwise perceiving, or something enough like seeing (say, understanding) to justify the metaphor that we all use'.[22] Wodehouse returns to her own version of this position in the conclusion of her *Mind* paper. Knowledge consists in presentation in the sense that 'there can be no knowledge, even the highest, without presentation, and presentation is all that is necessary...reality lies immediately before us whichever way we look. If we only see it "through a hole",[23] at all events the hole is nothing worse than the pupil of our eye.'[24] That is, in cognition, everything ultimately rests on seeing what is presenting itself; without this primitive (sense-perceptual or intellectual) 'seeing' there could be no knowledge at all—a position marked in the history of Western philosophy by the centrality of the notions of 'evidence' (from the Latin *e* 'from' + *videre* 'to see') and of immediately apprehending or 'intuiting' (from the verb *intueri*, 'to see, look at' and its derivate nouns *intuitus* and *intuitio*, 'the act of viewing, looking').

It is crucial to note, however, that the reality which 'lies immediately before us whichever way we look' is always presenting itself under a (partial and limited) mode of presentation determined by our subjective (partial and limited) perspective: in Wodehouse's phrase, the metaphorical as well as literal 'hole' through which each one of us can only and ever see reality under a specific mode of presentation. It is along these lines that she construes the distinction between 'content' and 'object'. A mental 'content' is not some shadowy mental thing one carries around in one's head. The only 'thing' which is there is the real, presented object. On the other hand, of this concrete and complex object one can ever only apprehend some very limited aspect.[25] *Content* is the term we may conveniently use for this apprehension, that is, for those limited aspects of the presented object which are consciously grasped.[26] Most importantly, this is not a mental copy of the object: 'to have a presentation', Wodehouse writes, 'is a much simpler thing than to make a copy; it is to see'.[27] To speak of a copy, she warns, is dangerous even in the case of remembering an object, because it suggests a reproduction of the

---

[20] Wodehouse 1909: 392.
[21] See Ayers 2019 for an extensive defence of this view. For a brief historical account of this tradition see, in particular, Ayers and Antognazza 2019: ch. 1.
[22] Ayers 2019: vii.   [23] Bradley 1883: 70.   [24] Wodehouse 1909: 399.
[25] Wodehouse 1910: 32: 'we could never grasp in one act of apprehension the inexhaustible reality of a real thing'.
[26] See Wodehouse 1910: 13–14.   [27] Wodehouse 1910: 15.

object in some other 'material' (akin to the reproduction of a landscape on a canvas and in the watercolours of a painting): rather, in memory, 'the object presents itself in its habit as it lived'.[28]

Why it is preferable to speak of presentation *in* consciousness rather than *to* consciousness is explained by Wodehouse's eagerness to avoid the danger of multiplying faculties beyond the necessary ('sense', 'thought', 'consciousness', 'apprehension', 'judgement', and so on, as if these were all faculties *to* which the object is presented). But be that as it may, Wodehouse's key thought is that the object itself is *presented*, as opposed to construing the object as *presentation*.[29] That is, as shown above, Wodehouse is no idealist: by her lights, the object is not a mentally constructed 'presentation' (be it, an 'experience' *à la* Bradley, a 'reality constructed by the individual' *à la* Bosanquet, or even a 'phenomenon' *à la* Kant), but some piece of an objective reality that manifests or presents itself to a cognitive subject.[30]

The last striking claim I would like to extract from Wodehouse's pieces is that the 'contact with reality' in which knowledge consists 'is just as close, just as immediate' in all the presentation fields we have: 'reality is presented in consciousness…not in sense only or in thought only' but 'in memory, in expectation, imagery, imagination, intuition, and any other sort of presentation that may be found. Every one of these departments gives the thing room for special manifestations of its nature.'[31] The claim is that 'what is presented to us in any field is quite truly and literally in our presence'.[32] That is, if 'presentation is of the essence of knowledge',[33] then any presentation of 'what is' in any mental field—say, my drinking a cup of coffee this morning as present to me in episodic memory; or the image of my cute brown cat presenting itself to me as I stroke a familiar, purring, furry object in the dark—counts as a cognitive contact with reality manifesting itself in the way allowed by that particular presentation field. And, insofar as that is a presentation, it is 'just as close, just as immediate' as any presentation of reality which is present to us. In other words, no knowledge is non-immediate 'in the epistemological sense of being out of touch with its object'. Whether inferred or not inferred, knowledge always implies the 'real presence and immediate vision of its object'.[34] Conversely, 'what is not a presentation is not knowledge'.[35] That is, I take it, if I am actually misremembering what I had for breakfast this morning, or if the object I am stroking in the dark is not my cute brown cat but the scary grey cat of my neighbour, then none of these cases will count as 'presentations' of 'what is' (i.e. of reality) in memory or in imagination. Hence, none of these cases will be cases of knowledge or 'contacts with reality' in that presentation field.

---

[28] Wodehouse 1910: 15.   [29] See Wodehouse 1909: 392, sect. 3 and note 1.
[30] See Wodehouse 1910: 75. Cf. Bosanquet (1888): i, 4.   [31] Wodehouse 1909: 394, 392–3.
[32] Wodehouse 1909: 395.   [33] Wodehouse 1909: 396.   [34] Wodehouse 1910: 72.
[35] Wodehouse 1910: 72.

2.2. Knowledge as a Primitive Fact of Consciousness

In the same period in which Wodehouse publishes her 1909 *Mind* paper and her 1910 book, the articles 'knowledge' and 'belief' appear in the *Catholic Encyclopaedia* (respectively in 1910 and 1907).[36] The author of the first article is Charles Albert Dubray, a French-born Marianist based in the United States with a strong background in both philosophy and psychology (notably, his doctoral dissertation on *The Theory of Psychical Dispositions*, submitted in 1905 for the doctoral degree in philosophy, and published as monograph supplement number 30 of the prestigious *Psychological Review*).[37] Even stronger credentials in experimental psychology, as well as philosophy and theology, characterize the author of the article 'belief', Francis Aveling.[38] Part of the interest of these two encyclopedia entries is their very place of publication: duly equipped with the necessary *nihil obstat* and *imprimatur* from the relevant church authorities, the articles are meant to give 'full and authoritative information' about views broadly endorsed in Catholic intellectual circles. For present purposes, they are, therefore, particularly significant as representative of an institutionalized conception of knowledge and belief very much alive at least as late as the first half of the twentieth century. As we shall see, it is a conception coming from an Aristotelian mould reshaped by the interests in the new scientific psychology and philosophy of mind of the articles' authors.

'Knowledge', Dubray writes at the beginning of his article, is 'a primitive fact of consciousness.' As such, it 'cannot strictly be defined; but the direct and spontaneous consciousness of knowing may be made clearer by pointing out its essential and distinctive characteristics'.[39] This opening statement comprises at least three important claims: first, knowledge is a primitive mental state; second, due to its primitiveness, it cannot be reductively analysed into more basic elements; third, the nature of this mental state can, nevertheless, be helpfully clarified by a

---

[36] The *Catholic Encyclopedia* was published in the United States between 1907 and 1912.
[37] Dubray 1905. Founded in 1894 by James Mark Baldwin (Princeton University) and James McKeen Cattell (Columbia University), the *Psychological Review* rapidly establishes itself as the most important psychology journal in North America, counting amongst its early contributors William James (1842–1910) and John Dewey (1859–1952).
[38] Born in Canada, Aveling studies at McGill University and Keble College, Oxford, before entering the Canadian Pontifical College in Rome, where he obtains a doctorate of divinity. Later on, he earns a doctorate in philosophy from the University of Louvain, as well as a doctorate of science (DSc) and a doctorate of letters (DLitt) from the University of London. Remarkably, the letter institutioned latter institution also awards him the Carpenter Medal for work of exceptional distinction in psychology. After a stint of teaching at University College London, he moves to King's College London where he holds the chair of psychology. From 1926 to 1929 he serves as the President of the British Psychological Society. On his death in 1941, the *American Journal of Psychology* describes him as 'one of the most outstanding personalities of British psychology', 'profoundly interested in epistemological problems'. 'One of his greatest contributions to knowledge', the obituary continues, 'resided in his relating the psychology of cognition to persistent problems of philosophy.' See Cattell 1941 (quotations on p. 608) and Spearman 1941.
[39] Dubray 1910.

non-reductive identification of its 'essential and distinctive' features (rather than its 'necessary and sufficient' conditions). The project of providing a definition of knowledge by breaking down the notion into supposedly more primitive elements is not only conspicuously absent: it is also explicitly declared undoable. What can be helpfully done instead is to provide an explanation that unpacks our own 'direct and spontaneous' experience of this primitive mental state—in itself a very different project, akin to the 'elucidation' or 'connective analysis' Peter Strawson contrasts with the 'reductive analysis' for which any successful charge of circularity would be damning.[40]

What, then, are the 'essential and distinctive' characteristics of knowing, intended as a mental state? 'Knowledge', Dubray explains, 'is essentially the consciousness of an object.' 'Object', in turn, is 'any thing, fact, or principle belonging to the physical, mental, or metaphysical order, that may in any manner be reached by cognitive faculties', for example 'an event, a material substance, a man, a geometrical theorem'. Most broadly taken, the object is a 'not-self' which impinges in some form or another on a 'self'. From the claim that knowledge is *essentially* the consciousness of an *object* broadly conceived as *not-self* it follows that knowledge:

> always possesses an objective character and any process that may be conceived as merely subjective is not a cognitive process. Any attempt to reduce the object to a purely subjective experience could result only in destroying the fact itself of knowledge, which implies the object, or not-self, as clearly as it does the subject, or self.[41]

Dubray plainly understands the self/not-self distinction as an ontological as opposed to a merely phenomenological distinction. On this basis, he rejects an idealistic reduction of the object of knowledge to an 'experience' of the subject on pain of undermining 'the fact itself' of knowledge as essentially an encounter between ontologically distinct subject and object (self and not-self).

One may wonder, however, whether the qualification of experience as *purely* subjective leaves space for an understanding of the object as a Kantian phenomenon. This possibility is swept aside later in the article: 'knowledge is not, as in Kantian criticism.... the filling up of empty shells—a priori mental forms or categories—with the unknown and unknowable reality'. Instead, Dubray urges, a conception of knowledge as essentially the consciousness of an object leads us back:

> to the old Aristotelian and Scholastic view, that all knowledge begins with concrete experience, but requires other factors, not given in experience, in order to reach its perfection. It needs reason interpreting the data of observation,

---

[40] Cf. Strawson 1992: 17–28 and Antognazza 2024.   [41] Dubray 1910: sect. 1.

abstracting the contents of experience from the conditions which individualize them in space and time, removing, as it were, the outer envelope of the concrete, and going to the core of reality.[42]

In other words (and not surprisingly), Dubray commends a traditional Aristotelian-Thomist approach according to which the starting point of cognition is empirical: our first contact with reality is with concrete material entities apprehended by the senses. To go beyond the accidental features under which the senses present concrete particulars (in Dubray's phrase, to remove their 'outer envelope'), and grasp their stable core, the intellectual capacity of abstraction is needed: namely, the capacity to abstract from the singularity of concrete entities to grasp their 'whatness'. The crucial difference with the Kantian approach, Dubray notes, is that 'even abstract knowledge reveals reality'. In other words, however inadequately, both sense-perceptual knowledge and intellectual knowledge grasp reality (by which he means, I surmise, things-in-themselves). Of course, 'knowledge is necessarily proportioned or relative to the capacity of the mind and the manifestations of the object'.[43] Infinitely many aspects of the object (or of reality) therefore remain unknown. But there is no barrier in principle between mind and things-in-themselves. The objects of knowledge are real, concrete objects that *manifest* or *present* (Wodehouse would say) themselves to the senses and the mind: they are given, or discovered (however partially and imperfectly), as opposed to being mentally constructed.

2.3. Assent, Knowledge, and Belief

'Belief', Aveling maintains in his entry, is (unlike knowledge) 'that state of mind by which it assents to propositions, not by reason of their intrinsic evidence, but because of authority'.[44] 'Though the term is commonly used in ordinary language, as well as in much philosophical writing, to cover a great many states of mind,' Aveling continues, it should be carefully distinguished 'from all other forms of mental assent'.

The first thing to be noted here is that 'mental assent' is regarded as a broader category than belief. The different forms of assent are distinguished from one another not by a difference in nature ('assent is of its nature simple and indivisible', Aveling writes) but by a difference in the *motive* of assent. That is, assent is always an indivisible mental 'yes' or an indivisible mental affirmation that things are as one is judging them to be (e.g., certain, uncertain, likely, or doubtful), but the motive why one is judging them to be such-and-such can vary. In the case of the

---

[42] Dubray 1910: sect. 3. [43] Dubray 1910: sect. 3.
[44] Aveling 1907. Unless otherwise noted, the citations below are from this entry.

'assent of knowledge', the motive of assent is the intrinsic *evidence* of their being such-and-such.[45] In the case of the assent of belief, the motive of assent can be reduced to two types: testimony and 'the partial evidence of reason'. Testimony, Aveling specifies, is 'a valid and satisfactory cause of assent' only if it is suitably authoritative. In other words, for our belief 'we may have recourse to the authority of those who know'. On the other hand, 'the partial evidence of reason' is evidence 'not sufficiently clearly presented to our mind to enable us to say we know': 'Probable opinions, conjectures, obscured or partially recalled memories, or any truths or facts of which we have not a consciously evidential grasp, are the main objects of a belief resultant upon partial evidence.'

In this, Aveling claims, lies the distinction between knowledge and belief. We *know* self-evident truths and truths which are reached demonstratively from self-evident principles.[46] Moreover, 'we know all facts and truths of our own personal experience, whether of consciousness or of objective nature. Similarly, we know the truth of the reports of memory that come clearly and distinctly into consciousness.' Conversely, 'we do not believe evident truths'.[47]

This last claim becomes clearer in the light of Aveling's complaint that:

> Belief... is often indiscriminatingly used for these [i.e.: intelligence, science or knowledge, doubt, opinion and conjecture] and for other states of mind from which for the sake of accuracy it should be as carefully distinguished as is possible. Though we may know a thing and at the same time believe it[48]..., it is in the interest of clearness that we should keep to the distinction drawn and not confound belief and knowledge, because of the fact that the same truth may simultaneously be the object of both.[49]

In sum, knowing and believing are distinct in kind as two different mental states:[50] one is a mental state in which assent to such-and-such being the case is given in virtue of its intrinsic evidence; the other is a mental state in which assent to such-and-such being the case is given in virtue of testimony or partial evidence insufficient for knowledge. Furthermore, there is an 'assent of knowledge' and an 'assent of belief'; assent and belief should not, therefore, be conflated. By contrast, Aveling notes, 'the distinction drawn between the assents of knowledge and belief

---

[45] I discuss the difference between intrinsic and extrinsic evidence in Antognazza 2024: 212–19.
[46] In Aveling's words: 'intuitional truths as well as all those that are indirectly evident in their principles'. This is, of course, the classical distinction between *nous* and *episteme*, *intellectus* and *scientia*, intuition and demonstration found in Aristotle, Aquinas, Descartes, and Locke, among others. More generally, Aveling's approach is clearly inspired by Thomistic views (cf. in particular Aquinas, *Summa Theologiae* IIa IIae, q. 1, a. 4 and a. 5). I discuss these views in Antognazza 2024.
[47] Cf. Cook Wilson 1926: 100: 'the man who knows does not believe at all what he knows'.
[48] It is not clear here whether 'we' is to be taken collectively or distributively, that is, whether the same thing can be simultaneously known and believed by the same person or by different persons.
[49] Aveling 1907.   [50] Cf. Aquinas, *Summa Theologiae* IIa IIae, q. 1, a. 5.

cannot be said to be observed at all closely in practice, where they are frequently confused'. 'It is none the less undoubtedly felt to exist,' he concludes, and given sufficient attention, 'the one can readily be distinguished from the other'.

3. Knowledge as Presence and 'Presentiality'

The view that the primary cognitive mode is a contact with reality essentially characterized by the presence—or 'presentiality'—of the object of cognition to a cognitive subject is strongly defended in later medieval philosophy by John Duns Scotus, Peter Auriol, and William of Ockham. As mentioned in Section 1, my aim is not to trace—or even suggest—specific influences of these much earlier thinkers on the twentieth-century authors discussed in Section 2. Although Dubray and Aveling certainly knew their history of philosophy and were part of a broadly Aristotelian-Scholastic tradition, I will not speculate on whether they knew and appreciated the Franciscan (and, in some respects, anti-Thomist) medieval tradition represented by Scotus, Auriol, and Ockham. Even less will I speculate on whether Wodehouse had any knowledge of or interest in this tradition whatsoever. Rather, my aim is to show that a conception of knowledge as presence and 'presentiality' is developed in remarkably interesting ways also in a historical period very far from the intellectual environment of Anglo-American twentieth-century philosophy to which Wodehouse, Dubray, and Aveling belong. By my lights, the very resurfacing of this type of conception in very different historical periods is a sign of its tracking something in the structure of human cognition which transcends historically and culturally conditioned discourses.

3.1. Grasping a Present Object as Present

Scotus, Auriol, and Ockham's theories of knowledge differ significantly from one another on key points. The three thinkers agree, however, on some broad issues which set the framework in which their theories are constructed. According to them, to know is, most fundamentally, the presence of reality to a cognitive subject. For the object to be known is to be present to the senses and the intellect. Cognition starts from this presence: that something exists and manifests itself to a cognizer is the primary evidence which neither can be demonstrated nor (most importantly) needs to be demonstrated.[51]

They agree, moreover, that we first encounter this reality via the senses: 'the intellect', Scotus writes, 'cannot have any knowledge of the terms of a proposition

---

[51] See Vanni Rovighi 2006: 142.

unless it has taken them from the senses'.[52] Now, what is distinctive of the external senses from which human cognition begins is that they cognize 'the object under the aspect of existence'.[53] This is the type of cognition which Scotus calls 'intuitive'; that is, for him, an intuitive act of cognition is a perceptual state exemplified, first of all, by sense-perceptual states in which an existing object is apprehended.[54] Precisely the capacity of sense perception to put us in 'contact with the object itself, as existing, and as it is present in real existence' is what constitutes the 'perfection' of sensory cognition as a cognitive mode.[55] A 'relation of contact' (*relatio attingentiae*)[56] is, in fact, what establishes this mode of cognition as superior to representational cognitive modes, which arrive at the object only 'in some diminished or derivative similitude of the object'.[57]

So far, there is no major difference from fairly typical Aristotelian views. Scotus's break with the Aristotelian tradition is to argue that, as a cognitive power superior to the senses, the intellect must also be capable of the *direct* cognitive contact with particulars of which the senses are capable. This particular debate, however, need not detain us here.[58] For present purposes, it is enough to focus on the claim that intuitive (that is, for Scotus, perceptual) cognition,[59] whether by the senses or by the intellect, is the most perfect (as well as primitive and fundamental) type of cognition *because* it is cognition of its object face to face, as it were, with no gap to be bridged between subject and object.[60] This is a cognitive act which is 'precisely of a present object as present, and of an existent object as existent'.[61] Most importantly, it can occur *only* if an existing object is actually present to a cognitive subject because this actual presence of the object is what *causes* the cognition itself: 'in intuitive cognition,' Scotus writes, 'the thing in its proper existence is per se what objectively moves' (technically, it is the *ratio formalis motiva*).[62] Of course, I could imagine a pink cat as existent, although there exists no such pink cat. Or I could imagine my existent brown cat, even though my brown cat is not actually present (when, for example, it is happily staying with my neighbour while I am on holiday). The point is that neither cognition would count as an intuitive cognition because neither is caused by the actual presence of

---

[52] Scotus, *Ordinatio* (*Opus Oxoniense*) I, dist. III, q. iv; translated in Wolter 1987: 108. Scotus hastens to add that 'once it has them, the intellect by its own power can form propositions with these terms'. In general, the Aristotelian inheritance is filtered in Scotus by a pervasive Platonic or Neoplatonic inspiration which reaches him via Avicenna.
[53] Scotus, *Quodl*, q. 13 (*Opera Omnia*, xxv, 522a).   [54] Cf. Pini 2014: 348.
[55] Scotus, *Quodl*. q. 6, n. 8 (*Opera Omnia*, xxv, 244a).
[56] Scotus returns repeatedly to the *relatio attingentiae* throughout the *Quaestiones Quodlibetales*.
[57] Cf. Scotus, *Quodl*. q. 6, n. 8 (*Opera Omnia*, xxv, 244a).
[58] I examine this debate in Antognazza 2023.   [59] See Cross 2014: 18.
[60] Scotus's ideal cognitive model here is the beatific vision of God face to face enjoyed by the blessed in the afterlife. See Scotus, *Quodl*. q. 6, n. 8 (*Opera Omnia*, xxv, 244b).
[61] Scotus, *Quodl*. q. 6 n. 8 (*Opera Omnia*, xxv, 243b–244a). See also Scotus, *Reportatio I-B, Prol.*, q. 3, p. 88, explaining that intuitive cognition is a mode of cognition in which a thing is 'actually present' (*praesens actualiter*).
[62] Scotus, *Quodl*., q. 13, n. 10 (*Opera Omnia*, xxv, 522b).

the cat. Ultimately, human cognition rests on a primitive acquaintance with actually present, existing things which are the cause (technically, the formal motive reason) of the cognition itself.[63]

3.2. Presentiality

For the matter at hand, it is in many respects more difficult to evaluate the position of Auriol. Also in his case, the starting point is our sense-perceptual cognition of the material individuals which surround us. In particular, visual cognition (*notitia ocularis*) is taken as paradigmatic of sense perception and as providing a prime example of what Auriol calls intuitive cognition (*notitia intuitiva*).[64] Intuitive cognition, he explains, is 'direct cognition, exhibiting presentiality of that over which it transits, objectively actuative, and positive, as it were, of existence' [cognitio directa praesentialis eius, super quod transit[,] obiective actuativa,[65] et quasi positiva existentiae].[66] The four conditions listed in this definition are illustrated through a contrast between visual cognition and imagination (*notitia imaginaria*). First of all, vision is characterized by *directness* (*rectitudo*) and *immediacy*. Intuitive cognition *transit* (goes over) a thing's existence in the direct and immediate way exemplified by the act of seeing. Second and most importantly for present purposes, visual cognition (and more generally, intuitive cognition) is characterized by *presentiality*: in intuitive cognition, the object is 'presented' to a cognitive subject. Third, intuitive cognition presents the object in its actuality (*actuatio obiecti*). Finally, visual intuitive cognition is *positiva existentiae*, that is, it posits the existence of the object. By contrast, imaginary cognition (*notitia imaginaria*) 'lacks and abstracts from this quadruple condition since it does not go over the object directly, or presentially [praesentialiter], or actuatively, nor does it posit the existence of the object imagined, even when it imagines that its object exists, is actual, and will be present'.[67]

Crucially, for Auriol, what is distinctive of intuitive cognition is not its object (what is seen, he reasons, can also be imagined) but the mode of presentation of its object, that is to say the way in which intuitive cognition presents its object directly and as present, actual, and existing. This view leads him to the conclusion that, provided there is this mode of presentation, cognition counts as intuitive, even if the object does not actually exist (as, for instance, in the case of

---

[63] Cf. Scotus, *Quodl.*, q. 13, n. 10 (*Opera Omnia*, xxv, 522b).
[64] See Boehner 1949: 296–98 and Friedman 2021: sect. 4.
[65] Correcting 'intuitiva', found in Auriol, *C I Sent.*, (ed. Sarnano). Cf. Auriol, *S I Sent.* i, 204: 'cognitio directa praesentialis eius, super quod transit obiective actuativa et quasi positiva existenter'.
[66] Auriol, *C I Sent., Pars Prima, Prologi Quaestio 2*, 27a C–D.
[67] Auriol, *I C Sent., Pars Prima, Prologi Quaestio 2*, 27b C.

non-existing objects we see in dreams).⁶⁸ In brief, contrary to Scotus's account, according to which a cognition is intuitive if and only if it is caused by a present and actually existing object, for Auriol there can be intuitive cognition of the non-existent.

Of course, this conclusion would raise glaring sceptical worries if what Auriol intended to do was to use intuitive cognition to demonstrate the existence of the external world. But this is not what Auriol (or, for that matter, Scotus) is up to. As noted above, for these thinkers, that there is 'something' (*aliquid*) with which the subject comes into contact in cognition is the primary *evidence* and not some doubtful hypothesis in need of demonstration. It may, then, be a matter of determining what is the nature of this something (the 'object') but not of doubting that the presence of some 'object' to a cognitive subject is of the very essence of cognition. It seems to me that what Auriol is doing is stressing that the primary mode of cognition is characterized by this 'presentiality' of the object—typically a concrete, material individual, presenting itself directly as present, actual, and existing as in a typical act of sense-perceptual vision, although we should be aware that the nature of this presented object can vary.⁶⁹

More generally, it seems to me that Auriol's considered view of human cognition is that knowing consists, most fundamentally, in the presence of a thing to the mind, and not in the construction of a mental thing akin to an *ante litteram* Kantian phenomenon.⁷⁰ Contrary to the phenomenist and representationalist interpretation of Auriol's notion of *esse apparens*,⁷¹ Auriol's *esse intentionale/esse obiectale/esse apparens* is not a mental image that mediates between the cognitive subject and the extra-mental thing, or a mental entity that the cognitive subject knows in order to know the extra-mental thing, or a mental object towards which cognition is directed.⁷² The *esse intentionale/obiectale/apparens* is the mode of existence or mode of being that the extra-mental thing has qua cognized.⁷³ This type of existence (*modus essendi*) is different from the kind of existence that this same thing has in the world; but it is still a type of existence or a mode of being of that very extra-mental thing. In other words, the extra-mental thing and the

---

⁶⁸ Auriol, *C I Sent., Pars Prima, Prologi Quaestio 2*, 27b B–C: 'intuitiva notitia est cognitio directa contra arguitionem, et quod est praesentialis contra modum absentem, quo imaginatio fertur super res praesentes, et quod est actuativa obiecti, et positiva existentiae, quoniam realem existentiam eius et actualem positionem eius facit apparere: esto etiam quod non sit.' Cf. Auriol, *S I Sent., Prooemium*, q. 2 (n. 83 in Pasnau 2002: 201).

⁶⁹ Cf. Perler 2004: 267–8. As Perler stresses, the focus of Auriol's inquiry is not *what* is present but *how* something is present in an intuitive act.

⁷⁰ The interpretation along these lines by Vanni Rovighi 2006: 144–7, 1978a, and 1978b (firmly grounded in a close reading of the primary texts) is, in my view, still persuasive. Vanni Rovighi grants that there are texts by Auriol which suggest a subjectivist interpretation but argues that those texts are an infelicitous application of his general theory of knowledge to sense-perceptual cognition in the absence of a modern scientific understanding of physical and physiological processes.

⁷¹ Cf., for instance, the classic study by Prezioso 1950.

⁷² See Auriol, *C I Sent., Pars Prima*, distinctio xxvii, art. 2, 625 b–626 a.

⁷³ See Friedman 2021: sect. 3; Perler 2004: 267–8; and Vanni Rovighi 1978a, 1978b.

cognized thing (the 'intention') are *not* two things (happily corresponding to each other in a good case). They are the same one thing under two different modes of existence.[74] To be sure, the actualization of the intentional/objective mode of being of that thing needs a perceiver. But this actualization is nothing else than the manifestation (the *apparere* or 'appearing') of that very extra-mental thing to the perceiver as an object of perception.[75] *Esse apparens* should be taken as 'manifested' being and not as 'appearance' to be contrasted with reality.

In particular, according to Auriol, intellectual knowledge (that is, knowledge by universals) is having something present ('habere aliquid praesens') through its manifesting itself to a cognitive subject.[76] What 'appears' is the thing itself observed by the intellect ('illa sit vera res, quam intellectus speculatur'), and not some psychical reality by means of which the intellect proceeds to external things ('quod per illum procedat intellectus ad res').[77] Auriol explains:

> Health as thought and health as existing outside are really one and the same [sunt unum, et idem realiter], although they differ in their mode of being [in modo essendi], because health, in the intellect, has an apparent and intentional being [habet esse apparens, et intentionale]; outside, however, in the body, it has existing and real being [habet esse existens, et reale]...they differ in fact in mode of being, although they are an identical thing [differunt quidem in modo essendi, quamvis sit eadem res].[78]

Furthermore, not only is the cognized thing not a *tertium quid* (a mental picture or a mental copy) which is in the mind like an item in a box: the cognized thing is also not a 'real' modification, or an accident, of the mind. That is to say, the cognized thing is not an ontological (or formal) constituent of the mind. This is the meaning, I suggest, of Auriol's contrast between *esse reale* and *esse intentionale*/ *esse obiectale*: a mental act (say, the act of vision) is, ontologically, a mode of being of the cognitive subject (*forma realis existens subjective*); by contrast, a cognized thing (say, a seen rose) is a mode of being of the extra-mental thing (a mode of being of the rose). The latter is in the cognitive subject 'intentionally'

---

[74] Auriol, *C I Sent.*, Pars Prima, distinctio ix, art. 1, 321 b E–322 a D–E:
res posita in esse obiectali, puta rosa apparens[,] non potest resolvi per intellectum in rem, et apparitionem passivam, tanquam in duo, immo rosa, quae obiicitur, videtur omnino simplex...unde conceptus rosae, licet non sit purum concipi, immo cum hoc est rosa, resolvi tamen non potest in realitatem rosae, et ipsum concipi, tanquam in duo, immo conceptum rosae obiicitur, tanquam aliquid quid simplicissimum, et impossibile separari in duo...immo est aliquid simplicissimum propter unitatem indistinctionis omnimodae.

[75] Friedman 2021: sect. 3 and Vanni Rovighi 1978a, 1978b.
[76] Auriol, *C I Sent.*, Pars Secunda, distinctio xxxv, art. 1, 752 a A: 'ergo manifeste apparet, quod non est plus de formali ratione ipsius intelligere, aut cognoscere in universali, nisi habere aliquid praesens per modum apparentis.'
[77] Auriol, *C I Sent.*, Pars Prima, distinctio ix, art. 1, 320 a C.
[78] Auriol, *C I Sent.*, Pars Prima, distinctio ix, art. 1, 320 a D–E.

(*intentionaliter*) or 'objectively' (*objective*), as opposed to 'really' (that is, as a mode of being or as a modification of the cognitive subject).[79] This intentional presence in the mind does not have any kind of distinct existence of its own apart from being a mode of existence of the extra-mental thing.[80]

3.3. The Direct Apprehension of Material Particulars

William of Ockham is even more radical in his direct realism. For him, knowledge is, in general, a mental state—a view he expresses by stating that 'knowledge is a certain quality which exists in the soul as its subject'. This ontological status applies to dispositional knowledge (in his vocabulary, *habitus* or 'habitual' knowledge) no less than to occurrent knowledge (an 'act of knowledge').[81] Human cognition starts with a direct awareness of extra-mental singular things[82]—that is, from the only sort of things which have mind-independent existence (as he writes in *Quodlibeta*, I, q. xiii: 'everything [omnis res] outside the mind is singular').[83] No *tertium quid* mediating between mind and world is needed to explain the immediate grasp of ordinary material particulars from which our cognitive journey begins: by its own nature (*ex natura sua*), an act of cognition is a natural sign of an external thing similarly to the way in which a word is a conventional sign of a thing.[84] In brief, a cognitive act is capable of directly signifying or presenting an extra-mental thing to a cognitive subject.

Ockham calls this direct apprehension of material particulars 'intuitive cognition' (*cognitio* or *notitia intuitiva*), contrasting it with 'abstractive cognition' (*cognitio* or *notitia abstractiva*). 'Intuitive cognition of a thing', he explains, 'is cognition that enables us to know whether the thing exists or does not exist, in such a way that, if the thing exists, then the intellect immediately judges that it

---

[79] Vanni Rovighi 1978a: 288–9.
[80] Auriol, *S I Sent.*, Dist. III, Sectio XIV, C b 31, ii, 698/C I *Sent.*, Pars Prima, distinctio iii, art. 1, 193 b D: 'Quomodocumque enim sit, constat quod illae apparentiae non sunt actus visionis, nec habent aliquod esse nisi cognitum intentionale et apparens.'
[81] Ockham, *Exp., Prologus* § 2 (in *OPh* iv, 4–5): 'scientia...est quaedam qualitas exsistens subiective in anima...non minus est scientia, quae est habitus, talis qualitas quam actus scientiae.' Translated in Boehner 1990: 3.
[82] See Ockham, *QS*, I, q. xiii (translated in Boehner 1990: 28): 'a singular thing...is what is first known...What is first known by such cognition is an extra-mental thing.'
[83] Boehner 1990: 28. On Ockham's direct realism, see Adams 1987: i, 495–550. Panaccio's claim that Ockham is a representationalist is based on an understanding of the cognitive act itself as a third entity between the mind and external things. However, even Panaccio grants that if by representationalism is meant the doctrine according to which the immediate object of cognition is always a representation rather than the external thing itself, and by direct realism the denial of this thesis, then Ockham's mature theory of knowledge is a straightforward case of direct realism (see Panaccio 2004: 16).
[84] See Ockham, *S I Sent., Distinctio.* II, q. VIII (in *OTh* ii, 289): 'ex natura sua ita est signum rei extra sicut vox est signum rei ad placitum instituentis.'

exists and evidently knows that it exists.'[85] That is, intuitive cognition is the kind of cognition by which we can be immediately aware of the existence of an object.[86] By contrast, abstractive cognition 'abstracts from existence and non-existence'.[87] It is clear, Ockham claims, that intuitive cognition is 'the first to be acquired' and has cognitive primacy over abstractive cognition, 'for abstractive cognition of a singular thing presupposes an intuitive cognition of the same object, and not vice versa'.[88] Furthermore, according to him, an intuitive cognition of a singular thing 'is immediately caused, or is of such nature as to be so caused, by this singular thing'.[89] In sum, for Ockham, intuitive cognition, understood as the direct apprehension of existing material particulars caused by those particulars, is the first and most fundamental kind of cognition. In modern parlance, it is a primitive mental state involving the world that has ontological priority, as well as cognitive primacy, over other cognitive mental states.

Most importantly, without this primitive cognitive contact with extra-mental things, we would have no evident knowledge of the truth value of contingent propositions about the present. As already taught by Aristotle in the *Metaphysics* and the *Posterior Analytics*, Ockham notes, knowledge of the sensible world acquired by experience begins with the senses.[90] This sensory intuition, Ockham reasons, acquaints us (for instance) with shapes and colours but is insufficient for a complex cognitive apprehension such as 'Socrates is white'. Ditto for the non-complex apprehension of its terms ('Socrates' and 'white'). In other words, the apprehension of terms (in Ockham's vocabulary, a non-complex cognition) and of a proposition formed by these terms (in Ockham's vocabulary, a complex cognition) is not a matter for the senses but for the intellect. Even more so for any judgement by which we may assent to or dissent from an apprehended proposition. Now, in the case of analytical propositions, we evidently know their truth value by grasping the meaning of their terms. By contrast, in the case of contingent propositions (e.g., 'Socrates is white'), their truth value can evidently be known only through the intellectual intuitive cognition of their terms, that is, through the only kind of cognition that 'enables us to know whether the thing exists or does not exist'.[91]

---

[85] Ockham, *S I Sent.*, *Prologus*, q. 1, a. 1 (in *OTh* i, 31) (translated in Boehner 1990: 23).
[86] I will not enter here into the complex issue of Ockham's account of intuitive cognition of non-existents. I will just mention that, according to him, 'if the divine power were to conserve a perfect intuitive cognition of a thing no longer existent,' we would correctly judge that the intuited object is non-existent (see Ockham, *S I Sent.*, *Prologus*, q. 1, a. 1 (in *OTh* i, 31) (translated in Boehner 1990: 23).)
[87] Ockham, *S I Sent.*, *Prologus*, q. 1, a. 1 (in *OTh* i, 31) (translated in Boehner 1990: 23).
[88] Ockham, *QS*, I, q. xiii (translated in Boehner 1990: 28).
[89] Ockham, *Qs*, I, q. xiii (translated in Boehner 1990: 28–9).
[90] See Ockham, *S I Sent.*, *Prologus*, q. 1, a. 1 (in *OTh* i, 33) (translated in Boehner 1990: 24). Cf. Aristotle, *Metaphysics* 980^b 25–982^a 2 and Aristotle, *Posterior Analytics* 100^{a}3–9.
[91] Ockham, *S I Sent.*, *Prologus*, q. 1, a. 1 (in *OTh* i, 31) (translated in Boehner 1990: 23).

through abstractive cognition no contingent truth, in particular none relating to the present, can be evidently known. This is clear from the fact that when Socrates and his whiteness are known in his absence, this non-complex knowledge does not enable us to know whether Socrates exists or does not exist, or whether he is white or is not white, and the same for other contingent truths.[92]

4. Conclusion

The thinkers discussed above share, from their different perspectives, a deep insight: namely that knowledge is, most fundamentally, the presence of an objective reality to a cognitive subject and that it is from this primitive presence that human cognition begins. I find this insight both persuasive and attractive. It is, at any rate, certainly resilient in its capacity to take new forms adapted to the spirit of the time. It might be tempting, for instance, to dismiss medieval thinking on these matters by arguing that medieval philosophers had not yet confronted robust forms of scepticism, or that after Kant no one could ever think again that the objects of our experience are given, as opposed to mentally constructed. As we have seen, the latter is certainly not the case: as Dubray puts it as late as the twentieth century, 'knowledge is not, as in Kantian criticism..... the filling up of empty shells—a priori mental forms or categories—with the unknown and unknowable reality'.[93] Rather, it is a process of discovery of a knowable, although never fully known reality which presents itself to a cognizer under different and always partial modes of presentation. Needless to say, the view that, in cognition, we do make cognitive contact with extra-mental, ordinary objects which are given to, although never exhausted by, our cognition, is also far from dead nowadays. Indeed, thinking of knowledge as, first of all, the encounter with material individuals which are present to perceiving subjects is still a natural (and, perhaps, the most natural) way to think of cognition. Its very naturalism helps explain why it keeps resurfacing even after Kant and the robust attacks of scepticism. Seen from the vantage point of modern, post-Kantian philosophy, the fact that this was the way in which medieval philosophers also tended to think of cognition can no longer be dismissed as a hopelessly naive approach to be relegated to the infancy of epistemology.[94] On the contrary, it seems to me that these distant thinkers are remarkably sophisticated in their grasp of what knowledge essentially is, and that there is a great deal to be learned by listening to them.

In sum, a conception of knowledge as presence and presentation is a major live strand which traverses the history of philosophy and which continues to resist the

---

[92] Ockham, *I Sent.*, *Prologus*, q. 1, a. 1 (in *OTh* I, p. 32) (translated in Boehner 1990: 24).
[93] Dubray 1910: sect. 3.
[94] This is why I have discussed medieval theories of cognition after forms of direct realism in the twentieth century.

attacks of rival conceptions. It is, I contend, a historically well-attested as well as a philosophically fertile version of 'knowledge-first' epistemology, intended as the view that knowing is a primitive mental state involving the world from which our cognitive journey begins.[95] The reappearance of this conception in distant historical periods and in very different intellectual contexts is in itself an indication, I have claimed, of its tracking something deeper than merely culturally and historically conditioned features of possible accounts of human cognition.

References

1. Primary Sources

Aquinas, Thomas (1886–7), *Summa Theologiae*. Textum Leoninum (Rome: Ex typographia Senatus).

Auriol, Peter (1596), *Commentariorum in Primum Librum Sententiarum Pars Prima*, ed. C. Sarnano (Rome: Ex typographia Vaticana). Abbreviated as *C I Sent*.

Auriol, Peter (1952–6), *Scriptum super primum sententiarum*, ed. E. M. Buytaert, 2 vols (St. Bonaventure, NY: Franciscan Institute). Abbreviated as *S I Sent*.

Ockham, William of (1974–88), *Opera Philosophica*, ed. Gedeon Gál et al., 7 vols. (St. Bonaventure, NY: Franciscan Institute). Abbreviated as *OPh*.

Ockham, William of (1967–86), *Opera Theologica*, ed. Gedeon Gál et al., 10 vols. (St. Bonaventure, NY: Franciscan Institute). Abbreviated as *OTh*.

Ockham, William of (1967), *Scriptum in Librum Primum Sententiarum Ordinatio: Prologus et Distinctio I*. (St. Bonaventure, NY: Franciscan Institute). Abbreviated as *S I Sent*.

Ockham, William of (1970), *Scriptum in Librum Primum Sententiarum Ordinatio: Distinctiones II–III*. (St. Bonaventure, NY: Franciscan Institute). Abbreviated as *S I Sent*.

Ockham, William of (1980), Quodlibeta Septem. (St. Bonaventure, NY: Franciscan Institute). Abbreviated as *QS*.

Ockham, William of (1985), *Expositio in Libros Physicorum Aristotelis: Prologus et Libri I–III*. (St. Bonaventure, NY: Franciscan Institute). Abbreviated as *Exp*.

Scotus, John Duns (1954), *Ordinatio* (*Opus oxoniense*). In *Opera Omnia*, vol. iii. (Vatican City: typis polyglottis Vaticanis).

Scotus, John Duns (1895), *Quaestiones Quodlibetales*. In *Opera Omnia*, vol. xxv (Paris: Vivès). Abbreviated as *Quodl*.

---

[95] Cf. Williamson 2013: 3: 'The most salient feature of knowing as the focus of epistemology is that it is a world-involving state.' See also Williamson 2000.

Scotus, John Duns (2005), *Reportatio I-B. Prologus*. In Klaus Rodler, ed., *Die Prologe der Reportata Parisiensia des Johannes Duns Scotus: Untersuchungen zur Textüberlieferung und kritische Edition* (Innsbruck: Studia).

Spinoza, Baruch (1925), *Ethica*. In *Spinoza: Opera*, ed. Carl Gebhardt, vol. ii (Heidelberg: Carl Winters Universitätsbuchhandlung): 41–308.

Spinoza, Baruch (1925), *Tractatus de Intellectus Emendatione*. In *Spinoza: Opera*, ed. Carl Gebhardt, vol. ii (Heidelberg: Carl Winters Universitätsbuchhandlung): 1–40.

2. Secondary Sources

Adams, Marilyn McCord (1987), *William Ockham*, 2 vols. (Notre Dame, IN: University of Notre Dame Press).

Antognazza, Maria Rosa (2015), 'The Benefit to Philosophy of the Study of its History', *British Journal for the History of Philosophy*, 23/1: 161–84.

Antognazza, Maria Rosa (2020), 'The Distinction in Kind between Knowledge and Belief', *Proceedings of the Aristotelian Society*, 120/3: 277–308.

Antognazza, Maria Rosa (2023), 'Intuitive Cognition in the Latin Medieval Tradition', *British Journal for the History of Philosophy*, 31/4: 675–92.

Antognazza, Maria Rosa (2024), *Thinking with Assent: Renewing a Traditional Account of Knowledge and Belief* (Oxford: Oxford University Press).

Arnauld, Antoine (1843), *Des vraies et des fausses idées* [1683], in *Œuvres philosophiques*, ed. C. Jourdain (Paris: L. Hachette/Ladrange): 27–264.

Aveling, Francis (1907), 'Belief', in *The Catholic Encyclopedia*, ii (New York: Robert Appleton Company), https://www.newadvent.org/cathen/02408b.htm, accessed 11 February 2024.

Ayers, Michael (2019), *Knowing and Seeing: Groundwork for a New Empiricism* (Oxford: Oxford University Press).

Ayers, Michael, and Antognazza, Maria Rosa (2019), 'Knowledge and Belief from Plato to Locke', in Michael Ayers (ed.), *Knowing and Seeing: Groundwork for a New Empiricism* (Oxford: Oxford University Press): 3–33.

Boehner, Philotheus (1949), '"Notitia Intuitiva" of Non Existents according to Peter Aureoli', *Rivista di Filosofia Neo-Scolastica*, 41/3: 289–307.

Boehner, Philotheus (ed. and trans.) (1990), *William of Ockham: Philosophical Writings: A Selection* (Indianapolis, IN: Hackett).

Bosanquet, Bernard (1888), *Logic, or the Morphology of Knowledge* (Oxford: Clarendon Press).

Bradley, F. H. (1883), *The Principles of Logic* (London: Kegan Paul).

Bradley, F. H. (1893), *Appearance and Reality* (2nd edn, with an appendix, 1897, London: Swan Sonnenschein).

Cattell, Raymond B. (1941), 'Francis Aveling: 1875–1941', *American Journal of Psychology*, 54/4: 608–10.

Cook Wilson, John (1926), *Statement and Inference with Other Philosophical Papers*, 2 vols (Oxford: Clarendon Press, repr., Bristol: Thoemmes Press, 2002).

Cross, Richard (2014), *Duns Scotus's Theory of Cognition* (Oxford: Oxford University Press).

Dubray, Charles (1905), *The Theory of Psychical Dispositions* (*The Psychological Review*: Monograph Supplements, 7.2), https://doi.org/10.1037/h0093005

Dubray, Charles (1910), 'Knowledge', *The Catholic Encyclopedia*, viii (New York: Robert Appleton Company), https://www.newadvent.org/cathen/08673a.htm, accessed 10 February 2024.

Friedman, Russell L. (2021), 'Peter Auriol', in Edward N. Zalta (ed.), *The Stanford Encyclopedia of Philosophy*. Summer 2021 Edition, https://plato.stanford.edu/archives/sum2021/entries/auriol/, accessed 10 February 2024.

Panaccio, Claude (2004), *Ockham on Concepts* (Aldershot: Ashgate).

Pasnau, Robert (2002), *The Cambridge Translations of Medieval Philosophical Texts*, iii: *Mind and Knowledge* (Cambridge: Cambridge University Press).

Perler, Dominik (2004), *Theorien der Intentionalität im Mittelalter* (2nd edn, Frankfurt am Main: Klostermann).

Pini, Giorgio (2014), 'Scotus on Intuitive and Abstractive Cognition', in Jeffrey Hause (ed.), *Debates in Medieval Philosophy: Essential Readings and Contemporary Responses* (London: Routledge), 348–65.

Prezioso, Fortunato (1950), 'La teoria dell'essere apparente nella gnoseologia di Pietro Aureolo', *Studi Francescani*, 46: 15–43.

Spearman, C. (1941), 'Obituary Notice, Francis Aveling, 1875–1941', *British Journal of Psychology*, 32: 1–4.

Strawson, P. F. (1992), *Analysis and Metaphysics: An Introduction to Philosophy* (Oxford: Oxford University Press).

Vanni Rovighi, Sofia (1978a), 'Una fonte remota della teoria husserliana dell'intenzionalità', in *Studi di filosofia medioevale*, ii: *Secoli XIII e XIV* (Milan: Vita e Pensiero): 283–98. Originally published in I. Bona (ed.), *Omaggio a Husserl* (Milan: Saggiatore, 1960): 49–65.

Vanni Rovighi, Sofia (1978b), 'L'intenzionalità della conoscenza secondo P. Aureolo', in *Studi di filosofia medioevale*, ii: *Secoli XIII e XIV* (Milan: Vita e Pensiero), 275–82. Originally published in *L'Homme et son destin* (Louvain and Brussels: Nauwelaerts, 1958 [1960]): 673–80.

Vanni Rovighi, Sofia (2006), *Storia della filosofia medievale* (Milan: Vita e Pensiero).

Warnock, Mary (2004), 'Wodehouse, Helen Marion', in D. Cannadine (ed.), *Oxford Dictionary of National Biography*. doi: 10.1093/ref:odnb/48473.

Williamson, Timothy (2000), *Knowledge and its Limits*, Oxford: Oxford University Press.

Williamson, Timothy (2013), 'Knowledge First', in M. Steup. J. Turri, and E. Sosa (eds), *Contemporary Debates in Epistemology* (2nd edn, Somerset: Wiley Blackwell), 1–9.

Wodehouse, Helen (1909), 'Knowledge as Presentation', *Mind* 18/1: 391–99.

Wodehouse, Helen (1910), *The Presentation of Reality* (Cambridge: Cambridge University Press).

Wolter, Allan (trans.) (1987), *Duns Scotus: Philosophical Writings* (Indianapolis, IN: Hackett).

4
Śrīharṣa on the Indefinability of Knowledge Events

Nilanjan Das

1. Introduction

In contemporary epistemology, it is widely recognized that states of knowing are subject to an *anti-luck condition*. Gettier (1963) showed that, in order to know, not only must an agent have a belief that is true and justified, but it must also be free from a certain kind of epistemic luck. But it turned out to be difficult—if not impossible—to articulate what this anti-luck condition on knowledge is without appealing back to knowledge itself. In the wake of Gettier, many epistemologists proposed non-circular analyses of knowledge: analyses that seek to characterize either knowledge itself (as an epistemological kind) or the application conditions of the word 'know' in knowledge-independent terms. But these analyses are subject to counterexamples. Given this miserable track record, some epistemologists beginning with Williamson (2000) have recommended a 'knowledge first' approach to epistemology. As fleshed out by Williamson, the approach involves at least two commitments.[1] First, it is committed to the view that knowledge should be treated as a *sui generis* mental state that need not be (metaphysically or conceptually) decomposable into a *mental* condition like belief and other *non-mental* conditions like truth and reliability. Secondly, it is committed to the view that knowledge should be treated as *explanatorily fundamental* in epistemology: other normatively significant notions in epistemology, such as evidence and justification, should be analysed in terms of knowledge.

Like history *simpliciter*, the history of philosophy too repeats itself.[2] In this chapter, my aim is to explore an analogous episode in the history of Sanskrit philosophy in which a number of epistemologists who were active in South Asia

---

[1] For discussion, see McGlynn (2014). For a helpful disambiguation of different ways of construing the 'knowledge first' approach, see Ichikawa and Jenkins (2017).
[2] Vaidya (2023) and Williamson (2023) have recently discussed the question of whether there are 'knowledge first' approaches in Sanskrit epistemology. I disagree with Vaidya's interpretation of the later Nyāya view as an example of the 'knowledge first' approach, because both the early and the later Nyāya epistemologists typically seek to analyse the notion of knowledge events (*pramā*) conceptually into mental conditions such as awareness events (*jñāna*) and non-mental conditions such as accuracy (*yāthārthya*). See Das (2021) for more details.

between the second half of the first millennium CE and the first half of the second millennium CE grappled with the problem of epistemic luck. These epistemologists were concerned not exactly with the notion of knowledge, but rather with the notion of *pramā*. Instances of *pramā* are mental events of *learning* or *knowledge acquisition*. Suppose I look out of my window and undergo a veridical perceptual experience as of there being a hawk on my fence. So, I perceptually learn—that is, acquire the knowledge—that there is a hawk on my fence. Or suppose I see a thin trail of smoke emanating from a hill at a distance and conclude that there is fire on the hill. So, I inferentially learn—that is, acquire the knowledge—that there is fire on the hill. Here, both my perceptual experience and my inferential judgement are awareness events (*jñāna*)—experiences or thoughts—in undergoing which I acquire some knowledge.[3] They are instances of *pramā*. For convenience, we shall call these *knowledge events*.[4] At least some Sanskrit epistemologists recognized that such knowledge events are subject to an anti-luck condition: an experience or a judgement that is accurate or true as a matter of luck cannot be a knowledge event.

Yet the lessons that they drew were varied. The *optimists*—for example, early Nyāya philosophers like Udayana (tenth/eleventh century CE)—thought that we could articulate an anti-luck condition on knowledge events without falling back on the notion of learning or knowledge acquisition. The *pessimists*—especially the non-dualist Vedāntins like Śrīharṣa (twelfth century CE) and his later followers like Citsukha (thirteenth century CE)—rejected this claim: they argued that there was no way of characterizing the anti-luck condition on knowledge events independently of our notion of learning or knowledge acquisition. Finally, the *ameliorationists*—especially, later Nyāya philosophers like Gaṅgeśa Upādhyāya (fourteenth century CE) and his commentators—agreed with the pessimists but revised the concept of knowledge events so that it would not only apply to experiences and judgements that are free from epistemic luck, but also to epistemically

---

[3] The term '*jñāna*' is sometimes translated as 'cognition'. Typically, philosophers and cognitive scientists take cognitive states to be mental states like beliefs and judgements whose contents can be directly used for theoretical reasoning, verbal reports, and controlling action. But some Sanskrit philosophers think that non-conceptual perceptual experiences—which count as '*jñāna*'—aren't like this. So, it is better to use a term like 'awareness'. Even though a construction like 'S is aware that p' in English ascribes a factive mental state insofar as it entails that p, philosophers use constructions of the form 'S is aware of o as being F', which don't always entail that o is F. I will use the latter kind of construction stipulatively: on my view, S is aware of o as being F if and only if S perceives/judges/suspects o to be F. None of these attitudes entails that o is F, even though they entail that o exists (which is an assumption shared by Śrīharṣa's Nyāya-Vaiśeṣika interlocutors).

[4] Not all states of knowing are knowledge events. First, knowledge events are awareness events, i.e. occurrent mental states like experiences and thoughts. By contrast, states of knowing can be occurrent as well as dispositional. Secondly, not all states of knowing are states through which we learn or acquire knowledge; for example, remembering is a paradigmatic state of knowing, but we needn't learn that p by remembering that p.

lucky ones.[5] In earlier work (Das 2021), I have explored the ameliorationist approach in detail. In this chapter, I wish to consider the view of the pessimists: a view developed by Śrīharṣa in *A Confection of Refutation* (*Khaṇḍanakhaṇḍakhādya*, henceforth the *Refutation*).

Śrīharṣa is a defender of non-dualistic Vedānta, a view that emerges from a certain reading of the Upaniṣads, which are the last part of the Vedic corpus and therefore sometimes called '*vedānta*' (literally, 'the end of the Veda'). Non-dualistic Vedāntins accept a form of monism: the view that there is a single entity that ultimately exists (*paramārthasat*), that is, exists independently of our attitudes like beliefs, desires, and judgements, namely consciousness (*vijñāna*). Nyāya and Vaiśeṣika philosophers reject this view. They make two claims. The first is an *ontological* claim: there are many kinds of entities that ultimately exist. The Vaiśeṣika metaphysicians offer a list of six ontological categories—substance (*dravya*), quality (*guṇa*), motion (*karman*), universals (*sāmānya*), ultimate differentiators (*antyaviśeṣa*), and inherence (*samavāya*)—that is supposed to exhaust everything that ultimately exists. The second is an *epistemological* claim: our ordinary methods of knowing can help us know various facts about ultimately existent objects. The Nyāya epistemologists (henceforth the Naiyāyikas) offer a list of four methods of knowing (*pramāṇa*)—perception (*pratyakṣa*), inference (*anumāna*), analogy (*upamāna*), and testimony (*śabda*)—which are supposed to give us epistemic access to the constituents of ultimate reality. In the *Refutation*, Śrīharṣa dissents from both these claims: he refutes the definitions (*lakṣaṇa*) that the Nyāya and Vaiśeṣika thinkers propose for their preferred ontological and epistemological categories. His aim is to show that neither the polycategorial ontology that the Vaiśeṣikas defend nor the Nyāya story about how we gain epistemic access to objective features of reality is defensible. While defending this claim, Śrīharṣa argued that knowledge events are *indefinable* precisely because there is no good way of articulating the anti-luck condition on knowledge events.

What is novel about Śrīharṣa's treatment of this problem is that he takes his arguments for indefinability of knowledge events also to undermine the view that knowledge events form a unified, *sui generis* kind of mental events. This, as I shall show, has to do with his commitment to a view about attributions of knowledge events:

The Epistemic Priority Thesis. Knowledge events are *epistemically prior* to other non-factive mental states and events: when we are trying to determine whether an agent has undergone a knowledge event, we don't initially ascribe to them

---

[5] See Matilal (1986); Ganeri (2017) closely follows Matilal's exposition. A complete translation of Śrīharṣa's *A Confection of Refutation* (*Khaṇḍanakhaṇḍakhādya*) can be found in Jha (1913/1986) and a partial one in Granoff (1978). For discussions of Śrīharṣa's philosophical views more generally, see Granoff (1978), Phillips (1999), Ram-Prasad (2002), and Das (2018).

some other non-factive mental event and then check whether that event meets some further conditions (like truth or reliability) necessary for it to count as a knowledge event; rather, we treat certain mental events by default as knowledge events until a defeater comes along.

Śrīharṣa argues that this thesis—when taken in conjunction with the arguments for the indefinability of knowledge events—should give us reason to doubt whether our ordinary attributions of knowledge events are reliably tracking any unified, *sui generis* kind of mental events. I argue that Śrīharṣa's arguments can be extended to states of knowing more generally. Thus, his arguments undermine not only the idea that knowledge is analysable, but also one of the key theses of 'knowledge first' epistemology, namely, that knowledge is a *sui generis* mental state.

2. Śrīharṣa's Argument

Śrīharṣa's argument against Nyāya epistemology exploits a tension between two commitments about knowledge events that many Naiyāyikas endorse. Many (if not all) Naiyāyikas accept the following definition of knowledge events:

The Nyāya Definition of Knowledge Events. An awareness event (*jñāna*)—an experience or a thought—is a knowledge event if and only if it satisfies two conditions:
  (i) It is a first-hand awareness event (*anubhava*): it is not a recollective awareness event.
  (ii) It is accurate (*yathārtha*): it represents the world the way it is.

This characterization of knowledge events imposes two necessary conditions on knowledge events. The first condition—call it the *non-mnemic condition*—says that a knowledge event cannot be a recollective awareness event. This may seem surprising, but it follows from the Nyāya conception of recollection (*smaraṇa*). Recollection, according to Naiyāyikas, just is *information retrieval*, that is, a process of retrieving bits of information one has acquired through earlier non-recollective awareness events. Understood in this way, recollection is not a *generative* source of knowledge: when we undergo a recollective awareness, we simply retrieve what we already were aware of; we don't thereby acquire any piece of knowledge that we didn't already possess. This implies that recollective awareness events aren't knowledge events. The second condition—call it the *accuracy condition*—says that a knowledge event must be accurate. Different Naiyāyikas explain this condition differently. But the basic idea is clear: if an experience or thought misrepresents the way the world is, then it cannot be an event of knowledge acquisition. While both these conditions can plausibly be treated as necessary conditions on knowledge events, it is not obvious that they are jointly sufficient.

The *Nyāya Definition of Knowledge Events* conflicts with another commitment of the Naiyāyikas:

Nyāya Infallibilism. An awareness event is a knowledge event only if it is produced by a totality of causal conditions (*kāraṇasāmagrī*) that could not have given rise to an inaccurate awareness event.[6]

Take three examples that Śrīharṣa considers in this connection:

Guesswork. You place a few shells in your fist and ask me, 'How many shells are there in my hand?' I have no idea. On a hunch, I judge, 'There are five shells in that fist.' So, I say out loud, 'There are five.' My awareness is correct: you have exactly five shells in your hand.

Mist and Fire. I look at a hill and see what looks like smoke emerging from it. So, I judge that there is smoke on the hill. I am wrong: all I see is a wisp of mist. I had previously observed (in kitchens, etc.) that smoke is always accompanied by fire. On the basis of those observations, I had judged that wherever there is smoke, there is fire. Now, I remember that generalization. So, I conclude that there is fire on the hill. My judgement turns out to be true: there is fire on the hill.

Horns and Cows. From a distance, I see an animal with horns. Earlier, I had observed many cows with horns. On the basis of these observations, I *falsely* judged that all animals with horns are cows. Now, I recall that generalization. So, I conclude that the animal is a cow. My judgement is true: the animal is a cow.

In these cases, it seems that I could easily have made a false judgement. Thus, my judgement is true as a matter of luck. According to *Nyāya Infallibilism*, therefore, these cannot be knowledge events: the totality of causal conditions that yield these judgements could easily have given rise to an error. Yet, according to the *Nyāya Definition of Knowledge Events*, the judgements that I make in these cases of epistemic luck are knowledge events: they are accurate, non-recollective awareness events. This is the tension. Call this the *problem of epistemic luck*. Śrīharṣa argues that this tension cannot be resolved by any definition of knowledge events.

---

[6] It is worth distinguishing *evidential* infallibilism from *causal* infallibilism. Evidential infallibilism says that an agent can come to know that *p* only if the evidence on the basis of which they believe (or judge) that *p* entails that *p*. The Nyāya thinkers like Udayana are not evidential infallibilists: they think that we can come to learn inductive generalizations, or facts on the basis of testimony, even though our evidence for judging the relevant contents to be true doesn't decisively rule out the possibility that they are false. However, they are causal infallibilists: they think that whenever an agent comes to know that *p*, their awareness is formed on the basis of causal conditions that couldn't lead to an accurate judgement. Thanks to Mark Siderits for pressing me on this point.

Any satisfactory (and therefore non-circular) definition of knowledge events will have to include an anti-luck condition that doesn't appeal back to the notion of learning or knowledge acquisition itself. But there is no such anti-luck condition.

In what follows, I will reconstruct Śrīharṣa's argument by paying closer attention to his text.

3. Response 1: Infallibilism

Śrīharṣa's argument against the Nyāya conception of knowledge events primarily targets a definition given by Udayana in his *Garland of Definitions* (*Lakṣaṇamālā*): 'A knowledge event is a first-hand awareness of the way something is (*tattvānubhūtiḥ pramā*)' (LM 9.1). This is a version of the *Nyāya Definition of Knowledge Events*. In an initial barrage of arguments, Śrīharṣa claims that neither the notion of first-hand awareness (*anubhūti*) nor the notion of the way something is (*tattva*) can be adequately characterized. But then he turns to the definition as a whole. Here, his argument hinges on a case like *Guesswork* (KKh 383.20–384.11). In that case, when you ask, 'How many shells do I have in my fist?', I think, 'There are five.' My awareness event is accurate: there are exactly five shells in your hand. And it is first-hand: since its content isn't derived from any earlier first-hand awareness event through recollection, it is non-recollective. Yet it is obvious that this cannot be a knowledge event: when I judge that you have five shells in your hand, I don't thereby come to know this. This is a problem for the *Nyāya Definition of Knowledge Events*.

Śrīharṣa considers two possible Nyāya responses to this problem. The first response seems to be the most natural: the way I arrive at my judgement in this case could easily have led me astray. Since I was randomly making up my mind about the number of shells in your hand, I could easily have made a false judgement about how many shells you had in your fist. Thus, Śrīharṣa's Nyāya interlocutor could revise their conception of knowledge events:

The Revised Nyāya Definition of Knowledge Events. An awareness event is a knowledge event if and only if it satisfies three conditions:
  (i) It is a first-hand awareness event: it is not a recollective awareness event.
  (ii) It is accurate: it represents the world as it is.
  (iii) It arises from a totality of causal conditions that couldn't give to rise any inaccurate or erroneous awareness.

This account preserves the spirit of *Nyāya Infallibilism*: it entails that an awareness can be a knowledge event only if its causal ancestry guarantees its accuracy. But we might wonder, what is it about the causal ancestry of knowledge events which explains why the knowledge events are infallible in this way? There are two different answers to this question—defended by Naiyāyikas and Bhāṭṭa Mīmāṃsakas respectively—which, in turn, imply two distinct ways of fleshing out the *Revised Nyāya Definition of Knowledge Events*.

3.1 Two Kinds of Infallibilism

Let us begin by distinguishing two kinds of infallibilism. The Bhāṭṭa Mīmāṃsakas—Kumārila Bhaṭṭa (seventh century CE) and his commentators—argued that the normal or default (*autsargika*) state of any awareness is to be a knowledge event. An awareness will deviate from this normal or default state—and become inaccurate—just in case the causal conditions are *abnormal*, that is, just in case the causal conditions that give rise to the awareness include certain epistemic defects (*doṣa*) that are normally absent. Thus, what is necessary for a knowledge event to arise is the absence of epistemic defects. This yields:

Defect Infallibilism. For any kind *K* of knowledge events (perceptual, inferential, testimonial, and so on), the totality of causal conditions that are necessary for producing any instance of *K* must include the absence of certain positive conditions—epistemic defects—which guarantee the inaccuracy of the resulting awareness event.[7]

Nyāya and Vaiśeṣika thinkers such as Jayanta Bhaṭṭa (ninth century CE), Śrīdhara (tenth century CE), and Udayana disagree with this claim (NM I 442.13–444.2; NK 516.1–2; NKA 211.1–220.2).[8]

---

[7] This is sometimes called the theory of intrinsic knowledgehood (*svataḥprāmāṇya*) with respect to production (*utpatti*); on this view, a knowledge event arises simply from the normal causes that give rise to awareness events of a certain kind (as long as those causes are non-defective); no positive factors such as epistemic virtues are necessary. Kumārila Bhaṭṭa's commentators—Umveka Bhaṭṭa, Sucarita Miśra, and Pārthasārathi Miśra—defend different variations of the theory of intrinsic knowledgehood in their commentaries on Verse 47 in *The Detailed Commentary in Verse* (*Ślokavārttika*) ad *Mīmāṃsāsūtra* 1.1.2 (ŚVTṭ 54.1–17; ŚVK 90.13–25; NRK 45.7–20).

[8] The disagreement revolves around the epistemic status of testimony. Both the Bhāṭṭas and the Naiyāyikas accept the status of testimony as a *sui generis* source of knowledge and accept the Veda—a text regarded as authoritative by all Brahmanical thinkers—to be a source of knowledge with respect to ritually appropriate action (*dharma*). But Bhāṭṭas think that testimony can be a source of knowledge only insofar as certain epistemic defects belonging to the speaker—which make testimony inaccurate—are absent. By contrast, the Nyāya thinkers think that testimony can be a source of knowledge insofar as the speaker not only lacks these defects but also possesses certain epistemic virtues (*guṇa*) that makes them trustworthy (*āpta*). This disagreement bears indirectly on the epistemic status of the Veda. Since Bhāṭṭas regard the Veda as an authorless text, they take it to be a source of knowledge precisely because it is not vitiated by the defects of an author. By contrast, the Naiyāyikas like Jayanta and Udayana regard the Veda as the creation of an omniscient, omnipresent God-like being called Īśvara; not only does Īśvara lack the epistemic defects that make testimony inaccurate, but They also possess certain epistemic virtues that make Them trustworthy.

Udayana notes that the question of whether *Defect Infallibilism* is true can only be settled by looking at specific sources of knowledge, such as inference (NKA 215.1–216.2). Take cases of defective inference like *Mist and Fire* and *Cows and Horns*. In *Mist and Fire*, the fire that I infer is the target property (*sādhya*), and the hill to which I ascribe that fire is the site (*pakṣa*) of the inference. The inferential mark (*liṅga*)—the perceived feature of the hill on the basis of which I infer the fire—is smoke. But since this smoke is not, in fact, present in the site, my judgement that there is smoke on the hill is erroneous. It is this epistemic defect that prevents me from acquiring knowledge in this case. Next, consider *Cows and Horns*. Here, the target property that I infer is the cowhood, while the site of the inference is the animal before me. The horns of the animal I see are the inferential mark on the basis of which I infer its cowhood. In this case, even though the inferential mark is present in the site, the target property doesn't invariably accompany or *pervade* the inferential mark; for not all animals that have horns are cows. This, in turn, makes my judgement that whatever has horns is a cow false. It is this epistemic defect which, in this case, prevents me from acquiring knowledge.

Udayana claims that the mere absence of such epistemic defects isn't sufficient to generate inferential knowledge events. In good cases of inference, other positive conditions must be present: the agent's inferential judgement must be based on prior judgements that accurately indicate (i) that the relevant inferential mark is present in the site and (ii) that it is invariably accompanied or pervaded by the target property. This suggests that the inferential knowledge events causally depend on certain positive conditions over and above the absence of the epistemic defects which generate awareness events that aren't knowledge events. This diagnosis seems to be true of other kinds of knowledge events, such as those derived from perception, analogy and testimony. The general view, then, is that knowledge events require not only the absence of epistemic defects but also the presence of certain epistemic virtues (*guṇa*) that guarantee their accuracy. This suggests:

Virtue Infallibilism. For any kind K of knowledge events (perceptual, inferential, testimonial, and so on), the totality of causal conditions that are necessary for producing any instance of K must include certain positive conditions—epistemic virtues—that guarantee the accuracy of the resulting awareness event.[9]

It is worth understanding the general picture that emerges from this discussion.

---

[9] Contemporary virtue epistemologists treat epistemic or intellectual virtues either as faculties or as traits that promote some intellectual good. Virtue reliabilists, like Sosa (1991), think of intellectual virtues as faculties or qualities that help the agent maximize their surplus of true beliefs over false ones. In contrast, virtue responsibilists, like Zagzebski (1996), treat intellectual virtues as traits of character that promote intellectual flourishing. Both camps, however, treat virtues as dispositions. However, the Nyāya epistemologists typically treat epistemic virtues as causal factors which are necessary for the production of knowledge events but may or may not be dispositional properties.

For both virtue and defect infallibilists, what distinguishes knowledge events from other kinds of awareness events—such as error and doubt—is that the causal history of knowledge events is different from the causal history of these other kinds of awareness events. According to the defect infallibilists, the causal history of knowledge events is characterized by the absence of certain positive conditions—the epistemic defects—whose presence would make the resulting awareness events inaccurate. By contrast, according to the virtue infallibilists, the causal history of knowledge events involves certain positive conditions—the epistemic virtues—over and above the absence of epistemic defects. These positive conditions—insofar as they guarantee the accuracy of the resulting knowledge events—explain why these are accurate.

3.2 Śrīharṣa on Virtue Infallibilism

A virtue infallibilist could say that, in cases of epistemic luck like *Guesswork*, these epistemic virtues go missing. In *Guesswork*, my guess that you have five shells in your fist cannot be a knowledge event even if it is accurate: what generates my awareness in that case is a cognitive process that could easily lead to inaccurate judgements in other cases, so the causal ancestry of that awareness doesn't include any epistemic virtue that could guarantee its accuracy.

Śrīharṣa is unhappy with *Virtue Infallibilism*. His unhappiness comes across clearly in his treatment of an infallibilist response to *Guesswork*:

[The opponent:] One should insert the qualifying clause 'produced by causal conditions that don't err (*avyabhicārin*)' [in the definition that a knowledge event is a first-hand awareness of the way something is].

[Reply:] No. For, then, the expression 'the way something is' (*tattva*) will be useless. And you cannot accept even an accidentally fact-conforming (*kākatālīyasaṃvāda*) awareness to be produced by a totality of causal conditions that are shared with erroneous (*vyabhicārin*) awareness events. This is because, then, since an erroneous awareness would not differ with respect to its causal conditions [from accurate ones], there would be the undesirable consequence that it would be accurate. For it is not the case that the accuracy [of the awareness under consideration] is causeless, since, then, a problem of overgeneration would follow due to the absence of a determining factor. Given that this [awareness] is not erroneous, it must necessarily be said that its causal conditions are indeed invariably connected to non-erroneous awareness events.

(KKh 387.1–7)

Śrīharṣa is making two claims in this passage. The first is relatively trivial: adding clause (iii) to *Nyāya Definition of Knowledge Events* makes the accuracy condition laid down by (i) redundant. We would no longer need to define a knowledge event as a first-hand awareness of how something is. The second point is more important: the reasoning that leads Udayana to *Virtue Infallibilism* should also compel him to say that accidentally accurate awareness events must arise from certain accuracy-guaranteeing epistemic virtues. Let's unpack this claim.

Udayana's argument for *Virtue Infallibilism* depends on a principle about causation (NKA 211.1–213.2), namely that if effects of a certain kind E are a species of effects of a more general kind E^*, then the totality of causal conditions which are necessary for producing any instance of E must include causal conditions that are not included amongst the causal conditions which are necessary for producing any arbitrary instance of E^*. Now, consider knowledge events of a particular kind (perceptual, inferential, etc.). Since these are a subspecies of awareness events of the relevant kind, the causal conditions necessary for producing knowledge events of that kind must include some further conditions that are not included amongst the causal conditions which are necessary for producing awareness events of that kind. These special causal conditions—which distinguish the causal history of knowledge events from mere awareness events of the relevant kind—are the epistemic virtues.

The problem is this: just like knowledge events, *accurate* awareness events of a particular kind (perceptual, inferential, etc.) too are a subspecies of awareness events of that kind. So, given Udayana's principle about causation, they too must be produced by certain specific causal conditions that are not included amongst the causal conditions which are necessary for producing awareness events of that kind. For, if these accurate first-hand awareness events were produced by exactly the same causal conditions that also produce other awareness events of the relevant kind (including inaccurate ones), then even those other inaccurate awareness events would be accurate. This reasoning, if sound, should yield the result that the causal history of accurate awareness events must be different from that of inaccurate awareness events. This is significant: it implies that even awareness events that are *accidentally accurate* must be produced by at least some causal conditions that play no role in the production of inaccurate awareness events. So, accidentally accurate awareness events—such as my lucky judgement that you are holding five shells in your fist—must also arise from causal conditions that could not give rise to any inaccurate or erroneous awareness. So, the infallibilist response fails.

A general concern about this argument is that it relies heavily on the assumption that *Virtue Infallibilism* can only be motivated by relying on Udayana's principle about causation. This assumption can be rejected. But Śrīharṣa does have a second response against *Virtue Infallibilism* that doesn't make this assumption (KKh 389.11–16).

The response depends on two closely related examples. The first is *Mist and Fire*, the case where I misperceive mist on a hill as smoke and infer the presence of fire on the hill on the basis of that smoke. The second is:

Extended Mist and Fire. I look at a hill and see what looks like smoke emerging from it. So, I judge that there is smoke on the hill. I am wrong: all I see is a wisp of mist. I had previously observed (in kitchens, etc.) that smoke is always accompanied by fire. On the basis of those observations, I had judged that wherever there is smoke, there is fire. Now, I remember that generalization. So, I conclude that there is fire on the hill. My judgement is true: there is *both* smoke *and* fire on the hill.

The difference between this case and *Mist and Fire* is that, in the latter, my judgement that there is smoke on the hill could be false; in this case, it is true. But in both these cases, the inferential mark on the basis of which I arrive at my judgement is defective: what I perceive as smoke is, in fact, not smoke; it is mist. Yet the inferential judgement that I make is accurate: there is, in fact, fire on the hill. Since this judgement is an accurate first-hand awareness, the defender of the *Nyaya Definition of Knowledge Events* is committed to the claim that the judgement is a knowledge event. Even though the problem here is structurally the same as in the case of *Guesswork*, this pair of examples is a bit more robust. First, in both these cases, my judgement is uncontroversially a state of certainty. So, the two cases cannot be ruled out by appealing to a response that is available in the case of *Guesswork*: since in that case I merely guess that you have five shells in your fist and there is nothing to make me certain about this, the relevant awareness is not a state of certainty (KKh 384.7–10). Secondly, in *Extended Mist and Fire,* the kinds of epistemic virtues that Naiyāyikas typically regard as necessary for knowledge events are indeed present: since there is smoke on the hill and smoke invariably accompanies fire, my final inferential judgement is based on my correct judgement that there is smoke on the hill and my correct judgement that wherever there is smoke, there is fire. So, at least *Extended Mist and Fire* cannot be excluded from the scope of knowledge events by appealing to the idea that certain epistemic virtues that are necessary for the production of inferential knowledge events have gone missing.

Of course, the Naiyāyika could indeed insist that the epistemic virtue that is required for the production of inferential knowledge events is not merely a correct judgement about the inferential mark's being present in the site or its being invariably accompanied by the target property. Something stronger is needed, namely that the agent must have *learnt* or come to *know* that the inferential mark is present in the hill and that it is pervaded by the target property. But the Naiyāyika cannot, strictly speaking, appeal to such an epistemic virtue within their definition of knowledge events without making that definition blatantly circular. So, *Virtue Infallibilism* fails.

3.3 Śrīharṣa on Defect Infallibilism

Given the failure of *Virtue Infallibilism*, the Nyāya infallibilist could always switch to *Defect Infallibilism*: they could argue that an accurate first-hand awareness is a knowledge event just in case it arises from a totality of causal conditions that doesn't involve any epistemic defects. In *Mist and Fire* and the extended version thereof, my final inferential judgement arises from a defective awareness of an inferential mark: what I take to be smoke on the hill is, in fact, mist. However, as Śrīharṣa himself emphasizes elsewhere, it is difficult to articulate what epistemic defects are without appealing back to the notion of knowledge events.

This argument occurs in a different context: while discussing the proposal that knowledge events are awareness events that are free from disconfirmation (*avisaṃvādijñāna*) (KKh 430.13–16). Under one interpretation of this proposal, it is equivalent to an indefeasibility analysis of knowledge events: the view that knowledge events are awareness events that cannot be defeated (*bādhita*)— indicated to be inaccurate—by other awareness events. As Śrīharṣa rightly notes (KKh 432.2–7), this account will lead to undesirable consequences unless it is properly restricted: erroneous experiences and thoughts can count as *defeaters* (*bādhaka*) against a knowledge event insofar as they can indicate, from the subject's perspective, that the relevant knowledge event is inaccurate. So, the only kind of defeaters that knowledge events should be invulnerable to have to be knowledge events themselves. This leads the opponent to say that a knowledge event is an awareness that cannot be defeated by an awareness that is produced by a non-defective method or instrument.

In reply, Śrīharṣ notes that this property of *being an awareness that is produced by a non-defective instrument* (*aduṣṭakaraṇajanyatva*) can itself be treated as a defining characteristic of knowledge events (KKh 432.7). But unless the opponent can independently specify what defectiveness consists in, the proposal in question will remain uninformative (KKh 432.7–8). Recall how we understood *Defect Infallibilism*: we took epistemic defects to be causal conditions of awareness events that guarantee or at least are conducive to their being inaccurate. Thus, the opponent initially claims that 'defectiveness is a specific characteristic which is conducive to an opposite awareness and which resides in the causal conditions of that awareness' (KKh 432.8–10). Śrīharṣa's response is simply that we don't know what 'opposite awareness' (*viparītajñāna*) means here (KKh 432.10–11). If an opposite awareness were just an inaccurate awareness, then the proposal under consideration would be equivalent to the view that a knowledge event is simply an awareness which is produced by a totality of causal conditions that could not have led to an inaccurate awareness. But this view would inherit the two problems for *Virtue Infallibilism*. First, given Udayana's principle about causation, even accidentally accurate awareness events could be taken to have been produced by causal conditions that couldn't have led to any inaccurate awareness. Secondly, in *Extended Mist and Smoke*, both the judgements that my inferential judgement is based on are accurate. Even though I misperceive the mist as smoke, my judgment that there is smoke on the hill is accurate. Moreover, I also know that fire invariably accompanies smoke. Thus, despite the defectiveness of the inferential mark, the presence of these epistemic virtues guarantees that the resulting inferential judgement will be accurate. So, it is unclear that *Defect Infallibilism* can be successful in ruling out accidentally accurate awareness events like my inferential judgement in *Extended Mist and Fire*.

In their desperation, the opponent could make one final gambit. They could argue that any epistemic defect that prevents an awareness from being a knowledge event is *just that*: it is a causal factor that is conducive to the production of awareness events that aren't knowledge events. Thus, in this context, the kind of opposite awareness that an epistemic defect yields is, quite simply, an awareness that isn't a knowledge event. But this makes the definition of knowledge events circular and, therefore, uninformative:

[The opponent:] Knowledge events are excluded by the expression 'opposite'.

[Reply:] No. For that is what is being defined. Given that the nature of those knowledge events, insofar as it is excluded from what isn't a knowledge event, remains unapprehended so far, what is it from which the exclusion is to be apprehended [by means of the expression 'opposite']? Without the awareness of that [nature of knowledge events] as excluded from what isn't a knowledge event, it is impossible for there to be awareness of that [nature] as excluded from what isn't a knowledge event. So, there will be either faults of reflexive dependence and symmetric dependence or a regress.

(KKh 432.13–18)

According to the proposed definition, knowledge events are just awareness events which arise from causal conditions that are free from epistemic defects. According to the last characterization of epistemic defects, these are just causal factors that are favourable to the production of awareness events that aren't knowledge events. So, in order to grasp what the distinguishing features of knowledge events are on the basis of the proposed definition, we need to know antecedently what distinguishes knowledge events from awareness events that aren't knowledge events. Under one interpretation, this solution makes the proposed definition straightforwardly circular: as Śrīharṣa says, there is either a fault of reflexive dependence (where knowledge events are characterized in terms of themselves) or a fault of symmetric dependence (where knowledge events are characterized in terms of defects, while defects are characterized in terms of knowledge events). Under another interpretation, this solution leads to a regress: since this definition—in order to be informative—requires us to know antecedently what distinguishes knowledge events from awareness events that aren't knowledge events, we would need a further definition that informs us of this distinguishing characteristic;

if that definition appeals to the notion of an epistemic defect, we will need another definition, and then another, and so on ad infinitum.

The upshot is this: the infallibilist strategy—favoured by virtue infallibilists like Udayana as well as defect infallibilists like Kumārila and his commentators—cannot solve the problem of epistemic luck: it will either fail to rule out cases like *Extended Mist and Fire* or will make our characterization of knowledge events circular. This dilemma has some similarity to the generality problem for process reliabilists, that is, the problem of individuating the causal process that give rise to a belief with the right fineness of grain.[10] If the causal process is individuated too coarsely, then it will be less reliable, making the resulting belief unjustified; if it is individuated too finely, then it will be more reliable, making the belief justified. Here too the problem is that of specifying the set of causal conditions that gives rise to a knowledge event. But unlike in the case of the generality problem, here the fineness of grain is not at issue. The problem, rather, is this: if the accuracy-guaranteeing causal conditions that give rise to a knowledge event were specified without reference to knowledge events, then those causal conditions might sometimes generate accidentally accurate awareness events. So, the infallibilist would have failed to solve the problem of epistemic luck. By contrast, if those causal conditions were specified with reference to knowledge events, then the infallibilist's characterization of knowledge events would be circular.

4. Response 2: Inaccuracy

A less conciliatory response to cases like *Mist and Fire* will be to say that, in these cases, my judgement that there is fire on the hill is not accurate at all. This response is conservative: it tries to reconcile the original *Nyāya Definition of Knowledge Events* with *Nyāya Infallibilism* by claiming that the putative 'accidentally accurate' awareness events aren't accurate at all. Śrīharṣa states this response as follows:

> Since that awareness arises from a defective instrument, its intentional object [e.g., the inferred fire] is, in fact, distinct from the actual target property and so on.
> (KKh 389.16–18)

The argument is this: in *Mist and Fire*, when I infer that there is fire on the hill, the fire that I infer is not the actual fire that is present on the hill; rather, it is a fire that accompanies the smoke that I erroneously take to be present on the hill when I see mist. So, the content of my inferential judgement is not that:

---

[10] See Conee and Feldman (1998) for a seminal treatment of this problem.

(1) The hill contains fire.

Rather, it is expressed by:

(2) The hill contains a particular fire that pervades the smoke I saw.

Since no such fire exists on the hill, my inferential judgement is false.

Śrīharṣa's initial response is concessive (KKh 389.18–19). Even if we grant that the particular fire that I infer to be present on the hill is distinct from the actual fire that is present on it, my inferential judgement could, nevertheless, be partially accurate insofar as it ascribes the presence of something of that kind—*some* instance of firehood—to the hill. So, with respect to that part of its content, the inferential judgement would still be a knowledge event according to the *Nyāya Definition of Knowledge Events*. This response won't be effective against the opponent (KKh 289.19–21). They could argue that this is not really a part of the content of the inferential judgement: when we infer the presence of a particular fire on the hill, we do not thereby also separately draw the more general conclusion that *some* instance of firehood is present on the hill.

In response, Śrīharṣa appeals to a type of case that he hasn't discussed so far: *Horns and Cows* (KKh 390.3–4; KKhPV 393.7–12). In that scenario, I infer that the animal before me is a cow on the basis of the fact that it has horns. On a natural construal of this case, what I inferentially ascribe to the animal is a universal, that is, cowhood. While there can be multiple instances of fire, universals like cowhood are unitary: there is only a single property of cowhood that is shared by all and only cows. Thus, even though the opponent may claim that the particular fire that I infer in *Mist and Fire* isn't really present on the hill, they cannot claim that the cowhood that I infer is, in fact, absent from the animal before me. If the animal is present before me is a cow, it will indeed possess cowhood. This, in turn, will make my inferential judgement accurate. But given that the inference is based on a defective inferential mark, that is, the possession of horns, which isn't invariably accompanied by the target property, that is, cowhood, the resulting inferential judgement can only be true as a matter of luck. So, it cannot be a knowledge event. Thus, the opponent's strategy of explaining away the accuracy of epistemically lucky inferential judgements won't succeed.

Śrīharṣa pre-empts two possible responses from his Nyāya opponent (KKh 390.4–6). First, they could claim that the inferred property of cowhood in *Horns and Cows* is an imaginary or conceptually constructed (*kalpita*) property which is distinct from the real cowhood that is present in the animal before me. Or they could claim that my inferential judgement in *Horns and Cows* ascribes cowhood to the animal before me by means of an imaginary or conceptually constructed relation of inherence (*samavāya*). But this response—as Śrīharṣa correctly notes—will be costly for his Nyāya opponent. The Naiyāyika is committed to a *realist theory of content*: the view that only ultimately existent particulars and properties can serve as intentional objects of awareness. This commits them to a misplacement theory of error (*anyathākhyātivāda*): the view that, even in cases where an object *o* is presented or represented to an agent as *F* when it is, in fact, not *F*, both *o* and *F*-hood, as well as the relation between the two, should ultimately exist.[11] If the Naiyāyika were to claim that, in such cases of error, either *F*-hood or the relation by which *F*-hood is ascribed to *o* in fact doesn't ultimately exist, then they will be jettisoning their own realist theory of content. In effect, they would be embracing an alternative theory sometimes attributed to the Mādhyamika Buddhists: the view that, in cases of error, non-existent particulars and properties can appear. This would undermine the realist ambitions of Nyāya epistemology. Given that it will often be difficult subjectively to distinguish erroneous awareness events directed at conceptually constructed objects from ordinary knowledge events that track how things are independently of our attitudes, we may not be able to show that our awareness events do, in fact, constitute knowledge events about ultimately existent particulars and properties. By contrast, the misplacement theory of error implies that, even in cases of error, our awareness event do in fact latch onto ultimately existent particulars and properties.

The second response that Śrīharṣa entertains is somewhat different: the claim is no longer that the inferential judgement in *Horns and Cows* ascribes an imaginary or conceptually constructed property or relation, but rather that it ascribes identity with cowhood to some other property present in the animal before me (KKh 390.6–7). So, the content of my inferential judgement is not that:

(3) This animal is a cow.

Rather, it is that:

(4) The property which pervades the possession of horns and which is present in this animal is identical to cowhood.

Since the property in question isn't cowhood (given that cowhood doesn't invariably accompany the possession of horns), my inferential judgement will be false. This will allow the Naiyāyika to maintain that so-called 'accidentally accurate' awareness events aren't accurate after all.

Śrīharṣa's response is twofold (KKh 390.7–11). First, even if (4) expresses the content of the inferential judgement, that content still implies—and has as its part—the content that the animal in question possesses cowhood. So, with respect to that part of its content, the inferential judgement will remain accurate and therefore would qualify as a knowledge event. But this is not a result that the

---

[11] For discussions of this view, see Dasti (2012) and Vaidya (2013).

Naiyāyika wants. Secondly, we should be sceptical of the proposal that (4) actually represents the content of the inferential judgement that I make in *Horns and Cows*. As Śrīharṣa notes, the causal conditions that give rise to my inferential judgement are, in fact, part of a cognitive process that necessarily yields ascriptions of an association (*saṃsarga*), that is, a relation other than identity, rather than those of identity. If I judge that an object *o* possesses a feature *X* and that whatever possesses *X* possesses *Y*, then those two judgements should (under favourable circumstances) give rise to the inferential judgement that the object *o* possesses *Y*. Here, the relation between *o* and *Y* is an association, not an identity. The same pattern of inference takes place in *Horns and Cows*.

To bolster this point, Śrīharṣa considers a variant of *Horns and Cows*. In this version of the example, I not only make an inference, but also express my reasoning out loud to an audience: 'The animal before me is a cow, because it has horns; whatever has horns is a cow, for example the animal in my byre.' A linguistically competent hearer who listens to my utterance and takes it at face value should judge that the animal before me is a cow and therefore ascribe an association with cowhood to the animal before me. For, in this scenario, the content of the sentence I utter *just is* an association between the referents of the words that are part of that sentence, that is, an association between the animal picked out by 'the animal before me' and the property of cowhood picked out by 'is a cow'. So, it would be perverse for a trusting hearer who understands my uttered sentence to make a judgement with a different content. Yet given that my argument is based on my earlier defective inference, it cannot give rise to any (testimonial) knowledge event in the hearer. Thus, this would be a case where the hearer will make an accurate judgement that fails to be a knowledge event.

Of course, the opponent could stubbornly insist that, even in this case, the content of the hearer's judgement is false because it involves the misascription of identity with cowhood to some other property. But then, this could lead to a problem of overgeneration elsewhere. For, now, the opponent could treat pretty much any case of error as involving a misascription of identity. If they were to do so, they would be blurring a distinction between two kinds of error: awareness events that are erroneous in virtue of misascribing identity and awareness events that are erroneous in virtue of misascribing an association. For example, when I mistake mother-of-pearl for silver, what I misascribe to the mother-of-pearl is an association with silverhood. By contrast, when I misidentify a man on the street for Devadatta, what I misascribe to the man is identity with Devadatta. The distinction between these two kinds of error is borne out by introspective evidence. In the first case, I introspectively judge myself to have ascribed the association with silverhood to the object before me. In the other, I introspectively judge myself to have ascribed the identity with Devadatta to the man before me. To claim that all error involves the misascription of identity is to blur the distinction in content between these two kinds of error. For example, the defender of the view that my inferential judgement in *Horns and Cows* is erroneous would also be committed to saying that my introspective judgement in *Horns and Cows*—which takes the form 'With respect to this [animal], an association with cowhood has been inferred by me; surely, this is just a cow'—is erroneous. Thus, the defender of this view will proliferate error not only amongst inferential judgements, but also amongst introspective ones.

Perhaps, the opponent can bite the bullet here: they could accept the consequence that we introspectively misconstrue the content of our inferential judgements in cases like *Horns and Cows*. Śrīharṣa explores one last way of convincing such an opponent (KKh 395.8–13). Consider the following variant of *Horns and Cows*:

Extended Horns and Cows. From a distance, I see an animal with horns. Earlier, I had observed many cows with horns. On the basis of these observations, I falsely judged that all animals with horns are cows. Now, I recall that generalization. So, I conclude that the animal is a cow. Then, I come closer to the animal and notice that it has other characteristics such as a dewlap, hooves, and so on (which jointly distinguishes cows from other kinds of animals). Earlier, I had observed many cows with those characteristics. On the basis of these observations, I correctly judged that all animals with characteristics like dewlaps and so forth are cows. So, I now conclude that the animal is a cow.

In this case, my second inference suffers from the fault of establishing what has already been established (*siddhasādhana*): its conclusion had already been established by the first inference. Yet Śrīharṣa's opponent is committed to saying that the first episode of reasoning—insofar as it is based on a deviating reason— cannot yield a true conclusion. By contrast, *ex hypothesi*, the second inference (unlike the first episode of reasoning) is not based on any defective inferential mark (since only cows have dewlaps and so forth) and therefore can yield an inferential knowledge event. But this can only happen if the conclusion of the second inference is true. So, Śrīharṣa's opponent faces a dilemma in cases like this (KKh §264): either they must implausibly say that the second inference in this case doesn't suffer from the fault of establishing what has already been established or they must abandon the view that the first defective inference leads to a false conclusion. The first option is risky: unless properly qualified, it could lead to the result that the fault of establishing what has been established never arises at all. The second option will undermine the *Nyāya Definition of Knowledge Events*: the opponent will be admitting that even a defective reason can help us to draw a true conclusion in cases like *Horns and Cows*.

The lesson: the Naiyāyika cannot easily explain away the accuracy of epistemically lucky inferential judgements in cases like *Mist and Fire* and *Horns and Cows*.

5. Knowledgehood and the Epistemic Priority Thesis

So far, we have seen how Śrīharṣa exploits a tension within the Nyāya conception of knowledge events. On the one hand, Naiyāyikas are committed to the simple view that a first-hand awareness is a knowledge event just in case it is accurate. On the other hand, they embrace a kind of infallibilism: they think that a knowledge event is produced by a totality of causal conditions that couldn't have led to any error. Cases of epistemic luck like *Guesswork, Mist and Fire,* and *Horns and Cows* create trouble for this combination of this views. In each of those cases, the final awareness seems accurate, but not a knowledge event because its causal conditions could easily have led the agent astray. As Śrīharṣa has argued, the Naiyāyika cannot exclude such cases from the class of knowledge events either by adding a blanket infallibility condition on knowledge events or by explaining away the accuracy of such awareness events.

What moral should we draw from this discussion? For a contemporary defender of a 'knowledge first' approach, this might just reveal a flaw in the Nyāya approach to knowledge events. The Naiyāyikas presuppose that knowledge events can be defined in terms of a *mental condition* like a first-hand awareness plus some *non-mental conditions* such as accuracy or reliability. However, a defender of a 'knowledge first' approach might argue that this assumption is wrong: if knowledge events are a *sui generis* kind of mental events, they may not after all be decomposable (either metaphysically or conceptually) into mental and non-mental conditions.

Śrīharṣa's Nyāya interlocutor Udayana himself seems to anticipate a proposal of this kind (NVTP 51.16–52.4 ad *Nyāyasūtra* 1.1.1):

Knowledge Events as a Natural Kind. An awareness event is a knowledge event if and only if it is an instance of the natural kind property (*jāti*) of *being a knowledge event* (*pramātva*), what we shall call *knowledgehood.*

Natural kind properties, on the Nyāya-Vaiśeṣika view, cannot be decomposed— either conceptually or metaphysically—into other properties. So, on this view, even though knowledge events are a subspecies of awareness events, they are unified by a property—knowledgehood—that cannot be decomposed (conceptually or metaphysically) into (i) a mental property like the property of being an awareness (*jñānatva*) or being a first-hand awareness (*anubhūtitva*) and (ii) a non-mental property like accuracy. In that sense, they are a *sui generis* kind of awareness. It is this latter feature of this definition that makes it analogous to a contemporary 'knowledge first' approach to epistemology. Even though defenders of this latter approach needn't treat states of knowing as a *natural* kind, they nevertheless hold the view that those states form a *sui generis* mental kind.[12] *Knowledge Events as a Natural Kind* makes a similar claim.

5.1 Not a Natural Kind

Like Udayana, Śrīharṣa too is sceptical of the idea that knowledgehood is a natural kind property. For Udayana, two natural kind properties cannot *cross-cut*: if K_1 and K_2 are natural kinds, it cannot be the case that (i) there exists an entity x that belongs to both kinds K_1 and K_2, (ii) there exists an entity y that is of kind K_1 but not of kind K_2, and (iii) there exists an entity z that is of kind K_2 but not of kind K_1.[13] This constraint on natural kinds—sometimes called the *cross-cutting constraint* (*saṅkarya*)—amounts to the constraint that natural kinds should be *categorically distinct*, that is, that there shouldn't be any smooth transition from one to another.[14] But if two kinds K_1 and K_2 were to cross-cut each other, there would be plenty of things that are of both kinds, but there would also be things that are of kind K_1 but not of kind K_2, and also things that are of kind K_2 but not of kind K_1. In that case, it would seem that the distinction between the two kinds is merely conventional; for nature itself doesn't really draw a clear boundary between them. In that case, they shouldn't be treated as natural kinds. Following Udayana, the problem that Śrīharṣa points out for knowledgehood is this (NVTP 51.13–52.11; KKh 444.2–3): for Nyāya-Vaiśeṣika philosophers, perceptual awareness events form a natural kind in virtue of instantiating the property of epistemic directness (*sākṣāttva*). But note that some perceptual awareness events are knowledge events, while others, for example inaccurate ones, are not. So, if knowledge events were to form a natural kind, there would be two natural kinds that cross-cut each other.

Śrīharṣa realizes that this argument isn't decisive. Someone who wishes to defend the proposal that knowledge events are a natural kind might just deny that

---

[12] Williamson's (2000, ch. 1) claim that knowledge is a *sui generis* mental state is best understood as the claim that particular states of knowing, e.g. my seeing here right now that there is a coffee mug on my desk, are instances of a *mental kind* that cannot be reductively analysed in terms of other kinds of mental states like belief and non-mental conditions like truth, or reliability. Even though knowledge cannot be reductively analysed in terms of other mental states and non-mental conditions on this view, particular states of knowing are, nevertheless, instances of a unified kind of mental state. This interpretation fits Williamson's claim that knowledge is the *most general factive stative attitude*, in the sense that other such factive attitudes, such as *perceiving* and *remembering*, are subspecies of knowledge. Nagel (2023), more recently, has cast her version of 'knowledge-first' epistemology in terms of knowledge being a type of mental state. Other authors—notably Kornblith (2002) and Kumar (2014), who are sympathetic to naturalism in epistemology—argue that knowledge is a natural kind; 'knowledge first' epistemologists don't have to accept this stronger view.

[13] In his commentary *Kiraṇāvalī* on Praśastapāda's *Padārthadharmasaṅgraha*, Udayana explains the distinction by appealing to a set of six kind blockers (*jātibādhaka*) (Kir 23.3–4). Cross-cutting (*saṅkarya*) is one of them. For discussion, see Pellegrini (2016).

[14] For a defence of this constraint, see Ellis (2001). For the claim that there are cross-cutting natural kinds, see Dupré (1993), Khalidi (1998), and Hacking (2007).

perceptual awareness events form a natural kind or that the cross-cutting constraint is a genuine constraint on natural kinds. And nothing crucial about the relevant conception of knowledge events really hangs on whether we recognize knowledge events as a *natural* kind. As long as there is a sufficiently non-disjunctive property of awareness events—knowledgehood—on the basis of which our attributions of knowledge events are made, it would be permissible to define knowledge events in terms of knowledgehood.

Therefore, instead of focusing on the question of whether knowledgehood is a natural kind property, Śrīharṣa raises a different question. If knowledgehood is supposed to capture the application condition (*pravṛttinimitta*) of the expression 'knowledge event', then it must be the condition that triggers our application of that term. Thus, knowledgehood should (causally) explain our use of the term 'knowledge event' in ordinary discourse. How does it do this? Śrīharṣa explores possible answers to this question while focusing on our *self-attributions* of knowledge events.

Śrīharṣa begins with the proposal that the presence of knowledgehood in various awareness events produces our attributions of knowledge events *by itself*, that is, in the absence of any awareness on our part that an experience or a thought has the status of being a knowledge event (KKh 444.3–6). Clearly, this is a non-starter. On this picture, we are just knowledge-ascribing automata whose ascriptions of knowledge events are directly manipulated by the presence of knowledgehood outside in the world. No judgements about knowledgehood are required on our part. But as Śrīharṣa points out, if this were the case, then we couldn't possibly be in doubt or be mistaken about whether an awareness is a knowledge event. For, then, whenever an awareness had the status of being a knowledge event, the knowledgehood present in that awareness episode would on its own make us correctly ascribe that epistemic status to that awareness. This seems bad.

The only other option is to say that knowledgehood explains our use of the term 'knowledge event' only insofar as our use of this term is triggered by our awareness of various experiences and thoughts as instances of knowledgehood. This, in turn, raises a different question. How do we determine whether an awareness is an instance of knowledgehood? There are two options: either we have *epistemically direct* access to knowledgehood or we have *epistemically indirect* access to knowledgehood. Śrīharṣa argues that none of these options really work.

5.2 No Direct Access

What does it mean to have *epistemically direct* access to knowledgehood? As Śrīharṣa understands it, the position is roughly this: We are equipped with an internal monitoring mechanism by which we can attend to our own conscious mental occurrences and thereby can become aware of them and their features. For instance, when I am undergoing a perceptual experience as of there being a wall before me, I may not only attend to the wall that is outside in the external world, but I may also simultaneously attend to the perceptual experience itself and become aware of myself as undergoing that perceptual experience. This internal monitoring mechanism—which enables me in this case to become aware of my perceptual experience—is what the Nyāya-Vaiśeṣika philosopher calls the *inner sense* or the *manas*.

The inner sense's access to various conscious mental occurrences is in most cases *epistemically direct* in the sense that, in order to become aware of their own conscious mental occurrences, an agent doesn't have to base their awareness on something else. This is supposed to be analogous to the case of sensory perception, where in order to become perceptually aware of their external environment, the agent doesn't have to become aware of some piece of evidence first and then infer various claims about the external world on that basis. This kind of epistemically direct access to one's own awareness events and other conscious mental occurrences is, therefore, construed as a form of 'inner perception' or 'introspection', and the *manas*, accordingly, is thought of as an 'inner sense'. The Nyāya-adjacent position that Śrīharṣa considers is this: just as we become aware of our own conscious experiences and thoughts by means of inner perception, so also we can detect the property of knowledgehood that belongs to those awareness events by means of inner perception.

Here is Śrīharṣa's response (KKh 445.12–15): we cannot ascertain whether an awareness is a knowledge event by inner perception alone. For, even when we are aware of all the introspectable features of an awareness by means of inner perception, we could still be in doubt or be mistaken about whether it is a knowledge event. The examples that Śrīharṣa considers are cases where *positive introspection* fails for knowledge events: cases where an agent comes to know something, but doesn't (or can't) come to know that they have come to know it, because they either doubt whether they know it or falsely think that they don't know it. A commentator on the *Refutation*, Ānandapūrṇa, describes an example similar to Radford's (1966) case of the unconfident examinee (KKhPV 446.6–8):

The Circumspect Jeweller. An apprentice to a jeweller, unbeknownst to themself, is an expert at discerning precious metals like silver. So, when they see a piece of jewellery made of silver, they can immediately tell that it is made of silver. But since they are not sure of their own ability to tell precious metals apart from ordinary ones, they doubt whether they have learnt that the jewellery is made of silver. So, they know that the piece of jewellery before them is made of silver, but still doubt whether they know this.

In this case, the agent might indeed know everything about their judgement that there is to know by introspection. But that still wouldn't dispel their doubts about its epistemic status. But if knowledgehood were, indeed, an introspectable feature of awareness events, this wouldn't be the case. If positive introspection for knowledge events can fail in this way, knowledgehood cannot be a feature of awareness events which we can detect by inner perception. Since inner perception is the only way we can have direct access to properties of awareness events, it follows that we don't have direct access to knowledgehood.

5.3 The Problems of Indirect Access

This leaves us with the possibility that we may have epistemically indirect access to knowledgehood. Śrīharṣa entertains two different ways of fleshing out this possibility (KKh 445.15–17). The first option is to say that an agent gains access to the property of knowledgehood inherent in their own awareness events by means of inner perception, but this kind of inner perception is *indirect*, that is, dependent on the agent's antecedent awareness of some *symptom* (*cihna*) that the relevant awareness events possess. In other words, when an agent becomes aware of their own experience or thought, they first pick up on this symptom, and that triggers an introspective recognition of that awareness as a knowledge event. The second option is to flesh out the relevant proposal without appealing to inner perception. On this approach, we become aware of knowledgehood by *inference* on the basis of some symptom possessed by the relevant awareness events. In either case, crucially, the symptom that forms the basis of our awareness of knowledgehood is something that can be introspectively grasped independently of knowledgehood itself. It is this feature of the two proposals that Śrīharṣa will exploit in his arguments against them.

Śrīharṣa's opening move is to say: 'Let's grant that we become aware of knowledgehood on the basis of certain symptoms. But are there many such symptoms or just one?' Suppose Śrīharṣa's interlocutor says that there is just one symptom which underlies our self-attributions of knowledge events (KKh 445.17–18). But if that is true, there is no reason to posit an unanalysable property such as knowledgehood. The thought is that when we defined knowledge events in terms of knowledgehood, our definition was supposed to capture the extension (or intension) of the term 'knowledge event' as it is commonly used by laying down its application conditions. But now it turns out that there is a single symptom which constitutes the reason for which we apply the term 'knowledge events' to our experiences and thoughts. Then, there is no reason to treat knowledgehood as the application condition of the term; the symptom itself should do the job.

What if there are many such symptoms? Śrīharṣa presents two distinct challenges here. First, Śrīharṣa challenges his interlocutor to say what these many symptoms are (KKh 445.18–19). Suppose there is a series of different symptoms $S_1, S_2, S_3, \ldots$, such that each S_i *decisively indicates* that the relevant awareness is a knowledge event. Śrīharṣa's argument is that his opponent won't be able to list any such symptom: for any symptom that the opponent may mention, it will suffer from one of the problems that Śrīharṣa has already described for the proposed definitions of knowledge events.

However, one needn't be convinced by this argument. One might argue that in order to infer the presence of knowledgehood on the basis of some symptom, the relevant symptom doesn't have to be a *decisive* indicator of knowledgehood and therefore needn't rule out all awareness events that are not knowledge events. For example, red spots on one's skin aren't a decisive indicator of measles, but they surely are a *reliable* indicator of measles. And on that basis, one can know that a person is suffering from measles. Similarly, certain features of an awareness—its accuracy, its possession of some kind of epistemic pedigree, and so on—may serve as a *reliable* indicator of knowledgehood under a range of circumstances, even though none of them may decisively indicate the presence of a knowledge event by ruling out all instances of epistemic luck.

Even though Śrīharṣa doesn't explicitly address this objection, the second challenge that he raises seems to speak to it. This challenge arises from a positive proposal about attributions of knowledge events: the *Epistemic Priority Thesis*. According to this proposal, knowledge events are *epistemically prior* to other non-factive mental states and events. When we are trying to determine whether an agent has undergone a knowledge event, we don't initially ascribe to them some other non-factive mental event and then check whether that event meets some further conditions (like truth or reliability) necessary for it to count as a knowledge event. Rather, we (if we're rational) treat certain mental events by default as knowledge events until a defeater comes along.

In Śrīharṣa's own work, the *Epistemic Priority Thesis* is articulated in two distinct ways. In some contexts, it is expressed as a thesis about *self*-attributions of knowledge events (KKh 445.19–20). On this version of the thesis, in order to judge that their own experience or thought constitutes a knowledge event, the agent doesn't need to check whether the epistemic credentials of that experience or thought are any good, for example whether it is produced by certain epistemic virtues or the absence of epistemic defects.[15] As long as there is no positive reason to suspect that the awareness is inaccurate or is produced by a defective set of causal conditions, the agent is required not to be uncertain about the status of the awareness as a knowledge event. Call this:

The Default Knowledgehood Thesis. If an agent undergoes an experience or a thought with the content that *p*, then, in the absence of any rebutting or

---

[15] This theory was defended by Kumārila Bhaṭṭa in vv. 52–3 in his *Detailed Commentary in Verse* (*Ślokavārttika*) on *Mīmāṃsāsūtra* 1.1.2. In the fourth chapter of the *Refutation*, Śrīharṣa tells us that he has defended this view in another text called *The Intent of the Lord* (*Īśvarābhisandhi*), a work that is lost to us.

undercutting evidence against their awareness, they are required by rationality not to doubt that they have come to know (or learnt) that *p*.

This is sometimes called the theory of *intrinsic knowledgehood* (*svataḥprāmāṇyavāda*). On this story, if a rational agent doesn't have any doubt about the epistemic credentials of an awareness, then—provided that they are aware of that awareness—they will typically never hesitate to ascribe the status of being knowledge event to that awareness. The agent's judgement that the awareness is a knowledge event won't be dependent on their antecedent grasp of any symptom—like accuracy or reliability—that the relevant awareness possesses over and above the mere fact that it is an awareness that portrays the world in a certain way.

Why should we think that this story about self-ascriptions of knowledge events is true? The best a priori argument for this theory is a regress argument offered by Bhāṭṭa Mīmāṃsakas like Kumārila Bhaṭṭa and his commentators. Suppose we reject this theory and say that, to judge that they have learnt something, an agent must always antecedently judge that their awareness has the epistemic credentials required for being a knowledge event, for example that it is accurate or that it is reliably formed. Now, take an agent who has formed such judgements. If the agent is rational, why should they rely on such judgements unless they also think that these judgements are knowledge events? To assure themself that these judgements are knowledge events, they might appeal to another set of judgements about the epistemic credentials of these judgements. This will lead to a regress. To avoid the regress, we must grant that there is at least one set of judgments whose status as knowledge events the agent rationally takes for granted without relying on a further set of judgements.[16] But then, why shouldn't we say that about the very first awareness?

In the fourth chapter of the *Refutation*, Śrīharṣa seems to generalize this story from the case of self-attributions of knowledge events to the case of attributions of knowledge events to others (KKh 1322.14–15). He argues that we can criticize a sceptic who refuses to recognize our ordinary waking experiences and thoughts as knowledge events by appealing to a kind of suppositional reasoning (*tarka*) which is driven by a default assumption (*utsarga*). Unlike other standard instances of suppositional reasoning accepted by Śrīharṣa's Nyāya-Vaiśeṣika interlocutors, the point of such reasoning is not to show that some undesirable consequence follows from the sceptic's view, but rather to show that the sceptic's position doesn't fit our default picture of how things normally are in the world. The underlying principle is this: for any two mutually incompatible and exhaustive features F_1 and F_2, if F_1 is *predominantly* or *normally* present amongst a class C of objects rather than F_2, then (in the absence of defeaters) we should accept that any arbitrary

---

[16] This argument occurs in v. 56 in Kumārila Bhaṭṭa's *Detailed Commentary in Verse* (*Ślokavārttika*) on *Mīmāṃsāsūtra* 1.1.2.

object chosen from C has F_1 rather than F_2. As Kumārila and his commentators claim, (given the threat of regress) we are entitled—if not required—to assume without further evidence that our awareness events are knowledge events under normal conditions, for example, when we are awake or when our awareness-generating mechanisms aren't malfunctioning. So, in the absence of any defeater that suggests that the conditions are abnormal, we should treat our awareness events (irrespective of whether they belong to ourselves or others) as knowledge events. Thus, Śrīharṣa writes by appealing to Kumārila:

> For example, this kind of suppositional reasoning would apply against someone who, in the absence of defeat, ascribes the absence of knowledgehood to an awareness that arises for a well-functioning and wakeful agent, even though there is no difference with respect to the presence of any source of knowledge (*pramāṇa*) that could determine the presence of knowledgehood or the absence thereof. However, it would not apply against someone ascribes knowledgehood [to such an awareness]. It is this suppositional reasoning by adopting which [Kumārila] has said: 'Therefore, the status of an awareness as a knowledge event is obtained in virtue of its having the nature of awareness. That is cancelled due to the awareness of the object's being otherwise, or of a defect that arises from the causes [of the awareness].'
>
> (KKh 1322.15–20)

As Śrīharṣa is careful to emphasize, a default assumption—like the assumption that our experiences and thoughts are knowledge events under normal conditions—is not a hypothesis that we are uncertain about or even treat as highly likely. A default assumption is not fundamentally different from a state of certainty, that is, a judgement or a determination (*nirṇaya*) (KKh 1322.22–1323.11). When we conclude that an awareness is a knowledge event on the basis of the default assumption that our experiences and thoughts under normal conditions are knowledge events, there remains no residual uncertainty about the epistemic status of that awareness. We simply judge that the relevant awareness is a knowledge event. Thus, in this way, a background default assumption not only leads to the destruction of uncertainty, but also functions—at least from our perspective—as a source of knowledge with respect to facts about whether we know. Once again, on this view, knowledge events are epistemically prior: to ascribe knowledge events to ourselves and others rationally, we don't need to determine whether the relevant awareness events satisfy any further non-mental conditions such as accuracy or reliability; given our background default assumption, in the absence of defeaters, we can rationally ascribe such knowledge events to ourselves.

What is important in this picture—but is left implicit by Śrīharṣa—is that we cannot rationally accept the default assumption that our experiences and thoughts are normally knowledge events on the basis of any judgements that—independently of that assumption—confirm or provide evidence that those experiences and thoughts are accurate or reliable. If such judgements were required to justify this default assumption, a Kumārila-style regress argument would be difficult to avoid.

This brings out a key feature of the position that Śrīharṣa is driving us towards. On this view, we simply don't have any independent evidence that our ordinary attributions of knowledge events are reliably tracking instances of a unified kind property—knowledgehood—in ourselves and others. Rather, if Śrīharṣa is to be believed, such attributions are typically based on two factors: one is independent of the context of attribution, and the other is not. The context-invariant factor is our default assumption that our experiences and thoughts are knowledge events under normal conditions. The context-dependent factor is the lack of any available evidence that suggests that the conditions are abnormal. When both these factors are present, we can—and often do—rationally ascribe knowledge events to ourselves and others. But neither of these two factors guarantees that our attributions of knowledge events are in fact tracking a unified or *sui generis* kind of mental events. First, the assumption that our awareness events are knowledge events under normal circumstances isn't justified by any independently acquired evidence. So, it may indeed be false. Secondly, even if that assumption is true, the context-dependent factor—namely the lack of evidence that suggests that conditions are abnormal—doesn't guarantee that conditions are, in fact, abnormal. So, it is compatible with this contextualist story that, in different contexts of ascribing knowledge events, we are treating very different kinds of awareness events as knowledge events. Thus, there is no way of showing that our ordinary attributions of knowledge events are reliably tracking a unified or *sui generis* mental kind.

6. Scepticism

The difference between Śrīharṣa and contemporary defenders of 'knowledge first' epistemology lies in the fact that the latter adopt an anti-sceptical stance about our ordinary attributions of knowledge to ourselves. They assume that there is a unified mental kind—the *most general factive stative mental attitude*—that is reliably tracked by our ordinary ascriptions of knowledge.[17]

By contrast, Śrīharṣa thinks that his arguments against the definability of knowledge events pave the way for thoroughgoing scepticism about our ordinary attributions of knowledge events. He states his conclusion as follows:

---

[17] See n 13. Nagel (2013, 2023) discusses this anti-sceptical assumption explicitly.

Moreover, whatever may be stated as the defining characteristic of knowledge events, if it gives rise to linguistic usage pertaining to knowledge events insofar it is not an object of awareness or insofar as it is merely an object of an awareness [which isn't a knowledge event], then there will be a problem of overgeneration. If it gives rise to such linguistic usage in virtue of being known, then that will be difficult to determine given that it hasn't been determined what knowledge events are.
(KKh 448.22–449.1)

Suppose our ordinary attributions of knowledge events reliably track a unified mental kind. Assume that what instances of that kind share is a property X, a defining characteristic of knowledge events. But if we reliably track that mental kind, then we must have the capacity to make attributions of knowledge events reliably only in cases where the property X is instantiated. But if we don't know what this property X is—because we are either unaware of this property or aware of this property but don't know that it distinguishes knowledge events from awareness events that are not knowledge events—then it is hard to explain how we might have such a capacity to make attributions of knowledge events reliably. By contrast, if this property X generates our attributions in virtue of being known to us but we cannot determine this property, even then it will remain hard to show that we know what the defining property of knowledge events is. In either case, we end up with a sceptical conclusion, namely that we cannot show that our ordinary attributions of knowledge events are reliably tracking a unified mental kind.

A tempting response to this problem is to say that even if we cannot determine any extensionally (or intensionally) adequate defining characteristic of knowledge events, we nevertheless can reliably track instances of that characteristic. Śrīharṣa is unmoved by this response:

[The opponent:] Let the defining characteristic be undetermined, but it is in fact such [i.e. gives rise to linguistic usage pertaining to knowledge events].

[Reply:] No. This is because then there will be the undesirable consequence that there will be no response to someone who says that [the defining characteristic] is in fact not such, and because it will follow that it is futile to determine what knowledgehood is. And let linguistic usage pertaining to the reality of objects such as a pot also proceed simply on the basis of a knowledge event [without any intervening ascription of knowledge events]. No further elaboration is needed.
(KKh 449.1–5)

The position, according to Śrīharṣa, faces three objections. The first two objections revolve around two flaws of the Nyāya position. First, if the Naiyāyika has no way of articulating what the defining characteristic of knowledge events is, then they have—by their own admission—no way of showing that our attributions of knowledge events are made in response to the presence of a defining property of knowledge events. But then, they have no way of refuting a sceptic who makes the opposite claim, namely that our attributions do not reliably track the presence of such a property. The second objection is ad hominem: if the Naiyāyika says that we reliably track the presence of the defining characteristic of knowledge events without, in fact, being able to determine what that defining characteristic is, then the whole Nyāya project of discovering such a defining characteristic will be pointless.

The third objection is better: the Naiyāyika claims that there is a defining characteristic of knowledge events which is reliably tracked by our ordinary attributions of knowledge events. Yet they cannot tell us any believable story about how we know that there is such a characteristic. If this were permitted, then we should also be allowed to claim that an ordinary object such as a pot exists without putting forward any story about how it is that we know such an object to be real. But surely, if an agent asserts that a pot exists, they can reasonably be asked, 'How do you know that the pot exists?'[18] But if the agent then fails to come up with an answer to that question, then it seems unreasonable for them to persist in asserting that the pot exists. But the Naiyāyika's stance seems to suggest that this charge of unreasonableness doesn't apply when it comes to the defining characteristic of knowledge events. This, then, raises a challenge for the Naiyāyikas: they must explain why the defining characteristic of knowledge events should be treated differently from that of ordinary objects such as pots.

A defender of 'knowledge first' epistemology will resist this sceptical argument. Śrīharṣa claims that it is unreasonable for his opponent to assert that there is a defining characteristic X of knowledge events, on the basis of which we make our attributions of knowledge events, without being able to say what this characteristic X is and how we recognize it. There are two—mutually compatible—ways of resisting this claim. The first is to say that our recognition of this characteristic is *tacit* or *implicit* and therefore not accessible to conscious reflection or verbal expression. So, even though we are able to know that this characteristic is instantiated by our awareness events, we cannot consciously determine or articulate what it is. Alternatively, one could appeal to failures of the KK principle, the principle that whenever one knows that p, one knows (or is in a position to know) that p. Thus, even though we may know that the defining characteristic X of knowledge events is instantiated by our awareness events, we don't know that we know

---

[18] This is one of the observations on the basis of which Williamson (2000, ch. 11) motivates the view that knowledge is the norm of assertion. Śrīharṣa himself states the principle in a stronger form (KKh 90.4–5): 'A person who is constrained by the sources of knowledge and speaks of the existence of a pot should state a source of knowledge with respect to that.'

this.[19] Due to the lack of such higher-order knowledge, we fail to articulate how we recognize it.

These responses miss the point of the argument that Śrīharṣa is offering here. Śrīharṣa's argument is *dialectical*, indexed to the context of a debate about the thesis that there is a defining characteristic of knowledge events in virtue of recognizing which we ordinarily make attributions of knowledge events. The point, more abstractly, is this: imagine a context of a conversation where the content that *p* isn't part of the stock of information shared by the participants in the conversation. Suppose that, in that conversation, an agent *S* asserts that *p* but then cannot answer the follow-up question from their interlocutor, 'How do you know that *p*?' Since it cannot be settled in that context whether *S* in fact knows *p*, the content of *S*'s assertion—even though the assertion may originally have been appropriate because it was based on knowledge—won't be accepted by the other participants. At that point, *S* cannot just persist in asserting that *p* without offering any further explanation of how it is that they know that *p*. Similarly, for the defender of the view that there is a defining characteristic of knowledge events that guides our ordinary attributions of knowledge events, it is inappropriate *to persist in asserting their view* when they cannot explain how they know this.

If Śrīharṣa's positive account of how we ascribe knowledge events is correct, this failure to answer the 'How do you know?' challenge isn't induced by a rectifiable epistemic defect, for example the tacitness of some piece of knowledge that could in principle be made explicit, or the lack of some piece of higher-order knowledge that in principle could be acquired. It is, in fact, *impossible* to show that our ascriptions of knowledge are made in response to *any* defining characteristic of knowledge events. For Śrīharṣa, we typically ascribe knowledge events to ourselves and others, *not* because we recognize some unifying feature of knowledge events, but rather because, first, we assume that our awareness events are normally knowledge events and, secondly, we have no reason to suspect that conditions are abnormal. But the problem is that the assumption in question is not justified on the basis of any independently acquired evidence, and the lack of evidence that conditions are abnormal doesn't guarantee that conditions are normal. This leaves open the possibility that, in different contexts of ascription, our ascriptions of knowledge events pick out heterogeneous mental events which have nothing in common with one another except perhaps that they called 'knowledge event' in those contexts.

---

[19] See Williamson (2000, chs. 4 and 5). As I have noted in Section 6.2, Śrīharṣa isn't committed to any strong introspection principle about knowledge events: he thinks that an agent can be subject to error and uncertainty about the presence and the absence of their own knowledge events. However, he would reject Williamson's strong anti-luminosity thesis that there is no non-trivial condition *C* such that whenever *C* obtains, one is in a position to know that it obtains. While defending the idea that consciousness is self-manifesting (*svaprakāśa*), he defends the claim that whenever we are conscious of something, we are in a position to know that we are conscious of something (KKh 81.1–8).

This throws the sceptical problem that Śrīharṣa develops here into sharper focus. Since the defender of the claim that knowledge events—or states of knowing more generally—form a unified mental kind cannot show that our ascriptions of such events or states reliably track any such kind, they cannot continue to assert that there is such a unified mental kind.[20]

References

1. Primary Sources and Abbreviations

Kir — Udayana's *Kiraṇāvalī* in *Praśastapādabhāṣyam: With the Commentary Kiraṇāvalī of Udayanācārya*. Edited by Jitendra S. Jetly. (Baroda: Oriental Institute, 1971).

KKh — Śrīharṣa's *Khaṇḍanakhaṇḍakhādya* in *Śrīharshapraṇītam Khaṇḍanakhaṇḍakhādyam Ānandapūrṇaviracitayā Khaṇḍanaphakkikāvibhajanākhyayā vyākhyayā 'vidyāsāgarī' ti prasiddhayā sametam Citsukha-Śaṇkaramiśra-Raghunāthakṛtaṭīkāvalambinyā tippaṇyā sanātham*. Edited by Gaṅganātha Jhā and Lakṣmaṇa Drāviḍa Śāstrī. (Benares: Chowkhamba Sanskrit Book Depot, 1904–14).

KKhPV — Ānandapūrṇa Vidyāsāgara's *Khaṇḍanakhaṇḍakhādyaphakkikāvibhujana* in *Śrīharshapraṇītam Khaṇḍanakhaṇḍakhādyam Ānandapūrṇaviracitayā Khaṇḍanaphakkikāvibhajanākhyayā vyākhyayā 'vidyāsāgarī' ti prasiddhayā sametam Citsukhaśaṇkaramiśraraghunāthakṛtaṭīkāvalambinyā tippaṇyā sanātham*. Edited by Gaṅganātha Jhā and Lakṣmaṇa Drāviḍa Śāstrī. (Benares: Chowkhamba Sanskrit Book Depot, 1904–14).

LM — Udayana's *Lakṣaṇamālā* in *Lakṣaṇamāla by Udayanācārya*. Edited by Śaśinātha Jhā. (Darbhanga: Mithila Institute, 1963).

NK — Śrīdhara's *Nyāyakandalī* in *Nyāyakandalī Being a Commentary on Praśastapādabhāṣya, with Three Sub-Commentaries*. Edited by Jitendra S. Jetly and Vasant G. Parikh. (Baroda: Oriental Institute, 1991).

NKA — Udayana's *Nyāyakusumāñjali* in *The Nyāyakusumāñjali of Śrī Udayanācārya with Four Commentaries: The Bodhinī, Prakāśa, Prakāśikā (Jalada) and Makaranda by Varadarāja, Varddhamānopādhyāya, Mecha Thakkura, and Rucidattopādhyāya and with Notes by Śrī Dharmadatta (Bachchā Jhā)*. Edited by Padmaprasāda Updhyāya and Dhuṇḍirāja Śāstrī. (Varanasi: Chowkhamba Sanskrit Series, 1957).

NM I — Jayanta Bhaṭṭa's *Nyāyamañjarī* in *Nyāyamañjarī: Sampādakagrathitanyāyas aurabhākhyaṭippaṇīsamanvitā*, i. Edited by K. S. Varadacharya. (Mysore: Oriental Research Institute, 1969).

---

[20] Thanks to Artūrs Logins, Rosanna Picascia, Mark Siderits, Davey Tomlinson, an anonymous referee for this volume, and audiences at the University of Oxford, University of Manchester, and Columbia University for their helpful comments.

NRK Pārthasārathimiśra's *Nyāyaratnākara* in *Ślokavārttikam Kumārilabhaṭṭapādaviracitaṃ Pārthasārathimiśraviracitayā Nyāyaratnākaravyākhyayā Sanātham*. Edited by Dwarikadas Sastri. (Varanasi: Tara Publications, 1978).

NVTP Udayana's *Nyāyavārttikatātparyapariśuddhi* in *Nyāyavārttikatātparyapariś uddhi of Udayanācārya*. Edited by Anantalal Thakur. (New Delhi: Indian Council of Philosophical Research, 1996).

ŚV Kumārila Bhaṭṭa's *Ślokavārttika* in *Ślokavārttikam Kumārilabhaṭṭapādaviracitaṃ Pārthasārathimiśraviracitayā Nyāyaratnākaravyākhyayā Sanātham*. Edited by Dwarikadas Sastri. (Varanasi: Tara Publications, 1978).

ŚVK *The Mīmāṃsāślokavārttika of Kumārilabhaṭṭa: With the Commentary Kāśika of Sucaritamiśra*. Parts I and II. Edited by K. Sāmbaśivaśāstri. (Trivandrum: CBH Publications, 1990).

ŚVTṬ *Ślokavārtikavyākhyā (Tātparyaṭīkā) of Bhaṭṭombeka*. Edited by S. K. Ramanatha Sastri. (Madras: University of Madras, 1940).

2. Secondary Sources

Conee, Earl, and Feldman, Richard (1998). 'The Generality Problem for Reliabilism', *Philosophical Studies* 89(1): 1–29.

Das, Nilanjan (2018). 'Śrīharṣa', in Edward N. Zalta (ed.), *The Stanford Encyclopedia of Philosophy*. Winter 2021 Edition, https://plato.stanford.edu/archives/win2021/entries/sriharsa/, accessed 12 February 2024.

Das, Nilanjan (2021). 'Gaṅgeśa on Epistemic Luck', *Journal of Indian Philosophy* 49(2): 153–202.

Dasti, M. R. (2012). 'Parasitism and Disjunctivism in Nyāya Epistemology', *Philosophy East and West* 62(1): 1–15.

Dupré, J. (1993). *The Disorder of Things: Metaphysical Foundations of the Disunity of Science* (Cambridge, MA: Harvard University Press).

Ellis, Brian (2001). *Scientific Essentialism* (Cambridge: Cambridge University Press).

Ganeri, Jonardon (2017). 'Śrīharṣa's Dissident Epistemology', in Jonardon Ganeri (ed.), *The Oxford Handbook of Indian Philosophy* (Oxford: Oxford University Press): 522–38.

Gettier, Edmund L. (1963). 'Is Justified True Belief Knowledge?', *Analysis* 23(6): 121–23.

Granoff, Phyllis E. (1978). *Philosophy and Argument in Late Vedānta: Śrī Harṣa's Khaṇḍanakhaṇḍakhādya* (Dodrecht: D. Reidel).

Hacking, Ian (2007). 'Natural Kinds: Rosy Dawn, Scholastic Twilight', *Royal Institute of Philosophy Supplement* 61: 203–39.

Ichikawa, Jonathan, and Jenkins, C. S. I. (2017). 'On Putting Knowledge "First"', in J. Adam Carter, Emma C. Gordon, and Benjamin W. Jarvis (eds.), *Knowledge First: Approaches in Epistemology and Mind* (Oxford: Oxford University Press): 113–30.

Jha, Ganganatha (1913/1986). *The Sweets of Refutation. An English Translation of the Khaṇḍanakhaṇḍakhādya of Shri-Harṣa* (Allahabad: 'Indian Thought Series'; repr. Delhi: Satguru Publications, 1986).

Khalidi, Muhammad Ali (1998). 'Natural Kinds and Crosscutting Categories', *Journal of Philosophy* 95(1): 33–50.

Kornblith, Hilary (2002). *Knowledge and Its Place in Nature* (Oxford: Oxford University Press).

Kumar, Victor (2014). ' "Knowledge" as a Natural Kind Term', *Synthese* 191(3): 439–57.

McGlynn, Aidan (2014). *Knowledge First?* (New York: Palgrave Macmillian).

Matilal, Bimal Krishna (1986). *Perception: An Essay on Classical Indian Theories of Knowledge* (Oxford: Oxford University Press).

Nagel, Jennifer (2013). 'Knowledge as a Mental State', in Tamar Szabó Gendler and John Hawthorne (eds.), *Oxford Studies in Epistemology*. Volume 4 (Oxford: Oxford University Press): 275–310.

Nagel, Jennifer (2023). 'Seeking Safety in Knowledge', *Proceedings and Addresses of the American Philosophical Association* 97: 186–214.

Pellegrini, G. (2016). 'Differentiating *jāti* and *upādhi*: Towards a Further Exegesis of the Six *jātibādhaka*s according to Navya Nyāya', *Proceedings of the Meeting of the Italian Association of Sanskrit Studies. Rivisita degli Studi Orientali* 28: 73–91.

Phillips, Stephen H. (1999). *Classical Indian Metaphysics: Refutations of Realism and the Emergence of 'New Logic'* (Chicago and La Salle, Illinois: Open Court).

Radford, Colin (1966). Knowledge: By Examples. *Analysis* 27(1): 1–11.

Ram-Prasad, Chakravarthi (2002). *Advaita Epistemology and Metaphysics* (London: Routledge).

Sosa, Ernest (1991). *Knowledge in Perspective* (Cambridge: Cambridge University Press).

Williamson, Timothy (2000). *Knowledge and its Limits* (Oxford: Oxford University Press).

Williamson, Timothy (2023). 'Vaidya on Nyāya and Knowledge-First Epistemology', *Oxford Studies in Epistemology* 7: 365–75.

Vaidya, A. J. (2013). 'Nyāya Perceptual Theory: Disjunctivism or Anti-Individualism?', *Philosophy East and West* 63(4): 562–85.

Vaidya, A. (2023). 'Elements of Knowledge-first Epistemology in Gaṅgeśa', *Oxford Studies in Epistemology* 7: 336–64.

Zagzebski, Linda (1996). *Virtues of the Mind* (Cambridge: Cambridge University Press).

PART 2
KNOWLEDGE AS A MENTAL STATE

5
How the Brain Makes Knowledge First

Robert M. Gordon

1. Introduction

In the two decades since the publication of *Knowledge and its Limits* (Williamson 2000), researchers have found considerable empirical evidence that knowledge and factive propositional attitudes are central to our understanding of other people. In important ways knowledge attribution has priority over the attribution of beliefs and other non-factive propositional attitudes. For example, Phillips et al. (2021) note that some individuals—non-human primates, young children, and certain cognitively impaired people—can attribute knowledge but not belief, while none attribute belief but not knowledge; and also that attributions of knowledge are "more automatic" than attributions of belief, which evidently requires additional processing.

Phillips et al. (2021) then ask why the capacity for knowledge representation "would have ended up being one that is cognitively basic." After all, they argue, this capacity is of only limited use in predicting (or in interpreting or explaining) the behavior of others. We can't always just "look at the facts" to predict or explain another's behavior, if the other doesn't "share"—that is, doesn't know, isn't aware of—those facts. The assumption by Phillips et al. seems to be that either knowledge attribution or belief attribution *might* have become the basic one, but a certain important function of knowledge attribution (namely allowing us to learn about the world from others—knowledge transmission) caused knowledge attribution to end up as basic. This is indeed an important function. It explains why, as Jennifer Nagel notes:

> we develop the capacity for *knowledge recognition*: it pays off over time to recognize situations in which people have a state of mind of a type that one can only have to truths, and as we discover through trial and error that we are largely able to do so, this reinforces our tendency to seek out signs of these truth-anchored mental states in each other.
>
> (Nagel 2023)

However, there are at least two problems with the further claim that this learning function somehow makes knowledge basic. First, it isn't clear that we can extricate the role of knowledge recognition from its explanatory role. After all, we learn about the extra-mental world not only from another's assertions, but often by way of the other's actions and emotional reactions. For example, we see someone running, and we note their frightened look. We want to know what it is about the world that might have frightened them and caused them to run; maybe they know something we don't know. Thus, we look behind them to see whether there might be something they are running from (which we might want to run from ourselves). Or, observing a happier expression, we might look for something ahead of them, some possible reward (to which we might want to run as well). The parent wants to know what it is about the environment that frightens or upsets the child; and in social referencing, the child wants to know what the caregiver is responding to, so that it can copy and learn the response. Thus, we learn about the extra-mental world by discovering the knowledge that explains the other's behavior.

The second problem concerns the notion that knowledge representation ended up being one that is "cognitively basic." I assume "cognitively basic" means not dependent on the capacity to represent and attribute belief or any other mental states. It is hard to see how the particular uses of knowledge attribution would have any bearing on whether knowledge is in this sense "cognitively basic." Knowledge attribution may in various ways be more useful than belief attribution. But to show that knowledge attribution does not require the capacity for belief attribution, we must look elsewhere. The same is true if we want to understand why knowledge attribution might be more automatic and require less processing than belief attribution.

2. Inverse Planning

Although knowledge and belief are topics within epistemology, they also fall under what is variously called theory of mind, mind reading, folk psychology, and mentalizing. The ultimate goal of a theory of mentalizing is to explain how we come to understand the intentions, goals, and reasons behind observed behavior, shedding light on the underlying motivations that make such behavior understandable and unsurprising. To address the question of how the brain interprets the observed actions of others, Baker, Saxe, & Tenenbaum (2009) suggest that we adopt a framework that has been particularly fruitful in studies of vision: Contrary to the widely held view that visual perception simply pastes together a complex scene from elements such as lines and edges, it is now thought that the process works in reverse. Our brains generate predictions about the incoming sensory information based on past experiences and learned patterns. These predictions help anticipate what we are likely to perceive in a given situation. When actual sensory input matches these predictions, the brain processes the information more efficiently, which leads to a sense of familiarity and reduced cognitive load. However, when there are discrepancies between predictions and actual input, our brains update their models to match the current environment better. This theory highlights the active role of the brain in shaping our perception of the world around us. The interpretation of a visual scene might involve, essentially, using in reverse the process of *producing* such a scene. Analogously, the interpretation of another's behavior might be understood as a comparable inverse problem (Baker, Saxe, & Tenenbaum 2011; Baker, Saxe, & Tenenbaum 2009):

> By analogy, our analysis of intentional reasoning might be called "inverse planning," where the observer infers an agent's intentions, given observations of the agent's behavior, by inverting a model of how intentions cause behavior.
> (Baker, Saxe, & Tenenbaum 2011)

The process is *inverted* in that, instead of proceeding forward from a given intention to its behavioral execution, it takes the behavior as the given and determines the intention most likely to have produced it. The planning process would thus be used as a mechanism for testing hypotheses about underlying intentions.[1]

Strictly speaking, however, the term "inverse planning" suggests that the very mechanism that is used to plan our own behavior may be reused as a platform for testing hypothetical explanations of the observed behavior of other agents. This would, in effect, be a way of *simulating* ways of generating the behavior. However, Baker, Saxe, & Tenenbaum (2011) actually propose something more complicated. The authors speak of inverting a *model* or *theory* of the planning process. As they point out, their project originated as an attempt to formalize an intuitive theory of mind thought to underlie our interpretations of behavior—the so-called "theory theory":

> On a theory-based interpretation, inverse planning consists of inverting a causal theory of rational action to arrive at a set of goals that could have generated the observed behavior.
> (Baker, Saxe, & Tenenbaum 2011)

The theory-based approach attributes to the brain a capacity for detachment: It *stands back from its own operations* and employs instead a general theory or model of these operations. As distinct from actual action planning, the theory

---

[1] In the broadest terms, inverse planning exemplifies hypothesis-testing as unconscious inference, an idea introduced in the perceptual realm by Helmholtz (1856). The proposal bears some resemblance to "hypothetico-practical" inference (Gordon 1986), modeled on a traditional model of the scientific method, hypothetico-deductive inference. Instead of forming hypotheses and deducing consequences that match observations, hypothetico-practical inference would form hypotheses and then act on them, producing consequences that match the observed behavior of the other agent.

theorist proposal is that in mentalizing about others the brain engages in *plan-theorizing*, *theorizing about* the steps in the other's planning process. The proposal assumes that we humans have an intuitive theory of mind and that our brains employ this theory not only in our explicit attributions of mental states but also in their unconscious subpersonal neural processing. I will call this *inverse plan-theorizing*. Thus understood, it does not make use of our capacity for planning: It is not inverse planning as such, that is, an inverse reuse of one's own action-planning system. Strictly speaking, what would be analogous to "inverse graphics," where perception involves searching among alternative hypothetical ways of building a scene, would be "inverse planning," understood as a search among alternative hypothetical ways of generating (planning) an action to find the most plausible simulation of the planning that might have generated the observed action.

Baker, Saxe, & Tenenbaum (2009) acknowledge that a simulation-based account would cover the data just as well as their theory-based account:

> On a simulation account, goal inference is performed by inverting one's own planning process—the planning mechanism used in model-based reinforcement—infer the goals most likely to have generated another agent's observed behavior.
> (Baker, Saxe, & Tenenbaum 2011)

If indeed such reuse of its own "first-person" planning system would be sufficient for goal inference, the following question arises: Why would the brain need to operate instead on a model of the planning process? Here again, using an existing system would avoid the overhead costs of storing and utilizing an information-rich theory or model. Moreover, first-person inverse planning would seem to be the proper analogue of the inverse-graphics account of vision. As inverse graphics is "the inversion of a causal physical process of scene formation" (Baker, Saxe, & Tenenbaum 2011), so inverse planning should be the inversion of *a physical process* of action determination—*not* the inversion of a causal *theory of* a physical process of action determination. The "vision is inverse graphics" idea is generally understood to be an analysis-by-synthesis paradigm, and analysis by synthesis is not analysis by a *theory of* synthesis.

2.1. Simulative Inverse Planning

There is at least one crucial difference between the simulation account of inverse planning (where the planning process itself is inverted) and the theory-based account (where a model of that process is inverted): On the simulation account, one and the same action-planning system has a double function: in addition to its primary use in generating one's own actions, a reuse—or secondary use—in which the planning process is inverted in order to infer the goals and reasons that lie behind another agent's observed behavior. Moreover, it appears likely that the secondary use of the action-planning system, namely inverse reuse for explanatory purposes, runs concurrently with its primary use for generating one's own actions. Otherwise, we would have to suspend our own actions in order to interpret the actions of others. Thus, the system is translating existing inputs into action and at the same time looking for hypothetical inputs that would explain the perceived actions of others. Concurrent processing for self-action and other-understanding would be consistent with evidence of "motor contagion," or interference effects between observed and executed actions. It has been suggested that motor contagion, first noted in the case of biological movements, may be "the first step in a more sophisticated predictive system that allows us to infer goals from the observation of actions" (Blakemore & Frith 2005). Indeed, recent research indicates that such interference is markedly increased when the observed movement is directed toward a visible goal (Bouquet, Shipley, Capa, & Marshall 2011). This interference suggests a competition for resources and thus that the same or strongly overlapping neural resources are employed concurrently in goal-directed action planning and in interpreting the goal-directed actions of others.

Such concurrent double employment raises the question: What, if anything, must *change* as the planning system switches from primary use to reuse and from self to other? Specifically, what happens to the existing inputs? When the system switches to inverse planning as it seeks to explain another's behavior, does it clear the slate and approach the task with no a priori top-down commitments? More specifically, for the inverse use, does the brain suspend the beliefs, desires, preferences, emotional valences, affordances, and other influences on one's own action planning? That is, does it expend energy to intervene and wipe away the inputs and start with a blank slate when simulating others? That would seem wasteful both in loss of information and in use of resources. At the opposite extreme, does the brain leave all inputs in place, add no others, and seek the best explanation of the other agent's behavior strictly on the basis of the beliefs, desires, preferences, emotional valences, affordances, and other influences on one's own action planning? That would seem highly limiting. The most plausible account would be for the brain to default to this do-nothing position and devote its limited energy to looking for problems. With its focus on exploiting redundancy and then checking for exceptions, it is much in line with a widely held view in cognitive science that neural systems tend to reduce metabolic and other expenses with a predictive coding strategy (Clark 2013). As in the case of vision, this is a strategy of "guessing ahead." Rather than waiting for the world to bombard us with new information, the system makes its latest best guess as to what will be coming in. This process of predicting input values minimizes the need for new information input, in that only discrepancies, or information that conflicts with the predicted values (prediction errors), need be encoded. This resembles compression schemes commonly used in the digital transmission and storage of graphic and video content (Gordon 1992). These schemes exploit the likelihood that the content will be redundant in a number of ways. For example, typically, little or no visual content changes in, say, the thirtieth of a second that separates one frame from the next. The compression program can bet that the next frame will be the same as the previous and focus its limited resources on detecting and correcting for exceptions.

3. Agent-Neutral Coding

I have argued (Gordon 2021) that the top-down inputs to inverse planning would default to what I call *agent-neutral coding*. That is, inputs, including factual inputs, would by default remain the same for self and other, that is, the same unless corrected, for example in response to predictive error. Coding begins as agent-neutral, in the sense that any differentiation would be the result of intervention of some sort: Identical coding for self and other would be the default. With agent-neutral coding, one's own actions and the actions of others are constrained by the same inputs unless there is reason for differentiation. The claim is not that *my* inputs are carried over, but rather that an *undifferentiated* input, neither mine nor the other's, becomes differentiated into mine and the other's. It is, of course, my own mental states that provide input to the forward planning of my own actions, and it is representations of the other's mental states that feed into the inverse use of the planning system to explain the other's behavior. It might be supposed that the system has to distinguish these in some way. But this is not so. Unlike intentions and motor plans, beliefs may remain happily undifferentiated, and failure to differentiate is not only not pathological, but it is the norm. What the system needs to "know" is, simply, that there is a puddle in the path; it can deal with undifferentiated, impersonal "facts" without marking them as facts-to-me, facts-to-you, or facts-to-another—or, in other words, as facts *as I believe them to be,* or you, or another. Moreover, as will be argued, simple "factive" explanations such as "She stepped to the side because there was a puddle in the path" are the preferred form of action explanation in contrast to "because she believed..." explanations. (Use of "because she believed..." is taken to imply that there was reason not to use the simple factive form.)

In reconstructing the processes behind the other's action, inverse planning locates the agent's reason or reasons for acting, as far as possible, within a shared world of facts; and likewise, as I discuss in Section 8, what the agent's emotions are about. Shared-world explanations have a number of advantages over those requiring explicit mentalizing: They can identify environmental threats and rewards, they are conceptually and linguistically less demanding, and they achieve greater code compression. If this is correct, then we must reject the common assumption that explicit mentalizing—or mental state attribution—is the paramount explanatory aim of the procedures we lump under the term *mentalizing*. The aim is rather to interpret behavior in terms of a shared world where this is possible and to diagnose cases where it is not.

We can, of course, add to any theory a stipulation that the interpretation start by importing the world of the interpreter. Rebecca Saxe, a leading proponent of the theory-based approach to mentalizing in neuroscience, writes:

> I agree that by far the bulk of action explanation in everyday life is accomplished by 'factive', 'agent-neutral' coding of beliefs (and indeed of desires!). When I try to explain this, I sometimes talk about the default naive realism we bring to understanding both the world and other people. Instead of beliefs or perceptions, we explain actions in terms of facts. Instead of desires, we explain actions in terms of what is valuable or good. Explanations in terms of mental states (what she saw, or didn't see, or thought, or wanted) are exceptions, corrections.
> (Pers. comm., July 6, 2020)

It should be remarked that agent-neutral coding requires a simulative account of inverse planning. It stipulates that top-down inputs are by default invariant between the direct or forward employment of the action-planning system and its inverse simulative use in interpreting another's behavior. If Saxe indeed accepts the simulative account of inverse planning with its reuse of the very system used for planning and generating one's own actions, all well and good: What are facts for us are portrayed as available to others' decision-making as well—and therefore, as I will argue, as something known to the others. If, on the other hand, it is simply plastered onto a formal theory or model, perhaps as a useful heuristic, then we can't speak of an automatic carry-over of an agent-neutral (same for self and other) coding.

Agent-neutral coding requires the simulation account of inverse planning with its concurrent use of the same system for generating actions and interpreting the action of others; and as I will argue, it is agent-neutral coding that explains why what we ourselves regard as *facts* get passed along to other (the target agent) as *known* facts. However, not all versions of the simulation theory of mentalizing support default agent-neutral coding. The simulation theory has sometimes been characterized as a two- or three-step process of first reading one's own mental states (by introspection or otherwise) and then inferring that the other agent has similar mental states. Many proponents as well as most critics of the simulation theory have supposed simulation to be founded on such an implicit inference from oneself to others. The form of inference is essentially the old argument from analogy (Mill 1869), which requires that one first recognize one's own mental states under actual or imagined conditions and then infer that the other is in similar states. This is usually linked to an introspectionist account of how one recognizes and ascribes one's own mental states (Goldman 1993). It is further assumed that, to recognize and ascribe one's own mental states and to transfer these states over to the other mentally, one would need to be equipped with the concepts of the various mental states. According to this account, in short, simulation is an analogical inference from oneself to others premised on introspectively based ascriptions of mental states to oneself, requiring prior possession of the concepts of the mental states ascribed. Goldman's account of simulation has been characterized as requiring three stages of processing in order to generate an interpretation of another's behavior:

Stage 1. *Mental Simulation*: Subject S undergoes a simulation process, which outputs a token simulated mental state m^*.
Stage 2. *Introspection*: S introspects m^* and categorizes/conceptualizes it *as* (a state of type) M.
Stage 3. *Judgment*: S attributes (a state of type) M to another subject, Q, through the judgment Q is in M.

(Barlassina & Gordon 2017)

In short, we (or our brain) must somehow read our own mental states, then describe or categorize them, and finally form a judgment that the other is in the same or a similar state. However, given the simple alternative of agent-neutral coding, with one and the same neural code indifferently serving both self and other, this elaborate intellectually loaded process seems both unnecessary and wasteful of time as well as of energy resources.

4. Perspective-Taking and Positional Correction

The most economical strategy for mentalizing, other things being equal, would be one that minimizes individuation, or information tagged to specific individuals. That is, it would minimize the need for explicit mentalizing, in the sense of judgments about mental states or processes. In the default case, with uncorrected agent-neutral coding, the actions of others would be interpreted in terms of a shared world—that is the world on the basis of which we ourselves act. Mentalizing, on this account, would be called on to complement or to correct what is passed along through agent-neutral coding. It would be reserved for cases in which a shared world proves inadequate to predict or explain the actions or emotions of particular individuals.

Spatial perspective-taking is probably the most familiar type of error correction in the interpretation of others' behavior. Moving mentally to the other's viewpoint, we may recognize that their view is partly or wholly occluded (they are in a different room), Or we recognize that they can see aspects of a scene that are hidden to us and consequently that they may know something we do not know. As Nagel writes:

the capacity to differentiate patterns of knowledge and ignorance in our fellow agents enables us to exploit their epistemic access to those parts of reality for which their vantage point is better than ours. If you want to know which way the coin in my palm is facing, you know you can ask me. While many primates show selective social learning from peers recognized as knowledgeable, humans show exceptionally active use of the knowledge of their peers (Tomasello, 2019), guided by an exceptionally well-developed sense of what others do and do not know, a sense informed by continual feedback from conversational exchanges (Westra & Nagel, 2021) and extraconversational encounters with reality.

(Nagel 2023)

In addition, rather than imparting different information, the altered viewpoint may account for a different emotional or motivational response. To a stranger observing the scene from a distance, the bear now approaching me is not likely to feel threatening, or in any case as threatening as it does to me. The threatening (or non-threatening) emotive quality of the bear may be seen as a function of one's location relative to the bear—or the bear's location and vector in egocentric space. With the ability to move mentally into another's spatial perspective, individual differences become mere positional differences. That is, it is a good starting bet that (unless there is evidence to the contrary) any individual in the same position will see the bear as threatening. With the operation of "putting ourselves in the other's place" by spatial perspective-taking, we are able to restore the economic advantages of a shared world. We allow the threatening quality to remain out there in the bear, or rather in the bear-from-a-point of view. We need not represent it as a function of individual mental makeup, even if some individuals may be found immune to the standard bear-approaching-me response.

Although it is spatial perspective-taking that gives us the general metaphor of "perspective-taking," "adopting the other's point of view," and "putting ourselves in the other's place," many other kinds of corrections may be considered broadly perspectival or positional. For example, differences in social or occupational role may be bridged by a kind of perspective shift: student/teacher, worker/manager, diner/waiter, patient/doctor, consumer/salesperson. In these cases, as in differences in spatial perspective, it may be sufficient to shift to a generic "point of view" or, as we say, to understand where the other is "coming from," to explain the other's actions without explicit mentalizing. That is, it may be a good starting assumption that a person in a given "position" will act in more or less the same "standard" way, an assumption that may underlie the notion of generic "scripts" of action sequences postulated by Schank & Abelson (1977). Such an assumption would exploit positional redundancies and limit new input to deviations from the standard.

By mentally adopting someone else's perspective, differences tend to become merely positional: People in the same position are more likely to see the bear similarly. This shared perspective helps us create a common understanding and economizes our interaction with the world. Besides spatial perspective-taking, various other corrections, like understanding different social or occupational roles, can be considered perspectival. These shifts in viewpoint help explain others' actions without the need for explicit mentalizing, relying on assumptions of standard behavior in specific positions.

5. An Evolutionary Perspective

For most of human history, social encounters would have occurred primarily within small, close-knit cultural groups with limited exposure to faraway lands and diverse cultures. As a result, to explain and predict behavior within the local group, "mentalizing" could have consisted largely of looking to the shared world and its common facts, emotive qualities, affordances, attractions, and repulsions. The environmental and cultural contexts of these small social groups led to the development of shared mental maps and a common understanding of their surroundings. Members of these groups would have agreed on which elements of their environment were significant, threatening, appealing, or repulsive. This shared understanding allowed for relatively straightforward predictions and explanations of one another's behavior, given the group's limitations and homogeneity. Of course, even in these close-knit communities, individual differences in temperament, sensory and cognitive capacities, knowledge, acculturation, and goals existed. However, such differences would have been relatively rare and likely observed against the backdrop of the more predictable shared background. In such situations, minor adjustments could be made to accommodate these individual differences.

The evolutionary advantage of this social predictive system lies in its ability to exploit, reinforce, and create redundancies within the group. The more shared understanding and predictability there is among group members, the smoother the social interactions and cooperation, which would lead to increased chances of survival and successful reproduction.

The process of social learning and prediction plays a vital role in fostering unity and cooperation within small groups. Infants and young children acquire knowledge by observing and imitating the behavior of trusted adult caregivers. Through social referencing, they learn how to react to various situations and stimuli on the basis of the responses of those they trust. By imitating similar responses, the child's behavior aligns with the group's norms and expectations, which leads to shared patterns of behavior that are strengthened and repeated.

However, as societies evolved and expanded, encounters with culturally distant and geographically separated groups became more frequent. In such encounters, the strategy of agent-neutral coding that worked reasonably well within small, homogeneous groups might no longer be effective. Understanding and predicting the behavior of people from vastly different cultures would require extensive corrections and adjustments, as their mental maps, norms, and affordances could vary significantly from one's own.

In summary, the evolutionary perspective suggests that the reliance on agent-neutral coding and shared mental maps was an effective strategy for understanding and predicting behavior within small, culturally cohesive groups. However, as human societies became more complex and interconnected, this strategy faced limitations in explaining behavior in culturally distant contexts, which necessitated the development of more nuanced and culturally sensitive approaches to cross-cultural understanding.

6. Ignorance and False Belief

How does inverse planning deal with ignorance? For example, we see someone do something surprising: In broad daylight they walk nonchalantly into a deep puddle. We are aware of the puddle, but apparently the other, engrossed in their cellphone, is not: Earlier I cited Nagel on knowledge recognition. For facts automatically passed along by agent-neutral coding, perhaps the more important capacity is *ignorance* recognition. We pick up on evidence of behavior that is *not* truth-anchored, and accordingly we modify the default input to inverse planning. We make the surprising behavior unsurprising by disconnecting or "decoupling" the fact that there was a puddle in their path from the input to inverse planning. Decoupling a fact from inverse planning is a way of marking ignorance of the fact. Ignorance, in turn, may engender false belief: because the puddle-walker was ignorant of the fact that there was a puddle. Out of touch with the facts concerning his current environment, they continued operating on the false default assumption of an ordinary puddle-free path. The puddle is there, but it is not there for the other—until it is.

Agent-neutral coding and the possibility of toggling between knowledge and ignorance would give us the neural underpinnings for two theses long held by the psychologist Josef Perner: first, that well before they have an explicit grasp of belief attribution, young children are quite capable of explaining action in terms of the external situation; and second, that older children and adults use the same type of explanation young children use, except in the occasional cases where it proves inadequate; then they must fall back on explanations that mention the mental states, especially the beliefs, of the agent. Young children and, where possible, older children and adults "make sense of intentional actions in terms of justifying reasons provided by 'worldly' facts (not by mental states)" (Perner & Roessler 2010).

The young child's conception is all we usually call upon, because it is typically all we need. This comes to saying that explaining and predicting actions in terms of actual situations or facts is our default mode of explanation and prediction, the mode we employ unless we find some reason not to. Only where this appears inadequate do we invoke beliefs in our explanation. In the classic "false belief" condition, you see individual A place her treasure at location x. You also see that *(m)* the treasure has been moved and is now at a different location y. If you were planning to steal the treasure, your action planning system would take account of *(m)* and direct you to location y. However, if your system is hypothetically generating A's plan to retrieve A's treasure, the questions arise: Does A know about the move? Is A aware that *(m)*? The possibility of attributing ignorance—or not knowing—is simply the possibility of decoupling the action-planning system from the fact that *(m)*. (*Egocentric* ignorance acknowledges that there are facts to which our own planning is not yet coupled or connected.) *Knowledge*, on the other hand, is represented simply by nonintervention. That is, one implicitly attributes knowledge that *(m)* simply by *not decoupling* the system from the fact that *(m)*. "Knowledge representations," accordingly, consist in nothing more than *access to facts*.

Attributing ignorance consists in decoupling from fact, which is an extra step beyond implicitly attributing knowledge. False belief requires decoupling as well as introducing into the planning process an "as if" fact, such as that the treasure is still at location *x*. True belief for the wrong reason would similarly entail introducing an "as if" fact. (Although it might produce the same actions as the "real" fact, the counterfactual dependencies would differ.) The upshot is that what is really basic is a shared world, where, prior to any corrective processing, everything we ourselves regard as the world, as the facts, is publicly accessible and thus available to others as possible reasons for action.

7. Knowledge-First

It is traditional to see factual knowledge as an achievement, as having a status that is to be earned by meeting certain stringent conditions. As Nagel (2023) suggests, we develop the capacity to recognize when those conditions indicate a state of mind of a type that one can only have in relation to truths. Consistent with this, however, is that knowledge is also a status granted by birthright, as it were. When we try to make sense of another's actions and emotions, we gift the other with access—for planning—and, I will argue, for emotion generation—to all the facts available to us in generating our own actions and emotions, that is, with knowledge of these facts. (There may be differences in attention, of course; for one thing, our own direction of gaze may differ from the other's. But this is often a bridgeable gap: we look around to previously unnoticed features of the environment—or more broadly, to aspects of the world that might be salient to the other.)

In summary, there is evidence that the human brain exploits a strategy that appears to operate in several other areas of cognition, a strategy of analysis by synthesis. Specifically, the brain interprets the behavior of others by testing hypothetical ways of *generating* that behavior. This would involve the inverse use of one's own system for planning and generating intentional action, concurrent with its primary "forward" use in generating one's own actions. The inverse use of the planning system for hypothetically generating the actions of others would ordinarily require adjustments of the top-down inputs to the system. These would include adjustments of the factual input, the set of facts that influence planning. In hypothetically generating another's actions, the planning system may be selectively decoupled (disconnected, unplugged) from some of these facts. In a predictive strategy, the actual world—that is, what we ourselves take to be the facts—serves as a starting point, an opening bid or bet, subject to revision ("correction") on the basis of new evidence. As our mechanisms for decision-making and planning are used to test hypothetical explanations of the actions of others, the carryover of agent-neutral inputs has the effect of projecting onto others a shared world within which we act and interact. Strictly speaking, the brain doesn't do anything to accomplish this; rather, it is not doing anything to modify or correct the top-down inputs in the concurrent use and reuse of action planning that gives us a shared world as a default. Withholding or diminishing the implicit attribution of knowledge, such as attributing a belief that falls short of knowledge, requires additional steps in neural coding and processing. Those extra steps, their added complexity, and their drain on resources suffice to explain the empirical findings: why (per Phillips 2002[1]) some individuals—nonhuman primates, young children, and certain cognitively impaired people—can attribute knowledge but not belief, while none attributes belief but not knowledge; and why attributions of knowledge are "more automatic" than those that require additional processing.

8. Factive Emotions and Knowledge: A Postscript

In discussing factive emotions more than a half century ago, I offered a hint of a knowledge-first thesis. It was definitely not a full-fledged knowledge first-epistemology, such as that presented in *Knowledge and its Limits* (Williamson 2000), but it did argue that our default attributions of factive emotions entail knowledge rather than mere belief.[2] Coming full circle, I now believe that the notion of default agent-neutral coding would explain why this is so.

The philosopher Irving Thalberg, Jr., noted (Thalberg 1964) that many of our attributions of emotion implicitly attributed "cognitive" states as well. Thalberg was concerned with emotion terms in English that take a sentential complement,

---

[2] Actually, I would probably not have considered knowledge an important category in philosophy of mind but for my good fortune in having Fred Dretske and Peter Unger as colleagues at the University of Wisconsin.

as in sentences of the form *S emotes that p*. Replace *emotes* with almost any emotion verb—*regrets, is glad, is embarrassed, is annoyed, is upset, is surprised,* for example—and the following condition holds: S emotes that p, only if S *believes* that p. This applies not only to the "that p" form, but to any sentential complement, for example, a gerund, as in "He's upset about (his) being late." Call these the *belief emotions*. It should be noted that a few emotion terms that take a sentential complement do not entail the corresponding belief. A person may fear or be afraid or worried or even terrified that p, without actually believing that p; likewise, one may hope or be hopeful that p, without the corresponding belief. Indeed, as Thalberg noted, the few exceptions appear to satisfy a contrary condition: S emotes that p, only if S *does not believe* that p. Both types of propositional emotions are discussed at length in my book *The Structure of Emotions* (Gordon 1987).

Building on Thalberg's paper, I argued (Gordon 1969) that all belief emotions are also *factive* emotions: For these, S emotes that p, only if p. Thus, S *is embarrassed, is annoyed, is upset, is surprised, that p,* only if S has a *true* belief that p. (On the other hand, S is afraid, is worried, is hopeful that p are neither factive nor belief-presupposing.) Indeed, a further generalization seems to hold for any state *e* that we intuitively classify as an emotion: An attribution of *e* is belief-presupposing *if and only if* it is factive.

This coupling of belief with truth appeared to be something more than a coincidence. Why should the description of emotion depend on whether the implied belief happens to be true or false? True belief, I suggested, is part of a larger package. The main thesis of my 1969 article was that all of Thalberg's belief emotions are actually *knowledge* emotions. For each of them, S emotes that p, only if S *knows* (or: is aware) that p.[3] Emotions are not in any straightforward sense planned and executed as actions. They may sometimes be expressed in action, as in "acting out of anger"; it is also possible to allow oneself to be angry, as well as possible to decide to interpret as anger interoceptive responses that are ambiguous. But in general, anger is not generated by action planning; and its interpretation by others is, therefore, not a function of *inverse* planning. However, it is plausible that the processes responsible for emotion generation, whatever their nature, can be interpreted by inverting them. In inverse emotion generation, we test hypothetical ways of generating something approximating the emotion we observe.

Suppose we see someone look startled, or frightened, or obviously pleased about something, but we can't easily tell the source of the emotion. Following the other's gaze, we find several objects or environmental features, any one or more of which might be the source; we need to pick out the *right* feature or features. Or

---

[3] Arguments I offered for this thesis included Gettier examples as well as inconsistencies such as "S emotes that p but doesn't know that p /isn't aware that p." For further support, see Dietz (2018),

suppose the person has already turned away from the source of the emotion. What do we do in such cases? We look around for a plausible target. That is, we look for something startling. Or if the other is frightened, we look for something that is frightening. If pleased, we look for something pleasing. To do this, we engage *our own* system for generating emotions out of our perceptions. We are also prepared to make positional adjustments, where necessary. For example, I see a competitor for an award and find them looking elated. On the wall nearby there is posted a list of award-winners. My own name on the list would indeed be pleasing; but I automatically shift to viewing the list through their eyes. We do this sort of thing so routinely that we aren't aware of doing it—and we fail to appreciate the sophistication of the maneuver we are engaging in (Gordon 1995b).

Bibliography

Baker, C. L., Saxe, R., and Tenenbaum, J. B. (2009). "Action Understanding as Inverse Planning." Cognition 113: 329–49.

Baker, C. L., Saxe, R., and Tenenbaum, J. B. (2011). "Bayesian theory of mind: Modeling joint belief-desire attribution." Proceedings of the Annual Meeting of the Cognitive Science Society 33: 33.

Barlassina, L. and Gordon, R. M., (2017). "Folk Psychology: as Mental Simulation." In Edward N. Zalta (ed.), *The Stanford Encyclopedia of Philosophy*. Summer 2017 edition, https://plato.stanford.edu/entries/folkpsych-simulation/, accessed February 13, 2024.

Blakemore, S.-J., and Frith, C. (2005). "The Role of Motor Contagion in the Prediction of Action." Neuropsychologia 43: 260–67.

Bouquet, C. A., Shipley, T. F., Capa, R. L., & Marshall, P. J. (2011). "Motor contagion: Goal-directed actions are more contagious than non-goal-directed actions." Experimental Psychology 58(1): 71–78. https://doi.org/10.1027/1618-3169/a000069

Clark, A. (2013). "Whatever next? Predictive brains, situated agents, and the future of cognitive science." Behavioral and Brain Sciences 36(3): 181–204. doi: 10.1017/S0140525X12000477

Dietz, C. H. (2018). "Reasons and Factive Emotions." Philosophical Studies 175: 1681–91.

Goldman, A. (1993). "The psychology of folk psychology." The Behavioral and Brain Sciences 16: 15–28.

Gordon, R. M. (1969). "Emotions and Knowledge." Journal of Philosophy 66: 408–13. Reprinted in David M. Rosenthal (ed.), *The Nature of Mind* (Oxford: Oxford University Press, 1991): 450–53.

Gordon, R. M. (1986). "Folk Psychology as Simulation." Mind and Language 1: 158–71. Reprinted in M. Davies & T. Stone (eds.), *Folk Psychology: The Theory of Mind Debate* (Oxford: Blackwell, 1995): 60–73. Reprinted in W. Lycan (ed.), *Mind and Cognition: An Anthology* (2nd edn, Oxford: Blackwell, 1998): 405–13.

Gordon, R. M. (1987). *The Structure of Emotions: Investigations in Cognitive Philosophy* (Cambridge: Cambridge University Press).

Gordon, R. M. (1992). "The Simulation Theory: Objections and Misconceptions." *Mind and Language* 7: 11–34.

Gordon, R. M. (1995a). "Simulation without Introspection or Inference from Me to You." In M. Davies & T. Stone (eds.), *Mental Simulation: Evaluations and Applications* (Oxford: Blackwell): 53–67.

Gordon, R. M. (1995b). "Sympathy, Simulation, and the Impartial Spectator." *Ethics* 105: 727–42. Reprinted in L. May, M. Friedman, & A. Clark (eds.), *Mind and Morals: Essays on Ethics and Cognitive Science* (Cambridge, MA: MIT Press, 1996): 165–80.

Gordon, R. M. (2000). "Sellars's Ryleans Revisited." Protosociology: An International Journal of Interdisciplinary Research 14: 102–14.

Gordon, R. M. (2021). "Simulation, Predictive Coding, and the Shared World." In M. Gilead & K. N. Ochsner (eds.), *The Neural Basis of Mentalizing* (Cham: Springer): 237–55.

Helmholtz, H. (1856). "LXIV. On the interaction of natural forces." The London, Edinburgh, and Dublin Philosophical Magazine and Journal of Science 11.75: 489–518.

Mill, J. S. (1869). *An Examination of Sir William Hamilton's Philosophy*. 6th edition. London.

Nagel, J. (2023). Sosa Prize lecture, Central Division meeting of the American Philosophical Association, February 24, 2023.

Perner, J., & Roessler, J. (2010). Teleology and causal reasoning in children's theory of mind. In J. Aguilar & A. Buckareff (eds.), *Causing Human Action: New Perspectives on the Causal Theory of Action* (Cambridge, MA: Bradford Book, The MIT Press): pp. 199–228.

Phillips, J., Buckwalter, W., Cushman, F., Friedman, O., Martin, A., Turri, J., Santos, L., & Knobe, J. (2021). "Knowledge before Belief." Behavioral and Brain Sciences 44: 1–37.

Schank, R. C., & Abelson, R. P. (1977). *Scripts, Plans, Goals and Understanding*. Hillsdale, NJ: Erlbaum.

Thalberg, I. (1964). "Emotion and Thought." American Philosophical Quarterly 1: 45–55.

Tomasello, M. (2019). *Becoming Human: A Theory of Ontogeny*. Harvard University Press.

Westra, E., & Nagel, J. (2021). Mindreading in conversation. Cognition 210: 104618. doi: 10.1016/j.cognition.2021.104618.

Williamson, T. (2000). Knowledge and its Limits (Oxford: Oxford University Press).

Yildirim, I., Siegel, M., & Tenenbaum, J. B. (2020). "Physical Object Representations for Perception and Cognition." In D. Poeppel, G. R. Mangun, & M. S. Gazzaniga (eds.), *The Cognitive Neurosciences* (6th edn, Cambridge, MA: MIT Press): 399–410.

6
Factive Mindreading in the Folk Psychology of Action

Carlotta Pavese

1. Introduction

A recent and growing literature suggests that, from an early age, humans possess the capacity to track factive mental states—the capacity for *factive mindreading*—and that this capacity plays an important role in our mindreading practices (Perner, 1993; Nagel, 2013, 2017; Phillips & Norby, 2019; Phillips et al., 2021; Westra & Nagel, 2021).[1] Infants can track perceptual knowledge in others from six months (Phillips et al. 2021). Preschool children learn factive epistemic vocabulary ("know," "knowledge") before they learn how to use non-factive epistemic vocabulary ("think," "thought," "belief") correctly (Nagel, 2013; Phillips et al., 2021). Successful attribution of factive mental states often emerges when children are aged three, well before successful attribution of mere belief states (Nagel, 2013; Phillips & Norby, 2019; Phillips et al., 2021).

Distinctive of factive mind reading is that it does not involve *decoupling*—the cognitive process whereby a subject represents the content of another agent's mental state in a way that conflicts with the content of the subject's primary and action-guiding representation of the world (Westra & Nagel, 2021: 2–3). Because factive mindreading does not require decoupling, it offers a less costly and all in all more efficient cognitive device for a variety of cognitive purposes, from predicting the behavior of others to finding the best communicative strategies in conversational settings (Phillips et al., 2021; Westra & Nagel, 2021).

Thus far, the discussion on factive mindreading has proceeded independently of the study of the *folk psychology of action*—of our capacity to track intentional and skilled actions. Yet the folk psychology of action has been studied extensively

---

[1] Indeed, recent work has made a persuasive case that primates are also capable of factive mind reading and that they employ it when predicting their mates' behavior (Horschler, Santos, & MacLean, 2019; Phillips et al., 2021; Williamson, Chapter 2 of this volume). There is also some evidence that some primates are capable of recognizing rational and goal-directed action (e.g., Povinelli et al., 1998; Wood et al., 2007; though see Tomasello, 2000 for a dissenting voice). On the assumption that nonhuman primates *can* recognize intentional action, it is an interesting question, though one that I will not be able to explore here, whether their recognizing intentional action involves factive mind reading.

in the last three decades: A huge amount of experimental work has been devoted to the question of how people track intentional action, specifically in connection with the concept of responsibility (e.g., Malle & Knobe, 1997; Knobe, 2003a, 2003b; Knobe & Burra, 2006; Nadelhoffer, 2004, 2005; Cova et al., 2012; Guglielmo, Monroe, & Malle, 2009, 2010). Some of this work has even focused on how people track skilled action (e.g., Malle & Knobe, 1997; Nadelhoffer, 2004, 2005). This literature suggests that adult human beings are quite proficient in tracking intentional and skilled behavior, which in turn suggests that this ability—which has been shown to be stable in different populations and interculturally robust (Knobe & Burra, 2006; Knobe, 2023)—is a core component of social cognition. Yet this research has not tackled the question of whether factive mind reading plays any role *vis-à-vis* our ability to track intentional and skilled action. Indeed, the role of factive mindreading in the folk psychology of action has thus far remained rather unexplored.

And yet the same considerations of expediency and efficiency that make factive mindreading a helpful cognitive device for predicting the behavior of others would presumably make it also an effective device for tracking intentional and skilled behavior. On this hypothesis, the easiness and reliability of factive mindreading would contribute to explaining the remarkable easiness and reliability with which we can track intentional and skilled action. Indeed, given how reliable and efficient we are at tracking intentional and skilled action, and given how pervasive factive mindreading seems to be in social cognition, it would be quite surprising if factive mindreading was found to play no role in the folk psychology of action.

Here is how the technical terms will be used henceforth. Let 'factive mindreading' refer to the ability to track factive mental states in ourselves and in others. A *factive mental state* is one that obtains only if its content is a true proposition. Clear examples of factive mental states are *understanding that, being aware that, seeing that, remembering that*, and *knowing that*. If every factive mental state involves knowledge (Williamson, 2000), then factive mindreading boils down to the ability to track knowledge. If not every factive mental state involves knowledge, then factive mindreading is a more general ability than the capacity for tracking knowledge. Let 'social cognition' refers to the way in which we process and use information in social contexts to predict our behavior and that of others. Let 'folk psychology' refer to the general ability that humans have to predict and understand others' behavior through mind reading (whether factive or not). Let 'folk psychology of action' refer to the specific ability to recognize and ascribe intentional and skilled action.

We are now in position to state my goals. This chapter aims to single out, to clarify, and to explore the following question: What role (if any) does factive mind reading play in the folk psychology of action? This question is part of the more general factive mindreading program—the exciting program in the theory of mind that aims at understanding the role of factive mind reading in folk psychology and in social cognition. A natural continuation of the factive mindreading program is to look at whether factive mind reading plays a role not only when it comes to predicting people's behavior but also when it comes to recognizing and ascribing intentional and skilled action. This is the sense in which I want to ask about the role of factive mindreading in the folk psychology of action. Of course, the study of factive mindreading is in its early stages; moreover, the evidence that I will overview is preliminary. My main aim in this chapter is to raise the central questions, to assess prima facie reasons for skepticism, to sketch the map of the terrain, and to individuate general issues that might prompt further investigation.

Here is the plan. Section 2 overviews knowledge-first approaches to the philosophy of action, which motivated some of the experimental work surveyed in this chapter. Section 3 discusses critically some recent empirical work that might be taken to suggest—erroneously I think—that people are not factive mind readers when ascribing intentional and skillful action. Section 4 overviews some experimental work about the role of know-how in the folk psychology of action and highlights its relevance for the question at hand; Section 5 overviews some experimental work that provides positive evidence for the role of propositional knowledge in the folk psychology of action. Section 6 identifies open questions for further investigation.

2. Knowledge-First Action Theory

The idea that factive mental states such as knowledge or awareness enter constitutively in a theory of intentional action has a rich history: It has roots in Aristotle, and it plays a starring role in the work of Elizabeth Anscombe (e.g., Anscombe, 1958; Hampshire, 1959; Gibbons, 2001; Thompson, 2011; Rodl, 2011; Pavese, 2018, 2020, 2021a, 2022; Kneer, 2021; Beddor & Pavese, 2022; Pavese & Beddor, 2023). This section overviews general trends in the literature on the role of knowledge and factive mental states in a theory of intentional action, including recent knowledge-first approaches to action theory (Gibbons, 2001; Pavese, 2013, 2016, 2018, 2020, 2021a, 2021b, 2022).

There are many different ways in which knowledge might enter into the theory of action. According to Anscombe (1958), practical knowledge enters as a requirement on intentional action—intentional action requires knowing what one is doing when doing it. All indicates that she understood practical knowledge in terms of propositional knowledge—as knowing *that something is the case* (Schwenkler, 2019; Pavese, 2022: Section 3 below). Many have followed Anscombe on this insight. Even those who have challenged the idea that a practical-knowledge condition applies to every instance of intentional action tend to retain *some* version of a practical-knowledge condition. For example, Setiya (2012) questions whether basic actions require practical knowledge but defends a version of a practical-knowledge condition for non-basic complex actions. Others argue that at least *self-awareness*, rather than knowledge, is necessary for intentional action (cf. Rodl, 2007), but they do understand self-awareness factively such that if one is self-aware that one is ϕ-ing, then one is ϕ-ing (cf. Schwenkler, 2019). Paul (2009) argues against a practical knowledge condition on habitual and automatic action but deems it plausible for deliberate conscious actions. Others respond that practical knowledge need not be consciously entertained at the time of the performance and yet might still play a role in explaining its intentionality (Setiya, 2008; Pavese, 2022).

Assuming that skilled action is always or typically intentional (Pavese, 2013, 2016, 2022; Pavese & Beddor, 2023), one might expect practical knowledge also to enter into a theory of skilled action. Consider Jackson Pollock's first 'drip' painting, *Free Form* (1946). According to an accredited reconstruction, Pollock began by painting an entire canvas red and then added black and white tangles and pools of paint by flinging and dripping diluted oil paint from a brush or stick. Suppose my 5 year-old niece, armed with a canvas, a brush, and white, black, and red oil colors, started dripping color on the canvas randomly and without following a plan. While it is, presumably, not impossible for my niece to drip oil on a canvas in such a way that the outcome turns out to look exactly like Pollock's *Free Form*, if she did manage to reproduce, by pure luck, the exact same colors and forms on a canvas, the difference between her so doing and Pollock's performance would be no less noteworthy. Indeed, even if their bodily movements turned out to be exactly the same, Pollock's execution would be skilled throughout; my niece's would instead be accidental, fortuitous, and unskilled. We would describe this difference by saying that while Pollock knew or was aware of what he was doing, my niece did not. Examples such as this motivate thinking that factive mental states such as practical knowledge ought to enter in a theory of skilled action too.

While many have recognized a role for practical knowledge in a theory of intentional or skilled action, a parallel debate on the nature of know-how has recognized a role for know-how to play in action theory too. Ryle (1949) argued that what distinguishes skilled and intentional action from unskilled unintentional action is whether the action manifests know-how. As an example, Ryle (1949) compared a clown who tumbles on purpose and whose tumbling is skilled, to a clumsy person who does not tumble on purpose and whose tumbling is not skilled. Several authors have followed Ryle on this point. Stanley and Williamson (2001: 442–3) claim that intentional actions are employments of know-how. Setiya (2012) argues that intentional action is guided by either knowing how to perform the action itself or knowing how to perform some other action that is a means to perform it. Gibbons (2001) argues that the concept of knowledge, rather than true beliefs, is required for intentional action, on the grounds, for example, that one cannot intentionally lose or win a fair lottery and that one cannot know how to win or lose a fair lottery. Indeed, this philosophical intuition that intentional action is closely connected to know-how or skills has been confirmed to be shared widely by non-philosophers too (Bengson, Moffett, & Wright, 2009). In a representative case, Irina, a novice figure skater, decides to try a complex jump called the salchow. Irina is seriously mistaken about how to perform a salchow. However, Irina also suffers from a severe neurological abnormality that often makes her perform actions that are different than those she thinks she is performing. By a fluke, whenever Irina attempts to do a salchow (in accordance with her misconceptions), her neurological condition causes her to perform the correct sequence of moves, so she ends up successfully performing a salchow. Intuitively, Irina does not skillfully or intentionally perform the salchow nor does she know how to perform it.

The connection between know-how and intentional action offers a new line of argument for the centrality of factive mental states in a theory of intentional and skilled action. On the basis of this insight, Pavese (2013, 2018, 2020, 2021a, 2021b, 2022) has developed a systematic knowledge-first account of intentional and skilled action. Start with standard action theory, according to which one intentionally Fs when one has a plan to F, where a plan to F is a knowledge state that specifies the means to F:

(Intentionality/knowledge): If s intentionally Fs, then there are some means $m_1, \ldots, m_n$ to F such that s knows that $m_1, \ldots, m_n$ are means for oneself to F.

Plausibly, moreover, intentional action employs (at least some degree of) relevant knowledge-how:

(Know-how/Intentionality): If s intentionally Fs, s employs (some degree of) knowledge how to F.

Suppose that (Intentionality/Knowledge) is true so that the intentionality of an action is to be explained at least in part in terms of propositional knowledge. Then by (Know-how/Intentionality) and (Intentionality/Knowledge), we get that if one intentionally Fs, one employs (some degree of) knowledge how to F and one has propositional knowledge of some means to F:

(Know-how, Intentionality, Knowledge): If s intentionally Fs, s employs (some degree of) knowledge how to F and for some means $m_1, \ldots, m_n$, s knows that means $m_1, \ldots, m_n$ are means for oneself to F.

As Pavese (2020) points out, a picture of know-how as involving propositional knowledge provides the best explanation for why (Know-How, Intentionality,

Knowledge) should hold. According to this explanation, (Know-How, Intentionality, Knowledge) is true not just because of a coincidental aligning of propositional knowledge and know-how in intentional action. Rather, its truth is grounded in the very nature of know-how, as involving propositional knowledge of the means of performing an action. To the objection that a know-how condition on intentional action might be too demanding (cf. Knobe, 2003b; Nadelhoffer, 2004, 2005), a possible response is that some degree of know-how might be all that is required for intentional action (Pavese & Beddor, 2023; Pavese & Henne, 2023) and degrees of know-how can be reduced to propositional knowledge too (see Pavese, 2017 for discussion). Qualitative gradability is about the quality of one's known answers to the practical question of how to perform the relevant task; quantitative gradability is about whether one knows part or all of that practical answer, where parts of practical answers are themselves propositions.

On this knowledge-first account of action, intentional action is itself *knowledgeable*. Here is yet another theoretical argument for thinking that know-how is key to understanding intentional action. Intentional actions are *creditable* to their agents. If a politician's policy ends up benefiting the environment but that outcome was not sought out and is entirely coincidental, we would not say that the politician is to be credited for benefiting the environment. Indeed, intentionality seems a necessary condition on creditability. On the other hand, actions manifesting know-how are *paradigmatically* creditable to their agents (cf., e.g., Sosa 2007). Consider a sprinter who scores a record time unhelped by luck or the wind, just by virtue of their know-how. In this case, the athlete should be credited for that success. On the other hand, if the success was due to luck or to an excessively strong wind, the record should not be awarded to them. If intentional action is an employment of (some degree of) know-how—we would have explained why intentional actions are creditable to their agents: in virtue of their being the employment of (some degree of) know-how.

Similar considerations apply from intentional action to skilled action, given the tight relation between skills and know-how. The idea that skills are closely connected to know-how has considerable pre-theoretic appeal. Ordinary speakers seem to use the terms, "know-how" and "skills," interchangeably, as do many philosophers and scientists (Ryle, 1949; Heider, 1958; Dreyfus, 2008; Setiya, 2012; Pavese, 2016; Cath, 2020). Skills are routinely ascribed by ascriptions of know-how even in those languages that lack a dedicated word for skills, such as Italian and French. Indeed, it sounds incoherent to affirm that someone is skilled at ϕ-ing while denying that they know how to ϕ. For example, it is weird to affirm that Mary is a skilled swimmer but she does not know how to swim or that Mark does not know how to make risotto but is, nonetheless, skilled at it.

This plethora of considerations provide some evidence that skills entail knowhow. Does know-how entail skills? This is more controversial. Consider Mark, a bumbling chef. Admittedly, it seems coherent to say "Mark knows how to make risotto, but I would not say he is *skilled* at it." However, this can be explained on the assumption that gradable adjectives such as "skilled" require that their argument exceed a certain threshold (Pavese, 2016). While one may know how to ϕ without counting as skilled, it is, nonetheless, true that knowing how to ϕ *sufficiently well* entails being skilled at ϕ-ing. Note that it *does* seem incoherent to say "Mark knows how to make risotto *very well*, but I would not say he is skilled at it."

We have thus found no good reason to abandon the idea that skills are a species of know-how. Indeed, plausibly, skills are know-how—as Ryle (1949) first alleged—and they differ from some abilities, such as instincts, in that they are learned and from yet other abilities, such as habits, in that they are acquired through deliberate practice (Pavese, forthcoming). Suppose that S skillfully ϕs. Presumably, that means that S's success in ϕ-ing is guided by S's skill at ϕ-ing. If skills are a species of know-how, it also follows that S's ϕ-ing is guided by S's knowledge of how to ϕ. If so, then there is room for a view on which skilled action is guided by a factive mental state about the means for acting.

To sum up, in several current strands in action theory, people have recognized a variety of roles for factive mental states to play in a theory of intentional and skilled action. Some take practical knowledge to be a factive mental state central to a theory of intention in action and of intentional action. Knowledge-first accounts of intentional action link intentional action with know-how and know-how with propositional knowledge about the means. Finally, given the link between skills and know-how, factive mental states might have a role to play in a theory of skills and skilled action too.

The discussion in this section has been limited to *philosophical theories of skilled and intentional action*. However, it would be surprising if such theories dramatically diverged from the *folk psychology of action*. After all, such philosophical theories are routinely tested against judgments that are supposed to be widely shared or even commonsensical. So an emerging knowledge-first landscape in the theory of action offers some initial motivations to investigate the question whether factive mind reading plays a role in the folk psychology of action too.

That said, it is also important to notice that although knowledge-first approaches to the theory of action encourage thinking that we are factive mind readers when it comes to ascribing intentional and skilled action, a view according to which we are factive mind readers in the folk psychology of action does *not* commit one to a knowledge-first approach to the theory of action. For it might be that the capacity to ascribe factive mental states plays a role in our capacity to track intentional action in a variety of different contexts, even though it does not play such a role in *every* context. Moreover, one ought not rule out a priori the possibility that factive mental states other than knowledge—such as awareness—play a larger role in folk psychology than knowledge itself.

With these complexities in mind, let us begin by looking at some preliminary reasons for doubting a substantive role for factive mind reading in the folk psychology of action.

3. Reasons for Skepticism

In recent experimental work, Vekony, Mele, and Rose (2021) have tested whether people's judgments of intentional and skilled action require practical knowledge in Anscombe's sense. The authors' primary intent is to put pressure on the *philosophical* theory of intentional action on which practical knowledge is a necessary condition for intentional action. However, these results are also relevant to whether factive mind reading plays a role in the folk psychology of action, since they concern people's judgments about intentional action and whether these judgements go together with judgments of practical knowledge and awareness—both plausibly factive mental states. It is worth looking at the experiments in some detail, since these are the only published experimental studies that might seem to answer the main question of this chapter negatively.

Vekony, Mele, and Rose (2021) focus on two *distinct* cases—one concerning skilled (and non-automatic, controlled action) and the other concerning habitual (automatic) action. In the first experiment, they assigned vignettes such as:

> **Basketball:** Andy is a 92% free-throw shooter. One evening, he is at the gym practicing his free throws. He lines up and takes the shot. But just as the ball leaves his hands, lightning strikes the building. The power goes out and it is pitch black. There is also a loud clap of thunder. Due to this, Andy cannot see or even hear whether he made the shot. He is completely unaware of whether he sank the shot. But he did, in fact, sink the shot.

Beneath the scenario, on the same page, participants responded to three test statements (presented in random order):

> When Andy was sinking the shot, he knew that he was sinking it. (Knowledge)
>
> While Andy was sinking the shot, he was aware of sinking the shot. (Awareness)
>
> Andy intentionally sank the shot. (Intentionality)

Vekony, Mele, and Rose (2021) found that in cases involving skilled action, participants were overwhelmingly inclined to say that Andy intentionally sank the shot, but they were considerably less inclined to say that Andy knew or was aware that he was sinking the shot.[2]

---

[2] As a referee observes, it would be interesting to see whether these results would replicate if *Basketball* was adjusted slightly so that the lights went out *just before* the ball was released, rather than just after. In this circumstance it is much less clear that the shot is intentional.

This experiment nicely details ordinary intuitions about whether intentional action ϕ requires knowledge or awareness that one is ϕ-ing. Does this experiment show that accurately recognizing intentional action does not require people to recognize factive mental states in others? Here is an explanation of what is going on, which is compatible with the factive mind-reading hypothesis. It might be that although the basketball player is judged not to know *that he is sinking the basket*, he is judged to know *some other propositions* about his performance. Vekony, Mele, and Rose's (2021) experiment was not devised to check whether the basketball player has been judged to act intentionally *because* he is judged to know that he is performing some action as a means of sinking the basket.

Let me develop this idea a bit further. Practical knowledge is *knowledge of what one is doing when ϕ-ing*; but what one is doing need not be *that one is succeeding at ϕ-ing*. Philosophers thinking about practical knowledge have long recognized that the most plausible formulation of the practical-knowledge condition is not one on which intentionally ϕ-ing requires knowing that *one is ϕ-ing*. Rather, the practical-knowledge requirement is best thought of as the requirement that intentionally ϕ-ing requires knowing *that one is taking certain means in order to ϕ*. This weakening of the practical-knowledge condition is required to deal with classical counterexamples, such as Davidson's (1971) carbon copier case, in which the subject is not sure that they will succeed at producing ten carbon copies, and yet seems to do so intentionally (Pavese, 2021b, 2022). Though the carbon copier does not know that they are succeeding in producing the ten carbon copies, they *do* know what means they are taking to that effect.³

For all we know from Vekony, Mele, and Rose's (2021) first experiment, it might very well be that subjects judge the basketball player to be sinking the basket intentionally only because they judge him to know that, for example, he is taking the means available to him in order to sink the basket—that is, is taking position, positioning his arms and hands in the right way, directing his attention at the basket, and taking a shot. Thus, it is compatible with Vekony, Mele, and Rose's (2021) first experiment that the basketball player is represented as being aware of these means for taking the shot, despite the blackout. So, since Vekony, Mele, and Rose's (2021) first experiment only targets a *particular* construal of the practical-knowledge condition, it should not be taken as evidence that factive mind reading does not play a role in the folk psychology of action.

Similar considerations hold for Vekony, Mele, and Rose's (2021) second experiment, which looks at habitual actions. They used the following vignette:

---

³ As a referee reminds me, even my preferred weaker formulation according to which intentionally ϕ-ing requires knowing that one is taking certain means in order to ϕ might need to be weakened further to deal with Paul's (2009) 'distracted driver' cases. In Pavese (2022), I suggest all one needs for intentionally ϕ-ing is *that one be in position to know that one is taking the means for ϕ-ing*.

Door: Suzy locks her door every morning as she leaves for work. On her way out to work one morning, she locks the door. But because she is preoccupied with thoughts about her day, she is completely unaware of doing so. She gets to her car, pauses, and wonders whether she locked the door. Because she was unaware of locking it, she didn't even remember locking it. So she walks back from her car to check whether she locked the door.

And they asked three questions (presented in random order):

When Suzy was locking her door, she knew that she was locking it. (Knowledge)
While Suzy was locking her door, she was aware of locking it. (Awareness)
Suzy intentionally locked her door. (Intentionality)

They found that a majority of participants say that Suzy intentionally locked her door, despite the fact that Suzy failed to satisfy the knowledge and awareness conditions regarding that action. They conclude that, on the ordinary concept of intentional action, neither knowledge nor awareness is required for intentional action.

Like the first, this second experiment only looks at whether knowledge or awareness *that one is ϕ-ing* is judged to be necessary for ascriptions of intentionally ϕ-ing. So this result is compatible with the hypothesis that subjects would be inclined to ascribe some *other* piece of knowledge to Susy. For example, it is rather plausible that they would be inclined to credit Susy with, for example, knowledge of where to find her keys. Thus, the considerations developed above about the first experiment apply equally to this second experiment.

In conclusion, Vekony, Mele, and Rose's (2021) experimental findings are an important contribution to how to understand the knowledge requirement on the ordinary concept of intentional action. But while they might also be taken to suggest that factive mind reading does not play a role in the folk psychology of action—intentional, skilled, or habitual—this conclusion would be too hasty. These findings are overall compatible with factive mind reading entering in the folk psychology of action.

4. Kraemer's Puzzle

This section discusses in particular a puzzle about ascriptions of intentional action and recent experimental work I have conducted, jointly with Paul Henne, which suggests that the puzzle arises because people's ascriptions of intentional action are affected by their ability to recognize and ascribe know-how (Pavese & Henne, 2023). At the end of the section, I speculate on how our results might also bear on the question of the role of factive mental states in our ability to recognize and ascribe intentional action.

Suppose Brown will win a game if he throws a six with an ordinary, fair dice. Brown rolls a six, so he wins the game. We are more prone to agree with 2 than with 1:

1. Brown intentionally rolled a six.
2. Brown intentionally won the game.

Rolling a six, however, is as likely as winning the game, so this pattern of judgments is puzzling. Specifically, it seems that agents bring about ends (e.g. winning the game) intentionally but also that they do not bring about the means that brought about the ends (e.g. rolling a six) intentionally, even though bringing about the ends and bringing about the means are equally likely. This contrast in judgments was first raised by Butler (1978) and sharpened by Kraemer (1978). Call it the *Kraemer effect* and the puzzle it raises as *Kraemer's puzzle*.

The Kraemer effect is mysterious: Why is it that people judge that agents bring about ends intentionally but they do not bring about the means that brought about those ends intentionally, even though bringing about the ends and bringing about the means is are equally likely? While some philosophers had discussed this puzzle before (e.g., Nadelhoffer, 2004, 2005; Cova, Dupoux, & Jacob, 2012), extant accounts have fallen short of a systematic discussion. Pavese and Henne (2023) have explored Kraemer's effect more systematically in order to see whether it could be explained by a related concomitant effect concerning judgments about know-how. In other words, they conjectured that what gave rise to Kraemer's effect was a perceived difference as to the degree at which the agent knew how to perform the means versus that of the ends.

To get the general motivating idea, consider the game example at the outset. In this scenario, we judge that there *is* a reliable way of performing the ends such that the agent knows: throwing a six is a perfectly reliable way of winning the game, and Brown knows that. By contrast, we do not judge that there is a reliable way of performing the means in these cases that the agent knows—in the fair dice game, there is just no reliable way such that Brown knows the way to throw a six. Thus, it is plausible that we judge that Brown knows how to win to a higher degree than he knows how to throw a six. As such, there is an apparent difference in the degree at which the agents know how to perform the ends and how to perform the means. We conjecture that this observation could explain the Kraemer effect; people's intentionality judgments vary between ends and means because of a more fundamental difference in the extent to which they represent the agents as knowing how to perform the ends and how to perform the means.

We call this the *Know-How Hypothesis*. The Know-How Hypothesis uniquely predicts that in the scenarios where there is the Kraemer effect, there should also be a *corresponding* effect for know-how ascriptions. For instance, it predicts that people should agree more with statement 4 than with statement 3:

3. Brown knows how to throw a six.
4. Brown knows how to win the dice game.

In several experiments, we found evidence for the Know-How Hypothesis (All materials, data, and analysis code for all experiments in this manuscript are available at https://osf.io/bj4np/.) Let me describe two experiments in particular. In Experiment 1, we asked the participants to read vignettes such as the following:

Vignette 1
Jane is a contestant on a game show. In the game, Jane is given the opportunity to push a button that will randomly open exactly one of the ten doors in front of her.

A brand-new car is behind one of the ten doors. If Jane pushes the button and the door with the brand-new car behind it opens, then she will win the car.

Jane has no idea which door will open if she pushes the button. But she does know that the brand-new car is behind door three. And Jane really wants to win that car. Hoping to win the car, Jane pushes the button. To her great satisfaction, door three opens, and Jane wins the brand-new car.

Before each statement, we asked participants "To what extent do you agree with the following statement about the passage you just read?" Participants who received the game show vignette responded to the following:

Jane knows how to win the brand-new car.
Jane knows how to open door three.
Jane intentionally won the brand-new car.
Jane intentionally opened door three.

For each question, we asked participants for their level of agreement with each statement on a −50–50 scale [−50 = strongly disagree, 0 = neutral, 50 = strongly agree].

We found that just as people are more inclined to judge that agents brought about the ends intentionally than the means, people also are more inclined to judge that agents know how to bring about the ends more than the means. That is, we conceptually replicated the Kraemer effect in a variety of non-moral scenarios (Nadelhoffer, 2004, 2005), and we found a new effect predicted by our new hypothesis: the Know-How effect. We also found that people's intentionality judgments that give rise to the Kraemer effect are fully mediated by people's know-how judgments.

Encouraged by these results, we planned more experiments to test the Know-How Hypothesis further. Here is a particularly significant one. The Know-How

Hypothesis holds that people's know-how judgments explain the Kraemer effect. One might think that perhaps there is another explanation of the effect that is just as plausible. Perhaps people judge that there is a reliable way for the agent to bring about the ends but no reliable way to bring about the means and that this difference in judgments independently explains both the know-how effect and the Kraemer effect. This alternative hypothesis predicts that if there is a reliable way to perform both the ends and the means, then there should be neither a know-how effect nor a Kraemer effect. The Know-How Hypothesis instead predicts that these effects should persist independently of the presence of a reliable way to perform the ends and the means when there is a difference in know-how.

To test these predictions, we used a modified version of the game show vignette from Experiment 1. In the modified vignette, there is a reliable way to perform the ends and there is a reliable way to perform the means: the agent can win the brand-new car by opening door three, and they can open door three by pushing the button, which is fixed. However, the agent has no idea how to open door three, since they do not know that the button is fixed. In this setting, the Know-How Hypothesis predicts both the know-how effect and the Kraemer effect. By contrast, the Common Cause Hypothesis predicts that both the Kraemer effect and the know-how effect would disappear when there is no difference in reliable ways to execute means and ends.

Again, we found a know-how effect and a Kraemer effect, which replicated our findings from Experiment 1. The Know-How Hypothesis predicted these results because, in this view, it is not the presence or absence of reliable ways to perform the means and the ends that is responsible for the know-how effect or the Kraemer effect. Rather, according to this view, it is the difference in know-how for the ends and the means (i.e., a know-how effect) that is responsible for a Kraemer effect. Critically, these results are incompatible with the Alternative Hypothesis, which predicts no know-how effect and no Kraemer effect when there is a reliable way for the agent to perform both the ends and the means. Pavese and Henne (2023) go on to replicate these results also for morally loaded versions of Kraemer's puzzle (Experiment 5 and Experiment 6).

The relevance of these findings for the topic of this chapter should be clear, given the discussion in Section 2, but it is, nonetheless, worth elaborating. To begin with, if the ordinary concept of know-how requires that of propositional knowledge, then these findings suggest that knowledge representation plays a role in folk ascribing intentional action, for they suggest that know-how representation is central to the ordinary practice of ascribing intentional action. Secondly, though Pavese and Henne (2023: 10–11) only briefly discuss this further complexity, their results are actually hard to explain on any view on which our concept of know-how is independent of propositional knowledge. Consider, for example, a view on which know-how is conceived as a mere ability of sort—understood as a reliable disposition to success, not further grounded in any factive mental state. In Vignette 1, subjects are presented as having the same ability to perform both means and ends, since means and ends are presented as just as likely. So, this view does not seem equipped to explain the know-how effect that we have found, since, in this case, the subjects are as disposed to succeed in performing the ends as they are in performing the means. Moreover, notice that in Experiment 3, manipulating the know-how *effectively* amounted to manipulating the subject's factive mental state—here Jane is presented as having no idea of how to open door three, so lacking awareness of how to open door three.

This observation goes in the direction of supporting the thought that the ordinary concept of know-how is at least partly intellectualistic—something that others have argued in recent literature as well (Gonnerman et al., 2018, 2021). So, these findings are not only compatible with the hypothesis that factive mental states play a role in explaining Kraemer's puzzle—on a closer look, they are *suggestive* of such a role.

5. Epistemic Luck and the Ordinary Concepts of Know-How and Intentional Action

Though our findings on Kraemer's puzzle are suggestive of a role for factive mental states in our capacity to track intentional action, they cannot be regarded as conclusively showing that *knowledge* specifically plays such a role. After all, in these experiments, we have not controlled for the possible difference between knowledge and other factive mental states such as awareness or for the possible difference between knowledge and mixed mental states such as true belief or justified true belief. This section discusses experimental findings on the ordinary concepts of know-how and of intentional action that provide evidence specifically for the role of knowledge representation in the folk psychology of action.

One respect in which propositional knowledge might be thought to differ from other factive mental states—such as awareness—or from mixed factive states—such as true belief—is that the former but not the latter would be defeated in Gettier scenarios and more generally in cases involving 'veritic epistemic luck' (Pritchard, 2005). Indeed, some recent experimental work shows that the folk concept of knowledge is sensitive to Gettierization (Nagel, San Juan, & Mar, 2013; Turri, 2013; Machery et al., 2017). These findings open up a novel avenue for research on factive mind reading. If the ordinary concept of knowledge is sensitive to Gettierization and to veritic epistemic luck, one way to ascertain whether knowledge representation plays a role in the folk psychology of action is to test whether epistemic luck also undermines the ordinary concept of intentional action.

This question can be investigated directly by looking at whether epistemic luck undermines people's inclination to ascribe intentional action. It can also be investigated *indirectly* by looking at whether epistemic luck undermines people's inclination to ascribe some *related* mental state concept that is plausibly related to that of intentional action. As we have seen in Section 2, the concept of know-how seems relevant to the concept of intentional action. Many philosophers and cognitive scientists have argued independently that the concept of intentional action is fundamentally related to the concept of *skills* (e.g., Ryle, 1949; Mele & Moser, 1994; Malle & Knobe, 1997; Malle, 2003; Guglielmo, Monroe, & Malle, 2009; Guglielmo & Malle, 2010; Setiya, 2012; Pavese, 2013, 2016; Cath, 2015; Pavese & Beddor, 2023). Moreover, it is commonly assumed that one is skilled at an action only if one knows how to perform it: skill requires know-how (e.g., Ryle, 1949; Setiya, 2012; Cath, 2015; Pavese, 2016). On this account, intentional action is fundamentally related to know-how and skills.

Thus, we might ask whether epistemic luck undermines people's inclination to ascribe know-how. If we found evidence for this claim, we would have some *indirect* evidence that epistemic luck undermines people's inclination to ascribe intentional action too. Let us begin to explore this indirect path.

In epistemology, it is often claimed that the folk concept of know-how is compatible with epistemic luck (e.g., Poston, 2009; Cath, 2011; Carter & Pritchard, 2015). One source of evidence for this claim are cases such as the following, adapted from Cath (2011, 2015):

Lucky Lightbulb: Charlie wants to change a lightbulb. Being unversed in such matters, he takes down a manual of everyday household tasks, looks up the instructions for lightbulb-changing, and proceeds to follow them. It turns out that the author of the manual was a prankster who riddled the book with inaccurate instructions. But by a fluke, when the instruction manual went to the printers, a correct set of lightbulb-changing instructions was substituted at the last minute, due to a misprint.

There is reason to question whether this case and other examples that have been proposed are genuine Gettier cases (cf. Pavese & Beddor, 2023). Indeed, in the following, I am going to suggest that this example and other examples that have been produced in the literature do not even have the same *structure* as Gettier's original cases.

In prototypical Gettier cases, the agent's belief is *unsafe*—that is, there is a nearby circumstance in which the agent forms *the very same belief* on similar grounds, but their belief is false. For example, consider the following variant of one of Gettier's (1963) examples:

Occupational Hazard: Suppose that Smith and Jones have applied for a certain job. And suppose that Smith has strong evidence for the following conjunctive proposition:

(d) Jones is the man who will get the job, and Jones has ten coins in his pocket.

Smith's evidence for (d) might be that the president of the company assured him that Jones would in the end be selected, and that he, Smith, had counted the coins in Jones's pocket ten minutes ago. Proposition (d) entails:

(e) The man who will get the job has ten coins in his pocket.

Let us suppose that Smith sees the entailment from (d) to (e), and accepts (e) on the grounds of (d), for which he has strong evidence. In this case, Smith is clearly justified in believing that (e) is true. But imagine, further, that unknown to Smith, he himself, not Jones, will get the job. And also, unknown to Smith, he himself has ten coins in his pocket. Proposition (e) is then true, though proposition (d), from which Smith inferred (e), is false. It is equally clear that Smith does not know (e).

In this example, there is a nearby world where either Smith did not get the job or Smith did not have ten coins in his pocket. In that world, Smith would have believed the *same* proposition (e), but his belief would have been false. So Smith's belief is unsafe. Indeed, the lack of safety appears to be the general mark of veritic epistemic luck (Sosa, 1999; Williamson, 2000; Pritchard, 2005; Beddor & Pavese, 2020).

By contrast, in **Lucky Lightbulb**, it is less clear that Charlie's belief is unsafe. In the nearby world where the instruction manual is free from misprints, Charlie would have formed a *very different belief* about how to change a lightbulb, since he would have come to believe an altogether different set of instructions. So there is no nearby world where he holds the very same belief falsely. Thus, **Lucky Lightbulb** does not even have the same structure as those of typical Gettier cases, since the main protagonist appears to have a safe belief.

Some might protest that safety principles should not hold fixed the content of the relevant belief, on pain of making all beliefs in necessary propositions trivially safe (Pritchard, 2012). Suppose I believe that that is a barn, where 'that' refers to a barn within sight. The content of my belief is necessarily true. So I could not have had the same belief falsely. And yet, intuitively, I might fall short of knowing that that is a barn. So a fix is needed for the standard formulation of a safety condition on knowledge and any such fix might extend to **Lucky Lightbulb**. On this ground, one might object that, on the right formulation of the safety principle, Charlie's belief in **Lucky Lightbulb** will come out unsafe after all.

However, this observation is simply incorrect. To see this, consider a prominent strategy that has been proposed for dealing with the problem of trivializing safety for necessary propositions. Pritchard (2012) proposes that a perceptually based belief B qualifies as safe if and only if any belief B' which is formed in response to the *same perceptual stimuli* would have been true. This formulation of safety deals with many cases of necessary but empirically formed beliefs, and it provides a desirable restriction on the relevant counterpart beliefs. It seems relevant to cases such as **Lucky Lightbulb** too, where the belief is formed on the basis of perception (as well as on the basis of reading skills). Notice, however, that if we apply this corrected definition of safety to **Lucky Lightbulb**, we still get that Charlie's belief is not unsafe. After all, if Charlie had received the manual with the misprint, he would have been in a different perceptual state, since he would have been reading a very different set of instructions. So, even by the lights of a formulation of safety for perceptual belief that does not run afoul of the problem of necessary propositions, Charlie's belief turns out to be safe.

Many putative examples of Gettiered know-how that the literature on know-how has produced are, just like **Lucky Lightbulb** and for the same reasons, actually cases of safe beliefs. Consider, for example, this example put forward by Stanley and Williamson (2001: 435) as an example of a Gettier case for know-how:

> there are indeed Gettier cases for know-how. Bob wants to learn how to fly in a flight simulator. He is instructed by Henry. Unknown to Bob, Henry is a malicious imposter who has inserted a randomizing device in the simulator's controls and intends to give all kinds of incorrect advice. Fortunately, by sheer chance the randomizing device causes exactly the same results in the simulator as would have occurred without it, and by incompetence Henry gives exactly the same advice as a proper instructor would have done. Bob passes the course with flying colors. He has still not flown a real plane. Bob has a justified true belief about how to fly.

Just as in **Lucky Lightbulb**, Bob's justified true belief about how to fly *is* safe—had the randomizing device provided Henry with different advice to give Bob, Bob would indeed have a false belief about how to fly, but it would not have been the same belief as the one that Bob turned out to have. That belief that Bob does have would have been true in that counterfactual circumstance too.

So several widely discussed counterexamples to the hypothesis that know-how can be Gettiered do not resemble paradigmatic Gettier cases closely enough, in that they are not cases of unsafe beliefs. The same holds for Carter & Pritchard (2015)'s variant of **Lucky Lightbulb**—originally designed to resemble the fake barns case more closely. On their variant, Charlie reads a manual that contains no misprints, but he could have easily received a phony manual with incorrect instructions. Here too, the earlier diagnosis applies: Had he received the phony manual, he would have held a false belief, but the content of the belief would have been importantly different.

Indeed, in this particular case, this diagnosis has received (unintended) empirical confirmation. Carter, Pritchard, and Shepherd (2019) have conducted an experimental study on the Know-How Question, with the goal of assessing

Intellectualism about Know-How—the view that knowing how to perform some task ϕ requires or consists in propositional knowledge about how to ϕ (Stanley and Williamson, 2001; Pavese, 2017, 2018). In particular, Carter, Pritchard, and Shepherd used the following vignette:

> **Lucky Manual:** Charlie needs to learn how to change a lightbulb, and so he goes to the 'how-to' section in his local library. He finds a shelf full of identical-looking books titled *Home Repair*. In each of these books are step-by-step instructions on the way to change a lightbulb—we'll call the way the book describes the way 'w'. Unbeknownst to Charlie, all the copies of *Home Repair* on the shelf are fakes, except for one. Pranksters have placed these copies there, and these fake copies contain mistaken step-by-step instructions on the way to change a lightbulb. Since Charlie does not know this, he reaches up and grabs the copy of *Home Repair* nearest to him. By sheer luck, he selects the only copy in the entire library that contains genuine and reliable step-by-step instructions for changing a lightbulb, and he reads the correct step-by-step instructions on the way to change a lightbulb. Had Charlie picked up any of the other guides—which he so easily could have—he would have believed the mistaken instructions were correct.

Carter, Pritchard, and Shepherd (2019) found that people tend to agree with the claim that Charlie knows how to change a lightbulb and take these results to be evidence that people attribute know-how in cases of epistemic luck.[4] However, there is reason to question Carter, Pritchard, and Shepherd's diagnosis. They meant their vignette as a case of *environmental luck*—the sort of luck present in fake barn cases (Pritchard, 2005). However, the extant experimental results on fake barns have been mixed, which suggests a greater willingness to ascribe knowledge in fake barn cases than in paradigmatic Gettier cases or in lottery cases. Moreover, Carter, Pritchard, and Shepherd's own results call into question whether epistemic luck is really present in **Lucky Manual**: they found that participants without philosophical training generally agreed with the claim that Charlie knows *that* way w is a way of changing a lightbulb—which suggests that people are willing to attribute *both* know-how and knowledge-that in this scenario. So, all in all, it is far from clear that **Lucky Manual** is an authentic case of epistemic luck.

So, in conclusion: Cath's original counterexample to the claim that know-how is not Gettierizable (**Lucky Lightbulb**) is questionable, since it does not have the same structure as Gettier's original cases—indeed, it does not even have the same modal profile as Gettier cases. The same is true for other putative counterexamples as well as for Carter, Pritchard, and Shepherd's variant. Indeed, Carter, Pritchard, and Shepherd's own experimental findings encourage this diagnosis.

---

[4] This line of argument has been pushed by Cath (2015).

It is now time to look at some positive evidence that the ordinary concept of know-how is sensitive to epistemic luck. Pavese, Henne, and Beddor (forthcoming) have conducted experimental work on the role of epistemic luck on know-how that differs from these recent works in that they focused on a variety of uncontroversial cases of epistemic luck which are also exact variants of Gettier's original cases, as well as in Dharmottara's desert traveler case, Russell's stopped clock case, in addition to lottery cases. In all of these cases, one of Pavese, Henne, and Beddor's (forthcoming) goals was to test whether this sort of epistemic luck undermines people's tendency to ascribe know-how. All of the vignettes they used feature someone acting on the basis of a belief that they have about how to perform an action. In the lucky condition, the agent's belief is Gettiered. In the control condition, a subject's belief is not Gettiered. In each condition, they asked participants the extent to which they agreed that the agent knows-that and knows-how.

For example, in the first study, they used two vignettes for condition (lucky/control). In the lucky condition, the vignette was:

Lucky: Alvin works at a barn supply company. Ed and Susan, Alvin's co-workers, are up for a promotion to supervisor. Kate, a typically trustworthy friend, tells Alvin that Ed got the promotion. Alvin also seems to remember that Ed has a personal email address: barns678@yahoo.com.

Alvin wants to congratulate the person who got the promotion. He believes that Ed got the promotion. So, he also comes to believe that the person who got the promotion has the email address: barns678@yahoo.com. So, Alvin writes a concise congratulatory email, addresses it to "Our New Supervisor," and then sends the email to barns678@yahoo.com, thinking that he is congratulating Ed.

It turns out that Alvin was wrong twice over. Susan had actually got the promotion. And Susan, not Ed, had the email address barns678@yahoo.com. As a result, Susan received Alvin's email.

Alvin's belief that sending an email to the email address barns678@yahoo.com is a means to send it to the person who got the promotion is Gettiered—it is true and justified but falls short of knowledge. Indeed, this vignette structurally matches Gettier's original coins in the pocket case. Interestingly, Pavese et al. (2023) found that participants who read about the agent in the control condition agreed to a greater extent that the agent knows-how ($M = 39.96$, $SD = 15.75$, $n = 237$) than participants in the lucky condition ($M = 3.78$, $SD = 35.36$, $n = 241$) ($b = 36.14$, $SE = 2.47$, $t = 14.58$, $p < .001$, CI_b [31.28, 41.01], $d = 1.33$).

As another example, in a third study, they tested the following vignette, which matches structurally Dharmottara's (770 CE: D:4429, 9a2–3) desert mirage case. In Dharmottara's desert mirage case, a desert traveler thinks that there is water upon seeing a mirage from far away, and when they reach the spot, there is actually water under a rock. They investigated a modified version of Dharmottara's case, where the traveler performs an action (leading a group to a location) based on their Gettiered belief. Here, they replicated the results of the first experiment: Participants who read about the agent in the control condition agreed to a greater extent that the agent knows that ($M = 9.27$, $SD = 27.63$, $n = 76$) than participants in the lucky condition ($M = -26.32$, $SD = 25.07$, $n = 83$) ($t(151.79) = 8.48, p < .001$, $d = 1.38$, CI [1.02, 1.73]). Participants who read about the agent in the control condition agreed to a greater extent that the agent knows how ($M = 18.11$, $SD = 24.85$, $n = 76$) than participants in the lucky condition ($M = -19.43$, $SD = 25.79$, $n = 83$) ($t(156.58) = 9.34, p < .001, d = 1.49$, CI [1.14, 1.85]).

In each case, Pavese, Henne, and Beddor (forthcoming) found that epistemic luck undermines people's tendency to ascribe know-how, which suggests that the folk concept of know-how *is* Gettierizable. These results fit nicely with the idea, voiced by others too (cf. Bengson, Moffett, & Wright, 2009; Gonnerman et al., 2018), that the folk concept of know-how is at least partly 'intellectualistic'—it is at least related to the concept of propositional knowledge, since this position *predicts* an effect of epistemic luck on ordinary ascriptions of know-how. These findings speak against those who have argued that people are purely anti-intellectualists with respect to know-how (cf. Harmon & Horne, 2016). They also strongly suggest that our ability to recognize and ascribe know-how requires knowledge representation. Why else would a distinctively epistemic kind of luck undermine people's ability to ascribe know-how?

Now, suppose the ordinary concept of know-how is sensitive to epistemic luck. Since the ordinary concept of intentional action is closely related to that of know-how, we should expect the ordinary concept of intentional action to be sensitive to know-how too. However, this conclusion has often been rejected without much argument. For example, Cath (2015) argues that the ordinary concept of know-how cannot require that of knowledge, since the ordinary concept of know-how goes together with the ordinary concept of intentional action and the latter is independent of the concept of knowledge.

Is it true, though, that the presence of epistemic luck is compatible with people's willingness to ascribe intentional action? In order to address this issue, in the same studies, Pavese, Henne, and Beddor (forthcoming) simultaneously checked for whether epistemic luck affected both people's willingness to agree with a know-how ascription and their willingness to agree with an intentional action ascription. For example, in Study 1 (Lucky) above, they asked whether Alvin intentionally sent the email to the person who got the promotion. Here is what they found: Participants who read about the agent in the control condition agreed to a greater extent that the agent intentionally performed the action ($M = 43.06$, $SD = 15.14, n = 237$) than participants in the lucky condition ($M = -9.82, SD = 37.72$, $n = 241$) ($b = 52.77, SE = 2.60, t = 20.24, p <.001, CI_b$ [47.66, 57.89], $d = 1.85$). Similarly, for Study 3, they asked whether the **traveler** intentionally brought the group to water. Here is what they found: Participants who read about the agent in the control condition agreed to a greater extent that the agent intentionally performed the action ($M = 28.30$, $SD = 25.54$, $n = 76$) than participants in the lucky condition ($M = -10.78$, $SD = 35.46$, $n = 83$) ($t(148.96) = 8.02$, $p < .001$, $d = 1.31$, CI [0.96, 1.67]). This result strongly suggests that. epistemic luck defeated people's inclination to ascribe intentional action.

Pavese, Henne, and Beddor (forthcoming) found very similar results in a lottery case and in a variant of Russell's clock case. Thus, far from epistemic luck sparing people's inclination to ascribe intentional action, the folk concept of intentional action, just like that of propositional knowledge, *is* sensitive to the presence of epistemic luck. This argument is reinforced by adding know-how to the mix: Since the ordinary concept of know-how is sensitive to epistemic luck in those scenarios too, if intentional action requires (some degree of) know-how, we should expect that the ordinary concept of intentional action is sensitive to epistemic luck too. Though more investigation is needed on this question, these findings are already strongly suggestive of a role for knowledge representation in the folk psychology of action.

6. Conclusions

This chapter has discussed the role of factive mindreading in the folk psychology of action. Granting that factive mind reading plays a role in our ability to predict and explain behavior, how does it enter (if at all) in our ability to track intentional and skilled action? I sharpened this question and motivated it by looking at several views which assign factive mental states a central role to play in action theory. After discussing and rebutting some prima facie reasons for skepticism, I overviewed some recent studies that suggest a role for factive mind reading in the folk psychology of intentional action. While these results are preliminary, they are strongly suggestive of factive mindreading in the folk psychology of action. Further experimental investigation might look more closely at people's judgments about skilled action and about the relation between skilled action and know-how; at the relation between knowledge representation and our ordinary concepts of culpability, responsibility, and intent; at the relation between knowledge representation and the ordinary concept of creditability, as well as at that between knowledge representation and legal and moral concepts.[5]

---

[5] I am grateful to Artūrs Logins and to an anonymous referee for comments that have improved this chapter. I'd like to thank the audiences at the symposium on factive mind reading at the Central APA 2023 in Denver for comments and suggestions and in particular Jennifer Nagel, Evan Westra, and Peter van Elswyk.

References

Anscombe, G. E. M. (1958). *Intention* (London: Basil Blackwell).

Beddor, B., & Pavese, C. (2020). Modal Virtue Epistemology. *Philosophy and Phenomenological Research*, *101*(1), 61–79.

Beddor, B.,. & Pavese C. (2022). "Practical Knowledge without Luminosity." *Mind* 131(523): 917–34.

Bengson, J., Moffett, M. A., & Wright, J. C. (2009). "The Folk on Knowing How." *Philosophical Studies* 142: 387–401.

Butler, R. J. (1978). "Report on Analysis "Problem" No. 16." *Analysis* 38(3): 113–14.

Carter, J. A., & Pritchard, D. (2015). Knowledge-How and Cognitive Achievement. *Philosophy and Phenomenological Research*, *91*(1), 181–199.

Carter, J. A., Pritchard, D., & Shepherd, J. (2019). "Knowledge-How, Understanding-Why and Epistemic Luck: An Experimental Study." *Review of Philosophy and Psychology* 10: 701–34.

Cath Y. (2011). "Knowing How without Knowing That," In J. Bengson & M. A. Moffett (eds.), *Knowing How: Essays on Knowledge, Mind and Action*. (Oxford: Oxford University Press), 113–35.

Cath Y. (2015). "Revisionary Intellectualism and Gettier." *Philosophical Studies* 172(1): 7–27.

Cath, Y. (2020). "Know How and Skill: The Puzzles of Priority and Equivalence." In E. Fridland & C. Pavese (eds.), *The Routledge Handbook of Philosophy of Skill and Expertise* (Abingdon: Routledge): 157–67.

Colaco, D., Buckwalter, W., Stich, S., & Machery, E. (2014). "Epistemic Intuitions in Fake-Barn Thought Experiments." *Episteme* 11(2): 199–212.

Cova, F., Dupoux, E., & Jacob, P. (2012). "On Doing Things Intentionally." *Mind & Language* 27(4): 378–409.

Davidson, D. (1971). "Agency." In R. Binkley, R. Bronaugh, & A. Marras (eds.), *Agent, Action, and Reason* (Toronto: University of Toronto Press): 43–61.

Dreyfus, H. L. (2006). "Overcoming the Myth of the Mental." *Topoi* 25: 43–9.

Gettier, E. (1963). "Is Justified True Belief Knowledge?" *Analysis* 23(6): 121–3.

Gibbons, J. (2001). "Knowledge in Action." *Philosophy and Phenomenological Research* 62(3): 579–601.

Gonnerman, Chad, Kaija Mortensen, and Jacob Robbins (2018). "The Ordinary Concept of Knowledge How." *Oxford Studies in Experimental Philosophy 2*, 104–115.

Gonnerman, C., Mortensen, K., & Robbins, J. (2021). Knowing how as a philosophical hybrid. *Synthese*, *199*(3), 11323–11354.

Guglielmo, S., Monroe, A. E., & Malle, B. F. (2009). "At the Heart of Morality Lies Folk Psychology." *Inquiry* 52(5): 449–66.

Guglielmo, S., Monroe, A. E., & Malle, B. F. (2010). "Enough Skill to Kill: Intentionality Judgments and the Moral Valence of Action." *Cognition* 117(2): 139–50.

Hampshire, S. (1959). *Thought and Action* (Notre Dame, IN: University of Notre Dame Press).

Harmon, I., & Horne, Z. (2016). "Evidence for Anti-Intellectualism about Know-How from a Sentence Recognition Task." *Synthese* 193(9): 2929–47.

Heider, F. (1958). *The Psychology of Interpersonal Relations*. (New York: Wiley).

Horschler, D., Santos, L., & MacLean, E. (2019). "Do Non-Human Primates Really Represent Others' Ignorance? A Test of the Awareness Relations Hypothesis." *Cognition* 190: 72–80.

Kilty, G. (2023). *Light of Samantabhadra: an explanation of Dharmakīrti's commentary on valid cognition*. Simon and Schuster, 2023.

Kneer, M. (2021). "Success and Knowledge in Action: Saving Anscombe's Account of Intentionality." In T. Ciecierski & P. Grabarczyk (eds.), *Context Dependence in Language, Action, and Cognition* (Berlin & Boston, MA: De Gruyter): 131–54.

Knobe, J. (2003a). "Intentional Action and Side Effects in Ordinary Language." *Analysis*, 63(3): 190–94.

Knobe, J. (2003b). "Intentional Action in Folk Psychology: An Experimental Investigation." *Philosophical Psychology* 16(2): 309–25.

Knobe, J. (2023). "Difference and Robustness in the Patterns of Philosophical Intuition across Demographic Groups." *Review of Philosophy and Psychology* 14(2): 435–55.

Knobe, J., and Burra, A. (2006). "Intention and Intentional Action: A Cross-Cultural Study." *Journal of Culture and Cognition* 6: 113–32.

Kraemer, E. R. (1978). "Intentional Action, Chance, and Control." *Analysis* 38(3): 116–17.

Machery, E., Stich, S., Rose, D., Chatterjee, A., Karasawa, K., Struchiner, N., Sirker, S., Usui, N., & Hashimoto, T., (2017). "Gettier across Cultures." *Noûs* 51(3): 645–64.

Malle, B. F. (2003). "The Social Cognition of Intentional Action." In P. W. Halligan, C. Bass, & D. Oakley (eds.), *Malingering and Illness Deception* (New York: Oxford University Press): 83–92.

Malle, B. F., & Knobe, J. (1997). "The Folk Concept of Intentionality." *Journal of Experimental Social Psychology* 33(2): 101–21.

Mele, A., & Moser, Paul K. (1994). "Intentional Action." *Nous* 28(1): 39–68.

Nadelhoffer, T. (2004). "The Butler Problem Revisited." *Analysis* 64(3): 277–84.

Nadelhoffer, T. (2005). "Skill, Luck, Control, and Intentional Action." *Philosophical Psychology* 18(3): 341–52.

Nagel, J. (2013). "Knowledge as a Mental State." *Oxford Studies in Epistemology* 4: 273.

Nagel, J. (2017). "Factive and Non-Factive Mental State Attribution." *Mind & Language* 32(5): 525–44.

Nagel, J., San Juan, V., & Mar, R.A. (2013). "Lay Denial of Knowledge for Justified True Beliefs." *Cognition* 129 (3): 652–61.

Paul, S. K. (2009). "How We Know What We're Doing." *Philosopher's Imprint* 9(11): 1–24.

Pavese, C. (2013). *The unity and scope of knowledge* (Doctoral dissertation, Rutgers University-Graduate School-New Brunswick).

Pavese, C. (2016). "Skill in Epistemology, I and II" *Philosophy Compass* 11(11): 642–60.

Pavese, C. (2017). Know-how and gradability. *Philosophical Review*, *126*(3), 345–383.

Pavese, C. (2018). "Know-How, Action, and Luck." *Synthese* 198(7): 1595–617.

Pavese, C. (2020). "Probabilistic Knowledge in Action." *Analysis* 80(2): 342–56.

Pavese, C. (2021a). "Knowledge, Action, and Defeasibility." In J. Brown & M. Simion (eds.), *Reasons, Justification, and Defeaters* (Oxford: Oxford University Press): 177–200.

Pavese, C. (2021b). "Knowledge and Mentality." *Philosophical Perspectives* 35(1): 359–82.

Pavese, C. (2022). "Practical Knowledge First", *Synthese* 200(5): 1–18.

Pavese, C. (forthcoming). *The Practical Mind* (Cambridge: Cambridge University Press).

Pavese, C. & Beddor, B. (2023). "Skills as Knowledge." *Australasian Journal of Philosophy*, 101(3): 609–24. doi: 10.1080/00048402.2022.2056753.

Pavese, C. & P. Henne (2023). "The Know-How Solution to Kraemer's Puzzle." *Cognition*, 238: 105490.

Pavese, C., Henne, P., & B. Beddor (forthcoming). "Epistemic Luck, Knowledge-How, and Intentional Action" *OSF*. https://osf.io/s4hyd, *Ergo*, 10(36). doi: 10.3998/ergo.4666.

Perner, J. (1993). *Understanding the Representational Mind* (Cambridge, MA: MIT Press).

Phillips, J., Buckwalter, W., Cushman, F., Friedman, O., Martin, A., Turri, J., & Knobe, J. (2021). "Knowledge before Belief." *Behavioral and Brain Sciences* 44. doi: 10.1017/S0140525X20000618.

Phillips, J., & Norby, A. (2021). "Factive Theory of Mind." *Mind & Language* 36(1): 3–26.

Poston, T. (2009). "Know How to Be Gettiered?" *Philosophy and Phenomenological Research* 79(3): 743–7.

Povinelli, D. J., Perilloux, H. K., Reaux, J. E., & Bierschwale, D. T. (1998). "Young and Juvenile Chimpanzees' (Pan Troglodytes) Reactions to Intentional versus Accidental and Inadvertent Actions." *Behavioural Processes* 42(2–3): 205–18.

Pritchard, D. (2005). *Epistemic Luck* (Oxford: Oxford University Press).

Pritchard, D. (2012). "Anti-Luck Virtue Epistemology." *Journal of Philosophy* 109(3): 247–79.

Rödl, S. (2007). *Self-consciousness*. Harvard University Press.

Rödl, S. (2011). Two forms of practical knowledge and their unity. In *Essays on Anscombe's "Intention"* (pp. 211–241). Harvard University Press.

Ryle, G. (1949). *The Concept of Mind* (London: Hutchinson).

Schwenkler, J. (2019). *Anscombe's Intention: A Guide* (Oxford: Oxford University Press).

Setiya, K. (2012, October). XIV—Knowing how. In *Proceedings of the Aristotelian Society (Hardback)* (Vol. 112, No. 3, pp. 285–307). Oxford, UK: Blackwell Publishing Ltd.

Shepherd, J. (2021). *The Shape of Agency: Control, Action, Skill, Knowledge* (Oxford: Oxford University Press).

Sosa, E. (1999). How to defeat opposition to Moore. *Philosophical perspectives*, 13, 141–153.

Sosa, E. (2007). *A Virtue Epistemology: Apt Belief and Reflective Knowledge*, i (Oxford: Oxford University Press).

Stanley, J., & Williamson, T. (2001). "Knowing How." *Journal of Philosophy* 98(8): 411–44.

Thompson, M. (2011). Anscombe's intention and practical knowledge. In *Essays on Anscombe's "Intention"* (pp. 198–210). Harvard University Press.

Tomasello, M. (2000). "Primate Cognition: Introduction to the Issue." *Cognitive Science* 24(3): 351–61.

Turri, J. (2013). "A Conspicuous Art: Putting Gettier to the Test." *Philosophers' Imprint* 13(10): 1–16.

Turri, J. (2017). "Knowledge Attributions in Iterated Fake Barn Cases." *Analysis* 77(1): 104–15.

Vekony, R., Mele, A., & Rose, D. (2020). "Intentional Action without Knowledge." *Synthese* 197: 1–13.

Vekony, R., Mele, A., & Rose, D. (2021). Intentional action without knowledge. *Synthese*, 199, 1231–1243.

Westra, Evan, & Nagel, Jennifer (2021). "Mindreading in Conversation." *Cognition* 210 (C):104618.

Williamson, T. (2000). *Knowledge and its Limits* (Oxford: Oxford University Press).

Wood, J. N., Glynn, D. D., Phillips, B. C., & Hauser, M. D. (2007). "The Perception of Rational, Goal-Directed Action in Nonhuman Primates." *Science* 317(5843): 1402–405.

7
Natural Curiosity

Jennifer Nagel

1. The Intrinsic Desire to Know

Knowledge is a naturally attractive state. As Aristotle saw it, "all men by nature desire to know" (*Metaphysics* A 1, 980ª21), but men are not alone in this. Curiosity, still characterized by at least some contemporary researchers as "the intrinsic desire to know" (Gottlieb & Oudeyer, 2018: 764), is evident in humans of all sorts from early in infancy (Liquin & Lombrozo, 2020); it is also said to appear in a broad array of other animals, including monkeys (Wang & Hayden, 2019), various types of birds (Auersperg, 2015), rats (Small, 1899), and octopuses (Byrne, Kuba, & Griebel, 2002). Even fruit flies show behavior that is taken to suggest a rudimentary form of curiosity (Lewis et al., 2017).

To say that curiosity is an intrinsic desire for knowledge is to say that curious creatures in some sense want knowledge for its own sake and not just for its contributions to securing other primary rewards such as nourishment. However, one might wonder whether curiosity, so understood, could really be present in such a broad range of creatures. Why exactly would an octopus need an intrinsic desire for knowledge, if that is indeed the best way of explaining its exploratory and playful behavior? Even if there are many things that octopuses must know in order to thrive, one might wonder why they couldn't learn these things through processes of trial and error driven by simpler incentives such as hunger. Indeed, the suggestion that nonhuman animals are pursuing knowledge for its own sake may sound somewhat ridiculous.

Nevertheless, several lines of evidence arguably point in that direction. Two important strands are outlined in a classic paper of Daniel Berlyne's, a paper that begins with the cautionary epigram, "Animals spend much of their time seeking stimuli whose significance raises problems for psychology" (Berlyne, 1966: 25). First, Berlyne observes that playful and exploratory behavior emerges too early in life to be explicable by an association with the satisfaction of other basic needs. Secondly, he notes that animals will sometimes attend to novel and complex stimuli even when it is hazardous to do so, and even in preference to satisfying immediate thirst or hunger. In his view, curiosity seems to have some serious independent weight of its own, a finding that he describes as "rather embarrassing" to early twentieth-century theories of motivation, theories which aimed to explain behavior strictly in terms of the pursuit of physical gratification and the avoidance of physical harm (Berlyne, 1966: 25).

Despite very substantial progress, some embarrassment lingers around curiosity today, with psychologists noting its importance and pervasiveness while lamenting a lack of scholarly consensus concerning its fundamental nature and purpose (Dubey & Griffiths, 2020; Kidd & Hayden, 2015). One source of difficulty concerns curiosity's target (or targets). Peter Carruthers, who accepts that many animals are curious, has argued that a desire for knowledge should be impossible for animals lacking the metacognitive ability to conceptualize that mental state (Carruthers, 2018). Carruthers now sees animal curiosity as guided by a kind of 'model-free metacognition', but he wavers (in ways to be examined in Section 3) on whether the target of this guidance is knowledge or mere belief (Carruthers, 2023: 15, 16).

Berlyne himself would not have described nonhuman animals as seeking knowledge. He draws a line between perceptual curiosity, described as aiming at "information-bearing stimulation" (Berlyne, 1966: 31), and epistemic curiosity, described as aiming at knowledge. In his theory, nonhuman animals have perceptual but not epistemic curiosity; humans have both. However, epistemologists may wonder whether this result can be traced back to Berlyne's decision to define knowledge as "information stored in the form of ideational structures" (1966: 31); perhaps a better way of understanding knowledge would have animal perceptual curiosity turn out to be knowledge-oriented as well. Meanwhile, among contemporary empirical researchers, many take all curiosity to be aimed at knowledge (Gottlieb & Oudeyer, 2018; Kang et al., 2009; Kobayashi et al., 2019; Loewenstein, 1994), while others speak in terms of drives or desires for information (Hsee & Ruan, 2016; Oudeyer & Smith, 2016). Still others combine the two, for example by defining curiosity as "a reward-learning process of knowledge acquisition or information seeking" (Lau et al., 2020: 531), or by characterizing curiosity as "a drive state for information" whose purpose is "to motivate the acquisition of knowledge and learning" (Kidd & Hayden, 2015: 450, 457). The relationship between knowledge and information is typically left unexplained in this literature, with the rare efforts to spell it out—"We define knowledge as information that is internal to the agent" (Silver et al., 2021: 5)—raising at least as many philosophical questions as they answer.

If the idea of knowledge as an internal agential state sounds unorthodox, there are other moves in this literature which might seem to lead us even further outside familiar epistemological territory. One influential paper on intrinsic motivations such as curiosity characterizes them as "based on mechanisms that drive learning of skills and knowledge, and the exploitation and energisation of behaviours that facilitate this, on the basis of the levels and the variations of such skills and knowledge directly detected within the brain" (Baldassarre, 2011: 3). The suggestion that levels of knowledge can be directly detected within the brain is surprising. It may sound especially jarring to 'knowledge-first' epistemologists who see knowledge as a factive mental state, a state whose objective, reality-matching correctness is its essential core (Williamson, 2000). This sort of passage might create the impression that empirical research on curiosity uses the word "knowledge" to pick out something quite different from whatever is meant by that word in epistemology, and that it will be hard to connect epistemological and empirical work in this area.

This chapter builds a fresh defense of the theory that curiosity is an intrinsic desire for knowledge, exactly by connecting knowledge-first epistemology to empirical work on natural curiosity. If it seems at first that empirical researchers and epistemologists are doomed to talking past each other, a closer look shows that their theories can be brought into contact, to the benefit of both sides. Knowledge-first epistemology can deliver a sharper theoretical characterization of the target of natural curiosity, and show how it is possible for animals to be curious without being reflective about their mental states. At the same time, empirical models of natural curiosity can clarify what it even means for knowledge to be a factive mental state, a state of a type that can only bind an agent to truths. Research into animal curiosity, together with related models in reinforcement learning, shows how knowledge can function as a special kind of adaptation of the agent to reality, an adaptation resulting in a type of mental state whose very existence depends essentially on the truth of its contents. Curiosity accelerates this adaptation by making it a direct goal for the agent, rather than a mere byproduct of the search for other goals. However, it will take some work to explain how this happens, and just why our adaptation to reality needs acceleration.

It will also take some work to clarify the relationship between information and knowledge. As an initial step, it may help to focus on an example of Jürgen Schmidhuber's (2010) involving a vision-based agent who encounters a television screen broadcasting random white noise. The display is terrifically information-rich in the classic signal-detection-theoretical sense (Shannon, 1948): At each moment, the precise array of pixels on screen is one of a vast range of possible arrays, and entirely unpredictable from everything that has preceded it. Regular patterns have redundancies that allow a compressed representation to transmit them with fidelity; the maximal disorder in the white noise means that it cannot be compressed, and can only be transmitted or reproduced exactly by means of a file with the same large size as the original. If curiosity were just a drive to encounter raw information, this visual buzz should be a source of endless fascination for a curious agent. The reason that it is not, Schmidhuber suggests, is that there are no patterns that the agent could make progress in compressing, no regularities that any agent could come to know. He applies this idea equally to what happens at the other end of the information spectrum, where a constantly darkened room affords minimal information. The dark room is also boring, but now because its regularity is learned at once, affording no further progress. What curious agents seek is not just raw information, but information at a level that poses an appropriate challenge to their current cognitive powers. Characterizing that level will turn out to be a surprisingly difficult problem, and a problem central to understanding the nature of curiosity.

The white noise example does not show that cognitive scientists are wrong to describe curiosity as involving information-seeking; rather, it raises questions about what sort of information is sought, and how. To answer these questions, we will need to look at a larger framework incorporating the relationship between the powers of the agent and the features of the environment producing informative signals, plus the structures in the brain producing metacognitive signals about the agent's level of adaptation to reality. With this larger framework in view, I will argue that the best way of making sense of curiosity is as a state aimed at knowledge gain. A quick advance sketch of the main ideas may be useful here. First, because our most basic form of learning is a kind of prediction-error correction, creatures like us gain knowledge when we are surprised, when events violate our expectations. (Note that the televised static which does not enable us to learn anything is information-rich but unsurprising, as we have no particular expectations about its configuration from one moment to the next.) Following a cue from research in reinforcement learning, we will examine the proximal signals behind natural curiosity, and formulate it as a kind of appetite for surprise. Surprise functions as a reward for the curious creature (in a technical sense of "reward" that will be explained), but because creatures like us gain knowledge from surprising situations, curiosity amounts to a desire for knowledge gain, or so I will argue. The resulting theory has broad applicability, because even animals lacking a reflective understanding of knowledge can still feel surprise. Curiosity is not strictly necessary for knowledge gain: A creature who must interact with the environment to satisfy basic extrinsic needs such as hunger and thirst will also learn at times when events violate its expectations. However, creatures who are curious benefit from an interaction between their reactive prediction-error correction processes and the active surprise-seeking force of their curiosity; this internally adversarial interaction accelerates knowledge gain in ways that are very helpful for biological agents in environments like ours.

After making a case that the best way of making sense of empirical research on curiosity is to understand this state as aimed at knowledge gain, I will need to explain what is going on in talk of detecting knowledge levels in the brain. Here I will situate curiosity among other motivational forces which also make use of proximal mechanisms in the brain to secure distal aims; when speaking loosely, cognitive scientists may sometimes fail to distinguish between markers of knowledge and knowledge itself, but this is not to say that the distinction is actually dispensable. But before tackling questions about the mechanisms that enable curiosity, and more abstract questions about the structure of curiosity itself, we can get a better sense of the target phenomenon by reviewing some data on how curiosity shows up in the natural world. Section 2 surveys research on apparently curious behavior in various types of animals, including humans.

2. Apparently Curious Behavior in Animals

The curiosity of the most-studied animal in comparative psychology has been remarked upon from the discipline's beginning. In his 1899 study of the development of the white rat, Willard Small insists that curiosity is "the most striking" of the animal's intellectual traits, emphasizing that "it is really curiosity, which is customarily spoken of as boldness by writers upon the natural history of the rat," and insisting that this curiosity develops early: "by the time they are three weeks old it is inordinate and overbalances fear" (Small, 1899: 99). In his view, "rats manifest curiosity apart from that curiosity which is directly associated with nutrition and reproduction" (Small, 1899: 90). This last observation has held up well under subsequent research. Exploratory behavior in the rat is not simply driven by immediate hunger, because rats will actively explore a maze even if they have just been fed. Indeed, the urge to explore is strong enough that hungry rats who are returned to their cages after being deprived of food for twenty-four hours will ignore openly available food if the bedding has been refreshed in their absence, and first "give themselves up for a while to explorations over and through their new bedding" (Dashiell, 1925: 208). Rats will also cross a floor that delivers a painful electric shock in order to explore new areas and will do so when they are neither hungry nor thirsty (Warden, 1931).

Exploratory behavior is not just random activity. Rats who have never been fed outside their cages will explore mazes systematically, showing a strong preference for visiting the options where they haven't most recently been: If they are relocated back to an earlier juncture, they significantly favor the right branch of a Y- or T-maze if they had previously explored the left, and vice versa, as opposed to choosing at chance (Dennis & Sollenberger, 1934). This tendency for 'spontaneous alternation' seems to be driven by the relative novelty of the place for the rat and not simply by the novelty of the motor activity of turning in a different direction. When these factors are disentangled, for example in mazes where the right and left fork swiftly lead to the same destination, rats no longer strongly prefer to avoid the path just taken (Montgomery, 1952; Sutherland, 1957). Exploration driven by relative novelty is better than random movement for foragers in a changing world, not only because it produces more efficient spatial discovery, but also because the longer one has been absent from a place, the greater the chance some food has appeared in one's absence.

Rats can be taught specific routes, or sequences of right and left turns, to gain extrinsic reward, but curiosity prompts the development of a more powerful form of spatial navigation, a cognitive map. Where meaningful routes have designated start and goal points, and a value contingent on the reward of reaching that goal, maps can be pressed into service from any direction, with no goal fixed in advance, enabling navigation along paths never taken before; in addition, maps are more robust in the face of environmental perturbations, where specific routes collapse at the introduction of an obstacle (O'Keefe & Nadel, 1978).

The cognitive maps developed by rats are maps in a broad sense of the word: They encode not only the spatial layout of reality, but also its causal features (Tolman & Brunswik, 1935; Wikenheiser & Schoenbaum, 2016). To flesh out the causal side of the map, rats seem to exhibit curiosity in their motor interactions with material objects, exploring new materials unprompted and without any apparent prospect of material reward. The benefits of this exploratory behavior become evident when novel problems must be solved. An illustrative example can be found in a study of the cognitive differences between rats raised in plain cages, with nothing beyond bedding, food and water, and rats raised in cages enriched with wooden toys, sections of tunnel, and metal enclosures (Renner, 1988). Researchers placed both types of rat in an arena with an escape route concealed under an obstruction box that could be entered only from the top; to simulate predation, the rats were chased by a noisy remote-controlled car. On their first time in the arena, all rats explored, but only the rats who had prior experiences of exploring materially enriched environments were able to escape through a cardboard ramp in the obstruction box within the three-minute experimental time limit (Renner, 1988: 52). Just as prior spatial exploration leads to mapping of a type that enables future navigation, prior material exploration equips rats with greater courage and skill in future interactions with various materials. These representations formed through these two types of exploration guide responses to unforeseen challenges and opportunities. Structurally similar types of cognitive mapping apply across a great range of task domains, including abstract nonspatial domains, and appear in a great range of animals, including humans (Behrens et al., 2018; Whittington et al., 2022).

Rats may show especially conspicuous curiosity, but many animals will approach and manipulate novel items. An early study of over 200 species of captive zoo animals investigated their responses to a range of objects: wooden blocks, steel chains, wooden dowels, rubber tubing, and crumpled paper, scaled roughly to the animal's size, and introduced to the animals' cages for a series of six-minute test sessions (Glickman & Sroges, 1966). These stimuli provoked active responses across taxonomic groups, with primates most engaged, and carnivores close behind. The reptiles were less engaged, the authors note, "with the notable exception of an Orinoco crocodile who lunged at, pushed, and bit all of the test stimuli"

(Glickman & Sroges, 1966: 164). It is hard to extract clear lessons about animal curiosity from this work, however: One might worry, in particular, that these particular human-selected items were shaped or structured to lend themselves better to the manipulation and chasing behavior of primates and carnivores, while other objects might have been more enticing to the lethargic snakes and armadillos. (Anatomical fit did make sporadic differences across animals; for example, anteaters scored high amongst the "primitive mammals" because they could insert their long tongues into the rubber tubing.) Even within a given species, there was considerable variation: One hedgehog scored zero in responsiveness, only bristling at the introduction of the objects, while another hedgehog chewed vigorously on the blocks and tubes and carried them around the cage. The same prehensile-tailed porcupine who was unresponsive to all the objects in the first test period grasped and chewed all of them in the second, while dancing on his hind legs (Glickman & Sroges, 1966: 173–4). This diversity in responses raises many questions; for example, one might wonder about the extent to which heightened responsiveness could have been a sign of confusion over whether the provided objects were edible, or dangerous, or perhaps some misapprehension interacting with the animal's current state of hunger, arousal, or fatigue.

More systematic and controlled investigation can resolve some of these ambiguities. Octopuses swiftly approach every object dropped into their surroundings, a tendency noticed by Aristotle, who saw it as a weakness: "The octopus is a stupid creature, for it will approach a man's hand if it be lowered in the water" (*History of Animals* viii (ix). 37, 622^{a}3–4). Contemporary theorists now draw quite a different conclusion, taking this behavior as evidence of the octopus's cognitive energy. Research on captive octopuses confirms that they do uniformly begin by approaching any novel object; one study tried edible shellfish versus similarly-sized cube- and snowflake-shaped plastic toys and found the octopuses approaching everything dropped into the tank within minutes (Kuba et al., 2006a). Following the initial approach, most of the time, objects were explored with a tentacle or two, and sometimes fondled into the central web near the mouth. Food was more likely to win tactile exploration when the octopus was hungry as opposed to sated, in contrast to the toys, which were explored equally often and with frequent touches, whether or not the octopuses were hungry. Equal attention to the toys in the hungry and sated conditions is one sign that the tactile exploration of the toys is not simply 'misplaced predation' by an animal confused about what it can eat. Signs of curiosity continued after the initial tactile exploration. After initial touching, food was either eaten or ignored, but the toys attracted ongoing attention. Most of the octopuses in a related study carried on to such play behaviors as passing the plastic toys repeatedly from arm to arm, and towing them across the water surface (Kuba et al., 2006b). It is natural to wonder what octopuses are gaining from this behavior, why exactly they are motivated to invest energy in their interactions with inedible and practically useless pieces of plastic, and indeed why they risk approaching everything in the first place, even (potentially octopus-hunting) human hands. Doubtless some benefits offset the costs. If their exploratory behaviors work to expand their general practical competence, it is noteworthy that this competence ends up being considerable: Octopuses have demonstrated the capacity to solve strategic problems calling for significant behavioral flexibility, for example where an extended series of steps must be performed correctly to gain food reward (Richter, Hochner, & Kuba, 2016).

Primates also show strong tendencies towards sensorimotor exploration. Given an elaborate mechanical puzzle solvable only by manipulating a series of six catches, clasps, and levers in the right order, rhesus monkeys manipulate it avidly until they can solve it with high accuracy, producing a learning curve that "does not appear to differ in any way from a typical learning curve obtained on animals under hunger or thirst motivation" (Harlow, 1950). This sequencing of fine motor skills is learned with no reward other than the presumed satisfaction of finding a reliable way to open the innermost metal flap, in a device that could be seen from the outset to contain nothing edible.

On the side of theoretical knowledge, curiosity in primates and other animals can be shown by their willingness to pay for information with no clear strategic value. Gambling paradigms have been used to show that rhesus monkeys are willing to forfeit some material reward (juice) to gain useless information about chance outcomes (Wang & Hayden, 2019). Strikingly, the amount of juice forfeited was proportional to the amount of information gained, with willingness to pay more where the chance outcome was closer to a fifty-fifty gamble for the monkey, the peak of informativeness in the formal entropic sense (Shannon, 1948).

Humans show some similar tendencies, in ways that are easier to probe, because humans can explicitly rate their level of curiosity. Humans report higher curiosity to see the early resolution of gambles with greater outcome uncertainty (van Lieshout et al., 2018). Indeed, we are willing to endure physical pain to see trivial but highly chancy matters resolved. In one ingenious experiment (Hsee & Ruan, 2016), participants were left in a room with a box containing some trick pens that would deliver a mildly painful electric shock when clicked, amid normal pens. Participants who were ostensibly waiting for the start of another study were told that they could click the pens to kill time, if they wished. Ten of the pens were marked with a red sticker, ten with a green sticker, and ten with a yellow sticker; the research assistant mentioned that the red stickers indicated a live battery which would always produce a painful shock on clicking the pen, the green stickers indicated a dead battery with no risk of shock, and the yellow ones were mixed. Left to their own devices for four minutes, participants spontaneously clicked more of the yellow-sticker uncertain-outcome pens ($M=4.16$, $SD=3.67$) than both of the other colors put together (green: $M=1.69$, $SD=2.29$;

red: $M = 1.03$, $SD = 1.79$). The unpredictability of the yellow-sticker pens seems to be part of their allure: Those who simply wanted to alleviate boredom through variety could more easily have done so by systematically selecting green or red pens at will (Hsee & Ruan, 2016: 664). The study is an elegant demonstration of the force of pure curiosity, both because the participants are willing to endure pain, while apparently gaining nothing of practical value by clicking the yellow pens, and because the green and red pens are tangible control stimuli whose value seems to differ only in its predictability. It is not easy to explain what is going on here while keeping in mind that curious humans do not feel a chronic temptation to flip coins.

Recent work has revealed deep similarities in the neural processing of human cravings for useless knowledge and for food. To elicit curiosity, participants can be asked a trivia question or shown a brief video of a magic trick, and then offered a chance to learn the answer or find out how the trick is done. The brain regions activated by such offers match those activated when hungry participants are shown an image of a snack and offered a chance to win it (Lau et al., 2020). In both cases, participants are then willing to take some risk of an electric shock to be told the answer or given the snack, accepting greater risk where the reported curiosity or craving is stronger. Decisions about these gambles for food or for trivial knowledge play out in the same striatal reward areas of the brain (Lau et al., 2020).

One robust pattern in human curiosity deserves special mention. Curiosity generally seems to be higher for questions on which we have some middling level of confidence (Loewenstein, 1994). This "inverted-U-shape" curve shows up in multiple domains. For example, trivia questions produce lower reported curiosity among those who report either very low or high confidence of getting the answer right; peak reported curiosity appears in most people for questions on which they report a level of uncertainty near the midpoint (Kang et al., 2009). Something similar appears in the attentional patterns of infants: They are most attracted to moderately challenging visual events, tending to look away from anything too simple or too complex, where complexity is a function of the predictability of the event, given the infant's prior experience (Kidd, Piantadosi, & Aslin, 2012). This "Goldilocks effect" of seeking partial familiarity is seen as a way of keeping cognitive resources engaged in the zone between what is already known and what is currently unknowable, the zone most promising for progress in learning.

3. Carruthers and the Metacognitive Challenge

Now that we have surveyed apparently curious behavior in a wide array of animals, the next task is to defend a unified account of this behavior. The view that curiosity is an intrinsic desire for knowledge has met with criticism from a philosopher who also sees it as widespread among animals. Peter Carruthers is ready to credit even bees with curiosity, showing up in their looping exploratory flights, for example. He has argued against "metacognitive" views of curiosity on the grounds that they demand too much self-reflection on the part of the curious animal. To desire something, he proposes, a creature must have at least some concept of it; so for example, "in order to want food, one must be capable of identifying (some) foodstuffs" (Carruthers, 2023: 5). On Carruthers's fairly minimal notion of what is needed for concept possession, bees can have concepts like FOOD and HOME, but they lack the kind of model of their own minds needed for a concept like KNOWLEDGE or BELIEF. Bees can be curious without having the power to represent states of knowledge, he contends, because they have motivational structures that tend to produce knowledge while bypassing the need to model it as a target. Following Dennis Whitcomb (2010) and Jane Friedman (2013), Carruthers sees curiosity as a motivational state whose contents are questions rather than propositions: The question picks out a set of alternatives, and the question-directed motivational state triggers behavior that settles the question in favor of one of them. We can describe these structured sets of alternatives as whatever is systematically designated by question words such as WHERE, WHICH, WHEN, and WHAT; Carruthers proposes that these question concepts fall within the cognitive capacity of very simple creatures. We could think of the WHERE concept, for example, as structuring the spatial composition of the bee's cognitive map of the environment. So, in Carruthers's view, the lost bee is not flying in search of something it represents as a change to its own mental state; rather, its exploratory flight is motivated by a question-embedding attitude, with a first-order content like *where the hive is*; likewise, "a monkey looking to see which of two hiding places contains food is motivated by a state with the question *where the food is*, or perhaps *which of these contains food*" (Carruthers, 2023: 5).

Carruthers's first (2018) version of this view involved a stark denial of metacognition in animal curiosity. As he saw it then, curiosity simply:

> recruits and motivates actions that have been sculpted by evolution and subsequent learning to issue in new knowledge (moving closer to the target of the question, looking at it, sniffing it, and so on). And just as fear can be apt to issue in safety without representing it (rather, safety is the normal effect of running away), so curiosity can be apt to issue in new knowledge without representing it.
> (Carruthers, 2018: 9)

In this edition of the anti-metacognitive view, the satisfaction of curiosity (coming to know an answer to the question) does not figure in any way in the bee's motivational profile; curiosity is simply a motivational force that ends up having learning as a result.

Carruthers has since moved a step closer to those who take curiosity to involve a representation of knowledge: He now holds that animal curiosity is produced and sustained by signals with the content *not known* and *learning is happening* (Carruthers, 2023). The modification is driven in part by the observation that subjective experiences of satisfaction are crucial to motivated learning: If hunger enables animals to learn new ways of getting food, this is because the state of hunger is aversive, and eating is especially pleasurable for a hungry animal. New behaviors that satisfy hunger are reinforced by these hedonic rewards. Likewise, "affective conditioning of successful curiosity-satisfying behavioral strategies can only happen when reward signals are created by learning the answer" (Carruthers, 2023: 15). Of course, the monkey who wonders which of two hiding places now contains food will gain (food) reward from investigative behavior that (also) results in knowledge, but this way of improving the animal's investigative behavior is already available without curiosity. The search for food is a straightforward instrumentally-motivated inquiry; by contrast, curiosity impels the hungry rat to turn down the hedonic promise of openly available food until it has thoroughly explored its fresh bedding. But the sheer fact that such non-instrumental exploration will answer a question (WHAT is there?—shredded paper) cannot release the needed hedonic signal unless the animal has some way of monitoring the satisfaction of curiosity.

The challenge for Carruthers is to explain the availability of signals for *not known* and *learning is happening* without positing some representation of knowledge in the animal. His inventive solution is what he calls 'model-free metacognition',[1] in which an ignorant animal's ambivalent reaction to an unknown stimulus itself comes to signal that the stimulus is unknown, and the resolution of this ambivalence is reward. There is precedent for this approach in other work on animal metacognition: Nate Kornell, in particular, has argued that animals can make decisions about their levels of confidence in gambling tasks on the basis of cues such as their own wavering or response times (Kornell, 2014). Animals do not need to engage in any introspection in order to respond systematically to such cues; their decision behavior in gambling tasks can be shaped by features of their own cognitive performance in ways that correlate nicely with their accuracy, without the animals needing to consult some inner model of this correlation.

To illustrate his theory of curiosity, Carruthers gives an example of a cat confronted with a new mechanical toy: The cat's attention is drawn by the noise of the toy, and a prediction error signal results when the cat fails to recognize it. The toy's size and motion will partially activate rival neural populations associated

---

[1] Section 4 will explore what it means for learning to be model-free (as opposed to model-based) in more detail; the main point of contrast for present purposes is that model-free cognition is habitual, requiring no representation of the goal state, where model-based cognition can also be strategic.

with roughly similar familiar dynamic objects (MOUSE, BALL, etc.) alongside a neural population representing NOT KNOWN. Each of these competing neural populations activates certain motor responses:

> The MOUSE-representation will activate the motor processes involved in stalking, pouncing, and biting; the BALL-representation will activate sequences of patting-and-chasing; and the PAPER-ON-STRING-representation will activate chasing and biting. Yet in competition with all these will be the investigative actions distinctive of curiosity (attending, approaching cautiously, patting). Since the representations underlying the latter build strength to the extent that the others don't (and because the item is not recognized), it carries the information *not known*. And given the role of that information in stabilizing the behaviour in question, and rendering it adaptive, that is what it represents, too.
> (Carruthers, 2023: 24–5)

This *not known* signal has both indicative and directive content, Carruthers observes.

Carruthers sees curiosity as always (or almost always) initiated by prediction error signals (2023: 21) and sustained by the *not known* signal until either the animal's question is answered as a result of the investigative behavior (the bee spots home and switches to its straight-line homing flight) or some other priority emerges. But epistemologists might wonder what it means to answer the question. At times, Carruthers frames things in terms of knowledge: "Curiosity is only satisfied in a way that is adaptive (in the way that it has been designed by evolution to be satisfied) when the agent comes to know some fact that answers the question embedded in the state of curiosity" (2023: 15). But he also uses disjunctive formulations involving belief and learning: "Curiosity about what something is will include within its content that one acquires a belief of the form *that is an X*, or that one learns what the thing in question is" (2023: 16). If curiosity is essentially a response to the shuffling ambivalence generated by an unrecognized object, then the cessation of that ambivalence could indeed be produced either by learning (coming to know) what the object is or by simply forming a belief (even a false belief) about its identity. We could try to reconcile these two ways of talking by reading the first (knowledge-based) formulation as about the idealized natural function of curiosity and the second as about its ordinary manifestation in us, where beliefs falling short of knowledge can indeed satisfy us at times, but not in the manner that nature intended. However, Carruthers elsewhere doubles down on the belief formulation: "States of belief figure among the referential satisfaction conditions of curiosity. It is belief-acquisition of the right sort (matching or answering the question) that removes curiosity and serves as curiosity's reward, as well as being curiosity's adaptive function" (2023: 16). Advocates of the view that curiosity aims at knowledge could grudgingly agree that states of belief figure among its satisfaction conditions, just on the strength of the entailment between knowledge and belief. But if all it takes for a belief to be "of the right sort" is that it matches or answers the question, then this characterization of the adaptive function of curiosity really is at odds with the earlier characterization in terms of knowledge. False answers and coincidentally correct answers are still answers, matching the form of the question. If we identify mere belief formation as the target of curiosity, it becomes somewhat harder to see its adaptive value: When animals enter into states of ambivalence, curiosity drives them to rehearse the kinds of actions that liberate them from these states and make them decisive again. But if their decisiveness or uncertainty reduction does not necessarily tend to steer them toward the truth, curiosity loses some of its appeal: in general, boldness might not be a benefit.

Of course, there are a number of ways out of this problem: for example, Carruthers could observe that natural selection will have ensured already that sensorimotor engagement with things will generally improve the accuracy of our judgments about them, so any struggle with a question is likely to leave us better off, epistemically. But an account of curiosity that does not make deliberate use of the special features of knowledge (as opposed to belief) may be missing something important, and Carruthers's account of curiosity does seem to leave a number of questions unanswered.

The way Carruthers describes it, curiosity is a reaction to perturbations of our usual homeostasis into ambivalence, which we are then keen to resolve by whatever innate or learned behaviors have resolved such ambivalence in the past. This does not quite seem to capture the way in which curious animals actively search out trouble, crossing electrified floors or plowing through the hidden reaches of their bedding, notwithstanding the openly visible bowl of food that one might expect to cue a more decisive and unproblematic motor response. It is not obvious that anything unexpected in the bedding needs to trip off a prediction error to motivate the curious search. More generally, we can become acutely curious about things that are outwardly familiar: The sealed package that one has promised not to open until one's birthday still looks exactly the same, sitting on the hall table three days after its arrival, while curiosity about its contents continues to build. One might also wonder about the extent to which curiosity triggers new behaviors, as opposed to reviving innate or previously learned ones; here we might think about the rats' material exploration, the anteaters' insertion of their tongues into those rubber tubes, or the octopuses' experiments with dragging plastic toys across the water surface.

To the extent that Carruthers sees curiosity as activating prior learned or innate patterns of investigation, he faces a special challenge in explaining how exactly curiosity-driven inquiries differ from instrumental inquiries. We can grant that knowledge is important for animals while still wondering why exactly they need a special motivational state whose adaptive function is to expand knowledge, as opposed to learning what they need to know on the basis of simpler motivations such as hunger. The latter type of learning could be enough to support even quite complex intelligent behaviors through secondary reinforcement.

According to Carruthers, there is no sharp line here: "the core difference between intrinsically motivated states of questioning like curiosity and interest, on the one hand, and instrumentally motivated inquiries, on the other, is that the former are appraised against long-standing interests and values, whereas the latter are appraised against current goals"(2023: 26). In an example he uses to illustrate this point, a visitor to a park might have her attention drawn by animate motion in a tree. Supposing that she is broadly interested in wildlife ("she likes to watch nature programmes and cares about the diversity of the natural world") and initially fails to recognize the creature, this will spark an affective state of curiosity in which she draws closer to examine it. Without that interest, a person might disregard the disturbance and continue walking. As Carruthers sees it, "Curiosity and interest are sustained by signals with the content *not known*, then. But such signals on their own are insufficient. One's ignorance also needs to be appraised as somehow relevant to one's goals or underlying values and interests" (2023: 25).

The example is a compelling one, but one may wonder whether it is missing some of the peculiarity of curiosity. Is the research participant who clicks the yellow-stickered pen something of a pen-fancier? What goals or underlying values drive the monkey who spends hours manipulating Harlow's empty metal device, or the octopuses with their plastic toys? These activities seem strangely independent of the ordinary goals of the agents involved; perhaps this independence from instrumental reward is an important feature of what makes curiosity its own intrinsic form of motivation, and not just a diluted or more diffuse version of ordinary learning. Carruthers does have a point that not just any experience of something as unknown will trigger curiosity, but here we might want an account with a greater capacity to predict just what will do the trick. One way to explain his wildlife case would be to return to the observation that curiosity is highest where we have partial familiarity, or more generally, that it is triggered by stimuli that present a manageable learning challenge. There is, after all, something that the yellow pen-clicker can easily learn, so perhaps what drives him is the abstract shape of the learning situation, rather than a mild interest in pens or shocks. A broad interest in a topic could suffice to produce partial familiarity, but perhaps it is the availability of a certain sort of challenge that really matters here: Perhaps curiosity drives us to learn in a way that is responsive to the level of our cognitive resources.

4. Curiosity in Reinforcement Learning

Research in the branch of artificial intelligence known as reinforcement learning (RL) has clarified the importance of marshaling cognitive resources well. In RL, artificial agents[2] discover through trial and error how to act in ways that tend to yield reward in artificially designed environments; as these environments become more realistic and complex, it becomes increasingly important for the agents to make efficient use of their capacities to absorb and process information. In research on humans and other animals, it can be hard to tell which aspects of intelligent behavior are innately specified and which are learned from experience; by contrast, RL research provides a cleaner slate for measuring differences between ways of controlling action and for testing the impacts of supplying the agent or the environment with various features.

One feature that can be added to the agent is some kind of intrinsic motivation for gaining knowledge. There are a number of ways of doing this (for a partial taxonomy, see Oudeyer & Kaplan, 2007); here I will not attempt an exhaustive survey, but instead highlight the approaches that are most relevant to a better understanding of natural curiosity. Our initial puzzle will then take a clearer form. If even fruit flies show signs of curiosity, we might wonder whether it is somehow essential to agency or essential to gaining knowledge of an environment. I will argue that it is not; completely incurious RL agents can gain knowledge incidentally, in pursuit of other objectives, and in some environments these incurious agents can perform very well, even optimally. If curiosity-free knowledge acquisition is possible for agents motivated only by the pursuit of non-epistemic reward, we can wonder exactly what agents ever gain from the addition of intrinsic motivation to pursue knowledge directly. To answer this question, we will look at environments and tasks where curious RL agents radically outperform their incurious counterparts, and we will see some commonalities with the natural world, and with the sorts of tasks that biological agents must succeed at in order to thrive.

RL research does not shy away from talk of knowledge; for example, an important class of RL agents is characterized as having "an adaptive world model...reflecting what's currently known [by the agent] about how the world works," together with "a learning algorithm that continually improves the model (detecting novel, initially surprising spatio-temporal patterns that subsequently become known patterns)" (Schmidhuber, 2010: 1). Granted, there are a few researchers who deny that RL agents can literally learn or come to know anything. For example, Selmer Bringsjord and colleagues, who start from the premise that knowledge is true belief for which the subject can produce an explicit justification, contend that RL agents do not gain knowledge so conceived and conclude that such agents do not learn in the literal sense of the word (Bringsjord et al., 2017). However, one way of

---

[2] Readers who think that only biological agents can have mental states can still see artificial agents as useful models of phenomena such as mental state possession; ultimately, humans and other animals also learn through similar processes of reinforcement. For simplicity, this chapter follows the common practice in RL of attributing mental states to artificial agents, rather than speaking of them as modeling mental state possession.

seeing what is wrong with this way of proceeding is to consider its application to the human case: As Cameron Buckner puts it, "This benchmark produces the surprising verdict that children do not really learn how to walk, talk, or recognize objects" (Buckner, 2023: 691). If we want to keep the idea that learning is literally knowledge gain, an epistemology that fits more smoothly with RL is the theory according to which knowledge is a mental state that is essentially factive, the type of state whose correctness is necessary for its existence. To see that RL agents can successfully achieve this kind of cognitive adaptation to their environments,[3] we can start by taking a closer look at how they are supposed to learn (this quick summary follows Sutton & Barto, 2020; for a more detailed tour of the philosophically interesting features of RL, see Haas, 2022).

In RL, causal influence runs both ways between the agent and the environment: The environment influences the agent by supplying a series of observations, and the agent influences the environment by producing a series of actions. The environment could be artificially simple (say, a tic-tac-toe game whose states are grid configurations of x's and o's) or arbitrarily complex. Observations are a signal of the state of the environment, sometimes a very direct and complete signal, such as board positions in a game like chess,[4] sometimes something more complex, such as the arrays of pixel values in consecutive frames of a video game. Given these observations, the agent computes the current state at every turn. This is a trivial computation in the tic-tac-toe environment, where the state is identical to the current observation, and more difficult in richer environments, where patterns of past observations are needed to differentiate superficially similar situations which are fundamentally distinct (like similar-looking doors leading to different rooms) and to compress superficially different situations which are fundamentally similar (like different-looking doors leading to the same room). Because of inevitable limitations in memory, time, and computational power, agents in complex environments cannot maintain a separate representation for each state, but must instead discover classes of relevantly similar states through processes of generalization, discounting noise in the observational signal from the environment, and discarding features of observations that are irrelevant to action.

---

[3] RL agents could know *more* than what they learn from experience: They could reasonably be seen as having some innate knowledge supplied by their designers, such as knowledge of the rules of a game like chess. Some of the initial (genetic) programming of biological agents could also constitute (innate) knowledge of certain stable features of the environment, where the accuracy of this programmed state is essential to its existence in the agent through natural selection. However, questions about innate epistemic states are set aside for present purposes; in what follows I focus on learning from environmental interaction within the lifespan of the agent.

[4] Because chess has rules about the repetition of board positions and about the one-time availability of castling actions, the state of the environment is not fully expressed in a single observation of the current board position, but only in the set of current and prior positions. That richer set of observations does, however, carry complete information about the state of the environment. Many environments are unlike chess in being only partially observable; however, even partially observable environments like the natural world have regularities that are knowable for an agent with adequate powers of memory and computation.

An action can be a move that will simply determine the next state that the agent will experience (such as taking one step forward in a simple maze); but more generally, state-action pairs set a probability distribution over the possible next state outcomes (like pressing the trigger on a weapon that sometimes misfires). Actions are selected in each computed state according to a rule known as the policy of the agent. The agent's policy dictates how it will act in any computed state by setting some probability distribution over the available actions for that state (so even a random selection of actions in every state could count as a policy, and indeed this might be a fine initial policy for RL agents starting to learn a new task). As time elapses, the agent's actions lead to new situations supplying fresh observations, perhaps including an experience of reward, and new possibilities for action.

The experience of reward plays a decisive role in refining the agent's policy over time. Reward is a special type of observation, a scalar signal that serves as a target for the agent, like points in a game for a player who has the sole objective of maximizing his score.[5] Patterns of behavior that yield positive reward are reinforced. The reward signal can be distributed densely or sparsely among the other observations: for example, in video games where the current score is displayed as a running tally, the score might either change frequently as time elapses, or it might sit at zero until very substantial progress has been made. Either way, the reward signal dictates what the agent will learn to do, although learning will generally be quicker in the presence of a dense reward signal, where steady "breadcrumbs" of reward frequently update the agent's evaluations of possible actions. (Curiosity will turn out to be especially important in scenarios with sparse extrinsic reward.)

A central puzzle in goal-directed action is how future reward can have a bearing on the present moment of choice. In RL this puzzle is solved by the agent's evolving representation of value, a measure of the extent to which the immediately available actions in each state have historically tended to produce reward. The value of an action in a given state is not the reward this action immediately produces, but the total average long-term reward it can be expected to lead to, conditional on the agent's policy, taking past experience as a guide.[6] Crucially, when reward is finally encountered, the values assigned to the earlier state-action

---

[5] Because reward in RL is definitive of the agent's goal, it does not quite align with the meaning of "reward" in animal learning experiments, where it typically refers to a substance or event. Unlike RL reward, substances can lose their motivational power: after consuming a large amount of juice, for example, a chimpanzee might no longer aim to get more. To describe the chimpanzee's motivational profile in the more abstract terms of RL, we could instead say that the animal experiences reward when its energy or hydration level approaches a homeostatic set point; perhaps some complex set of such points could operationalize animal well-being (Juechems & Summerfield, 2019).

[6] This representation of value is typically subject to some temporal discounting function to favor reward that comes sooner. Meanwhile, there are many further degrees of freedom in RL theorizing that I am passing over to keep this summary brief. For example, I focus on the value of state-action pairs; some RL value functions are expressed in terms of states. The policy that is used in the value function calculation may be the agent's current policy, or it may be a variant.

pairs that led to it are then updated to reflect the later payoff.[7] Over time, in environments where there are meaningful state-action-reward relationships to be discovered, repeated experimentation with different state-action pairings allows the development of a meaningful representation of value through these backtracking computations of the ensuing reward. Effective RL algorithms use representations of value to guide agents to forgo small short-term gains and endure unrewarding actions in order to get to situations where larger rewards can be reaped. A high-value action might itself deliver no reward but set the agent up so a subsequently available action will be rewarding (such as the position of being able to checkmate in two moves, no matter how the opponent plays). The computational backtracking of assigning high value to actions on paths that end up yielding reward is a species of prediction-error learning; projected reward estimates get revised, over time, to match reality.

This matching between assigned and real value ends up being modally robust, given the character of the training. An RL agent learning to play chess could start with nothing more than the rules of the game and rewards of +1 for a win, zero for a draw, and −1 for a loss; such an agent's initially random valuation of actions might by chance lead to an initial win against a weak adversary. But this valuation will not last on the strength of an accidental success, where the agent would have lost if the adversary had played slightly differently. In the course of training, the RL agent initially relying on the random valuation will soon be pitted against multiple adversaries playing slightly differently, and revise its valuation as it wins and loses. After millions of appropriately varied games, the agent's ranking of the value of moves in different types of situations will generally become reflective of their real tendency to promote victory, not least because the agent's compression of what counts as a relevantly different type of situation will be continually improving. An initially blank-slate agent of this type, AlphaZero, now outperforms prior world champion AI agents trained on expert human game data, just through repeated self-play training (Silver et al., 2018). Chess has a very large state space, so even the best RL agent will not always know what to do, but for many states of the game, AlphaZero can appropriately be described as knowing which move to take. At least in many states later in the game, if AlphaZero ranks one move over others, this valuation is not just correct, but safely correct; in the state AlphaZero currently occupies, and indeed in any close state,[8] the move that

---

[7] Various RL algorithms enable earlier value updating, for example when the reward payoff is still on the horizon, but becoming more predictable. In particular, model-based RL algorithms allow value updates prior to the actual experience of reward, on the basis of a cognitive model that may itself be learned from reward.

[8] A close state here is any state that AlphaZero is compressing together with the actual current state (recalling that in large state spaces it is not possible to maintain a separate representation for every possible state). AlphaZero is not just representing states that it has actually experienced; it is generalizing to cover possible states that it could encounter. Note that knowledge of which move is best does not necessarily require that AlphaZero knows the precise value of the move; if one move is much

AlphaZero represents as best is, in fact, the best move. In these cases of successful adaptation, the reason why AlphaZero has stabilized on ranking one move higher than the alternatives is that this move actually does lead to the highest reward in relevantly similar predicaments. This safely accurate representation is, therefore, a factive mental state: factive because its truth is what accounts for its stable existence in the trained agent, and mental because of its role in guiding the trained agent's choice of move.

Good policies favor actions that have shown high value for the relevant situation, exploiting what has been learned to date, together with some exploration of other actions, to test whether undiscovered higher value elsewhere should prompt a further update to the policy.[9] One simple example is the ϵ-greedy policy, which chooses a random 'exploratory' action some small percentage of the time and otherwise takes the 'greedy' action currently rated as having highest value, exploiting what has been learned to date. More sophisticated policies gradually explore less when the environment is better known, or in ways that are sensitive to what is at stake.

Any effective policy will ensure that illusions about value naturally tend to be dispelled, over time: States or state-action pairs that are currently assigned high value will be revisited often because of that high valuation, but if they end up failing to yield high reward, their valuations will drop. In biological agents, this process is known as extinction: Dogs will salivate at the sound of a metronome if this sound has in the past been followed by the provision of meat, but if the meat stops being provided after the sound, the metronome will soon cease to provoke a response (Pavlov, 1927). In this way biological agents are protected from being misled by merely coincidental patterns of reward and are sensitive to changes over time in the reward landscape.

Throughout learning, agents are guided by their current value representations in all but their exploratory actions, but these exploratory actions are crucial to the legitimacy of the agent's value representations. Viewed in isolation, exploratory actions might look like the antithesis of rational agency: They are independent of the agent's best current representation of value, even random. However, as long as the environment is not yet fully known, agents must incorporate some exploratory actions into their overall activity in order to avoid being trapped in local optima while larger reward lies elsewhere; exploration is needed to ensure that the agent's subjective valuations reflect the objective landscape of reward.

The experience of reward precedes learning in this framework: Acting randomly, naive agents can stumble upon reward without yet having learned anything.

better than the alternatives, then the ordinal judgment that this move is best can be safe even if there is imprecision or slight inaccuracy in its valuations.
[9] For the sake of simplicity, this chapter treats exploration and exploitation as distinct classes of action, but some dynamic environments will allow actions to serve both purposes simultaneously in what has been called 'exploration by exploitation' (Leibo et al., 2019).

Indeed, amnesiac agents who fail to learn anything can go on accruing some ongoing reward by chance. However, agents who learn from their reward-capturing experiences will outperform random agents over time, assuming that there are regularities in the environment of types that the agents can exploit to form suitable action-guiding mental states. The agent with a false or coincidentally true belief can act in a way that happens to yield reward, on the basis of a current pattern of observations aligning with that belief; the agent with knowledge can act in a way that tends to yield reward, on the basis of successful generalizations over its observations, where the truth of these generalizations explains their presence in the agent.

To characterize the mental states of RL agents, it will help to distinguish two styles of RL. Some agents update their value functions purely on the basis of experienced state-action-reward contingencies; this is model-free RL, the kind of learning that underpins habitual action. However, it is also possible for agents to develop cognitive representations of the relationships between states, creating shortcuts for updating their value functions. In model-based RL, still driven purely by reward, the agent builds a cognitive model of the environment that enables the simulation of never experienced state-action sequences, simulation that can be used in flexible planning. When the reward landscape changes, a model-free RL agent must experience the new state-action-reward contingencies multiple times to bring its valuations into line with the new reality (through extinction or through actually stumbling upon new rewards); a model-based RL agent can use its model strategically to revise valuations for novel state-action pairings in advance of visiting them.

Humans and many other animals, including rats, are capable of both model-based and model-free RL (Daw, Niv, & Dayan, 2005; Dayan, 2009). Because model-free RL caches or stores values for particular state-action pairings, it allows easy but inflexible action when familiar states are visited (driving home on mental autopilot, I take my usual route, switching lanes when triggered by the sight of the exit sign). Model-based RL allows more taxing but flexible on-the-spot updates (having heard on the radio that my exit is closed for emergency bridge repair, I simulate my options using a mental map and take an earlier exit, perhaps for the first time). Peter Dayan characterizes the contrast between model-free and model-based control as a contrast between imperatives and declaratives. Model-free control is procedural in character—"it specifies directly the choice of action at each state or location as an imperative command"—where model-based control "provides a set of (semantic) facts about the structure of the environment and the subject in the form of a forward or generative model," where ideally these facts will entail that some particular action is optimal (Dayan, 2009: 214). Model-free RL agents can often know what to do, given their training and what they are now observing; model-based RL agents can also know what is the case in a more detached way.

In model-based RL, successful learning again results in states that are robustly accurate; because incorrect predictions frustrate the pursuit of reward, models tend to improve over time. The idea here is not that everything that the agent incorporates into its model necessarily constitutes knowledge; especially in the early stages of training, the agent can be expected to model various misconceptions about its environment. The idea is rather that knowledge is the natural endpoint of reinforcement learning, the basin of attraction toward which the agent's representations should ultimately converge. Errors in the model will generally drive the agent to behave in ways that tend to correct those errors; safely accurate representations will be stabilized by their propensity to support the capture of reward.[10]

In model-based RL, the agent uses its observations to construct a model of the environment. Observations are a signal of the underlying state of the environment, and RL models extract reward-relevant differences in these underlying states. Every time I drive home, the sensory stream of observations I receive from the various roads I travel will be different, given slight variations in my lane position, traffic, conditions of illumination, and weather. For the purposes of efficient navigation, a learned model of the roads will not retain all these variations, but instead distill whatever features make a difference to successful travel. A useful mental map might distinguish the states of being on the main highway and being on the lower-speed side access road, without further distinguishing states involving small differences in cloud cover or illumination. A model whose state space is too fine-grained will tax the memory and processing capacities of the agent, impeding the effective valuation of actions (at the limit, by making the agent take every trip as if it is her first, because the clouds are slightly different this time). A model that is too coarse-grained will bar the agent from taking advantage of some reward-relevant contingencies (for example, if the model only maps spatial relationships, the agent may never learn that an alternative route is faster during rush hour).

With this overview of RL in hand, we can examine the addition of curiosity to RL agents. All RL agents must explore in order to bring their subjective valuations in line with objective reality, and curiosity "aims to provide qualitative guidance

---

[10] Objection: how can the propensity to gain (future) reward be secured by representations formed by a (past) history of interaction with the environment? One way of handling this problem would be to adopt something like Cameron Buckner's (2022) forward-looking theory of content, which draws on the resources of prediction-error correction models of learning such as those in RL. Backward-looking teleosemantic theories such as those of Fred Dretske (1983) and Ruth Millikan (1987) anchor content in the causal history of the individual animal's experiences, or the evolutionary history of the species. Buckner observes that these theories have struggled with explaining how misrepresentation is possible and with problems of indeterminacy. His forward-looking theory instead takes advantage of the way representations naturally improve over time as we interact with relevant environmental features. In his view, "a representation's forward-looking content (F+) in some environment is thus what it indicates at the limit of its likeliest revision trajectory, given that environment's informational structure" (Buckner, 2022: 383).

for exploration" (Bellemare et al., 2016: 1). With no qualitative guidance at all, uncurious exploration works by periodically inserting completely random actions in the agent's behavior, but this can be inefficient, for example when the random exploratory actions are wasted in probing situations whose outcomes are already known, while important zones further away are left unexplored. Simple count-based methods add reward for visiting rarely visited states, but these are best for small, deterministic domains, with states likely to be visited multiple times. These methods would also require the reward-allocation function to consult memory prior to each exploratory action to check which options had already been explored and how often. For agents more like us, better qualitative guidance for exploration is summarized as "explore what surprises you" (Bellemare et al., 2016: 1). Rather than demanding a memory check, reward can be allocated more simply for the experience of events that violate the agent's expectations. As an illustration of the contrast here, Schmidhuber's (2010) television offers a novel, previously unvisited state at every moment we observe it, but it is unsurprising, as we have no expectations concerning the particular configuration of the display at any moment. Stimuli with partial familiarity, on the other hand, set up expectations that can be proven wrong, generating prospects for surprise.

There are various ways to operationalize reward for surprise. Existing methods add reward either for actions that maximize the prediction error of the agent's world model or for prediction improvement over time (Achiam & Sastry, 2017).[11] Artificial curiosity can combine these approaches (Ten et al., 2021) or even add a self-model reflecting the agent's awareness of its inner state, enabling a more strategic pursuit of surprise (Haber et al., 2018). In general, agents who experience surprise as reward do better if they are making predictions involving lasting features of the environment as opposed to predictions of raw sensory stimulation for reasons Deepak Pathak and colleagues spell out as follows in a discussion of RL agents in video game environments:

> Making predictions in the raw sensory space...is undesirable not only because it is hard to predict pixels directly, but also because it is unclear if predicting pixels is even the right objective to optimize. To see why, consider using

---

[11] It is hard to allocate reward for prediction improvement over time in part because the agent can come to make better predictions simply by switching attention:

> the possible naive implementation comparing prediction errors between a window around time t and a window around time $t - \theta$ is in fact nonsense: this may for example attribute a high reward to the transition between a situation in which a robot is trying to predict the movement of a leaf in the wind (very unpredictable) to a situation in which it just stares at a white wall trying to predict whether its color will change (very predictable).
> (Oudeyer and Kaplan 2007: 8)

To solve this problem, prediction improvement methods need to define a "sensorimotor context" for any given exercise of curiosity; it is suggested that this is not, in general, a tractable problem (cf. Pathak et al., 2017: 3, "there are currently no known computationally feasible mechanisms for measuring learning progress").

> prediction error in the pixel space as the curiosity reward. Imagine a scenario where the agent is observing the movement of tree leaves in a breeze. Since it is inherently hard to model breeze, it is even harder to predict the pixel location of each leaf. This implies that the pixel prediction error will remain high and the agent will always remain curious about the leaves. But the motion of the leaves is inconsequential to the agent and therefore its continued curiosity about them is undesirable. The underlying problem is that the agent is unaware that some parts of the state space simply cannot be modeled and thus the agent can fall into an artificial curiosity trap and stall its exploration.
> (Pathak et al., 2017: 3)

The pixelated moving leaves represent two problems here: They form patterns too complex for the agent to master, and their motion is an "inconsequential" feature of the environment, so the agent derives no extrinsic reward from standing entranced by it. To protect agents from such fruitless curiosity traps, Pathak and colleagues transform the sensory input in their model into a feature space just representing aspects of the environment relevant to action. To learn this feature space, a network is trained on the inverse dynamics task which specifies two subsequent states occupied by the agent and asks the network to predict how the agent must have acted to get from the first state to the second (a task that motivates the network to disregard observations irrelevant to action, encoding only features that the agent can control or features that have an impact on how the agent acts). The next steps introduce a role for surprise:

> We then use this feature space to train a forward dynamics model that predicts the feature representation of the next state, given the feature representation of the current state and the action. We provide the prediction error of the forward dynamics model to the agent as an intrinsic reward to encourage its curiosity.
> (Pathak et al., 2017: 2)

This forward dynamics model predicts how things will turn out for the agent as it acts, generating reward for those actions whose outcomes are contrary to its predictions, that is, for surprising outcomes. If curious animals are similarly driven by a mandate to do things whose consequences are unpredictable, this helps to explain the innovative quality of their behavior.

In difficult 3-D video game navigation tasks, Pathak and colleagues' curious RL agents outperform rivals trained only on extrinsic (game point) reward, while also avoiding nuisance curiosity traps of white noise. In contrast to randomly exploring agents who get stuck in the loops of local minima, these curious agents swiftly learn to navigate hallways systematically, and visit many rooms in large mazes (Pathak et al., 2017: 7–8). Indeed, variations of these curiosity-driven agents can do remarkably well at video game play across a large range of games, even when learning *purely* on intrinsic reward, with no guidance from game score, doubtless in large measure because games are designed to mesh with natural human mechanisms for intrinsic reward (Burda et al., 2018). However, these agents remain vulnerable to curiosity traps of other types. In particular, if they have the power to generate stochastic events such as coin flips, or if they find a TV whose channel changes randomly in response to some action of theirs, then they can get stuck generating reward for themselves by repeatedly witnessing these mildly surprising actions within their control, ceasing larger exploration or progress within the game.

It is a good question how animals harvest the benefits of curiosity without getting stuck in the traps. Animals do seem to learn from surprise; indeed, the standard model of classical conditioning makes the stronger claim that "organisms *only* learn when events violate their expectations" (Rescorla & Wagner, 1972: 75, emphasis added). It is now thought that the phasic dopamine crucial to learning is released not only when animals experience surprising reward, but for surprising experiences of all types (for a review, see Barto, Mirolli, & Baldassarre, 2013). Of course, if surprise functions as reward, reinforcement learning will teach agents to forgo small, short-term surprise in favor of actions with the potential to produce more surprise in the longer term. Interacting with the pens in Hsee and Ruan's (2016) experiment differs from coin flipping in this respect: The coin flip produces a single, unexpected observation of a familiar type, with no consequences for the future, whereas clicking a yellow-stickered pen might give a novel sensation (so one learns how that feels) while also enabling one to classify the lasting object itself as a shocker or a dud. Having categorized it one way or the other in one's model of the environment creates further expectations that may later be violated, which yields additional possibilities for later surprise (if, for example, a shocker pen at some point ceases to shock). More generally, stronger long-term expectations can be produced by actions that reveal broader patterns of underlying causal structure, for example in the patterns of explanation-seeking questioning and causal experimentation that start early in human development (Liquin & Lombrozo, 2020). Theories with greater generality create the possibility for surprising counterexamples, so actions that lead to the formation of such theories will be reinforced.

If surprise functions as reward, state-action pairs will seem good to an agent when similar state-action pairs have in the past led to surprise; more strategically, agents who can anticipate that they don't know what will happen if they act a certain way will be drawn to do so. This is not to say that surprise will always be produced by these actions. Prey-stalking behavior can seem attractive to a predator even if most stalking ends in disappointment, as long as it sometimes pays off; so also, curious behaviors like mailbox-checking can be reinforced by very occasional surprises, even if the most common outcome is a relatively unsurprising empty box. As for avoiding traps, it may help that nonhuman animals typically lack easily available ways of generating stochastic outcomes, and it should be conceded that sometimes humans do get stuck flipping channels or playing mildly surprising but pointless games. Human self-consciousness could also give our curiosity the kind of strategic form that would keep us from dwelling on low-level chancy events. In reinforcement learning, artificial agents can be structured to develop both a world-model (predicting the consequences of the agent's action) and a self-model that tracks the types of situations in which the world model fails; these agents can adversarially choose larger sequences of actions where the world-model can be expected to fail, systematically expanding the boundaries of the agent's knowledge (Haber et al., 2018).

The question of why exactly biological agents need curiosity can now be addressed more directly. Knowledge can be gained even if it is not actively pursued; the basic mechanisms of reinforcement learning work for agents driven strictly by extrinsic reward. AlphaZero is such an agent, with a reward function strictly limited to winning and losing games ($+1/-1$), and no curiosity whatsoever. In the course of its training, this completely incurious agent nevertheless develops extensive, indeed superhuman, knowledge of how to play chess. A relevant feature of chess is that it is a fully observable environment, with games averaging forty moves per side. Whenever AlphaZero acts, it is not long before the environment supplies instructive feedback on its success or failure. By contrast, the natural world is very much a partially observable environment, with extrinsic rewards such as nourishment and reproductive opportunities only sparsely distributed among a massive flood of other sensory signals, which in turn provide only limited information about the local causal reality. In such sparse reward scenarios, incurious agents do poorly. So, for example, AlphaZero's successor MuZero is superhuman at chess and many Atari games, but humans beat it easily at games of long-range strategic exploration (Schrittwieser et al., 2020: Supplementary Table S1). In the Atari game *Montezuma's Revenge*, for example, the player must navigate an extended 99-room labyrinth, searching for keys, amulets, and other devices to unlock doors and defeat enemies later. The first reward is a key that can be grasped only through navigating a precise path along ladders and ropes, and jumping over a skull; it is estimated that random action sequences will attain this first reward only once every 500,000 attempts (Salimans & Chen, 2018). An average human will score about 4,700 points on this game; incurious MuZero is unable to score a single point after a million rounds of training, with its pure focus on game score. Curious RL does well, however; indeed, artificial agents driven purely by curiosity, with no reward for scoring game points, can do surprisingly well (Burda et al., 2018).

One reason why curiosity is helpful in partially observable environments is that it is up to the exploring agent to decide what to observe, and under the time pressure of a changing world, it is important not to waste time exploring what is already well known. Another reason relevant to biological agents is that curiosity can scaffold the pursuit of extrinsic rewards such as nourishment, whose acquisition in a competitive environment may require extended sequences of action.

Gianluca Baldassare describes the challenge posed by sparse extrinsic reward signals as follows:

> Learning mechanisms of animals fail to function when there are long delays between the performed behaviours and the learning signals they cause. Moreover, there are few chances to produce, by trial-and-error, complex behaviours and long action chains that result in a positive impact on homeostatic needs. As a consequence complex behaviours and chains would never be learned based only on extrinsic motivations.
>
> (Baldassarre, 2011: 3)

The fact that biological learning mechanisms fail after long delays is not something that is easily overcome; we need processes of forgetting and extinction to keep us up to date in a changing environment. However, if curiosity can deliver knowledge of lasting features of the environment that are only indirectly relevant to extrinsic reward, these can function as what Baldassare describes as "readily available building blocks" (2011: 3) that can support complex actions later, as needed. In complex environments, animals who experience primary (unlearned) reward only for nourishment and reproductive actions will be outperformed by animals who also experience primary reward for knowledge gain; under the pressure of natural selection, we can expect curiosity to become a favored trait in the primary reward functions (or natural instincts) of animals who may need to learn complex behaviors to satisfy their other needs (Singh et al., 2010).

Baldassare was the theorist who spoke of the direct detection of levels of knowledge in the brain (2011: 3). He did so in a passage distinguishing extrinsic motivations such as thirst from intrinsic motivations such as curiosity. In his view, extrinsic motivations such as thirst use fitness proxies in the visceral body, which trigger innate and learned behaviors to keep the animal within safe homeostatic limits. For thirst, this role is actually played by neurons in the forebrain, outside the blood-brain barrier, which measure changes in ion concentrations (Leib, Zimmerman, & Knight, 2016). Intrinsic motivations use proxies properly inside the brain itself, such as surprise in the case of curiosity. In either case, these proximal mechanisms work to secure the distal aim of enhancing fitness. Thirst makes us drink, as curiosity makes us investigate. Cellular function is generally optimized when our fluid balance falls within a narrow range; the adaptive function of thirst is not to produce a certain ion concentration in the forebrain but to maintain the fluid balance of the whole body, which thirst does both by making it pleasurable to drink (positive reinforcement) and by being an aversive experience (negative reinforcement). The proxy can occasionally come apart from the target, for example in thirst-disrupting diseases, but when all is well, the reward signals of thirst ensure that animals can learn behaviors that keep their bodies appropriately hydrated. On the side of curiosity, when the brain detects significant discrepancies between its expected and actual experiences, the resultant feelings of surprise serve as markers of knowledge gain, delivering the pleasure of discovery, while the absence of surprise is generally indicative of a well-known environment. Strictly speaking, what is directly detected in the brain is surprise; however, this signal generally marks a change in our level of knowledge. Again, the proxy is to be distinguished from the target; occasional illusory experiences could be surprising, and could prompt the formation of false beliefs rather than knowledge. The adaptive function of curiosity is not to produce surprise signals in the brain, but to motivate animals to act in ways that accelerate their accumulation of knowledge, an acceleration that seems to be vital for the survival of organisms in challenging environments such as ours.[12]

References

Achiam, J., & Sastry, S. (2017). "Surprise-Based Intrinsic Motivation for Deep Reinforcement Learning. *arXiv*. doi: 10.48550/arXiv.1703.01732.

Aristotle. (1984). *The Complete Works of Aristotle: The Revised Oxford Translation*, ed. J. Barnes. Princeton, NJ: Princeton University Press.

Auersperg, A. (2015). "Exploration Technique and Technical Innovations in Corvids and Parrots." In A. B. Kaufman & J. C. Kaufman (eds.), *Animal Creativity and Innovation*. Amsterdam: Elsevier, 45–72.

Baldassarre, G. (2011). "What Are Intrinsic Motivations? A Biological Perspective." Paper presented at the 2011 IEEE International Conference on Development and Learning (ICDL).

Barto, A., Mirolli, M., & Baldassarre, G. (2013). "Novelty or Surprise?" *Frontiers in Psychology* 4(907). doi: 10.3389/fpsyg.2013.00907.

Behrens, T. E., Muller, T. H., Whittington, J. C., Mark, S., Baram, A. B., Stachenfeld, K. L., & Kurth-Nelson, Z. (2018). "What is a Cognitive Map? Organizing Knowledge for Flexible Behavior." *Neuron* 100(2), 490–509.

---

[12] For discussion and comments on this material, I am grateful to Sara Aronowitz, David Barnett, Nilanjan Das, Jane Friedman, Eliran Haziza, Artūrs Logins, Jessica Moss, Daniel Munro, Juan Piñeros-Glasscock, Sergio Tenenbaum, Brian Weatherson, Mason Westfall, Evan Westra, Timothy Williamson, audiences at Princeton University, the University of British Columbia, Lehigh University, and Georgia State University. Thanks also to an anonymous reviewer for Oxford University Press for helpful feedback.

Bellemare, M., Srinivasan, S., Ostrovski, G., Schaul, T., Saxton, D., & Munos, R. (2016). "Unifying Count-Based Exploration and Intrinsic Motivation." *Advances in Neural Information Processing Systems*, 29, 1–9.

Berlyne, D. E. (1966). "Curiosity and Exploration." *Science* 153(3731), 25–33.

Bringsjord, S., Govindarajulu, N. S., Banerjee, S., & Hummel, J. (2017). "Do Machine-Learning Machines Learn?" Paper presented at the 3rd Conference on "Philosophy and Theory of Artificial Intelligence."

Buckner, C. (2023). "Black Boxes or Unflattering Mirrors? Comparative Bias in the Science of Machine Behaviour." *British Journal for the Philosophy of Science* 74 (3), 681–712.

Buckner, C. (2022). "A Forward-Looking Theory of Content." *Ergo, an Open Access Journal of Philosophy* 8 (37), 367–401.

Burda, Y., Edwards, H., Pathak, D., Storkey, A., Darrell, T., & Efros, A. A. (2018). "Large-Scale Study of Curiosity-Driven Learning." *arXiv.* doi: 10.48550/arXiv.1808.04355.

Byrne, R. A., Kuba, M., & Griebel, U. (2002). "Lateral Asymmetry of Eye Use in Octopus Vulgaris." *Animal Behaviour* 64(3), 461–8.

Carruthers, P. (2018). "Basic Questions." *Mind & Language* 33(2), 130–47.

Carruthers, P. (2023). "The Contents and Causes of Curiosity." *British Journal for the Philosophy of Science,* doi: 10.1086/716609.

Dashiell, J. F. (1925). "A Quantitative Demonstration of Animal Drive." *Journal of Comparative Psychology* 5(3), 205.

Daw, N. D., Niv, Y., & Dayan, P. (2005). "Uncertainty-Based Competition between Prefrontal and Dorsolateral Striatal Systems for Behavioral Control." *Nature Neuroscience* 8(12), 1704–11.

Dayan, P. (2009). "Goal-Directed Control and its Antipodes." *Neural Networks* 22(3), 213–19.

Dennis, W., & Sollenberger, R. T. (1934). Negative adaptation in the maze exploration of albino rats. *Journal of Comparative Psychology,* 18(2), 197–206.

Dretske, F. (1983). *Knowledge and the Flow of Information.* Cambridge, MA: MIT Press.

Dubey, R., & Griffiths, T. L. (2020). "Reconciling Novelty and Complexity through a Rational Analysis of Curiosity." *Psychological Review* 127(3), 455.

Friedman, J. (2013). "Question-Directed Attitudes." *Philosophical Perspectives* 27(1), 145–74.

Glickman, S. E., & Sroges, R. W. (1966). "Curiosity in Zoo Animals." *Behaviour* 26(1–2), 151–87.

Gottlieb, J., & Oudeyer, P.-Y. (2018). "Towards a Neuroscience of Active Sampling and Curiosity." *Nature Reviews Neuroscience* 19(12), 758–70.

Haas, J. (2022). "Reinforcement Learning: A Brief Guide for Philosophers of Mind." *Philosophy Compass* 17(9). doi:10.1111/phc3.12865.

Haber, N., Mrowca, D., Wang, S., Fei-Fei, L. F., & Yamins, D. L. (2018). "Learning to Play with Intrinsically-Motivated, Self-Aware Agents." *Advances in Neural Information Processing Systems* 31, 1–12.

Harlow, H. F. (1950). "Learning and Satiation of Response in Intrinsically Motivated Complex Puzzle Performance by Monkeys." *Journal of Comparative and Physiological Psychology* 43(4), 289.

Hsee, C. K., & Ruan, B. (2016). "The Pandora Effect: The Power and Peril of Curiosity." *Psychological Science* 27(5), 659–66.

Juechems, K., & Summerfield, C. (2019). "Where Does Value Come from?" *Trends in Cognitive Sciences* 23(10), 836–50.

Kang, M. J., Hsu, M., Krajbich, I. M., Loewenstein, G., McClure, S. M., Wang, J. T.-y., & Camerer, C. F. (2009). "The Wick in the Candle of Learning: Epistemic Curiosity Activates Reward Circuitry and Enhances Memory." *Psychological Science* 20(8), 963–73.

Kidd, C., & Hayden, B. Y. (2015). "The Psychology and Neuroscience of Curiosity." *Neuron* 88(3), 449–60.

Kidd, C., Piantadosi, S. T., & Aslin, R. N. (2012). "The Goldilocks Effect: Human Infants Allocate Attention to Visual Sequences That Are Neither Too Simple Nor Too Complex." *PloS One* 7(5), e36399.

Kobayashi, K., Ravaioli, S., Baranès, A., Woodford, M., & Gottlieb, J. (2019). "Diverse Motives for Human Curiosity." *Nature Human Behaviour* 3(6), 587–95.

Kornell, N. (2014). "Where is the 'Meta' in Animal Metacognition?" *Journal of Comparative Psychology* 128(2), 143–9.

Kuba, M. J., Byrne, R. A., Meisel, D. V., & Mather, J. A. (2006a). "Exploration and Habituation in Intact Free Moving Octopus Vulgaris." *International Journal of Comparative Psychology* 19(4), 426–38.

Kuba, M. J., Byrne, R. A., Meisel, D. V., & Mather, J. A. (2006b). "When Do Octopuses Play? Effects of Repeated Testing, Object Type, Age, and Food Deprivation on Object Play in Octopus Vulgaris." *Journal of Comparative Psychology* 120(3), 184.

Lau, J. K. L., Ozono, H., Kuratomi, K., Komiya, A., & Murayama, K. (2020). "Shared Striatal Activity in Decisions to Satisfy Curiosity and Hunger at the Risk of Electric Shocks." *Nature Human Behaviour* 4(5), 531–43.

Leib, D. E., Zimmerman, C. A., & Knight, Z. A. (2016). "Thirst." *Current Biology* 26(24), R1260-R1265.

Lewis, S. A., Negelspach, D. C., Kaladchibachi, S., Cowen, S. L., & Fernandez, F. (2017). "Spontaneous Alternation: A Potential Gateway to Spatial Working Memory in Drosophila." *Neurobiology of Learning and Memory* 142, 230–35.

Leibo, J. Z., Hughes, E., Lanctot, M., & Graepel, T. (2019). Autocurricula and the Emergence of Innovation from Social Interaction: A Manifesto for Multi-agent Intelligence Research. *arXiv preprint arXiv:1903.00742*.

Liquin, E. G., & Lombrozo, T. (2020). "Explanation-Seeking Curiosity in Childhood." *Current Opinion in Behavioral Sciences* 35, 14–20.

Loewenstein, G. (1994). "The Psychology of Curiosity: A Review and Reinterpretation." *Psychological Bulletin* 116(1), 75.

Millikan, R. G. (1987). *Language, Thought, and Other Biological Categories: New Foundations for Realism*. Cambridge, MA: MIT Press.

Montgomery, K. C. (1952). "A Test of Two Explanations of Spontaneous Alternation." *Journal of Comparative and Physiological Psychology* 45(3), 287.

O'Keefe, J., & Nadel, L. (1978). *The Hippocampus as a Cognitive Map*. Oxford: Clarendon Press.

Oudeyer, P.-Y., & Kaplan, F. (2007). "What Is Intrinsic Motivation? A Typology of Computational Approaches." *Frontiers in Neurorobotics* 1, 1–14.

Oudeyer, P.-Y., & Smith, L. B. (2016). "How Evolution May Work through Curiosity-Driven Developmental Process." *Topics in Cognitive Science* 8(2), 492–502.

Pathak, D., Agrawal, P., Efros, A. A., & Darrell, T. (2017). "Curiosity-Driven Exploration by Self-Supervised Prediction." Paper Presented at the International Conference on Machine Learning.

Pavlov, P. I. (1927). *Conditioned Reflexes: An Investigation of the Physiological Activity of the Cerebral Cortex*. London: Oxford University Press.

Renner, M. J. (1988). "Learning During Exploration: The Role of Behavioral Topography during Exploration in Determining Subsequent Adaptive Behavior in the Sprague-Dawley Rat (Rattus Norvegicus)." *International Journal of Comparative Psychology* 2(1), 43–56.

Rescorla, R. A., & Wagner, A. (1972). "A Theory of Pavlovian Conditioning: Variations in the Effectiveness of Reinforcement and Nonreinforcement." In A. H. Black & W. F. Prokasy (eds.), *Classical Conditioning II: Current Research and Theory*. New York: Appleton-Century-Crofts, 64–99.

Richter, J. N., Hochner, B., & Kuba, M. J. (2016). "Pull or Push? Octopuses Solve a Puzzle Problem." *PloS One* 11(3), e0152048.

Salimans, T., & Chen, R. (2018). "Learning Montezuma's Revenge from a Single Demonstration." arXiv. doi: 10.48550/arXiv.1812.03381.

Schmidhuber, J. (2010). "Formal Theory of Creativity, Fun, and Intrinsic Motivation (1990–2010)." *IEEE Transactions on Autonomous Mental Development* 2(3), 230–47.

Schrittwieser, J., Antonoglou, I., Hubert, T., Simonyan, K., Sifre, L., Schmitt, S.,...Graepel, T. (2020). "Mastering Atari, Go, Chess and Shogi by Planning with a Learned Model." *Nature* 588(7839), 604–9.

Shannon, C. E. (1948). "A Mathematical Theory of Communication." *The Bell System Technical Journal* 27(3), 379–423.

Silver, D., Hubert, T., Schrittwieser, J., Antonoglou, I., Lai, M., Guez, A.,...Graepel, T. (2018). "A General Reinforcement Learning Algorithm That Masters Chess, Shogi, and Go through Self-Play." *Science* 362(6419), 1140–4.

Silver, D., Singh, S., Precup, D., & Sutton, R. S. (2021). "Reward Is Enough." *Artificial Intelligence* 299, 103535.

Singh, S., Lewis, R. L., Barto, A. G., & Sorg, J. (2010). "Intrinsically Motivated Reinforcement Learning: An Evolutionary Perspective." *IEEE Transactions on Autonomous Mental Development* 2(2), 70–82.

Small, W. S. (1899). "Notes on the Psychic Development of the Young White Rat." *The American Journal of Psychology* 11(1), 80–100.

Sutherland, N. (1957). "Spontaneous Alternation and Stimulus Avoidance." *Journal of Comparative and Physiological Psychology* 50(4), 358.

Sutton, R. S., & Barto, A. G. (2020). *Reinforcement Learning: An Introduction. 2nd edn.* Cambridge, MA: MIT Press.

Ten, A., Kaushik, P., Oudeyer, P.-Y., & Gottlieb, J. (2021). "Humans Monitor Learning Progress in Curiosity-Driven Exploration." *Nature Communications* 12(1), 1–10.

Tolman, E. C., & Brunswik, E. (1935). "The Organism and the Causal Texture of the Environment." *Psychological Review* 42(1), 43.

van Lieshout, L. L., Vandenbroucke, A. R., Müller, N. C., Cools, R., & de Lange, F. P. (2018). "Induction and Relief of Curiosity Elicit Parietal and Frontal Activity." *Journal of Neuroscience* 38(10), 2579–88.

Wang, M. Z., & Hayden, B. Y. (2019). "Monkeys Are Curious about Counterfactual Outcomes." *Cognition* 189, 1–10.

Warden, C. J. (1931). "Animal Motivation: Experimental Studies on the Albino Rat." In *Animal Motivation: Experimental Studies on the Albino Rat*. New York: Columbia University Press, 353–67.

Whitcomb, D. (2010). "Curiosity Was Framed." *Philosophy and Phenomenological Research* 81(3), 664–87.

Whittington, J. C., McCaffary, D., Bakermans, J. J., & Behrens, T. E. (2022). "How to Build a Cognitive Map: Insights from Models of the Hippocampal Formation." *arXiv*. doi: 10.48550/arXiv.2202.01682.

Wikenheiser, A. M., & Schoenbaum, G. (2016). "Over the River, through the Woods: Cognitive Maps in the Hippocampus and Orbitofrontal Cortex." *Nature Reviews Neuroscience* 17(8), 513–23.

Williamson, T. (2000). *Knowledge and its Limits*. New York: Oxford University Press.

8
The Point of Knowledge...is to Make Good Decisions!

Moritz Schulz

1. Introduction

Humans have various needs. They have to eat. They have to drink. Given these needs, it is no wonder that they search for food and water. And once a language is in place, one expects there to be words for food and water. This way, humans can conceptualize and think about the things they need. And they can communicate and coordinate how best to satisfy everyone's needs. In an environment of limited resources and challenging risks, humans also have a need for good information. Good information can input an agent's decision-making processes and help them to satisfy their more basic needs, say, for water or food, without risking too much. And once a language is in place, one expects there to be a word for good information. This way, humans can conceptualize and think about what information to rely on. And they can communicate and coordinate what is and what is not good information, as well as where to get it.

Edward Craig in his *Knowledge and the State of Nature* (1990) famously argued that thinking about what humans need can shed light on the concept of knowledge. He writes:

> Instead of beginning with ordinary usage, we begin with an ordinary situation. We take some prima facie plausible hypothesis about what the concept of knowledge does for us, what its role in our life might be, and then ask what a concept having that role would be like, what conditions would govern its application.
>
> (Craig 1990: 2)

This program of providing a "practical explication" (Craig 1990: 8) of a given concept can, I think, be summarized as follows (cf. Craig 1990: ch. 1; Hannon 2019: ch. 1; Kelp 2011: 54). A practical explication starts with identifying a basic human need, say, the need for food or water, or a somewhat more abstract need for forming true beliefs about the world. In a second step, one then argues that satisfying the given need would be helped if the agent or a group of agents possessed a certain kind of concept, say, the concept of water or the concept of knowledge. One may then, thirdly, consider how the concept would be further shaped, given the constitution of the agent, their (social) environment, and other forces not yet considered.[1] If what one predicts about the concept in question coheres with how the concept actually behaves, one reaches one's primary conclusion: that one has produced defeasible evidence that the concept one wished to explicate has the function of satisfying the need one has identified. In this way, one is able to answer the question what the concept is good for, or what its point is in our lives.

From a methodological viewpoint, a practical explication can take the form of an evolutionary explanation, broadly construed (cf. Craig 1990: 10). In a broad sense, an evolutionary explanation is not confined to random mutation and natural selection but may comprise any kind of features that prove beneficial for the continuous satisfaction of a certain need. The fact that practical explications often take a *genealogical form* is, I think, best accommodated by construing the genealogical story to be essentially a *thought experiment*.[2] By hypothetically starting with a very simple situation and adding complexity as one goes along, one tries to identify forces that have shaped the concept in question and are responsible for its lasting existence. In other words, the point of such a thought experiment is merely to get some idea of what reasons there might have been (and still are) for choosing a particular concept. The point of such a thought experiment is not to suggest that the order in which one adds complexity represents the temporal order of the evolution of the concept. In this way, the envisaged explanation is only evolutionary in the sense of identifying certain evolutionary forces. But it is not evolutionary in the sense of giving a temporally adequate description of actual evolution.

According to Craig's practical explication, the function of the concept of knowledge is to *flag good informants* (Craig 1990: 11).[3] Our need for information is well served when we can conceptualize those members of our community that know the answer to a given question. In this way, Craig thinks, the concept of

---

[1] In this third step, the process Craig (1990: ch. 10) calls "objectivisation" might take place. According to Craig, the original need may call for a concept ("protoknowledge" in the sense of Kusch 2009) that is heavily relativized to the actual situation of the agent. At this stage, the need might favor, for example, having a concept for informants that are currently available as well as identifiable. Ultimately, however, the concept might evolve into one that abstracts from some or all of these agent-specific features.

[2] Craig (2007) tries to make his methodology more explicit. He makes it clear that the simplified assumptions about a hypothetical "state of nature" need not reflect a state in the distant past, nor does it have to match any state in history for that matter. Craig further emphasizes that one must only introduce general assumptions about the human condition that are actually true, so that one has some reason to conclude that the account one provides uncovers causal relations that actually obtain. For relevant discussions of how best to construe Craig's methodology, see Hannon (2019: ch. 2.6) and Queloz (2021: ch. 6).

[3] See Millikan (1984, 1989) for a classical account of (proper) functions. See Simion (2021) and Queloz (2022) for more recent treatments that fit well, in my view, with the project of the present chapter. And see Hannon (2019) for a comprehensive defense as well as further development of Craig's central tenets.

knowledge is determined by a certain role some concept must play in a community of information-gathering agents. The fact that the concept of knowledge is universal in the sense that every language has a word for it (Goddard 2010) is evidence that there is indeed a universal need for something like knowledge (Craig 1990: 2; see also Hannon 2015).

Interestingly, Craig objects to a similar but simpler story. Let us consider water again. Access to water is crucial for survival. In order to survive, humans must be able to trace sources of water. For that, they may not even need the concept of water, for one can trace a certain condition without (yet) being able to have a concept that identifies the condition. Nevertheless, given the eminent importance of water, it is no wonder that humans tend to have a word for it.[4] But the purpose of this word is just to denote something that is important for us as humans.

Craig does not wish to accept a similar story about knowledge:

Couldn't it just be that knowledge, like water, is common and important stuff, and that the purpose of the concept is simply to enable us to think and talk about it?

Though I would be hard put to it to argue the point, I am fairly confident that this is mistaken. Knowledge is not a given phenomenon, but something that we delineate by operating with a concept which we create in answer to certain needs, or in pursuit of certain ideals. The concept of water, on the other hand, is determined by the nature of water itself and our experience of it.

(Craig 1990: 3)

My aim in this chapter is to show that there is a point to *tracing* knowledge—the state itself—that is prior to any advantage that having a concept of knowledge might have. In one respect at least, the concept of knowledge is similar to the concept of water.[5] The point to tracing knowledge is, I propose, to enable good decision-making.

The view I propose conflicts with a strong reading of Craig on which "knowledge is not a given phenomenon" that agents could trace prior to having a concept for it. However, as Queloz (2021: ch. 6.1) points out, one may still save the weaker claim that the concept of knowledge exist primarily for pragmatic, need-based reasons. I agree that the concept of knowledge is in at least one key aspect closely linked to social practices. There is a point to *ascribing* knowledge that goes beyond the evident advantage of conceptualizing something that is important to

---

[4] The concept of water seems to be universal as well (Goddard 2012). However, according to the *natural language metalanguage program* (Goddard 2010), the concept of water might differ from the concept of knowledge in being a 'semantic molecule' rather that a 'semantic prime'.

[5] See Kornblith (2002: ch. 2.7) for a related view that construes knowledge as a natural kind very much like water. My discussion will stay neutral on whether knowledge is a natural kind or merely a phenomenon sufficiently objective for being traceable.

us as decision-makers. This point of ascribing knowledge, I propose in a second step, is quite different from what Craig thought it would be: I suggest that ascribing knowledge helps us to uphold a social practice of assertion. It puts us in a position to monitor whether speakers assert only things they know and thus allows us to blame those who violate this norm.

2. The Point of Tracing Knowledge

We can distinguish between *tracing a condition*, *possessing a concept* that uniquely applies to this condition, and *having a word* that expresses the concept in question.

In tracing a condition, one shows a sensitivity to when the condition obtains and when it does not. Thus, one may be able to trace sources of water by being able to react in a systematic fashion to sources of water. Overall, tracing a condition requires that one is disposed to show patterns of behavior sensitive to whether one is confronted with the condition or not. For example, tracing water means that some aspects of one's behavior regularly and systematically result from a causal chain originating from the presence of water and running through one's nervous system to produce a certain behavioral output. To be sure, not any causal influence will do: If in a one-off event one finds oneself in a swamp in danger of drowning, one will certainly react in some way to the presence of water. But this would not yet mean that one has the capacity of tracing water if one were not in many other ways sensitive to the presence or absence of water.

It seems clear that lower animals can trace water without having the concept of water. Their behavior systematically relies on the presence or absence of water. But they cannot form thoughts about water, for example by asking themselves where the next source of water could be or by contemplating ways in which it might be possible to store water. Hence, it seems possible to trace water without having the concept of water. Conversely, when one has the concept of water, one can—unfavorable circumstances aside—trace the condition the concept determines.

Similarly, one may possess a concept without (yet) having a word for it, at least not in a common language. For example, one may latch onto the phenomenon of 'mansplaining' or 'languishing', start being able to conceptualize it and having thoughts about it, without yet having a word for it.[6] Conversely, when one masters a word for a concept in a certain language, one is capable of having thoughts that involve the concept in question.

So, having a word for a concept is more demanding than possessing the concept, which in turn is generally more demanding than being able to trace the

---

[6] See Fricker (2007: ch. 7) on hermeneutical injustice, particularly the discussion on pp. 149–50 about how the term 'sexual harassment' was coined.

condition determined by the concept. Nevertheless, there is likely to be a tendency for one step leading to the other. If it is important for an organism to trace a certain condition, and if that organism is capable of concept development, one would expect that the organism starts to conceptualize the condition when the benefits of doing so outweigh the costs (which they often will). And if, in addition, the organism is part of a speech community and a reasonable number (of reasonably powerful) speakers have an interest in tracing and conceptualizing the relevant condition, one would expect that they add a word for it to their language.[7]

Is there a point in tracing knowledge? Or can we, as Craig seems to have thought, best understand what (the concept of) knowledge is for when we consider the need to distinguish between good and bad testimony?

2.1. Sources of Information

At various points, one can get the impression that for Craig (1990) cases of testimony are the primary factor in shaping the concept of knowledge. For instance, he writes ('on-board' sources of information cover, in Craig's terminology, perception and reasoning):

> I shall not for the moment be concerned with the evaluation of what I have called 'on-board' sources. In the ordinary way we simply take it that the beliefs they mediate are true. To find oneself in possession of a belief on the question whether *p* pre-empts inquiry; to take a self-conscious look at one's own apparatus with the doubt in mind that it may have delivered a falsehood calls for a considerable degree of sophistication. Our investigation ought to start from the position in which we as yet have no belief about *p*, want a true belief about it one way or the other, and seek to get it from someone else.
>
> (Craig 1990: 11)

The important observation for Craig seems to be that ordinarily "we simply take it that the beliefs they [perception and reasoning] mediate are true" (1990: 11). For the sake of argument, let us grant this point. But what would it show?

It could indicate that our uptake of perceptual information does not call for the concept of knowledge, or at least not strongly so. If our responses are usually automatic, there is no space for evaluating perceptual information before a corresponding belief is formed. This may be different in the case of beliefs based on testimony. Here it may help if we have the concept of knowledge and use it to evaluate the potential informant.

---

[7] The added qualification is supposed to cover cases of hermeneutic injustice (Fricker 2007: ch. 7).

Thus, cases of testimony may be particularly important for why we have *the concept of knowledge*. But one should not assume that the same is true for *tracing knowledge*. As I wish to show now, perception is just as relevant as testimony for the question of why we trace knowledge rather than some other state.

Even if our response to perceptual information is usually automatic, this does not mean that our response system was not shaped by evolutionary forces. More precisely, it does in no way suggest that evolution could not have shaped the uptake of perceptual information in such a way that we are normally prepared to believe something if and only if the perceptual information enables us to know.

To make the point more vivid, just note that perceptual information can greatly vary in quality. Imagine you are approaching an object from great distance, say, a date palm. Seeing it from very far, we may assume that it is a palm tree. But is it a date palm or some other palm? As we get closer, the possibility of seeing a date palm gets more and more likely until it becomes a virtual certainty. At which point do we believe that it is a date palm? At which point are we prepared to rely on it being a date palm in our decision-making?

It may be that we, as we are constituted now, no longer have a say in this. At the present state of evolution, we may form the belief in question at a certain point in a more or less immediate fashion. But this does not mean that this process cannot have been shaped by evolutionary forces. We can easily imagine ourselves in other worlds forming a belief slightly earlier or later in our example and being prepared to rely on the information slightly earlier or later. In other words, we could have been epistemically more risk-seeking or epistemically more cautious.

If we were epistemically more risk-seeking, we could avail ourselves of more information more quickly. This would be an advantage. The flip side would be that the information would be a little less secure. On the other hand, if we were epistemically more cautious, it would take longer until we take information on board. That is a downside. But on the upside, the information we would use would be more secure.[8]

So, whether our beliefs are based on testimony or not, there is an evolutionary question to be answered. Why do we rely on a piece of information only when it satisfies a certain epistemic standard? Why this standard and not some other standard?[9]

---

[8] The present considerations vary the themes "Believe truth! Shun error!" from James (1896: 18). But the kind of pragmatism James arrives at is very different from the decision-theoretic argument I put forward. For James, the fact that there is a trade-off between being epistemically cautions and being epistemically risk-seeking gives us a certain amount of liberty to decide what we want to believe (e.g. we may take the risk of believing in God), where this choice may be influenced by practical factors. On the account I am about to sketch, no such consequences are endorsed. Rather, only evolution had a certain "choice" as to which epistemic standard best suits our decision-making.

[9] We may note that this question remains a live one even when one assumes that the epistemic standard can vary with context, say, with the stakes of the decision. Suppose you think that for a decision involving n-high stakes, a certain epistemic standard s should be satisfied. One can still ask: Why

Overall, I think our discussion so far has indicated that in looking for the role of knowledge, there is (a) reason to consider all sources of information and (b) reason to think that there is a point in tracing knowledge that is largely independent of the point of ascribing knowledge.[10] In Section 2.2, I take up the question of what the point of tracing knowledge could be.

2.2. Insurance against Our Own Fallibility

Almost all accounts of the point of knowledge I am aware of postulate a close connection between knowledge, decision-making, and subsequent action. For example, Craig holds:

> In seeking information we are seeking to come by true beliefs;...these beliefs, since they are beliefs (and not mere entertainings) can guide our actions—and guide them to success because they are true.
> (Craig 1990: 13)

For Craig, we want true beliefs and turn to knowledgeable informants to get them. Christoph Kelp (2011: 63–64) adjusts Craig's proposal by holding that knowledge serves rather to mark when one has *adequately terminated inquiry*, so that one could act on it. And even someone like Mikkel Gerken (2011, 2015), who sees only looser ties between knowledge and action, still thinks that in normal situations knowledge coincides with information one should be prepared to act on.

The question I would like to ask is: What happens to the point of knowledge when one puts the link between knowledge and action, specifically decisions, first? The thesis I wish to defend is that the function (the point) of tracing knowledge is to facilitate good decisions:

Point of tracing knowledge. The point of tracing knowledge is to provide optimal information for one to rely upon in decision-making.

To substantiate this thesis, I shall first say something about the role information plays in decision-making. I will then sketch an argument why knowledge might be well suited to play this role.

---

an s-high epistemic standard for decisions with n-high stakes? Why not a more or less demanding epistemic standard instead? As a matter of fact, when one relativizes standards to stakes (or contextual factors more generally), the evolutionary question becomes harder, not easier, for there are more possible functions relating stakes to standards than there are options for a single invariant epistemic standard.

[10] See also Kelp (2011: 64), who argues that the most fundamental function of knowledge concerns the quality of information, not the quality of informants.

Let me start by saying something about the relation between decision-making and information uptake. In order for our decision-making to be effective, we have to rely on certain information. This is information we can use as premises in our practical reasoning (cf. Williamson 2000: 99). Thus, when thinking about what to do, we must divide logical space into a (hopefully small) region of uncertain information and a (hopefully large) region of information we are prepared to rely on, that is, information we treat as certain or as facts (cf. Ross and Schroeder 2014; Wedgwood 2012). We can then either work with a probability function conditionalized on this information to calculate (rather slowly) expected values.[11] Or we can use some other decision rules that may be faster or show specific sensitivity to other relevant factors. But no matter what decision rule we use, there is a need for relying on certain information, or at least this is what I shall presume.

If this is on the right track, then decision-making requires a specific kind of *epistemic filter*. Such a filter would have been optimized to grant access to the "reliance module" only to a certain kind of information. Thus, when it functions properly, such a filter would only let a specific kind of information through (as we shall see below, we cannot assume that it always functions properly). The question would then be what kind of information gets positively marked as a proper basis for being relied upon in our decision-making.

Holding this model of information uptake fixed, we can hypothetically vary the strength of the envisaged epistemic filter.[12] This leads to an evolutionary question: Which setting of the epistemic filter proves evolutionary to be most advantageous for agents like us in a world like ours? Of course, the answer I would like to give is *knowledge*. So let us see how one might argue for this claim.

Perhaps the first observation should be that for us as humans a perfect epistemic filter is out of reach. There are no methods of information acquisition available to us that would let only truths through and would block all falsehoods. In general, the only guarantee we could have for not believing anything false would be to believe hardly anything (possible exceptions might include very basic a priori truths). But this would be very ineffective from a decision-theoretic point of view: Almost every decision would have to be made as if we knew nothing at all.

So, our ways of gathering information are fallible. There is surely an evolutionary story to be told about why our information gathering devices (eyes, ears,

---

[11] Such a probability function may reflect our credences, or at least a certain kind of credence we employ for the purpose of decision-making (cf. Schulz 2021). Probabilistic information can also enter our decision-making in another way by being the content of the information we use (e.g. knowledge that something is probably so-and-so likely; cf. Hawthorne and Stanley 2008).

[12] Arguably, strength is but one relevant feature. For instance, one could ask whether the filter should be such that any time two pieces of information pass the filter, their conjunction should be suitable for passing the filter as well. This would be asking whether there is a decision-theoretic benefit of relying on information that is apt for closure. Although I am optimistic that a positive argument can be made in this regard, I must leave this and related issues (such as the question of whether the filter should be invariant or sensitive to contextual factors; see Henderson 2009 and Rysiew 2012) for another occasion.

introspection, reasoning, etc.) have the degree of fallibility they in fact have (why do humans have comparatively good vision but not such a good sense of smell?). For our purposes, however, we can set these questions to one side. Even after this story has been told, there remains a question of how we handle our own fallibility. For example, what epistemic quality must perceptual information have so that we should be prepared to rely on it in decision-making? Or, in other words, given the methods of information uptake available to us with their respective degree of fallibility, how do we set the epistemic filter safeguarding our decision-making?

To get us started, we may note that fallibility matters little in a world without risks. It matters greatly, however, in a world full of risks. In a world of small risks, being wrong would not cost us as much as in a world with big risks. For example, being wrong about a bridge being safe does not cost us as much when it leads us over a small river as when it crosses a deep canyon. Hence, it is reasonable to assume that there is one factor putting evolutionary pressure on having a fairly strict epistemic filter: The more risks we face in our day-to-day decision-making, the stricter the filter should be (the more tigers live in our world, the more care we should take before we believe that there is no tiger in the underwood).

On the other hand, we can also expect pressure for not having an epistemic filter that is overly strict. Any information blocked by an epistemic filter potentially harms our decision-making. If you want to exchange goods with your neighbor, but the information that they are trustworthy is blocked by the epistemic filter, you may pass up an opportunity by not deciding to trade with them. As more information generally improves our decision-making, there is pressure against setting the bar for actionable information too high. This point can be reinforced by observing that a higher bar requires more time and energy that could instead have been spent elsewhere. In our example, one would first have to gather more information about the neighbor before deciding to trade with them. In sum, a higher bar causes our decision-making to be less effective.

What we face then, it seems, is an optimization problem. In light of the fallibility of our epistemic methods, what would be an optimal point for setting the epistemic filter that best deals with the risks we normally face, while at the same time reaping as high an amount as possible of the rewards of informed and effective decision-making?

I venture the hypothesis that knowledge is, evolutionarily speaking, a solution to this optimization problem. Knowledge clearly shows signs of being a concept that strikes a middle ground. For instance, it seems to come with something like a safety condition of intermediate strength: If we know p, we could not easily have come to a false belief about p or a similar proposition on the same or similar grounds.[13] Safety only requires that we do not err in a set of close worlds. It does

---

[13] At various points Craig (1990) comes close to imposing something like safety. For example, he writes: "reliability must include the counterfactual property that the methods would still have produced true beliefs had the world been somewhat different" (Craig 1990: 133).

not require that we do not err in far removed worlds. A safety condition of this kind and almost all conditions that have been proposed in its place (e.g. cognitive skill, sensitivity, causality) stay shy of being maximally strong.

Any proposal along these lines faces in some shape or form the following challenge: When putting forward a safety condition, one needs to answer the question why it should matter that one still believes truly in some non-actual worlds, be they close or not. For example, Craig (1990: 19) puts this question as follows:

> Why should our inquirer be interested in what is the case in possible worlds? After all, he wants to be told the truth in this world, the actual world, so whence the interest in other, and merely possible, worlds, however 'close' they may be to this one?

To begin with, let us observe that there will be a range of conditions where our disposition to believe gets triggered despite the information not being knowledgeable. This simply reflects the fallibility of our belief-forming methods. In the range in which our methods do not deliver knowledge, there will be a number of close-to-normal conditions in which the agent still believes truly due to safety. And there will be number of conditions that are far from normal but that still appear to be normal, and so our belief forming dispositions get triggered too, even though the proposition in question may not even be true.

I contend that the protection we get from tracing knowledge is one that pays off precisely when we find ourselves in situations close to normal.[14] Imagine such a situation, a world w, and suppose we do not know (say, we believe that in front of us is a date palm but we are slightly too far away for this belief to constitute knowledge). Our disposition to rely only on what we know has wrongly been triggered. But our world, the actual world w, was assumed to be close to a normal situation. That is, there will be a close world w_1 in which nothing unusual happens and so we do know (in this world, we may assume, we stand a little closer to the palm tree so that our belief does constitute knowledge). If we apply the safety condition to w_1, we see that we must believe truly in the actual world w.[15]

In this way, a disposition to rely only on knowledge helps us by managing our own fallibility: When not everything goes, epistemically speaking, according to plan, we are still protected against the risk of relying on false information, at least as long as we are still close to a world in which we do know. Thus, we minimize to

---

[14] Talk of normalcy in this context is meant to capture those conditions in which our belief-forming mechanisms function properly (and so deliver knowledge). As it stands, normalcy is appealed to in order to explain the decision-theoretic advantage of knowledge. It is not invoked as some kind of ingredient in something like an analysis of knowledge.

[15] I presuppose that closeness is symmetric: If w is close to w_1, the world w_1 is close to w. If one had qualms with this, one could rephrase the argument by framing it in terms of a converse relation, closeness*, defined by saying that w is close* to w_1 iff w_1 is close to w.

a certain degree the number of situations in the actual world in which we shall be relying on false information. And this is, I take it, an obvious advantage.[16]

Before we move on, here is a quick summary of where we stand: According to the present story, there is a point to tracing knowledge that is visible even before we consider testimony. We trace knowledge because overall this proves advantageous for managing our own fallibility. Tracing knowledge secures that we still rely on true information in situations that depart somewhat from those normal situations in which our methods would deliver knowledge. This gives us some protection, while at the same time securing that we can still make effective decisions by availing ourselves of a sufficiently great variety of information. Thus, the particular properties of knowledge reflect, on the one hand, a balance between the risks we face in our world and, on the other hand, the advantage of availing ourselves rather quickly of as much information as possible. In short, knowledge solves an optimization problem for fallible agents in a risky world.[17]

3. The Point of Ascribing Knowledge

The discussion so far has shown, I hope, that knowledge is a condition worth *tracing*. In the light of their own fallibility, humans profit from tracing a condition that is strong enough to protect them against the risks they face. At the same time, such a condition should be weak enough to facilitate effective decision-making. As it stands, these considerations would even apply to solitary agents. Why, then, do almost all linguistic communities have a word for knowledge? What is the point of *ascribing* knowledge?

As promised, there is a baseline explanation for why we have a word for knowledge on which there is nothing special about knowledge. Just as we have a word for water because water is central for our nutritional system, one may expect that we have a word for knowledge because knowledge is central for our decision-making system. I call this a 'baseline explanation' because I think that the importance of tracing knowledge is a central factor in an explanation of the universality of 'knowledge'. But I also think that it may not be the only factor.

---

[16] The present explanation proceeds in terms of *safety* rather than knowledge. Does this mean that decision-theoretically safety is more fundamental than knowledge? Probably not. As safety implies truth, and the input to proper decision-making is safe *belief*, the present story invokes something very close to knowledge: (true) belief that is safe. If one further assumes that the notion of safety conceptually depends on knowledge, then one is free to assume that knowledge is safe (true) belief for a suitably calibrated notion of safety (cf. Grundmann 2018). So, one would not have given an explanation that is independent of the concept of knowledge. Rather, one would have explained which feature of knowledge makes it decision-theoretically advantageous.

[17] The present discussion is reminiscent of Plato's Meno problem. As good decision-making surely has some value, at least part of the value of knowledge could stem from its function in good decision-making.

In this section, I outline an account of the point of ascribing knowledge in three steps, taking some inspiration from Elizabeth Fricker (2015). First, I criticize Craig (1990) for not assigning assertion any role in his story about the point of knowledge. Next, I argue that a social practice of assertion would be best served if it is norm-governed. This gives rise, I hold, to the knowledge norm of assertion. In a final step, I indicate that a norm of assertion is best upheld if norm violations can be criticized ("You did not know!"). The (main) point of ascribing knowledge, I propose, is to monitor norm compliance with a knowledge norm of assertion.

3.1. Assertion: A Blindspot in Craig's Model?

If tracing knowledge serves our decision-making well, it is clear that communities of agents would benefit from being able to exchange knowledge. It would consume a lot of time and energy if everyone tried to find out everything for themselves. So much, I think, is uncontroversial.

More controversial is what kind of practice would serve knowledge exchanges best. On Craig's theory, it can seem that information exchange is primarily explained in terms of individual activity rather than social practice:

> A very large part of the art of acquiring correct information consists in being able to recognise the sort of person (or book, or whatever) that will have the right answer. So long as the inquirer is right in thinking that it has it, he will not have to concern himself with how it may have come by it, whether by a reliable method, or as a causal consequence of the relevant facts. So no such clause will appear in the concept which we are constructing—only the condition that the subject possess some detectable property that is a good indicator of true belief on the matter under discussion.
>
> (Craig 1990: 26)

So, on Craig's picture, agents in a state of nature would be looking for subjects that have a property they can fairly easily identify and that correlates well with being right about the question of interest. Such 'indicator properties' may include the perceived reliability of a potential informant.

There is, I think, something missing in this story. To see this, picture yourself in a state of nature, looking for a certain piece of information. Now a fellow human being comes along and utters a series of words, a sentence we may assume. You may then go on to evaluate this agent for reliability, trustworthiness, and the like. But in a way there is little sense in doing this if you did not first determine something else: Did the potential informant even intend to tell you something? Or was his utterance just a guess, part of some story, a question even?

Fricker (2015: sect. 3) goes even further. She thinks Craig's description of a hypothetical "state of nature" is *incoherent*. In order to gather information from others, there must exist a speech act of *telling* somebody something to begin with. Fricker then argues that one can only productively engage with tellings if one has the concept of knowledge. So, she concludes, the concept of knowledge cannot emerge from information-gathering activities—it must already exist for those activities to make sense.

The point I wish to make is slightly weaker. As I hope to have shown in Section 3, humans like us in a world like ours have a need for knowledge. This exerts evolutionary pressure to share knowledge. Such a goal is probably best achieved with a tailor-made speech act designed for this purpose. Without any kind of speech acts, not even loose prototypical ones, there is no way of sharing information. But I think it is at least possible that the concept of knowledge evolved in parallel to developing a speech act of assertion and went through various intermediate stages in a search for an optimal design. If this is possible, then it is not strictly necessary to have a concept of knowledge in order to seek information from others.

Nevertheless, it seems clear that there is strong evolutionary pressure for speech communities to develop a practice of speech acts, especially one of assertion. It is surprising that Craig (1990) nowhere discusses assertion. One may be under the impression that Craig has overlooked the most general and far-reaching indicator property of all: (the property of) assertion.

Speech communities would greatly benefit from a social practice of assertion, and they would benefit more the better assertions provide (or indicate) the kind of information other agents are after. To a certain extent, it is under the control of a speech community to create a practice that indicates the desired kind of information well. For how well assertion indicates good information depends on how well a speech community controls that only good information gets asserted. How can this be best achieved? As I hope to describe in Sections 3.2 and 3.3, the answer is in terms of a norm-governed speech act of assertion. Ultimately, the reason why we have the concept of knowledge and use it to ascribe knowledge can be well explained in terms of the need for having a speech act of assertion.[18]

3.2. Assertion

Tracing knowledge is important to individuals, for it enables good decision-making. Once one grants that there is a point in tracing knowledge, sharing

---

[18] I hope this closes a gap in Craig's (1990) theory by awarding assertion the importance it deserves. Putting particular emphasis on a norm for assertion is not meant to suggest that nothing else can help a community to pool information well. For instance, Williams's "virtues of truth" (2002: 7), i.e. truth or knowledge related character traits, may be important, as well as abilities to correct for biases in receiving testimony (Fricker 2007). On the other hand, assigning assertion a prominent role could also make a number of elements in Craig's theory superfluous: There is no longer a need to derive somehow properties of the concept of knowledge (e.g. a reliability condition) from certain detectable properties (the 'indicator properties') of informants; see Kelp (2011) for a critique of this aspect of Craig's theory.

knowledge can be seen to have an immediate benefit, for it would greatly benefit communities by benefiting, on balance, everyone. If this is so, there is evolutionary pressure on favoring communities that find effective ways of sharing knowledge. Having a norm-governed speech act of assertion would seem to be an effective strategy to achieve this.

On the present picture, the point of assertion would be to enable agents to share information they can rely on in their decision-making. Thus, an assertion would have the function of expressing what the speaker treats as information one can rely on in one's decision-making. If all goes well, it provides the hearer with information they can subsequently rely on in their own decision-making. Thus, one would arrive at the following idea:

Point of Assertion. The point of assertion is to share optimal information for one to rely upon in decision-making.

As knowledge is, on the present picture, made to be relied upon in decision-making, it would seem to be equally correct to say that the point of assertion is to share knowledge. In this way, one would be able to derive something like the knowledge norm of assertion (Williamson 1996). But to my mind there is at least a difference in relative priority. As an evolutionary explanation, it strikes me as more plausible that the human need for epistemically protected decisions is what gave assertion its (primary) point. That assertions are governed by a knowledge norm can then be explained in terms of the fact that knowledge is the optimal epistemic standard for good decision-making.

3.3. Blame

As agents are free to either lie or otherwise assert things they do not know, it is fairly clear that a social practice of assertion is most effective if it is treated as normative. This would mean that agents are usually blamed if they assert things they do not know.[19] And this is, I contend, the ultimate or at least a major reason why we *ascribe* knowledge:

Point of Ascribing Knowledge. The point of knowledge ascriptions is to monitor compliance with the norm of assertion.[20]

---

[19] See Beebe (2012) for a comprehensive argument that the point of knowledge may be connected to blame more generally.
[20] For a similar view, see Reynolds (2002), who develops an account of the concept of knowledge based on the idea of what we would *praise* testimony for.

We may note that we can trace knowledge and even share knowledge through assertions without ever ascribing knowledge. But having a concept of knowledge, and with it a word for it, is beneficial for upholding a norm of assertion. Once we have a word for knowledge, we can blame other people ('You didn't know!'), we can defend ourselves ('I (thought I) knew.'), and we can double-check ('Do you really know this?'). Generally speaking, the concept of knowledge puts us in a position to monitor, evaluate, and correct the practice of assertion. Locating the point of ascribing knowledge close to the norm of assertion does not mean that ascribing knowledge is not also useful in other ways. Of course, if knowledge signals choice-worthy information, then being able to ask the question "Who knows?" is extremely helpful in ways similar to how Craig (1990) supposes. So, if one adopts the view that a strong evolutionary force favors ascribing knowledge in order to uphold a social practice of assertion, one does not have to deny that there are other, related forces pointing in a similar direction.[21]

This is, then, the three-part story for why there is such strong evolutionary pressure to come up with a word that expresses the concept of knowledge. First, the need for good decision-making favors agents that are capable of tracing knowledge. Secondly, the point of tracing knowledge benefits communities that have a speech act designed for exchanging knowledge: It enables members of the community, as well as the community as a whole, to trace more effectively the kind of information that makes for good decisions. Thirdly and finally, such a speech act is best implemented when it is treated as normative, that is when it constitutes a norm-governed practice. In order to uphold a norm of assertion that requires knowledge on the part of the speaker, communities need a word that expresses knowledge in order to monitor norm compliance.

4. In What Sense Is Knowledge Social?

By way of conclusion, I would like to end with a few comments on whether and in what sense knowledge is social. Recall Craig's (1990: 3) remarks cited at the beginning of this chapter to the effect that "Knowledge is not a given phenomenon, but something that we delineate by operating with a concept which we create in answer to certain needs, or in pursuit of certain ideals." For Craig, the concept of knowledge serves a social purpose. It is made for flagging good informants. Unlike water, knowledge does not have a nature of its own that a concept could latch onto.

---

[21] Thus, the picture sketched here is compatible with a pluralist view on which (the concept of) knowledge may serve more than one function (see Elgin 2021). However, the way I have described it, some functions are more basic than others.

One of the main points of the present chapter was to show that there may be a point in *tracing* knowledge. Even before we operate with a concept, there is a need for tracing information that is, on balance, best suited to input our decision-making. If this is right, then knowledge is, at least to a certain extent, very much like water.

On this picture, knowledge reflects important aspects of the human condition. That we trace knowledge rather than a stronger or a weaker state reflects that we are fallible to a certain degree and live in a world with a certain amount of risks. For this reason, the fact that we trace knowledge rather than some other state tells a story about what we need, namely a certain kind of epistemic protection. This is not yet a sense in which knowledge is robustly social. But it is a sense in which knowledge is made for us. Agents with different epistemic capacities or agents living in a world with a different amount of risks might be better served by tracing a different condition.

Moreover, the *concept of knowledge*—this was my second point—has a social function. It serves to uphold a norm of assertion. Given that knowledge is worth tracing, knowledge is also worth trading. This makes it valuable to have a speech act—assertion—that signals knowledge on the part of the speaker. Such a practice of exchanging knowledge works best if it is treated as normative, that is, if assertions that do not constitute knowledge can be criticized for precisely this reason. In this way, the concept of knowledge arises because one can only trade a condition worth tracing if one is in a position to conceptualize when speakers violate the conditions for proper information exchange. This indicates that the point of having the concept of knowledge is partly social. However, it does not indicate that what this concept determines—knowledge, the state itself—is any more social than what we have already acknowledged.

Miranda Fricker builds on Craig's account and points to a further way in which knowledge could be social: "[The foregoing considerations] suggest that knowledge is connected at core—only at core—with structures of social power, through its necessary dependence on the norm of credibility" (Fricker 1998: 176). Fricker refers here to a variant of Craig's notion of 'indicator properties'. She thinks that a practice of information exchange inevitably comes with a 'norm of credibility' (Fricker 1998: 168). The norm of credibility regulates how much credibility is assigned to various epistemic subjects. In an ideal world, what the norm of credibility ascribes perfectly corresponds with 'rational authority' (Fricker 1998: 167). However, in the actual world, it often does not, which gives rise to various forms of epistemic injustice.

The story I sketched placed little weight on the role of indicator properties in fixing the concept of knowledge. It is the value of tracing knowledge and the value of upholding a norm of assertion that I think should be the primary explanatory factors. Nevertheless, putting only little emphasis on the norm of credibility being constitutive of (the concept of) knowledge is fully compatible, at least to my mind, with endorsing the kind of critical theory Fricker advances to identify epistemic injustice. It would just be that power structures would not be part of the story of how the concept of knowledge is determined. But given that knowledge is the standard of proper assertion, knowledge can still be what is denied of agents in situations of epistemic injustice.

One may even, though this must remain a tentative suggestion for now, go a step further and try to offer a more comprehensive story of why epistemic injustice is (so) bad. For if the present story is correct, then knowledge partly constitutes proper decision-making. So, being denied one's knowledge may amount to or at least be connected to being denied proper agency (this may concern individual choices, but it can also mean that one is denied proper participation in joint decision-making). Even though what one said or the way one acted was perfectly in order—after all, one does know—one is treated as if this were not the case.[22]

References

Beebe, J. R. 2012: "Social Functions of Knowledge Attributions." In J. Brown and M. Gerken (eds.), Knowledge Ascriptions. Oxford: Oxford University Press, 220–42.

Craig, E. 1990: Knowledge and the State of Nature. Oxford: Oxford University Press.

Craig, E. 2007: "Genealogies and the State of Nature." In A. Thomas (ed.), Bernard Williams. Cambridge: Cambridge University Press, 181–200.

Elgin, C. Z. 2021: "The Function of Knowledge." Analysis 81, 100–7.

Fricker, E. 2015: "Know First, Tell Later: The Truth about Craig on Knowledge." In D. Henderson and J. Greco (eds.), Epistemic Evaluation. Oxford: Oxford University Press, 46–86.

Fricker, M. 1998: "Rational Authority and Social Power: Towards a Truly Social Epistemology." Proceedings of the Aristotelian Society 98, 159–77.

Fricker, M. 2007: Epistemic Injustice. Oxford: Oxford University Press.

Gerken, M. 2011: "Warrant and Action." Synthese 178, 539–47.

Gerken, M. 2015: "The Role of Knowledge Ascriptions in Epistemic Assessment." European Journal of Philosophy 23, 141–61.

Goddard, C. 2010: "The Natural Semantic Metalanguage Approach." In B. Heine and H. Narrog (eds.), The Oxford Handbook of Linguistics. Oxford: Oxford University Press, 459–84.

Goddard, C. 2012: "Semantic Primes, Semantic Molecules, Semantic Templates: Key Concepts in the NSM Approach to Lexical Typology." Linguistics 50, 711–43.

Grundmann, T. 2018: "Saving Safety from Counterexamples." Synthese 197, 5161–85.

Hannon, M. 2015: "The Universal Core of Knowledge." Synthese 192, 769–86.

Hannon, M. 2019: What's the Point of Knowledge? Oxford: Oxford University Press.

---

[22] I would like to thank two anonymous referees and the editors for their very helpful comments. An earlier version of this chapter was discussed in a research seminar on "Knowledge and Decision" in Dresden. Many thanks to all its participants for extremely valuable feedback.

Hawthorne, J., and Stanley, J. 2008: "Knowledge and Action." Journal of Philosophy 105, 571–90.

Henderson, D. 2009: "Motivated Contextualism." Philosophical Studies 142, 119–31.

James, W. 1896: "The Will to Believe." In James, W., The Will to Believe, and Other Essays in Popular Philosophy, first published 1897. New York: Longmans, Green and Co., 1–31.

Kelp, C. 2011: "What's the Point of "Knowledge" Anyway?" Episteme 8, 53–66.

Kelp, C. 2014: "Two for the Knowledge Goal of Inquiry." American Philosophical Quarterly 51, 227–32.

Kornblith, H. 2002: Knowledge and its Place in Nature. Oxford: Oxford University Press.

Kusch, M. 2009: "Testimony and the Value of Knowledge." In A. Haddock, A. Millar, and D. Pritchard (eds.), Epistemic Value. Oxford: Oxford University Press, 60–94.

Millikan, R. G. 1984: Language, Thought, and Other Biological Categories. Cambridge, MA: Bradford Books/MIT Press.

Millikan, R. G. 1989: "In Defense of Proper Functions." Philosophy of Science 56, 288–302.

Queloz, M. 2021: The Practical Origins of Ideas. Oxford: Oxford University Press.

Queloz, M. 2022: "Function-Based Conceptual Engineering and the Authority Problem." *Mind* 131, 1247–79.

Reynolds, S. L. 2002: "Testimony, Knowledge, and Epstistemic Goals." Philosophical Studies 110, 139–61.

Ross, J., and Schroeder, M. 2014: "Belief, Credence, and Pragmatic Encroachment." Philosophy and Phenomenological Research 88, 259–88.

Rysiew, P. 2012: "Epistemic Scorekeeping." In J. Brown and M. Gerken (eds.), Knowledge Ascriptions. Oxford: Oxford University Press, 270–94.

Schulz, M. 2021: "Partial Reliance." Canadian Journal of Philosophy 51, 436–51.

Simion, M. 2021: "Knowledge and Reasoning." Synthese 199, 10371–88.

Wedgwood, R. 2012: "Outright Belief." Dialectica 66, 309–29.

Williams, B. 2002: Truth and Truthfulness. Princeton, NJ: Princeton University Press.

Williamson, T. 1996: "Knowing and Asserting." Philosophical Review 105, 489–523.

Williamson, T. 2000: Knowledge and its Limits. Oxford: Oxford University Press.

PART 3
KNOWLEDGE AS EXPLANATORILY PRIME

9
Knowledge-First Philosophy of Science

Alexander Bird

1. Introduction and Overview

Epistemological philosophy of science has, in my opinion, paid insufficient attention to developments in mainstream or 'core' epistemology. Not everything in the latter merits attention from philosophers of science. But much does. And knowledge-first epistemology is a prime example.

Knowledge has not been regarded as important by philosophers of science. For sure, they may use the term 'knowledge'. But the concept *knowledge* does not play a central role—or even a peripheral role—in philosophy of science. For example, Karl Popper talks about 'knowledge' and one of his well-known books is entitled *Objective Knowledge* (1972). But Popper's own views about induction imply that we cannot have a justified belief in any scientific theory that implies a universal generalization and that our favoured theories are almost certainly false. Indeed, Popper claims that scientists do not, in fact, believe their theories. Thus, Popper holds that such scientific theories do not have any of the three properties that standard epistemologists take to be necessary conditions on knowledge: they are not true, they are not believed, and even if they were believed, those beliefs would not be justified. By the lights of standard epistemologists, Popper must hold that there is no theoretical knowledge in science.

Even non-sceptical realists are disinclined to take knowledge seriously as a tool in the philosophical analysis of science. For very many of them are impressed by the pessimistic meta-induction. The history of science shows, so the argument goes, that our favoured theories will in due course be refuted and replaced. There are two standard realist responses to this. One agrees with Popper that it counts as a progressive improvement if each theory, even though false, has greater verisimilitude (truthlikeness) than its predecessor. This realist, unlike Popper, regards it as rational to prefer well-confirmed theories: an optimistic induction that our theories do show increasing verisimilitude partially offsets the pessimistic one that full truth will not be achieved (Niiniluoto 1987). The other realist response, structural realism, maintains that, even though theories are rejected, there is, in fact, some component of the theory that is retained in successor theories (the mathematical structure of the theory, for example). So one can be realist about that component (Worrall 1989). (These two approaches are not mutually inconsistent.) Either way, the theories themselves are always false and so cannot have the status of knowledge (as standard epistemologists understand 'knowledge'). So, while the non-sceptical realist does take (for example) verified experimental predictions to confirm a theory, she is concerned with incremental confirmation—when a piece of evidence speaks in favour of a hypothesis; this is not absolute confirmation—when the evidence is sufficient to support outright belief.

As I shall briefly explain, I do not regard the pessimistic induction as a reason either to abjure use of the term 'knowledge' or to use it in a non-standard way. It is *possible* to know the truth of scientific theories. The philosopher qua philosopher should not make the stronger claim that we *actually* know the truth of scientific theories (since that is clearly an a posteriori claim). Nor should anyone, philosopher or not, make blanket claims about what is known (or not) across all of science. Nonetheless, it strikes me that there are no known facts inconsistent with the proposition that *some* theoretical claims in science are known. So theoretical knowledge is not only metaphysically possible; it is epistemically possible.

If we start with the idea that scientific knowledge, including knowledge of the truth of scientific theories, is possible, it is, then, a plausible idea that the purpose of science is to generate such knowledge and that science progresses when it achieves that goal. Science aims to get to know the truth of theories by making inferences from evidence. This suggests a functional account of evidence: evidence is that from which you can make knowledge-generating inferences. That, in turn, implies Williamson's equation of evidence and knowledge, $E=K$, since only knowledge can fulfil this functional role. $E=K$ allows us to reject the empiricist claim that only observational/perceptual propositions can be evidence propositions. We can also reject the Duhem–Quine thesis, since *knowledge* of the truth of an auxiliary hypothesis means that *it* cannot be responsible for an experimental outcome that appears to refute a hypothesis under investigation. Evidence that, in fact, decisively refutes a hypothesis is possible. Our methods are laden with theories. When we know those theories to be true, those theory-laden methods will generate new knowledge. New knowledge of theories can inform new methods, driving the exponential progress of science.

2. The Aims of Belief

A central tenet of knowledge-first epistemology is (Williamson 2000: 47, 208):[1] **belief aims at knowledge.** My own reason for endorsing this central knowledge-first claim is a functionalist one (Bird 2019). The function of our cognitive, belief-forming systems is to produce truth, since it is by producing true belief states that

---

[1] See also Peacocke (1999) and Engel (2004).

those cognitive systems evolved. That does not mean that the aim of belief is merely truth rather than knowledge. I interpret 'the aim of belief' as referring to the correctness conditions of belief.[2] Let an evolved system have the function of producing Fs. It is not sufficient for some X produced by S to be correct that X is an F. It is necessary also that S produces X in the right way (the way it was evolved to produce Fs). For example a patient's heart may pump blood. But it is not functioning correctly if what makes it pump is only an artificial pacemaker rather than the heart's own natural pacemaker. Likewise, for a belief to be correct, the cognitive system that produces it must be producing truth in the right way. True belief produced in the right way (i.e. in ways that rule out Gettier cases) is knowledge. Hence, belief aims at knowledge.[3]

This claim has, we shall see, very significant consequences for the philosophy of science. Among these are the rejection of empiricism and consequently the rejection of a whole class of anti-realist positions and arguments.

3. Scientific Progress and the Aim of Science

The term 'science' in English has two principal uses. It can refer to a social institution, as in 'Can science help solve the problems of climate change?' or 'The Nobel prize is science's greatest accolade' and so on. It can also refer to a body of knowledge, as in 'Do you know much science?' and 'AI is predicted to contribute significantly to the progress of science'. The knowledge in question is, as we shall see, social knowing—knowledge possessed by the scientific community. In this section I argue that science (the institution) has a constitutive goal and that this goal is indeed the production of science (the body of knowledge). In so doing I draw on the parallel with individual belief having knowledge as its aim.

Institutions can have goals and in some cases those goals are *constitutive* of the institutions in question. If institutions of type T have a constitutive aim A, it is in the nature of institutions of that type that they may be judged according to whether or not they achieve A. If, indeed, an institution fails even to attempt to achieve A, then its claim to be an institution belonging to the type T is called into doubt. It is a constitutive aim of a hospital, qua hospital, that it should aim to improve the health of it patients. It may be judged a success or failure qua hospital on that basis. It ought also to have the aim of treating its employees with respect and paying them a decent salary. But the hospital has such an aim not qua hospital but qua employer. It would be failing as an employer but not as a hospital if it did not do those things. If, on the other hand, the hospital finds other revenue

---

[2] See Chan (2013) for a collection of essays on this topic. See also Velleman (2000); Wedgwood (2002); Owens (2003); and Sullivan-Bisset (2017).
[3] Simion (2019) develops a very similar 'knowledge-first functionalism'.

streams more lucrative than caring for the sick and ceases to do this, then, however well it treats its employees, it is not a good hospital and indeed may no longer be properly regarded as a hospital at all.

Scientific institutions have as their constitutive aim the production and/or dissemination of scientific knowledge—so I shall argue. The Royal Geographical Society (RGS) was founded in 1830 as the Geographical Society of London 'as an institution to promote the advancement of geographical science'.[4] According to some historians it also acquired the aim of promoting the interests of the British Empire. It is the first of these aims that makes the RGS a *scientific* institution.

An institution such as the RGS is a formally constituted institution, but some institutions are more informal and organic in nature. Sometimes the latter are made up, in part, of many instances of the former, in virtue of their shared aims, values, and interests, as well as their resulting interactions. We often use terms such as 'the press' or 'football' in such a way (as in 'The freedom of the press is paramount' or 'Football must do more to address racism,' etc.). Science, the institution, is like this.

The idea that science has a single overriding aim, whether that is knowledge or something else, is contentious. There is more to science than the knowledge of individual scientists, it will be retorted. Science is full of a multitude distinctly scientific practices—and so science does not solely aim to produce knowledge.[5] Electron microscopy, for example, including the preparation of samples for examination, is a practice. Samples have to be fixed and dehydrated. Then, for transmission electron microscopy, the sample has to be embedded in resin and then sliced very thinly with an ultramicrotome. When viewing the resulting image, the scientist has to be adept at distinguishing artefacts of the fixation process from genuine features of the original sample. This is what actual science is like, and knowledge is not part of the story (so the objection goes).

Even if knowledge (as a product of science) is not part of the story of *this* practice, it is, nonetheless, the reason why the practice exists. Electron microscopy exists in order to help scientists gain knowledge of the structure of things. And this, in turn, may help scientists generate and test hypotheses about those things. Electron microscopy is a practice because it has established procedures and craft skills that the scientists and technicians need to master. The reasons why such

---

[4] While the RGS talks of the advancement of *science*, other institutions talk of the advancement of *knowledge*. These formulations seem interchangeable, as my view would expect. For example, the American Psychological Association says 'Our mission is to promote the advancement, communication, and application of psychological science and knowledge to benefit society and improve lives'; the International Society of Hypertension (ISH) 'is committed to promoting and encouraging the advancement of scientific research and knowledge and its application to the prevention and management of heart disease'; the Society for the Environment operates under a Royal Charter which mandates it 'to promote the advancement of, the dissemination of, knowledge of, and education in good environmental practice for the public benefit'; first among the charitable objects of the Faculty of Public Health is 'to promote knowledge in the field of public health'; and so on for many others.

[5] Such a view is prominent, for example, in the Sociology of Scientific Knowledge, some of whose proponents will claim that science is not even about the production of knowledge in the epistemologists' sense of 'knowledge'.

procedures exist and those skills need to be acquired are that they make make electron microscopy reliable and so a source of knowledge. Without the practice, someone using an electron microscope might not be able to produce a usable image; and even if they do, they would not be able, for example, to recognize the artefacts for what they are and so will end up with false beliefs. That science aims at producing knowledge explains why practices such as this exist.

The aim of science is not exclusively (or, maybe, even primarily) the knowledge of individuals. The aim of science is the production of 'social knowing', knowledge that is ascribed to a scientific community as a whole (Bird 2010). And this, I argue, cannot be reduced to individual knowing; nor can it be reduced to the mental states of individuals more generally. That debate, whether the aim of science is individual knowing or social knowing, is orthogonal to the claim currently under discussion, whether the aim of science is knowledge at all. Nonetheless, the question of the role of social knowing within knowledge-first epistemology is an interesting one. The reason why we should take social knowing seriously is a sociologically functionalist one. As Durkheim (1893), Spencer (1874–96), Parsons (1961), and others have argued, we should see institutions as having social functions. The function of science is cognitive, paralleling the cognitive capacities of individual human (and animal) thinkers. Science aims to give the relevant communities collective states of knowing. Those communities range from the scientific subcommunity of specialists in the field to society more broadly. Just as individual states of knowing affect human behaviour, states of social knowing enable social groups, ranging from communities of scientists to nation states, to engage in actions such as building the Large Hadron Collider, putting people on the moon, or slowing climate change—actions that are actions of the group rather than actions of individuals.

So, according to this line of thought, social institutions can have constitutive aims just as biological structures such as organs have a function. An institution and an organ may both, in fact, do other things, or there might be other things that it is desirable that they do. But these need not be the aim or function of the institution or organ. Scientific institutions and science as the overarching institution of which they are a part have a constitutive cognitive aim, just as sense organs and processes of the brain have cognitive functions.

Since belief aims at knowledge, scientific belief aims at scientific knowledge. Therefore, **the aim of science is the production of scientific knowledge.** An activity that has a goal of achieving (more) X makes progress when it does indeed bring about more X, or when it does things directly conducive to bringing about more X. If Somerset County Council has the aim of cleaning up the beaches along its coastline, it is making progress when more beaches are clean or each beach is cleaner than before. It also makes progress when it makes a polluting factory change its ways. Therefore, I claim (Bird 2007): **science makes progress when it adds to the stock of scientific knowledge.** It also makes progress when it does things directly conducive to the production of knowledge (e.g. the development of new techniques).

The cumulative knowledge view of progress was one that was rejected by both realist and anti-realist philosophers of science alike. Insofar as the latter accepted any idea of scientific progress, they articulated that progress in terms of increasing problem-solving power (Kuhn 1962; Laudan 1981). The former analysed progress in terms of increasing verisimilitude (Niiniluoto 1984, 2014; Oddie 1986). Despite their differences, both groups are motivated by the pessimistic meta-induction. As mentioned, this argues that because in the past theories are in due course falsified, we should not expect our current best theories, however successful, to be entirely true—they too will be falsified in due course. Kuhn's *The Structure of Scientific Revolutions* (1962) makes a central feature of the repeated rejection of paradigms following crises in science. Nonetheless, one chapter of that book is entitled 'Progress through Revolutions' and argues that the power of paradigms to solve scientific puzzles increases even through revolutions. Scientific realists have tended to argue that even if all our theories are false, their truth content increases and they get closer to the truth—they increase in verisimilitude (Psillos 1999; Niiniluoto 1980, 2014; Cevolani and Tambolo 2013). Both sides agreed that knowledge is not increasing, since theories are not true and knowledge requires truth. This ignores, on the realist side anyway, the fact that propositions of the form 'approximately p' can be true and known to be true, even if p is false and not knowable. If a sequence of propositions is getting closer to the truth, there will be another sequence of propositions, ones employing operators such as 'approximately…' or 'within a 5% margin for error', etc., that are all true, and which are knowable (if appropriate epistemic conditions are met), and which, if known, show an increase in knowledge.

In any case, the pessimistic meta-induction is overstated.[6] We do not any longer expect well-established theories to be falsified. The examples typically referred to (theories of phlogiston and caloric, the electromagnetic aether, etc.) come from the early history of science. As Fahrbach (2009) notes, the exponential growth of science means 'early' should not be measured in years, but in the quantity of science performed. More than 95% of all science has been conducted in the twentieth and twenty-first centuries, and so examples from earlier are not representative of modern science. Of all of the Nobel Prizes in science awarded since 1901, only one was awarded for research that is now regarded as fundamentally false. We now know a lot in science that we used not to know. That is progress.

4. Scientific Evidence

Science is in the business of producing knowledge by making inferences from scientific evidence—so says the knowledge-first philosophy of science I have been

---

[6] For more discussion, see Bird (2022: 42–5, 232–9).

developing. What, then, is scientific evidence? The role of evidence in inference allows us to construct a functionalist account of evidence. When an inference is used in order to produce knowledge, its success depends on two factors: the inference procedure from the evidence to the conclusion, and the propositions that are the input into the inference. The inference procedure might be as good as it could possibly be, but if the input propositions, the premises, are not good enough, then any belief in the conclusion will fail to amount to knowledge. This will be the case, for example, when the input propositions are false or are themselves lacking in justification. My functionalist proposal regarding evidence is that a proposition is evidence when it is good enough to be the input into a knowledge-generating inference, should the inference procedure itself be good enough (Bird 2018). In short, **a proposition is evidence if and only if it is possible to gain knowledge by inference from that proposition.**

The next question then is: What properties does a proposition have to have in order to be evidence? That is, how good does a proposition have to be in order to ensure that a satisfactory inference procedure will take us from that proposition to knowledge? I argue that it is necessary that the premises of an inference, if that inference really does depend on them, must themselves be known if the conclusion is to be known. This is the principle I call 'No Unknown Lemmas'. For if a premise is not true, then the conclusion, even if true, is not known ('No False Lemmas'). And if a premise is not justified, then the conclusion cannot be justified and so is not known either ('No Unjustified Lemmas'). The best explanation of these two principles is that an inference from premises that are themselves not known cannot produce knowledge. I also argue that if the premises of an inference are knowledge, then that is sufficient for the inference to produce knowledge, so long as the inference procedure is itself faultless. If one has a perfectly good inference procedure, then, for the inferred proposition to be known, the premises do not need to be any *better* than knowledge. Putting these two principles together, we learn that it is precisely the class of *known* propositions that can realize the function of being inputs into inferences that can produce knowledge. Given the functional definition of evidence, we may conclude that the class of evidence propositions is the class of known propositions. That is, **a proposition is evidence if and only if it is known.** This, of course, is Williamson's (1997, 2000) well-known equation between knowledge and evidence, $E = K$.

5. Observation

$E = K$ had profound consequences for epistemology and for philosophy of science in particular. It is widely held among philosophers of science that evidence in science is *observational*—evidence is gained by observing things. Thus, all evidence concerns entities that are observable. This is a central source of the debate between scientific realists and anti-realists. Anti-realists maintain that, from this evidence base, no justified inferences may be drawn concerning what is unobservable. Realists reply that inference procedures such as Inference to the Best Explanation do allow justified inferences from premises concerning the observable to conclusions concerning the unobservable. Hence, a key debate in the philosophy of science concerns the rationality of Inference to the Best Explanation. This debate is made particularly acute since both sides agree that observation is essentially a perceptual process. There is disagreement about whether such perception is always unaided or may be supplemented by perception-enhancing instruments. But even the weaker claim that observation includes aided perception leaves a great gulf between the evidence—the observable—and the hypotheses of science concerning the 'unobservable' (e.g. facts about magnetic field strengths, about processes at the centre of the sun, about events within the first few seconds after the Big Bang, and about the properties of subatomic particles).

Now let us consider how this debate looks in the light of $E=K$. The equation tells us that anything can be evidence that can be known. The realist thinks that facts about 'unobservables' (i.e. imperceptibles) can be known. The realist should not concede, therefore, as an assumption of the debate, that only facts about observables can be *evidence*. To concede that is to concede that only facts about observables can be known, which is the anti-realist's conclusion. To put this another way, **an anti-realist argument that assumes that our evidence is limited to the observable is question-begging.**

The view that our evidence is always observational is a manifestation of the empiricism that, in a modest form at least, is widely assumed among philosophers of science.[7] On that view the source of all our synthetic knowledge is perception. (We have noted the shared assumption of realists and antirealists alike that observation is perception, perhaps aided, perhaps not.) In my view an externalist about knowledge—not just the knowledge-firster—has no reason to be an empiricist. While the knowledge-firster rejects the reliabilist's project of providing an analysis of knowledge, we can agree that there is something right about the idea that what is required for knowledge is the existence of a reliable link between the subject and the fact known. There isn't anything special about perception or the senses—this is just the way that, contingently, we human animals gain information about our immediate environment. Realism-inclined philosophers of science are tempted to think that science is successful because it *extends* our senses, for example with optical telescopes and microscopes. This, I think, is misleading, because much of modern science is not about extending our senses but about

---

[7] Similar views are shared outside philosophy of science, even by some knowledge-firsters. Littlejohn (2011), for example, thinks $E=K$ should be limited to non-inferential knowledge. It is true that Williamson's arguments for $E=K$ do not exclude that limitation. But I think that the gap in Williamson's case for $E=K$ (1997) can be filled (Bird 2004).

replacing them.[8] Indeed, for many scientists the extent of their perceptual engagement with an object of study is no more than the reading of analysed data on a computer screen. The physical engagement with the object (collisions in a particle accelerator, a gravitational wave, a genome) is carried out by a machine whose operation is automated, as are its acquisition and analysis of data.[9] (See below for an example.)

The term 'observation' as used by scientists bears little relationship to the way that philosophers understand it. Scientists regard as observable all manner of entities (gravitational waves, subatomic particles, magnetic fields, etc.) that the philosophers take to be paradigmatically unobservable. If we ditch the empiricism of the standard philosopher of science, we can make sense of the scientists' concept of observation. Observation is a matter of gathering evidence that is basic relative to the inquiry being undertaken or to the relevant subfield. Typically it will not be absolutely basic—on the contrary, it may well itself be the result of extensive inference. For example, the Laser Interferometer Gravitational-Wave Observatory (LIGO) experiments involved making an observation of a gravitational wave. The reason that this is valuable is that it provides confirmation of a prediction of Einstein's general theory of relativity. Relative to that inquiry, facts about the gravitational wave are basic evidence. That is consistent with its being the case that our knowledge of the gravitational wave is itself inferred. That knowledge is inferred from data generated by the LIGO detectors—movement in the arms of a large interferometer. To show that this is not the result of seismic or other such activity, this data is compared with background data that would not be generated by a gravitational wave. There are two distinct inferential processes here. One infers the existence of a wave with certain characteristics. The other infers the confirmation of general relativity from the existence of that wave and its properties. The first establishes the observation of the wave. It is an observation because of the role it plays in the second (or could play in similar inferences). There is nothing in this conception of evidence that links it to perception.

The interferometer in the LIGO experiments is similar in conception to that used by Albert Michelson and Edward Morley in their eponymous experiment. In it, Michelson and Morley observed the interference patterns through a 'telescope' (an eyepiece). In their case, observation was indeed a perceptual experience—they had to look at the interference patterns and assess whether the patterns had shifted and, if so, by what amount. However, in the case of the LIGO experiments, there is no perceptual engagement with the interference patterns. Instead photodiodes transform the incident light into electrical signals. The latter

---

[8] Paul Humphreys (2004) articulates this process very well. Although he talks of 'enhancement', what he describes includes what I take to be replacement. Indeed, Humphreys imagines a post-/non-human automated science.

[9] On the latter, see Leonelli (2016).

constitute a data source that is used for a variety of computerized processes. The data is used in the first instance to control the experiment itself (e.g. to align components of the apparatus). For our purposes, more important are the computerized collection and analysis of the data—an example is the automated search for signals that are candidate indicators of a gravitational wave produced by a 'burst event' such as a collision of black holes. The production and analysis of the data that result in an observation are here entirely mediated by computers. For these scientists, unlike Michelson and Morley, there is nothing interesting to see—they see only their computer screens. The LIGO experiments are entirely characteristic of modern science in the replacement of our senses by automated and computerized instruments.[10]

6. The Duhem–Quine Thesis

The data that scientists collect do not bear directly on the theory under test. As we have just seen, there is an inference from the data regarding the LIGO detectors to the observation (as the scientists would say) that a gravitational wave with such-and-such characteristics has occurred. And that inference will depend upon a number of 'auxiliary' theoretical assumptions—for example concerning how light will behave in the interferometer, causing interference patterns.

Now imagine that an observation proposition, O, is obtained that directly contradicts the target theory, Einstein's general theory of relativity, GR. (In this example we will not assume that GR is true.) For simplicity, imagine that O is inferred from the data set, D, plus a single auxiliary theory, AT. One might think that, having obtained O, we should regard GR as refuted. On the other hand, one might come to think that O is itself mistaken. O was derived from D and AT. So we could say, instead, that the conjunction D & AT is inconsistent with GR—or, equivalently, that D is inconsistent with the conjunction GR & AT. If we drop the simplifying assumption of a single auxiliary theory, we should say that D is inconsistent with GR & AT & … & … (where '… & …' are the other auxiliary assumptions).

So it looks as if we have not refuted GR with O, but have only refuted the conjunction GR & AT & … & … with D. Should we wish to 'save' GR from refutation, we can maintain that the source of the conflict with D is not GR but is AT or one of the other auxiliary theories. The idea that we cannot test individual theories but only combinations of theories is the Duhem–Quine thesis (Duhem 1954; Quine 1951). This leads in the direction of confirmational holism—the thesis that science faces the tribunal of experience as a body. The Duhem–Quine thesis and confirmational holism have antirealist implications. For if refutation by

---

[10] For more on automated processes in data production and analysis, see Bird (2022: 7–10).

experimental test may be avoided by adjusting other theoretical commitments, it looks as if confirmation by experimental test is correspondingly weakened too. The tribunal of experience is really quite limited compared with the huge extent of science. The Duhem–Quine thesis suggests that multiple distinct bodies of science might equally well be able to give a good account of themselves in front of that tribunal.

Externalist, knowledge-first philosophy of science simply rejects the Duhem–Quine thesis. Observation O does refute GR if O is evidence and O and GR are inconsistent. According to E=K, O is evidence iff O is known. So the scientist knows that O and knows that O and GR are inconsistent and so the scientist can know by inference that GR is false (in our imaginary example).[11] So a scientist can know that a specific theory is false on the basis of inference from observational evidence. Hence, **the Duhem–Quine thesis is false.**

Is it feasible to desist from taking GR to be refuted, on the ground that O itself was inferred from D and AT? If AT were false, would it not be a mistake to reject GR on that basis? Note first that if, in fact, one knows O, then by failing to believe that GR is false, one would thereby be failing to come to know something important that one is in a position to know. There is clearly something rationally suboptimal about that. The supporter of the Duhem–Quine thesis might claim that even if one is in a position to know that GR is false, one is not thereby *certain* that GR is false. Remaining doubt over O makes it rationally permissible not to reject GR. This response assumes that the norm for assent in science is something stronger than knowledge—it is certainty. If, as the knowledge-first philosopher of science has argued, the aim of science is knowledge, then this norm is too strong. For the knowledge-firster, whether it is scientific belief or belief of another kind, it is an error to withhold assent in cases where to believe would be to know. Nor, for that matter, do scientists act as if certainty is the goal of science.

So it is not a plausible position to assert that a subject should withhold belief in the falsity of GR even though they know O and that O is inconsistent with GR. The defender of the Duhem–Quine might, therefore, try to deny that O can indeed be known. That, in turn, will typically depend on whether the auxiliary theory AT is known. If AT is the only theory involved in generating O, then it might be that we know that O if and only if we know that AT. So the Duhem–Quine strategy works here only if we do not know AT to be true. As a general thesis then, the Duhem–Quine thesis holds only if we do not know any auxiliary theory or hypothesis to be true. That is to assume anti-realism. So, as the basis for an argument for anti-realism, the Duhem–Quine thesis is question-begging. Even if it is not considered as an argument for anti-realism, one does not have a reason to accept the thesis unless one is already committed to anti-realism.

---

[11] This employs the principle of closure. Whatever doubts one might have about closure in relation to sceptical scenarios do not apply here.

7. Knowledge and the Growth of Science

Far from being a problem, the theory-ladenness of observation is a strength of science. It is because we use theories in our instruments and observational techniques that we are able to make observations that bear on the truth (or falsity) of quite esoteric scientific theories that deal in things that are utterly remote from human perception—such as gravitational waves. If we did not have theory-laden methods for making such observations, we could not devise experiments to test such theories. It is because the auxiliary theories are themselves sufficiently well confirmed that they are known to be true, that the observations laden with those theories do indeed tell us about the truth or falsity of those target hypotheses.

Quine (1951) writes, 'As an empiricist I continue to think of the conceptual scheme of science as a tool, ultimately, for predicting future experience in the light of past experience.' According to this picture, it is really only experience that confirms any theory. When scientists talk of evidence or observations that are not experiential in nature, what they are referring to is standing proxy for some set of experiences.

The picture of science that knowledge-first epistemology helps us develop is one that is radically different from Quine's. Science aims not at predicting experience but at giving us knowledge of the world. When science investigates some hypothesis, that hypothesis may start out as a conjecture and develop into a tentative theory. If all goes well—and it may not or it may take a long time to go well—sufficient evidence may be gathered that will allow the hypothesis to become known. That constitutes scientific progress. Furthermore, it enables further progress to be made.

First, since the hypothesis is now known, it too is evidence. To some, it may seem odd to think of a *theoretical* claim being evidence. But not only is that the lesson of $E=K$; it also conforms to what scientists say, for the idea of 'theoretical evidence'—evidence that comes from theory—is a common one in science.

Secondly, hypotheses that are sufficiently well confirmed to be knowledge are suited to form the basis of our theory-laden methods. For example, the development of electromagnetism following Ørsted's discovery that a magnet and a current carrying wire will exert a force on each other led to knowledge of general laws relating electric current, magnetic field strength, and force (the Biot–Savart law, Ampère's law, etc.). These laws now form the basis of instruments used to measure currents and magnetic-field strengths. If some such measurements were to be inconsistent with a hypothesis under test, it would not be a rational response to save the hypothesis by calling the Biot–Savart law into question. It is known to be true; the hypothesis under test is not. At the end of the nineteenth century, radioactivity was at the forefront of scientific research, having been first identified and studied by Marie Curie and Henri Becquerel. Ernest Rutherford and Frederick Soddy formulated the law of radioactive decay in 1902, and in 1913

Soddy hypothesized the existence of isotopes—subtypes of elements with different radioactive behaviours. By the middle of the twentieth century, a large body of knowledge regarding radioactive decay had been acquired. This included the knowledge that the processes of decay involve nuclei of one isotope decaying into an isotope of another element, then into a third isotope, and so on, forming a characteristic series. Furthermore, the decay rates for each of these isotopes were known. These facts allowed scientists to infer the age of a rock sample from the proportions of different isotopes of elements such as uranium and lead that it contains. Likewise the age of an organic sample could be determined from the proportions of different isotopes of carbon found in the sample. Radiometric dating thereby came to be an essential tool in the methods of geologists, evolutionary biologists, and archaeologists. The fact that the underlying theories were *known* is what allows us to use them as components of methods that themselves will produce knowledge (e.g. concerning the dates of fossils) that is thereby evidence that can be used to assess theories (e.g. concerning the evolutionary relationships of extinct species).

In my view, this explains the exponential growth of science referred to above. The following is not an especially knowledge-first view but fits with the knowledge-first epistemology of science I have constructed above. One might imagine that there is such a thing as the 'scientific method' and that it is the application of this method that accounts for the production of scientific knowledge since the scientific revolution. My own view is that this is a myth. There is not one scientific method but many methods in science. These are theory-laden products of science itself. This leads to the exponential growth of science. For example, one method might lead to five distinct discoveries. If each of these discoveries generates a theory-laden method, then we now have six methods, and so we are able to generate thirty new discoveries in the next phase of science. And so on. While the production new science has grown exponentially, we have seen that the refutations of theories have not kept pace. So, overall, the proportion of falsity in many—but not necessarily all—fields of science is decreasing (Fahrbach 2011) and the methods of science are increasing in reliability.

8. Conclusion

Knowledge-first epistemology allows us to construct a view of science that is radically different from the standard empiricist picture, whether realist or anti-realist. The realist empiricist takes it to be a primary task of the philosopher of science to explain how observations, which for the empiricist are the evidence of one's senses, can rationally support some degree of belief in our best theories (or, at least, in some aspects of those theories). The anti-realist accepts that the starting point of science is the same—the evidence of scientists' senses—but denies that this can support rational belief or high degrees of belief in any theory.

Knowledge-first philosophy of science enables an anti-empiricism that denies the shared assumption of both realists and anti-realists. It is not the case that the starting point of a scientific inference is always, in any interesting sense, the sense experiences of scientists. A scientific investigation starts or should start from what we already know. What we already know may well be highly theoretical or theory-laden, which is not a problem when those background theoretical propositions are themselves known. (To deny that we already have theoretical knowledge or that the theories with which our claims are laden are known to be true is to be an anti-realist. This is not an assumption that the realist should make. Nor should the anti-realist make this assumption, on pain of their arguments being question-begging.) Indeed, far from being a problem, theory-ladenness is what makes science so productive. Scientists make theoretical inferences from what they already know. Those inferences, when science is being done well, produce new knowledge. That new knowledge can be the basis for producing more new knowledge. In some cases, it does that by being the theoretical underpinning of a new method, technique, or instrument which then produces yet further new knowledge. In other cases, the knowledge generates even more new knowledge by providing the premises of a knowledge-producing inference—in which case we call those premises 'evidence'. Knowledge-first philosophy of science takes the aim of science to be the production of scientific knowledge. It is not a given that science finds itself in the fortunate position just described where knowledge-producing methods generate both valuable scientific knowledge and also new knowledge-producing methods. Indeed, it might be that some fields are in this position and others are not. But when science or a subfield of science does achieve its aim of producing knowledge, then we have scientific progress.

References

Bird, A. 2004. 'Is Evidence Non-Inferential?' *The Philosophical Quarterly* 54: 252–65.

Bird, A. 2007. 'What Is Scientific Progress?' *Noûs* 41: 64–89.

Bird, A. 2010. 'Social Knowing,' *Philosophical Perspectives* 24: 23–56.

Bird, A. 2018. 'Evidence and Inference,' *Philosophy and Phenomenological Research* 96: 299–317.

Bird, A. 2019. 'The Aim of Belief and the Aim of Science,' *Theoria* 34: 171–93.

Bird, A. 2022. *Knowing Science*. Oxford: Oxford University Press.

Cevolani, G., and Tambolo, L. 2013. 'Progress as Approximation to the Truth: A Defence of the Verisimilitudinarian Approach,' *Erkenntnis* 78: 921–35.

Chan, T. (ed.) 2013. *The Aim of Belief*. Oxford: Oxford University Press.

Duhem, P. 1914/1954. *La Théorie physique, son objet et sa structure*. Paris: Chevalier et Rivière. Translated as *The Aim and Structure of Physical Theory* by P. Wiener, Princeton, NJ: Princeton University Press, 1954.

Durkheim, E. 1893. *De la division du travail social*. Paris: Alcan. Translated as *The Division of Labor in Society*, by W. D. Halls, New York: Free Press, 1984.

Engel, P. 2004. 'Is Truth the Aim of Belief?' in D. Gillies (ed.), *Laws and Models in Science*. London: King's College Publications, 77–97.

Fahrbach, L. 2009. 'Pessimistic meta-induction and the exponential growth of science,' in A. Hieke and H. Leitgeb (eds.), *Reduction–Abstraction–Analysis*. Frankfurt am Main: Ontos, 95–111.

Fahrbach, L. 2011. 'How the Growth of Science Ends Theory Change,' *Synthese* 180: 139–55.

Humphreys, P. 2004. *Extending Ourselves: Computational Science, Empiricism, and Scientific Method*. Oxford: Oxford University Press.

Kuhn, T. S. 1962. *The Structure of Scientific Revolutions*. Chicago, IL: University of Chicago Press.

Laudan, L. 1981. 'A Problem-Solving Approach to Scientific Progress,' in I. Hacking (ed.), *Scientific Revolutions*. Oxford: Oxford University Press, 144–55.

Leonelli, S. 2016. *Data-Centric Biology*. Chicago, IL: University of Chicago Press.

Littlejohn, C. 2011. 'Evidence and Knowledge,' *Erkenntnis* 74: 241–62.

Niiniluoto, I. 1980. 'Scientific Progress,' *Synthese* 45: 427–62. (Reprinted as ch. 5 of Niiniluoto 1984.).

Niiniluoto, I. 1984. *Is Science Progressive?* Dordrecht: Reidel.

Niiniluoto, I. 1987. *Truthlikeness*. Dordrecht: Reidel.

Niiniluoto, I. 2014. 'Scientific Progress as Increasing Verisimilitude,' *Studies in History and Philosophy of Science Part A* 46: 73–7.

Oddie, G. 1986. *Likeness to Truth*. Western Ontario Series in Philosophy of Science. Dordrecht: Reidel.

Owens, D. J. 2003. 'Does Belief Have an Aim?' *Philosophical Studies* 115: 283–305.

Parsons, T. 1961. *Theories of Society: Foundations of Modern Sociological Theory*. New York: Free Press.

Peacocke, C. 1999. *Being Known*. Oxford: Oxford University Press.

Popper, K. 1972. *Objective Knowledge*. Oxford: Clarendon Press.

Psillos, S. 1999. *Scientific Realism: How Science Tracks Truth*. London: Routledge.

Quine, W. V. 1951. 'Two Dogmas of Empiricism,' *Philosophical Review* 60: 20–43.

Simion, M. 2019. 'Knowledge-First Functionalism,' *Philosophical Issues* 29: 254–67.

Spencer, H. 1874–96. *The Principles of Sociology*, i–iii. London: Williams and Norgate.

Sullivan-Bisset, E. 2017. 'Biological Function and Epistemic Normativity,' *Philosophical Explorations* 20: 94–110.

Velleman, J. D. 2000. 'On the Aim of Belief', in *The Possibility of Practical Reason*. Oxford: Oxford University Press, 244–81.

Wedgwood, R. 2002. 'The Aim of Belief', *Philosophical Perspectives* 16: 267–97.

Williamson, T. 1997. 'Knowledge as Evidence', *Mind* 106: 1–25.

Williamson, T. 2000. *Knowledge and its Limits*. Oxford: Oxford University Press.

Worrall, J. 1989. 'Structural Realism: The Best of Both Worlds?' *Dialectica* 43: 99–124.

10
Wilful Hermeneutical Ignorance to the (Qualified) Rescue of Knowledge-First

Veli Mitova

1. Introduction

In the last two decades, knowledge-first has increasingly become the in thing. Thus, philosophers have proposed a knowledge norm on belief and assertion, on epistemic justification, practical rationality, action, and so on.[1] How should we judge the merits of knowledge-first? According to its godfather, Timothy Williamson, we should do so by evaluating 'its fruitfulness as a research program, compared to its competitors' (Williamson 2013: 6–7). Many have taken up this challenge, trying either to undermine the programme or to extend it in friendly ways.[2] But surprisingly, no one (as far as I am aware) has done so in relation to the programme's *ethical* fruitfulness. The present chapter tries to fill this lacuna. In particular, I argue that knowledge-first gets somewhat unexpected, albeit qualified support from thinking about epistemically unjust phenomena such as so-called wilful hermeneutical ignorance, the deliberate ignorance of the epistemic resources of the oppressed (Pohlhaus 2012).

The argument is this. One of the most unpalatable consequences of knowledge-first is that factors beyond our ken can determine our beliefs' normative status, such as their justification or evidential support. Although knowledge-firsters have ways of dealing with this hurdle—by distinguishing between justification and excuse—many have remained unconvinced (e.g. Brown 2018; Gerken 2011). By now, the back-and-forth has grown sufficiently involved to merit looking for an arbiter from outside the debate. This is what I provide here. I show that the only way to think of wilfully ignorant belief as unjustified is by appealing to some factors beyond the ignoramus's[3] ken. Thus, if we think that justification cannot be determined by external factors, we would be implausibly forced to think of the ignoramus's beliefs as justified. This is both epistemically and morally

---

[1] See, respectively, Williamson (2000); Littlejohn (forthcoming, 2022); Hawthorne and Stanley (2008); Williamson (2018).
[2] For just a handful of examples, see Boult (2017); Gerken (2011); McGlynn (2014); Meylan (2017); Shechter (2017).
[3] I borrow this way of referring to a wilfully ignorant person from Medina (2013: 76).

unacceptable—epistemically, because such beliefs are the paradigm of unjustified beliefs, and morally, because if the ignoramus's beliefs are justified, so are, arguably, their ensuing racist, sexist, and other discriminatory actions. Thus, knowledge-first is shown to get the epistemic and moral contours of the phenomena better than at least *some* of its competitors—the internalist ones—meeting the superiority desideratum posited by Williamson. That said, the argument falls short of supporting knowledge-first against *all* competitors, since it also supports other externalist views.

Why should we care about this sort of project? For at least two reasons, apart from the direct concern of this volume with seeing how far we can put knowledge-first to work. First, if the argument here succeeds, it clears an important hurdle not just for knowledge-first but for all externalist views (whether factive or not) of normative notions such as reasons, blame, and justification.[4] Such views deny that all factors relevant to the normative status of a belief must be knowable by the believer, and this thesis is the chief source of resistance to them as much as it is to knowledge-first. (This is unsurprising, of course, as knowledge-first is an externalist view.) Thus, the argument developed here removes a main motivation for resisting these views more generally.

The second reason for caring about the present argument is that the way we remove the motivation allows these views to catch up with an important recent development in epistemology—the acknowledgement that knowledge and knowers are irreducibly social. This is now becoming somewhat of a platitude in many epistemological circles;[5] yet knowledge-firsters (and other externalists) have remained curiously unconcerned about making room for it in their accounts, continuing to treat core epistemic normative notions in completely individualistic terms.[6] By hitching an argument for such views to social epistemic phenomena

---

[4] I follow Gerken (2018) and Ichikawa (2018) in distinguishing factive from externalist views. Factive views maintain that normative concepts such as reasons and justification entail truth. Thus, for instance, reasons are facts or true propositions. Factive views other than knowledge-first include factualism (Alvarez 2010; Dancy 2000), factive versions of propositionalism (e.g. Neta 2008), and truthy psychologism (Mitova 2015, 2017). Externalist views are all views that deny that only factors within our ken determine normative status, e.g. Broome (2013) and Parfit (2011) in metaethics, and Goldman (1999a) and Sosa (1991) in epistemology. Since facts, true propositions, etc. can be beyond our ken, all factive views tend to be externalist in my current sense, but not all externalist views are factive (e.g. Gerken 2018).

[5] These range from feminist and standpoint epistemologies, epistemologies of ignorance, and epistemologies of resistance (e.g. Collins 2017; Harding 1991; Alcoff 2007; and Medina 2013, respectively), on the one hand, to more mainstream analytic areas of epistemology such as Goldman's social epistemology (e.g. Goldman 1999b) and the epistemology of testimony (e.g. Fricker 2006; Lackey 2010) and disagreement (e.g. Lackey 2008).

[6] Some have tried to connect the knowledge-first programme to group knowledge (e.g. Faria 2022). (Thanks to Arturs Login for this point and the reference.) But this is still not treating knowledge *itself* as an inherently social phenomenon, since it is the group in 'group knowledge' that adds the social dimension. Others *give us the resources* for a more social kind of knowledge-first programme by treating knowledge itself as a social phenomenon (e.g. Bird 2010; Kusch 2002; McKenna forthcoming). (Thanks to an anonymous reviewer for making me think of such views.)

such as wilful hermeneutical ignorance, we open the way for these views to start accommodating the sociality of knowledge.

Here is the plan. In Section 2, I say a bit more about the hurdle, as well as the most popular way of overcoming it. Section 3 introduces two kinds of wilful hermeneutical ignorance—white ignorance (Mills 2007) and the ignorance involved in epistemic exploitation (Berenstain 2016). Section 4 motivates the claim that the beliefs we form in such ignorance have two features: (i) they are intuitively unjustified, but (ii) not all the factors that make them so are accessible to the believer. Thus, friends of the hurdle are unable to accommodate the intuition that such beliefs are unjustified, while knowledge-firsters can. In Section 5, I consider two objections by way of refining and strengthening my response to the challenge knowledge-first faces. In Section 6, I discuss two ways in which the argument provides only a qualified defence of knowledge-first: it gives us neither reason to prefer pure knowledge-first over hybrid views, nor knowledge-first over more radical kinds of externalism.

2. The Hurdle

Knowledge-first epistemology involves two axes of theorizing.[7] The first revolves around the concept of knowledge as unanalysable. The second is about the primacy of knowledge for epistemic and other kinds of normativity. It is at this latter level that knowledge-firsters make claims that give rise to the hurdle which thoughts about wilful ignorance can overcome. In this section, I give a sense of the back-and-forth around the hurdle, making a prima facie case that we'd do well to step outside the debate if we want to make progress in it.

Here is how the hurdle comes into view. Knowledge-first ties core epistemic concepts to knowledge. Thus, for instance, Williamson (2000) originally argued that one's total evidence consists of all and only known propositions—the famous $E=K$ principle. And Clayton Littlejohn maintains the related $J=K$, that a belief is justified if and only if it constitutes knowledge. (Littlejohn forthcoming, 2022). There are many subtle and varied ways of spelling out such principles in terms of both how to understand the equal sign that relates knowledge to other epistemic concepts and the concepts themselves.[8] But the differences are unimportant for our purposes, because the problem doesn't depend on them: all knowledge-first views imply that factors outside the believer's ken can fix the normative status of their beliefs; and this strikes many philosophers as implausible.

---

[7] I borrow this way of thinking from Schechter (2017).
[8] See Dutant and Littlejohn (2021); Ichikawa (2018; Meylan (2017); and Williamson (forthcoming) for just a handful of examples.

The implausibility is meant to be dramatized by the New Evil Demon Problem (NED), developed by Stewart Cohen (1984). Suppose that two believers are identical in all relevant respects except their environments: one of them is 'bedevilled', to use Littlejohn's (forthcoming) apt term—he is the systematically deceived victim of an evil demon—while the other believer is like us. It seems pretty obvious to many that the two believers are equally justified and rational in holding the beliefs that they do, even though the beliefs of the bedevilled subject don't constitute knowledge, while at least some of the other believer's beliefs do. After all, the two are following exactly the same procedures in acquiring their beliefs, so it seems implausible to credit the one with justification and not the other.[9] But if so, then justification and evidence cannot be identified with knowledge in the way some knowledge-firsters envisage.

Many have found this thinking compelling, including knowledge-firsters themselves, with Littlejohn (forthcoming: 2) calling it 'the single most important objection' to knowledge-first:

> The hard part [about defending J = K] is defending the idea that the conditions we couldn't have known about that prevent us from knowing prevent us from believing with justification.
>
> (Littlejohn forthcoming (b): 1–2)

Let us make this a bit more general, so as to apply to all normative statuses:

The Hurdle: Knowledge-first implausibly implies that justification and/or other normative statuses can be determined by factors beyond the believer's ken.

I have deliberately formulated this claim vaguely, as involving factors beyond one's 'ken', in order to allow for a variety of ways of spelling out the internalist intuition driving the resistance to knowledge-first. First, such factors could be *propositions* that one doesn't know, *facts* that are beyond one's reach, and so on. Second, these factors may be *in principle* beyond one's ken or simply *psychologically* inaccessible due to structural defects of one's epistemic environment. (More on the latter in Sections 3 and 4.2.) The loose formulation allows the argument here to work against the motivation for all externalist views (whether factive or not), hence giving the argument the broader philosophical significance I claimed it has. It also allows the Hurdle to be fuelled by either form of internalism available in the literature—'mentalism' or 'accessibilism'. According to both, only one's mental states determine the justificatory status of one's beliefs. But accessibilism restricts justifiers further to introspectively accessible mental states alone. The

---

[9] This, of course, is the internalist way of describing things. The whole point of externalist views is that the two subjects are *not* following the same procedures—the bedevilled believer is following one that doesn't issue in true beliefs.

loose formulation is neutral between the two. But since Littlejohn's formulation of the Hurdle favours the accessibilist one, I will from now on take this view as the internalist target of my argument.[10]

As one might expect, knowledge-firsters have said plenty in response. The most popular—and, to my mind, most promising—line of defence is to argue that we can do justice to our NED intuitions without granting that bedevilled subjects are justified, by appeal to excuses. Cameron Boult summarizes the distinction between justification and excuse like this:

> *Justifications* are appropriate when the agent has a sufficient reason for ϕ-ing.
>
> *Excuses* are appropriate when the agent does not have sufficient reason for ϕ-ing, but they manifest a kind of rational excellence, or a kind of right concern for the relevant reasons, in ϕ-ing.
>
> (Boult 2019: 151; italics in original)[11]

We can, thus, acknowledge that the NED victim has followed the same belief acquisition procedures as the non-victim, without being forced to conclude that the victim's beliefs are justified. NED victims do not have sufficient reason (factively construed) to believe as they do. But since they are using their rational capacities in the way we do, they are excused for believing as they do. The identification of justification and knowledge is thus not threatened by NED:

> On this account of excuses, the kind of sympathetic response we feel towards bedeviled subjects is a sign that the subject's actions or attitudes should be excused because they result from the excellent use of the subject's rational capacities but (crucially) this response does not indicate that the subject's actions or attitudes are justified as that requires that the subject conformed to the relevant standards.
>
> (Littlejohn forthcoming : 8)

---

[10] For the distinction between accessibilism and mentalism, see Conee and Feldman (2001). See also Srinivasan (2020: 400) for a more recent example, as well as for someone who takes externalism to be antithetical to accessibilism in the first instance (though she also makes room for anti-mentalism in Section 5). An anonymous reviewer has objected that there might be a form of non-factive mentalism that escapes my argument. I am seriously doubtful about this. The way the NED challenge is usually spelt out is in terms of mental duplicates, where that includes, of necessity, non-factive states only. So, the challenge is meant to tease out precisely the *conjunction* of intuitions: that non-factive states are (a) what fixes epistemic normative status and (b) the sorts of things we do have access to. Thus, a defence of externalism—the view that we needn't have access to all justifiers—can hardly be said to be compatible with non-factive mentalism. It would, of course, be compatible with a *factive* mentalism—a view on which both factive and non-factive mental states fix justification. But this is a form of externalism, since, on this view, some justifiers—the factive ones—will be inaccessible to the subject. I take it that this is the original point of distinguishing mentalism from accessibilism—to allow for such factive, inaccessible justifiers.

[11] This is his summary of Littlejohn's (forthcoming) distinction between justification and excuse. Boult also considers alternative understandings, e.g. Williamson's (Boult 2019: 152–53; 2017a). For Littlejohn's defence of his view against Williamson see Littlejohn (2022: 2693–4). The subtle differences between these excuse-accounts don't matter here for my overarching argument.

Needless to say, this 'excuse manoeuvre'—as Gerken (2011) has sceptically called it—has attracted plenty of crossfire. Thus, some have accused it of ad hocery (Gerken 2011), others of being too coarse-grained to capture importantly different ways in which a belief can be blameless (Madison 2014).[12] Still others have argued that it gets altogether wrong the normative contours of the NED situation—an excuse is a negative normative status, while the intuition that the excuse move is supposed to accommodate is about the positive normative status a NED victim's beliefs enjoy (Brown 2018).

One of the considerations that knowledge-firsters invoke in response to these objections is that the excuse move dovetails with moral and practical evaluations in ways that are congenial to an independently plausible unified account of practical and theoretical normativity (e.g. Littlejohn 2022; Williamson forthcoming). I find this response persuasive, but it seems others don't, as the back-and-forth has by now reached quite a crescendo. In light of this, I think that it will be helpful to make independently plausible the thought that factors outside our ken can determine whether our beliefs are justified. This is what I do here with the help of wilful hermeneutical ignorance.

3. Wilful Hermeneutical Ignorance

Wilful hermeneutical ignorance occurs 'when dominantly situated knowers refuse to acknowledge epistemic tools developed from the experienced world of those situated marginally' (Pohlhaus 2012: 715). Such ignorance is made possible by the interaction of two factors—our 'situatedness' and our 'epistemic interdependence' (Pohlhaus 2012: 715). Let me quickly explain these notions, as they are important for shaping our knowledge economy more generally, resulting in the sort of epistemic gaps that will be crucial for my argument that the lack of justification of wilfully ignorant belief is partly due to factors outside our ken.

The basic idea behind situatedness is that our social position affects what we are likely to know: the common challenges we face and the concerns that arise out of these challenges 'can lead to habits of expectation, attention, and concern, thereby contributing to what one is more or less likely to notice and pursue as an object of knowledge in the experienced world' (Pohlhaus 2012: 717). When one is in a vulnerable position—whether economically, politically, or socially—one must, as a survival strategy, attune oneself to the expectations of those to whom one is vulnerable (Pohlhaus 2012: 717). This means that one needs to attend to

---

[12] Some proponents of the excuse move are not prone to this charge. For instance, Littlejohn (forthcoming, 2022) distinguishes between two kinds of blamelessness—excuse and exemption—and shows that at least some of the opposition to the excuse move comes from thinking of exemption-involving examples instead of the correct excuse-involving ones (2022: 2690).

what the powerful are likely to notice and expect (Pohlhaus 2012: 721). Thus, from a position of vulnerability, one needs two sets of epistemic resources—one's own and those of the powerful.[13]

The idea behind interdependence is that the epistemic resources on which we rely to make sense of the world around us (including our own experiences) are dependent on the community in which we find ourselves. Given our situatedness, this means that some social positions count more in developing and distributing the epistemic resources on which we depend simply in virtue of the power that comes with such positions. If I am in a dominant position, I will not need to be attuned to marginalized experiences and so will not need marginalized epistemic tools to be part of the dominant epistemic framework. Take a concept like sexual harassment (to use an example from Fricker 2007: 149–50). For a long time it did not exist in our conceptual repertoire, and it was in many people's interest to keep things that way, classifying instances of such harassment as 'just flirting', 'showing appreciation of the female form', and so on.

The result of the interaction of situatedness and interdependence, in short, is that our shared epistemic resources are not equally good for making sense of all our experiences (Pohlhaus 2012: 719). Wilful hermeneutical ignorance exploits this asymmetry—the dominant knower remains deliberately ignorant of the resources of the marginalized, which enforces her dominance by excluding those resources from the knowledge economy.[14] And here is the important point for our purposes: because these resources are excluded, they become literally unavailable to many knowers as potential reasons for belief. This is what I meant earlier by saying that factors relevant to justification could be beyond one's ken due to structural defects of one's epistemic environment.

I now consider two more concrete instantiations of wilful hermeneutical ignorance in order to clarify the phenomenon. I then show how it results in beliefs that are unjustified (Section 4.1) but whose justification is affected by factors beyond the believer's ken (Section 4.2).

3.1. White Ignorance

White ignorance, as defined by its godfather Charles Mills is: 'a non-knowing, that is not contingent, but in which race—white racism and/or white racial domination and their ramifications—plays a crucial causal role' (Mills 2007: 20). White ignorance erases white privilege from the white person's view, thereby conveniently

---

[13] Some readers will be reminded of W. E. B. DuBois's notion of double-consciousness—'this sense of always looking at one's self through the eyes of others, of measuring one's soul by the tape of a world that looks on in amused contempt and pity' (DuBois 2007/1903: xiii). See also Pohlhaus (2012: 728).
[14] Some forms of this phenomenon are known in the literature as 'contributory injustice' (Dotson 2012).

erasing the ways in which slavery, colonialism, and the continued oppression of Black communities has been essential for white people's flourishing.

Mills gives the phenomenon a rich and subtle characterization, but what matters most for my argument here is just how wide its scope is in terms of both the kinds of *cognitions* it ranges over and the spectrum of *beliefs* that it spans. Regarding the former, Mills argues that white ignorance is a form of 'group motivated irrationality' (Mills 2007: 34) in which white group interest affects all aspects of cognition—what he calls perception, conception, memory, and testimony. An example of perceptual white ignorance is the way white normativity has, for centuries, centred the world's map around Europe, making the tiny space a continent, and representing it as vastly bigger than it in fact is (Mills 2007: 26). Examples of the way white ignorance plays out in conception are historical conceptual categories such as the 'savage' in need of civilizing, the idea that Europeans were 'discovering' 'empty lands', and, more recently, the notion of 'colour-blindness' (Mills 2007: 26–8). Concerning memory, Mills makes a persuasive case for white ignorance as a kind of 'collective amnesia', achieved through textbooks (e.g. the Belgian 'Great Forgetting' of the Congo Holocaust), monuments, and the myth of the self-made man (Mills 2007: 28–9). An example of the way white ignorance affects testimony was the 1930s South-West African decree that a white person's testimony in court could only be controverted by the testimony of seven African testifiers (Mills 2007: 32). (See also Section 3.2 for another example of how testimony is affected by white ignorance.)

White ignorance not only ranges over all cognition but also over a large spectrum of belief content—from purely descriptive beliefs such as ones concerning institutionalized police brutality towards Black men to ethically thicker beliefs such as the belief that Black and white people have the same socio-economic opportunities, to outright moral judgements such as the one that not seeing colour is a way of overcoming racism rather than one of its most pernicious varieties.

Notice that white ignorance isn't some crackpot, isolated phenomenon. A structurally similar ignorance pervades all dominant groups' cognition—male, able, straight, and so on. Again, these kinds of ignorance range over all cognition and all sorts of belief content.

3.2. Epistemic Exploitation

A practice that often goes hand in hand with white ignorance is that of epistemic exploitation. This is a form of epistemic oppression in which the oppressor compels the oppressed to explain the nature or aspects of their oppression and even sometimes to justify that it is properly thought of as oppression (Berenstain 2016:

570).¹⁵ Suppose I touched a Black friend's hair in fascination with its texture and my friend pointed out that this is a textbook racist micro-aggression. I could apologize, shut up, and learn from this. Or I could start asking her to explain to me how this could possibly be an aggression when I was simply admiring her hair. In the latter case, I am engaging in epistemic exploitation.

Such engagement comes with a lethal mix of (at least) five features. First, the exploiter feels a sense of entitlement to the time and energy of the oppressed (Berenstain 2016: 575). Second, the exploiter often doesn't recognize that she is asking for both emotional and epistemic labour from the oppressed (Berenstain 2016: 576). Third, the exploiter feels and typically expresses pre-emptive scepticism about the claims the exploited will make—either about the accuracy of the description of what the oppressed person is experiencing or about its being part of a larger system of oppression (Berenstain 2016: 570-8). Fourth, such requests are tendered in the guise of a desire to expand one's mind, and couched in expressions such as 'just asking a question', 'making a well-intentioned effort to learn', and so on (Berenstain 2016: 571). Finally, such requests put the exploited in a double bind (Berenstain 2016: 575-8). On the one hand, she could refuse to engage in the exploitative request, which will typically be perceived as an affront—given the entitlement of the exploiter—and as an affirmation (to the exploiter's mind) of stereotypes such as the angry Black woman. On the other hand, she could engage the request at the cost of being emotionally drained through having to relive related oppressive experiences and justify the claim to their oppressiveness, and all this in the knowledge that it will be a pointless exercise given the default scepticism of the exploiter.

3.3. An Example

To see these features at work specifically in the context of white ignorance, consider the following example.¹⁶ Suppose that all the scholarships got given yet again to white graduates by an all-white selection panel that already has a strong reputation for racism. Suppose that a Black student pointed out that he expected this all along, given how members of the panel have treated him in the past. And suppose a white student asked him to clarify. What does he mean, she wants to know. How can he say such nasty things about her nice professors?

---

¹⁵ The term 'epistemic oppression' was initially introduced by Fricker (1999) and later developed by Kristie Dotson as a 'persistent epistemic exclusion that hinders one's contribution to knowledge production' (2014: 115). For an argument that certain forms of inclusion can also be oppressive, see Pohlhaus (2020).
¹⁶ The example is adapted from Berenstain (2016: 582) to feature race rather than gender in order to combine epistemic exploitation and white ignorance. But as mentioned at the end of Section 3.1, wilful hermeneutical ignorance is not restricted to the *racially* dominant.

The white student is shifting the burden of proof onto the Black student. First, the shift assumes epistemic authority that she doesn't have. (After all, she could hardly have any experience of being the victim of racism.) Second, she is doing so without realizing that she is asking the Black student for intellectual and emotional labour, since he would have to recall and relive the traumatic racist experiences to persuade her. Third, her tone is already one of sceptical disbelief, so persuasion is highly unlikely. And yet, fourth, the request is tendered as a genuine request to be educated. Finally, the request puts the Black student in the double bind of either ignoring it at the price of appearing confrontational or honouring it at a great emotional cost and for the sole benefit of being disbelieved in any case.

4. Wilfully Ignorant Beliefs to the Rescue

I now argue that wilfully ignorant beliefs are intuitively unjustified but some of the factors relevant to their justification are beyond the subject's ken due to the defects in the epistemic environment that wilful hermeneutical ignorance fosters. This means that anyone who is gripped by the Hurdle doesn't get right the normative contours of epistemic situations involving wilful hermeneutical ignorance.

4.1. Wilfully Ignorant Beliefs Are Unjustified

I take it for granted that most would agree that wilfully ignorant beliefs, such as the one that the scholarships got awarded on merit, are unjustified. Most simply, ignorance is never a good basis for belief no matter how one got to be ignorant.[17] But wilfully ignorant beliefs aren't simply based on ignorance; they are additionally based on group interest, rather than the evidence. Indeed, Mills describes them as a form of group motivated irrationality. Citing empirical research, he writes:

> central to the shaping of white opinion, it turns out, is [whites'] perception of their group interests...whites generally see black interests as opposed to their own. Inevitably, then, this will affect white social cognition—the concepts favored (e.g., today's "color blindness"), the refusal to perceive systemic discrimination, the convenient amnesia about the past and its legacy in the present, and the hostility to black testimony on continuing white privilege and the need to eliminate it to achieve racial justice.
>
> (Mills 2007: 35)

---

[17] Indeed, some have argued that it is a defeater in the technical sense of the term (Dutant and Littlejohn 2021).

Although, to my knowledge, we do not yet have an account of group motivated irrationality, we could certainly concede that beliefs that are based on interest rather than the evidence cannot be justified.[18] Take the white-ignorant belief that Black men are violent, supposedly supported by statistics about incarceration. This supposed support is clearly defeated by all sorts of facts about routine and institutionalized police brutality, suspect interrogation practices, and so on. When one's interests suppress knowledge of these facts, we have a clear instance of unjustified belief by anyone's lights. Or take the earlier epistemic exploiter's belief that touching a Black person's hair can be an innocent act. Once the Black person has offered epistemically authoritative testimony to the contrary, it is a clear instance of an unjustified belief.[19]

4.2. Fans of the Hurdle, Can't Think These Beliefs Unjustified

We now have all the pieces for making the central argument of this chapter: some of the factors that affect the justificatory status of the ignoramus's beliefs are beyond her ken, in the sense that they are unavailable to her due to structural defects of the environment. So, the fan of the Hurdle must either deny the plausible intuition that wilfully ignorant beliefs are unjustified or give up the Hurdle and consequently her resistance to knowledge-first.

The reason some of the justificatory factors are beyond the ignoramus's ken is that these forms of ignorance foster what José Medina calls meta-blindness—blindness to one's own ignorance and to the reasons for thinking oneself ignorant. And this kind of blindness, I submit, when cultivated by dominant knowers, in turn creates the sort of epistemic environment in which certain reasons become unavailable to certain knowers.

Here is how Medina describes meta-blindness:

> the meta-blind ignoramus arrogantly assumes that there is nothing else to perceive beyond what she or he can see or hear. And it is this persistent, stubborn denial that defines meta-blindness: *the inability to recognize and acknowledge one's limitations and inabilities.* This meta-blindness *protects the first-order forms of blindness*, which become particularly recalcitrant and resistant to change and improvement.
>
> (Medina 2013: 76; my italics)

---

[18] For the aficionados, I am thinking here of the basing relation, which on a pretty standard view is a necessary condition for (doxastic, as opposed to propositional) justification and knowledge (see, e.g. Neta 2002). Thus, I am not saying that any belief that *aligns* with or *serves* one's interest would be unjustified, but only ones that are *based on* or *driven* by that interest rather than by the evidence. (Thanks to an anonymous reviewer for making me realize that I could be misunderstood in this way.)

[19] In case the reader is worrying that I am begging the question against the internalist here, I address this worry in Section 5.1.

But, we can continue the argument, the trouble is that these kinds of ignorance create and exacerbate what Miranda Fricker (2007: 151) calls hermeneutical lacunas—gaps in our collective self-understanding especially when it comes to understanding the experiences of the marginalized. This is a direct consequence of the dynamic between our situatedness and interdependence described at the beginning of Section 3. But once these gaps are in place, certain reasons become literally unavailable to the ignoramus, including reasons to believe that she is ignorant, which enforces her meta-blindness. For instance, before we had the concept of sexual harassment, reasons featuring this concept were literally unavailable to both harassed and harasser, which made it impossible to diagnose the lack of justification of their beliefs (and actions) in terms of factors available to these believers.

This is one way in which reasons can be unavailable through wilful ignorance—when we lack the relevant concepts due to the gaps in the environment that the ignorance of the dominant creates. But reasons can also be unavailable to a group through lack of uptake of the relevant concepts even when these concepts are available in the general knowledge economy. Hence, one still hears the infamous 'it's just flirting' even though the concept of sexual harassment has been in circulation for a good four decades. This is a clear result of the power that socially dominant knowers have to affect which epistemic resources get legitimated and are allowed to feature in acceptable explanations.

Couldn't the internalist object at this point that the notion of justification I ascribe to her is too demanding, implausibly requiring grasp of all relevant concepts?[20] I think that whether this charge sticks would depend on the way we describe the content of the belief whose justification we are discussing as well as the justifiers themselves. I hope that at least under some descriptions the larger point stands: if you live in a society that doesn't have the conceptual resources to call wrong what you believe is wrong, then it is unclear in virtue of what considerations available to you we can call justified your belief that something is wrong.

But in case the objection lingers, let me return to the scholarship example, which doesn't depend on such a demanding conception of justification. The trouble here is that a white-ignorant person is likely to see the award of the scholarship as evidence that the white graduates were the most able candidates in a pool of candidates who all had a genuinely equal opportunity to get the scholarship. This conveniently erases race in at least four respects: (i) the racial homogeneity of the panel, (ii) the strange coincidence of their race and the successful candidates', (iii) the panel's reputation for racism, and (iv) the fact that the unsuccessful candidates who supposedly had this equal opportunity are all Black.

---

[20] Thanks to Artūrs Logins and Jacques Vollet.

This erasure of race, in turn, amounts to an erasure of all sorts of evidence against the belief that merit was all that mattered in the selection procedure: that the institution in which the selection process has taken place is unjust (i and iii); that the panel is likely to maintain the racist status quo (ii and iii); and that not all candidates have had the same chance (iv and iii). Making unavailable such evidence is bad enough in itself. But it gets worse once we notice that these bits of evidence are also evidence against white-ignorant beliefs that are essential for maintaining the white-ignorant framework itself, such as the beliefs in the myth of the self-made man and in the virtues of colour-blindness. White ignorance, in other words, deprives its owner of reasons (a) against her beliefs in white-ignorant propositions and (b) her commitment to the white-ignorant framework, as well as of (c) reasons to believe that she is ignorant in these ways. But if so, then according to a friend of the Hurdle the white ignorant person's beliefs are justified: only reasons within her ken matter for the justification of her belief; and since those support her beliefs, these beliefs are justified.

The same goes for the epistemically exploitative episode that followed in our example (Section 3.3). When the exploiter asks the Black student to justify his claim that the selection panel is racist, she is already poised not to absorb his testimony. This starts her on the way to depriving herself of reasons to believe as she should. But it gets worse: the double bind in which the exploiter places the exploited typically ensues in the victim's pre-emptively silencing himself in expectation of being disbelieved.[21] Now add that the exploiter is situated in an environment which structurally favours her point of view and marginalizes that of the exploited. And the result is that the latter's testimony—evidence against the exploiter's beliefs—literally becomes unavailable to the exploiter. Again, the body of evidence includes both evidence against individually wilfully ignorant beliefs and larger reasons for doubting the entire wilfully ignorant framework and one's ignorance.

In contrast to friends of the Hurdle, and somewhat trivially, the knowledge-firster is in a perfect position to make sense of why many of the ignoramus's beliefs are unjustified: they are based on bad reasons—propositions that the ignoramus believes but doesn't know, because they are false.

5. Refining the Argument

If these thoughts are on the right track, we have at least a prima facie argument against the Hurdle: those who are impressed by it get wrong the normative contours of a sizeable portion of the epistemic terrain, while knowledge-firsters get it right. In this section, I refine the argument by countering two natural objections to it.

---

[21] Some forms of this phenomenon are known as 'testimonial smothering' (Dotson 2011: 237).

5.1. Justification and Rationality

The first objection which the internalist might raise is that I have begged the question against her when arguing that white-ignorant beliefs are unjustified (Section 4.1).[22] The argument was that these beliefs are a paradigm instance of motivated irrationality and hence must be unjustified by anybody's lights. But the internalist can retort that for irrationality claims to stick without begging the question against her—and without appealing to factors external to the agent—there must be some inconsistency within the agent's perspective itself. If such an inconsistency is present within her perspective, however, then she has in her possession reasons against some of her white-ignorant beliefs within her perspective. And if so, the internalist does, after all, have the resources to say that the white-ignorant person's beliefs are unjustified: whatever bits of evidence I am saying are inconsistent with her white-ignorant beliefs can be used by the internalist to diagnose the lack of justification of those beliefs. Conversely, once I have shown that there are no reasons available to the white-ignorant against her beliefs (Section 4.2), the internalist cannot accept my argument that such beliefs are irrational and hence unjustified (Section 4.1).

I think that the objector misunderstands the dialectical situation here. Both the claim to irrationality and the move to lack of justification can be staked independently of the present fight over the Hurdle. First, that white-ignorant beliefs are irrational is not something that I need to argue for, since this is taken for granted in the epistemic-injustice literature. Mills diagnoses such beliefs as a form of motivated irrationality and all motivated belief is *epistemically* irrational, since it is based on pragmatic considerations rather than the evidence.[23] Notice that this claim is neutral on the externalism–internalism debate.[24] It only relies on the thought that justified beliefs are based on the evidence/good epistemic reasons rather than on interest and bias. But this thought is silent on the issue which divides externalists and internalists—whether all epistemic reasons need to be accessible to us in order to make a contribution to the normative status of our beliefs.

Second, the move from a belief's lack of rationality to its lack of justification should be uncontroversial *for the internalist*. It is *her* view that rationality and

---

[22] Thanks to Artūrs Logins and Jacques Vollet for a version of this objection.

[23] In case this needs saying, obviously, the beliefs can be *practically* very rational, as they can be seen as promoting one's peace of mind and general well-being (assuming we don't have a knowledge norm on practical rationality or a very close link between morality and practical rationality). I am skirting over the thriving debate over whether pragmatic reasons can be reasons for belief (see, e.g. Meylan 2021 and Reisner 2009).

[24] I am making this point in order to pre-empt the following worry raised by an anonymous reviewer: the epistemic injustice literature perhaps already presupposes an externalist view of justification, the worry goes, and so using their justification verdicts to argue for externalism is circular. While I am not clear on the general stance on justification of epistemic injustice theorists, the line I develop here shows that, at all events, nothing *I* have said about the two epistemically unjust phenomena presupposes externalism.

justification go hand in hand. (Hence her insistence that the bedevilled subject is as justified as the normal one.) It's the externalist who is happy to drive a wedge between rationality and justification. Hence, it is *dialectically* unproblematic for an externalist to move from irrationality to justification in the context of an anti-internalist argument. And if I am right that the claim that such beliefs are irrational is *independently* plausible, then the present objection misfires. Indeed, I suspect that we could go further and argue that, given the often structural and veiled nature of the way white interest affects such beliefs, we could make an argument for going factive and externalist about rationality itself, but I will not press this point here.

5.2. Justification and Responsibility

The second natural objection for the Hurdle friend to raise at this point is that I have underestimated her resources for making sense of justification claims. After all, she has normative notions at her disposal other than reasons and rationality. Thus, she can make perfect sense of the lack of justification of the ignoramus's beliefs in terms of responsibility: the ignoramus is epistemically irresponsible—motivated belief being the paradigm of such irresponsibility—and hence her beliefs are unjustified. Since this response makes no appeal to factors beyond her ken, hinging instead on a standard internalist notion of justification, my argument miscarries.

The trouble with this response is that it just kicks the can down the road. Let us grant, as I think we ought, that the ignoramus's belief formation is irresponsible. The problem is that wilful hermeneutical ignorance and the kind of structurally defective environment it cultivates make the reasons for believing that the ignoramus is being irresponsible as unavailable to her, as I argued it makes unavailable the direct evidence against her first-order, white-ignorant beliefs. I now develop the argument for this response by showing how a general internalist condition on responsibility, applied to the epistemic domain, blocks the internalist from being able to say that the ignoramus is irresponsible. The move to responsibility, then, will not help the internalist resurrect the Hurdle.

Suppose that by pressing F9 on your computer you would end my career as a professional philosopher. And suppose you don't know this. As philosophers' stories rarely end well, you press F9. Are you blameworthy for ruining my career? The standard answer is that you aren't, because you violate a basic condition on responsibility—the so-called 'epistemic condition': 'S is blameworthy for bringing about consequence C by φ-ing only if S knew that in φ-ing she would bring about C' (Graham 2017: 163). Since you didn't know that by pressing F9 you would end my career, your action violates the epistemic condition, and you cannot be held responsible. This is an internalist condition on moral responsibility, and as the reader has probably noticed, it wears its affinity to the Hurdle on its sleeve: only factors within the agent's ken can contribute to determining whether she is responsible for her action.[25]

Now let us go to epistemic responsibility and the ignoramus. The internalist's contention was that the ignoramus was epistemically irresponsible in forming her beliefs, and this allowed the internalist to make sense of the claim that these beliefs are unjustified. But how *could* the ignoramus be irresponsible by the internalist's lights? As I argued, some of the reasons against her beliefs, *including reasons to believe that she is being ignorant*, are unavailable to her due to the defects in the epistemic environment created by white ignorance. Hence, by believing as she does, she breaches the epistemic condition on responsibility, and she cannot—according to the internalist whose condition this is—be held irresponsible for believing as she does.

Could the internalist not maintain that even though those reasons are unavailable to the ignoramus, they *ought* to have been available; she *ought* not to have been colour-blind and hence made all this evidence unavailable to herself.[26] After all, a plausible internalism would only allow ignorance to exculpate when the ignorance itself is non-culpable. Thus, for instance, if you were culpably ignorant of the fact that pressing F9 would end my career, we *would* think that you were blameworthy for ending it. Similarly, since wilful ignorance is culpable, it does not excuse.

This response once again kicks the can down the road: some of the fuel for wilful ignorance is implicit bias, that is, deep-seated bias whose existence is simply unavailable to the ignoramus. Of course, it *should* be available, but only the externalist can say this. Otherwise, internalism loses its distinctive tenet—that only factors within the subject's ken affect the normative status of her beliefs.[27] Since whether you have complied with an epistemic ought is equally a determinant of normative status, external oughts can't be used by the internalist to determine normative status. The point is enforced if you think that oughts are fixed by your conclusive reasons. Since the internalist only allows reasons available to you to count, moving to ought would still not allow the unavailable reasons to play a role.[28]

So it looks as if appeal to neither rationality nor responsibility will help the internalist block my argument against the Hurdle. Knowledge-first is still in business.

---

[25] It could also be argued that the condition is perspectivist rather than internalist. (Thanks to Artūrs Logins and Jacques Vollet.) I discuss this possibility in Section 6.2.

[26] Thanks to Artūrs Logins for this objection.

[27] The mentalist may have the resources to handle this objection. (Thanks to Artūrs Logins for making me realize this.) But I suspect only the factivist kind of mentalist, who would still be externalist. See n. 10 above.

[28] Artūrs Logins has also pointed out that the move to oughts seems to undermine an important dialectical motivation for internalism, talk of reasons being far more congenial to tying normative verdicts to the perspective of the actor and believer.

6. A Qualified Defence of Knowledge-First

I said at the beginning that the present argument will constitute a *qualified* defence of knowledge-first. The most obvious qualification has already been implicit throughout: the argument works in favour of all forms of externalism, even non-factive ones such as Gerken (2018) and more traditional views such as reliabilism (e.g. Goldman 1999a). This is because all such views posit justification determinants—such as the reliability of the belief-forming process—that may be inaccessible to the believer. The present argument doesn't get us all the way to factive views, since it just helps us resist a commitment shared by factive and non-factive externalists. I now discuss two further qualifications: the defence does not adjudicate in favour of knowledge-first as opposed to hybrid knowledge-first views (Section 6.1); nor does it give us any reason to prefer knowledge-first to more radical forms of externalism (Section 6.2).[29]

6.1. Back to the Bedevilled

The first qualification comes into view when we return to the excuse manoeuvre. According to knowledge-first, the bedevilled are unjustified but excused. According to the argument so far, the wilfully ignorant are unjustified and *not* excused—they are epistemically blameworthy. But now, given that in both cases we have reached these verdicts on the basis of factors beyond the believer's ken, the challenge for the knowledge-firster becomes to give a principled account of the difference between the two cases. In the absence of such an account, she fails to capture Brown-style intuitions that the bedevilled enjoy a positive epistemic status (which the white ignorant clearly lack), and thus the excuse manoeuvre remains ad hoc.

I have already foreshadowed the resources that knowledge-firsters have for handling this worry. Recall the way Boult spelt out the applicability of excuses: they are only applicable to agents who 'manifest a kind of rational excellence, or a kind of right concern for the relevant reasons, in φ-ing' (Boult 2019: 151). Likewise, Littlejohn insists that excuses are only appropriate for 'wrongful responses that manifest virtue and rational excellence' (Littlejohn 2022: 2690). The bedevilled subject certainly manifests the sorts of epistemic virtues, rational excellence, and concern for reasons that her non-bedevilled duplicate does. But clearly, the white ignorant subject does not. As I suggested (after Mills 2007), white ignorance is a form of motivated irrationality, thus undermining the possibility of rational excellence and right concern for reasons. And as I argued

---

[29] I am really grateful to Artūrs Logins for making me realize both these limitations to the defence.

(with Medina 2013), white ignorance produces and deepens meta-blindness, putting epistemic virtue beyond reach.

This is one of several resources that the knowledge-firster has at her disposal for deflecting charges of ad hocery. But notice that whatever resource we deploy here, it will not be a purely knowledge-first one. Virtues, excellences, and concern for reasons are character traits. Using them to help knowledge-first out means that we are not letting knowledge alone fix normative status. Thus, the view that can avoid the Hurdle is a hybrid one. My argument from wilful ignorance, correspondingly, falls short of defending a pure knowledge-first against this alternative hybrid view. The knowledge-firster will need to come up with an additional, independent argument if she is interested in staying pure.

6.2. Radical Externalism

The second qualification to my defence of knowledge-first through the present argument is this. We first notice that with the Hurdle out of the way, the motivation for having the agent's perspective as a determinant of normative status altogether disappears. But if so, then we open the door to much more radical forms of externalism than the one presupposed by knowledge-first friends. These friends may allow for factors beyond one's ken to determine normative status but that is because of the factivity of knowledge. Knowledge, however, is still a mental state of the agent's on this view (Williamson 2000: ch. 1), and hence the determinants of normative status still remain at least partly within the agent's perspective—only those propositions which are known count as evidence and fix normative status. Thus, knowledge-first is a form of externalism that is still 'perspectivist' (Fassio 2021). Once we remove the Hurdle, however, we remove the requirement that the agent's perspective is relevant to determining normative status at all. Thus, the argument here is also compatible with a defence of 'objectivism', the view that 'what an agent ought to do (believe, like, fear,...) depends on all kinds of facts, including facts not accessible to the perspective of the agent' (Fassio 2021: 184).

Could we not make a case for knowledge-first over objectivism by appeal to the consideration just developed that knowledge-first is, as a matter of fact, better off when it comes to making sense of the difference between the NED victim and the wilful ignoramus? A totally externalist view, presumably, would not be able to do this: both victim and ignoramus are transgressing objective oughts, so their epistemic status is, counter-intuitively, equivalent. But this move won't help knowledge-first. First, as just argued, the thing in virtue of which knowledge-first is better off—virtue, excellence, right concern for reasons—is not, in fact, a distinctively knowledge-first tool, so it is available to others. Second, the radical externalist has principled, distinctively radical externalist tools for distinguishing between these cases: the NED victim violates objective norms of reliable belief formation; the white-ignorant believer violates the objective evidence norm (though neither knows this).[30]

If the considerations in this section are compelling, the argument I have offered here doesn't take us all the way to knowledge-first; it just clears the way for it. The knowledge-firster still needs an independent argument if she wants to stay factive, pure, or moderate. For the argument clears a hurdle about access to justifiers, but such views are as non-accessibilist as is knowledge-first.

7. Conclusion

I have tried to make the case here that the supposedly most unpalatable feature of knowledge-first (and other externalist views)—that it makes normative status depend on factors beyond our ken—is not, in fact, so unpalatable. On the contrary, unless we embrace it, I have argued, we can't make sense of the negative epistemic status of epistemically and morally pernicious phenomena such as wilful hermeneutical ignorance. Such phenomena are instances of group-motivated irrationality and hence unjustified, I have argued. But only a view that allows external factors to affect justificatory status can accommodate this verdict. Knowledge-first is such a view.

A more detailed argument along these lines would, of course, have to say more about how exactly group-motivated irrationality works. In particular, one would need to tell a bigger-picture story about how epistemic responsibility distributes from a group to its members in cases where the members often have no access to the factors that affect their epistemic status. This much I think we owe to the internalist: although my response to her objections is *dialectically* correct, a more *satisfying* response would do more explanatory work as well, especially on this nexus between group responsibility and the individual's. One possibility here would be to retain the internalist intuition that drove the Hurdle by making these reasons internal to the group and allowing them to transmit to the individual in virtue of her membership. I tell a story along these lines elsewhere (Mitova 2022). Here I just hope to have said enough to make at least prima facie plausible the claim that knowledge-first and other externalist views have better resources than

---

[30] Two additional reasons for preferring radical externalism are provided by Fassio's (2021) persuasive argument against perspectivism and Srinivasan's (2020) argument that externalism provides a better account of justification verdicts in conditions of systematic oppression. (Srinivasan focuses on the beliefs of the victims rather than on those of the perpetrators as I have done here. A fuller account along these lines should explore how the two mesh.)

their internalist competitors for getting right the normative contours of epistemically unjust phenomena such as wilful hermeneutical ignorance.[31]

References

Alcoff, L. M. (2007), 'Epistemologies of Ignorance: Three Types', in S. Sullivan and N. Tuana (eds.), *Race and Epistemologies of Ignorance* (Albany, NY: State University of New York Press), 39–57.

Alvarez, M. (2010), *Kinds of Reasons: An Essay in the Philosophy of Action* (Oxford: Oxford University Press).

Berenstain, N. (2016), 'Epistemic Exploitation', *Ergo* 3/22: 569–90.

Bird, A. (2010), 'Social Knowing: The Social Sense of "Scientific Knowledge"', *Philosophical Perspectives* 24: 23–56.

Boult, C. (2017), 'Epistemic Normativity and the Justification-Excuse Distinction', *Synthese* 194: 4065–81.

Boult, C. (2019), 'Excuses, Exemptions, and Derivative Norms', *Ratio* 32: 150–58.

Broome, J. (2013), *Rationality through Reasoning* (Oxford: Wiley-Blackwell).

Brown, J. (2018), *Fallibilism: Evidence and Knowledge* (Oxford: Oxford University Press).

Cohen, S. (1984), 'Justification and Truth', *Philosophical Studies* 46: 279–96.

Collins, P. H. (2017), 'Intersectionality and Epistemic Injustice', in I. J. Kidd, J. Medina, and G. Pohlhaus Jr. (eds.), *The Routledge Handbook of Epistemic Injustice* (London: Routledge), 115–24.

Conee, E., and Feldman, R. (2001), 'Internalism Defended', *American Philosophical Quarterly* 38/1: 1–18.

Dancy, J. (2000), *Practical Reality* (Oxford: Oxford University Press).

Dotson, K. (2011), 'Tracking Epistemic Violence, Tracking Practices of Silencing', *Hypatia* 26/2: 236–57.

Dotson, K. (2012), 'A Cautionary Tale: on Limiting Epistemic Oppression', *Frontiers: A Journal of Women's Studies* 1: 24–47.

Dotson, K. (2014), 'Conceptualizing Epistemic Oppression', *Social Epistemology* 28/2: 115–38.

---

[31] Research on this chapter was funded by the European Research Council (ERC) under the European Union's Horizon 2020 Research and Innovation Programme (Grant agreement no. 740922). Huge thanks to Artūrs Logins, Jacques Vollet, and an anonymous reviewer for really helpful comments on earlier drafts of this chapter, as well as to the members of the *Normative and Moral Foundations of Group Agency* at Vienna University, the Vienna Forum for Analytic Philosophy, and the ZEGRA group at Zurich Philosophy for their feedback on some of the ideas defended here and presented at events they kindly hosted.

Du Bois, W. E. B. (2007/1903), *The Souls of Black Folk* (Oxford: Oxford University Press).

Dutant, J., and Littlejohn, C. (2021), 'Defeaters as Indicators of Ignorance', in J. Brown and M. Simion (eds.), *Reasons, Justification, and Defeat* (Oxford: Oxford University Press), 223–46.

Faria, D. (2022), 'A Knowledge-First Account of Group Knowledge', *Logos and Episteme* 13/1: 37–53.

Fassio, D. (2021), 'Perspectivism, Accessibility and the Failure of Conjunction Agglomeration', *Ethics* 131: 183–206.

Fricker, M. (1999), 'Epistemic Oppression and Epistemic Privilege', *Canadian Journal of Philosophy*, 29 (Supplement): 191–210.

Fricker, E. (2006), 'Second-Hand Knowledge', *Philosophy and Phenomenological Research* 73: 592–618.

Fricker, M. (2007), *Epistemic injustice: Power and the ethics of knowing*. New York: Oxford University Press.

Gerken, M. (2011), 'Warrant and Action', *Synthese* 178/3: 529–47.

Gerken, M. (2018), 'The New Evil Demon and the Devil in the Details', in V. Mitova (ed.), *The Factive Turn in Epistemology* (Cambridge: Cambridge University Press), 102–22.

Goldman, A. (1999a), 'Internalism Exposed', *Journal of Philosophy* 96/6: 271–93.

Goldman, A. (1999b), *Knowledge in a Social World* (Oxford: Oxford University Press).

Graham, P. (2017), 'The Epistemic Condition on Moral Blameworthiness: A Theoretical Epiphenomenon', in P. Robichaud and J. W. Wieland (eds.), *Responsibility: The Epistemic Condition* (Oxford: Oxford University Press), 163–79.

Harding, S. (1991), *Whose Science? Whose Knowledge? Thinking from Women's Lives* (Ithaca, NY: Cornell University Press).

Hawthorne, J., and Stanley, J. (2008), 'Knowledge and Action', *Journal of Philosophy* 105/10: 571–90.

Ichikawa, J. (2018), 'Internalism, Factivity, and Sufficient Reason', in V. Mitova (ed.), *The Factive Turn in Epistemology* (Cambridge: Cambridge University Press), 66–83.

Kusch, M. (2002), *Knowledge by Agreement: The Programme of Communitarian Epistemology* (Oxford: Oxford University Press).

Lackey, J. (2008), *Learning from Words: Testimony as a Source of Knowledge* (Oxford: Oxford University Press).

Lackey, J. (2010), 'What Should We Do When We Disagree?' in T. S. Gendler and J. Hawthorne (eds.), *Oxford Studies in Epistemology*, iii (Oxford: Oxford University Press).

Littlejohn, C. (2022), 'A Justification for Excuses: Brown's Discussion of the Knowledge View of Justification and the Excuse Manoeuvre', *Philosophical Studies* 179/8: 2683–2696.

Littlejohn, C. (forthcoming), 'A Plea for Epistemic Excuses', in F. Dorsch and J. Dutant (eds.) *The New Evil Demon Problem* (Oxford: Oxford University Press).

McGlynn, A. (2014), *Knowledge First?* (London: Palgrave Macmillan).

McKenna, R. (2022), 'Knowledge as a Natural Phenomenon', *Inquiry*. https://doi.org/10.1080/0020174X.2022.2135823

Madison, B. (2014), 'Epistemological Disjunctivism and the New Evil Demon', *Acta Analytica* 29: 61–70.

Medina, J. (2013), *The Epistemology of Resistance: Gender and Racial Oppression, Epistemic Injustice, and Resistant Imaginations* (Oxford: Oxford University Press).

Meylan, A. (2017), 'In Support of the Knowledge-First Conception of the Normativity of Justification', in J. A. Carter, E. C. Gordon, and B. W. Jarvis (eds.), *Knowledge First: Approaches in Epistemology and Mind* (Oxford: Oxford University Press), 246–58.

Meylan, A. (2021), 'Doxastic Divergence and the Problem of Comparability: Pragmatism Defended Further', *Philosophy and Phenomenological Research* 103/1: 199–216.

Mills, C. (2007), 'White Ignorance', in S. Sullivan and N. Tuana (eds.), *Race and Epistemologies of Ignorance* (Albany, NY: State University of New York Press), 13–38.

Mitova, V. (2015), 'Truthy Psychologism about Evidence', *Philosophical Studies* 172/4: 1105–26.

Mitova, V. (2017), *Believable Evidence* (Cambridge: Cambridge University Press).

Mitova, V. (2022), 'The Collective Epistemic Reasons of Social Groups', *Asian Journal of Philosophy*, 1/47: 1–20.

Neta, R. (2002), 'S Knows That P', *Noûs* 36/4: 663–81.

Neta, R. (2008), 'What Evidence Do You Have?', *British Journal of Philosophy of Science* 59: 89–119.

Parfit, D. (2011), *On What Matters* (Oxford: Oxford University Press).

Pohlhaus, G. (2012), 'Relational Knowing and Epistemic Injustice: Toward a Theory of Willful Hermeneutical Ignorance', *Hypatia* 27/4: 715–35.

Pohlhaus, G. (2020), 'Epistemic Agency under Oppression', *Philosophical Papers* 49/2: 233–51.

Reisner, A. (2009), 'The Possibility of Pragmatic Reasons for Belief and the Wrong Kind of Reasons Problem', *Philosophical Studies* 145: 257–72.

Schechter, J. (2017), 'No Need for Excuses: Against Knowledge-First Epistemology and the Knowledge Norm of Assertion', in J. A. Carter, E. C. Gordon, and B. W. Jarvis (eds.), *Knowledge First: Approaches in Epistemology and Mind* (Oxford: Oxford University Press), 132–59.

Sosa, E. (1991), *Knowledge in Perspective: Selected Essays in Epistemology* (Cambridge: Cambridge University Press).

Srinivasan, A. (2020), 'Radical Externalism', *Philosophical Review* 129/3: 395–431.

Williamson, T. (2000), *Knowledge and its Limits* (Oxford: Oxford University Press).

Williamson, T. (2013), 'Knowledge First', in M. Steup, J. Turri, and E. Sosa (eds.), *Contemporary Debates in Epistemology* (2nd edn, Wiley-Blackwell) 1–9.

Williamson, T. (2018), 'Knoweldge, Action, and the Factive Turn', in V. Mitova (ed.), *The Factive Turn in Epistemology* (Cambridge: Cambridge University Press), 125–141.

Williamson, T. (forthcoming), 'Justifications, Excuses, and Skeptical Scenarios', in F. Dorsch and J. Dutant (eds.), *The New Evil Demon Problem* (Oxford: Oxford University Press).

11
Reasons and Knowledge

Christina H. Dietz and John Hawthorne

1. Introduction

In other work we have defended a link between certain kinds of reason ascriptions and knowledge. Dietz (2018) and Hawthorne and Magidor (2018) defend the view that for a proposition to serve as a motivating reason, it has to be known. Moreover, Hawthorne and Magidor defend the view that, in order for a normative reason to be possessed, the reason has to be known. In this chapter, we elaborate on this framework, defend it against various objections, and compare it with some alternative approaches. Recent work by Juan Comesaña (some co-authored with Matt McGrath) and Mark Schroeder will serve as our main foil. Those authors develop approaches that are diametrically opposed to the one we defend, approaches that deny that the relevant kinds of reasons need to be true, let alone known. Our larger goal is further to motivate a picture according to which reasons are facts that get possessed by knowing them.[1,2]

2. Factivity

There is a good prima facie case that motivating reasons and possessed normative reasons must be known. Let's start with propositional motivating reasons, the phenomenon picked out by paradigmatic uses of constructions of the form 'S's reason for *v*-ing was that P'.[3,4] First, it seems that sentences of this form entail

---

[1] For the purposes of this chapter, we assume that facts are true propositions. We realize that some (for example, Vendler 1972) have challenged this, but we shall set aside the question whether they are right, as well as the question how the discussion that follows should be tweaked to accommodate this.

[2] Note also that our preferred picture has interesting consequences for old debates about the relation between reasons and causes, though we shall not explore the connection here. For further discussion, see Dietz (2016).

[3] We should not forget that there is also the construction 'S's reason for *v*-ing was to F' (a construction that gets relatively little attention in the literature on reasons). This last kind of construction seems to pick out a motivating goal rather than a motivating fact. A knowledge–reason connection is not plausible here. Hawthorne and Magidor (2018: 140, n. 1) suggest that this is perhaps elliptical for something along the lines of 'S's reason for V-ing was that her goal was to V'. Given the awkwardness of this construction, the suggestion seems rather speculative. And in any case it would not be a good basis for defending a constitutive knowledge link, since there are cases where one has a motivating goal without knowing that one does.

[4] Philosophers tend to use 'factivity' to encode an entailment thesis. An operator O is factive just in case the truth of 'OP' entails 'P'. By contrast, linguists tend to use 'factivity' to encode something about presupposition: An operator is factive in this alternative sense just in case 'OP' *presupposes* the truth of

the proposition expressed by the complementizer phrase 'That P'. In this connection, notice that the claim:

1. Smith's reason for leaving was that he had promised to be home by 10 p.m. but Smith had not promised to be home by 10 p.m.

sounds contradictory. Secondly, claims of the relevant form do not seem true in cases where the complementizer phrase expresses a proposition that is true but is not known. Suppose Jones is at a party and mistakes Maud for Mindy when Mindy is in fact at the party but in the next room. Suppose Jones then leaves because they don't like the thought of being at a party with Mindy present. It seems wrong to say:

2. Jones's reason for leaving the party was that Mindy was there.

An important caveat is in order here. The possessive construction is notoriously flexible (think of the myriad possible meanings of 'John's horse') and there are, in fact, a few different uses of 'S's reason' that need to be distinguished.[5] Consider the sentence:

3. Jones's reason for going to see Smith was that they believed they had twelve tropical diseases.

There are two different uses of this claim.[6] One use is in one important respect parallel to 'Jones's reason for leaving was that the house was on fire'. In this last case, supposing the claim is true, there is a fact that Jones becomes aware of—the house being on fire—and this very fact motivates Jones to leave the house. A parallel use of 3 would describe a case where Jones becomes aware of a certain psychological fact—their belief that they had twelve tropical diseases—and went to a psychiatrist, Smith, on this basis. This is the paradigmatic use of 'S's reason' and what we have in mind when we talk about motivating reasons. But there is another setting in which 3 is used. Suppose Jones went to a tropical disease

---

'P'. (So for example 'It is true that' is factive in the philosophers sense but not that of the linguists.) We intend the philosophers' use. Obviously there are cases where a sentential environment both presupposes and entails some embedded sentence and thus is factive in both senses. (We think 'S regrets that P' is an example of this. By contrast, 'S doesn't regret that P' merely presupposes the content of 'P'.) The factivity issue discussed here should be sharply distinguished from a second factivity thesis, namely that claims of the form 'P is a reason why Q' are factive with respect to 'Q'. For a persuasive case against this second factivity thesis, see Nebel (2019).

[5] As one would expect from the possessive, there are plenty of other, less common uses as well. In a setting where John and Christina are each handed a reason for Smith to v, written down on a piece of paper, 'John's/Christina's reason was that P' might refer to the information on the relevant piece of paper. (Thanks for discussion with Mark Schroeder here.)

[6] See Hornsby (2007, 2008) for relevant discussion.

doctor, Smith, and the ascriber is dubious of the truth of 'Jones had twelve tropical diseases'. In this case, factivity forbids:

4. Jones's reason for going to see Smith was that they had twelve tropical diseases.

In a setting like this we tend to switch to a different, *fallback* use of 'Jones's reason' where it no longer picks out the fact in the light of which the relevant actor acted. In a setting like this, the agent was moved by a consideration that turned out to be false. To respect factivity one does not insert that consideration as the complementizer phrase but instead a propositional attitude ascription that displays the fact of one's belief in the proposition that served as the consideration. In this fallback construction, 'Jones's reason' is working in a different way. In the sense it which it is true that the fact that Jones believed they had twelve tropical disease is Jones's reason in the psychiatry case, it is false that this fact is Jones's reason in the tropical disease specialist case. 4 only gets to be true in the context of the tropical disease specialist because a deviant use of 'Jones's reason' is in play.

Let's turn briefly to possessed normative reasons. As with the motivating reason construction, there seems to be a factivity entailment for normative reasons: 'That James has just won a million dollars is a reason for him to celebrate, but James has not just won a million dollars' is scarcely intelligible. How about the purported knowledge requirement on possession? We have just noted that possessive reason constructions are highly flexible. It is no surprise then that talk of 'possessed normative reasons' could, depending on context, denote a variety of phenomena. To fix ideas, Hawthorne and Magidor make clear that their target is a kind of possession that makes propositions *available* as motivating reasons, and they think that one very standard use of 'S is a reason S has' is to denote a state of affairs that involves such availability. And on this use, they suggest, the possessive expresses a relation that carries a knowledge requirement with it for reasons tightly connected to the fact that such a requirement obtains for motivating reasons. (Obviously this could all be precisified further by saying more about the intended meaning of 'available'.)

So far, this has all been recap. And we don't pretend that the knowledge-theoretic picture of reasons is new. The remarks in Dietz (2018) and Hawthorne and Magidor (2018) are substantively indebted to work by such authors as Alvarez (2010), Hornsby (2007, 2008), Hyman (1999, 2011, 2015), Unger (1975), and Williamson (2000). To move things forward, we wish in this section to examine some work that has challenged the factivity assumptions that drive this picture.

In their 'Having False Reasons' (2014), Comesaña and McGrath recognize the oddity of sentences like 1 but wish to explain their oddity without relying on a factivity diagnosis. Against that diagnosis they point out that while 'simple cancellations' like:

5. Sally's reason for turning down the job was that she had another offer, but she didn't have another offer

are problematic, the following sound rather better:

6. Sally's reason for turning down the job was that she had another offer; and that made perfect sense; however, her source was lying—she never had the other offer.

(Comesaña and McGrath 2014: 73)

7. Sally's reason for turning down the job was that she had another offer, but she was misinformed about the other offer—it was not a job offer after all but only a request for more materials.

(Comesaña and McGrath 2014: 74)[7]

They then offer an alternative picture: 'X's reason for v-ing was that P' merely *presupposes* that X believes that *p*, but then, unless one is given evidence to the contrary, it will be natural for audiences to assume that the backgrounded belief is true. This is why, if 'P' means that *p*, we naturally assume that *p* when we hear 'Jones's reason for V-ing was that P'.

Do 6–7 show that the factivity hypothesis is wrong after all? We don't think so. Here it is important to be aware of the following kind of phenomenon: we begin by narrating things from the perspective of some agent and then, in effect, take back part of what is narrated. Consider, for example:

8. Sally knew she was going to win. All the signs pointed that way. But alas, her sources were misleading her. She came in third.

This sounds *a lot better* than:

9. Sally knew she was going to win, but she was going to lose.

But no one should take 8 as decisive evidence against the factivity of 'know'. Similarly consider:

---

[7] Comesaña and McGrath also evidently think sequences like the following are good (cf. their discussion in 2014: 74): 'Sally's reason for leaving the room was that there was a dog in the room. You see, she falsely believed a dog-shaped stone to be a dog.' We are less impressed by sequences like these. Interpolating extra material improves things a bit. For example: 'Sally's reason for leaving the room was that there was a dog in the room. You see, she really doesn't like dogs. And on this occasion she falsely believed a dog-shaped stone to be a dog.' Our suspicion is that what is going here is that the interpolations distract the reader from the semantic oddity by creating some distance between the offending pair of sentences. We also suspect that this is part of what is going on in the examples in the text (so, for example, interpolations like 'and that made perfect sense' help in just this kind of way).

10. Jones had found the island with buried treasure.

We take it as obvious that this entails that there was buried treasure on the island.[8] Nevertheless 12–13 sound much better than 11:

11. Jones had found the island with buried treasure, but there was no buried treasure.
12. Jones had found the island with buried treasure. That made perfect sense. The map had shown the way. But the map Jones had trusted was a fabrication. There was no buried treasure on the island.
13. At last, Jones had found the island with buried treasure. But Jones had been misinformed. It wasn't treasure that was buried there, only fake jewellery.

As we see it, what is going on with 8, 12, and 13 is that we narrate from an agent's false point of view, reveal the point of view is false, and then, in effect, take back the claim we began with (rather like the sequence: 'Jones had found the island with buried treasure. Or so they thought'.) And we want to suggest that this is what is going on with 6 and 7. One way to test this diagnosis is to look at what happens when the order of information is reversed.

14. The map that Jones had trusted was a fake. There was in fact no buried treasure on the island. Jones had found the island with buried treasure.
15. Jones had been misinformed. There was no buried treasure on the island, only fake jewellery. Jones had found the island with buried treasure

These sequences are hard to make sense of.

Let us turn to the 'reason' examples, with the order of information reversed:

16. Sally's source was lying—Sally never had another job offer. And Sally's reason for turning down the initial job offer was that she had another offer.
17. Sally thought she had another job offer but was misinformed. It was not a job offer after all but only a request for more materials. And her reason for turning down the initial job offer was that she had another offer.

These sequences sound much worse to us. But this is not predicted on the Comesaña and McGrath diagnosis. Consider similarly:

18. There was no dog in the room, just a dog-shaped stone that Sally believed to be a dog. And Sally's reason for leaving was that there was a dog in room.

---

[8] If the reader somehow finds the presuppositional effects of the definite distracting, we invite them to run the examples with an indefinite.

Again, Comesaña and McGrath's framework predicts that this should be perfectly fine. But it doesn't sound very good at all to us.

Comesaña and McGrath point out that the data that interests them can be replicated for constructions of the form 'X V'd because P'. Thus, they claim the following is fine:

19. Sally turned down the job because she had another offer. You see, she falsely believed she had another offer.

We think 'fine' is a bit of an overstatement. Furthermore we think that when the order is reversed things degrade further:

20. You see, Sally falsely believed that she had another offer. So she turned down the job because she had another offer.

Interestingly, Schroeder, while also denying factivity for motivating reason constructions, parts company with Comesaña and McGrath on 'because' claims, remarking that '"because P" obviously entails P' (see Schroeder 2021: 85). We agree with Schroeder on this last point. But note that if one agrees with Schroeder here, one should look at McGrath and Comesaña's data with particular suspicion, since (as McGrath and Comesaña are aware), much of it can be replicated for 'because':

21. Sally turned down the job because she had another offer; and that made perfect sense; however, her source was lying—she never had the other offer.

(Note also that insofar as one likes the inference from 'S V'd for the reason that P' to 'S V'd because P', one should be particularly wary of Schroeder's split verdict.[9]) In repudiating the factivity of 'because p', Comesaña and McGrath note that there are perfectly good uses of 'explanation' that are not factive (see 2014: 77). They are right about this. The following pairs seem OK, for example:

22. His/One explanation for the bridge falling down is that there were too many Y-rivets and hers/another is that there are too few.

But they are wrong in thinking that this phenomenon carries over to 'because'. After all, the following is terrible:

---

[9] As an anonymous referee remarked, the following speech sounds very strange: 'Sarah bought biscuits for the reason that they reminded her of her childhood, but not because they reminded her of her childhood'.

23. The bridge fell down because there were too many Y-rivets and because there were too few.

And the remarks above about the factivity of 'S's reason was that P' carry over to 'because'. Here the data is perhaps even clearer. Thus, consider the striking infelicity of:

24. There was no dog in the room, just a dog-shaped stone that Sally believed to be a dog. And Sally then left because there was a dog in room.

Let us turn to some of Schroeder's remarks. For now we'll pick up on just two themes (and move to some larger theoretical considerations later). One theme is that the kind of data we have been alluding to merely tells us how we 'talk about reasons'. That is not how we see it. Suppose, having noted the infelicity of 'They used a fork without prongs', someone retorted 'But that just tells us how we talk about forks, not what forks are like'. That would be quite strange. For what the data does is remind us how we ourselves think about forks—we are uncovering our own view of the world.[10] In this case the data reminds us that, on our current view of things, you can't have a fork without prongs. In the case of factivity data, we are reminded that your reason for running cannot be that the house is on fire unless the house is on fire.

Schroeder's actual way of putting the worry involves some unusual terms of art:

> judgments about reports only tell us something interesting about how we *talk* about reasons, not about what must be true in order for there to be act-oriented factors that figure in the competition that determines what it is rational or correct for someone to believe or to do. And arguably, they do not even establish the claim that they need about how we *talk* about reasons.
>
> (Schroeder 2021: 81)

> The problem with this argument, I believe, is that it shows us more about how we can use the expression "her reason is that P" to report subjective reasons, than it does about what factors must be like in order to count in an act-oriented way in the determination of what it is rational for the agent to do.
>
> (Schroeder 2021: 82)

We do not find these remarks particularly helpful. These paragraphs raise new questions about what it takes for 'act-oriented factors' that enter into a 'competition' and which determine what is rational. But we are interested in what it is for a

---

[10] Of course, if we were somehow to discover that our view of forks was somehow contradictory or badly thought through, we would be ready to change it.

proposition to be someone's reason for acting. It is a further question—one that we will address shortly—whether motivating reasons determine what is rational. Similarly, it is obvious enough that there is some natural sense in which false propositions can be 'act-oriented factors'. If one believes a false proposition that belief causes one to act, then there is clearly some sense in which that proposition is an 'act-oriented factor'. But that does not tell us whether that proposition is one's reason for acting.

A second theme concerns how we react in our reason-theoretic thinking to discovering that someone acted on a false belief. Thus, Schroeder considers a case where we believe Bernie is about to drink a gin and tonic, Bernie's favourite drink. At that point we think:

25. That the glass contains gin and tonic is a reason Bernie has for drinking it.

We then learn that while Bernie believes the glass contains gin and tonic, it actually contains gasoline. Here, Schroeder admits that you would be less willing to say 25 but argues that our views about Bernie's reasons haven't, intuitively, changed:

> Here you report Bernie's reason differently based on what *you* believe about whether his glass contained gin and tonic. But it doesn't seem to me that you have changed your mind about what subjective reason he has to take a sip. If I pressed you on it, you shouldn't admit that you were wrong about what his reason is, but only about whether his glass contained gin and tonic.
> (Schroeder 2021: 82)

(Here 'subjective reason' is Schroeder's label for reasons that Bernie has). Given his remark above about 'because', it is clear that Schroeder does think you should admit you were wrong about a certain 'because' thought: one's later self should admit that one's earlier self thought that Bernie was taking a sip because it contained gin and tonic but that one's earlier self was wrong to think this. Moreover Schroeder's use of 'subjective' indicates that he is aware that one can also reasonably convict one's earlier self of a false-reasons thought expressed without the possessive construction. On a natural reading 'That the glass contains gin and tonic is a reason for Bernie to drink it' is false, even by Schroeder's lights (a claim he would classify as an objective reason claim, since it does not ascribe possession). So Schroeder is misleading at best when he suggests that you were wrong 'only about whether his glass contained gin and tonic'. Even by his own lights there are mistakes you made in the language of reasons, even if not in the language of possessed reasons. The key idea is that our earlier thoughts about reasons Bernie possessed did not figure among those mistakes.

On our own view, the natural fallback after the discovery is to the secondary use of the possessive on which, for example, 'Bernie's reason for taking the sip was that he believed it contained gin and tonic'. And the proposition that we express by this fallback sentence is one that we believed correctly both before and after the discovery of gasoline. That said, there doesn't seem to be anything intuitively compelling about the thought that while our earlier self expressed a falsehood by 'That there is gin and tonic is a reason for Bernie to take a sip', our earlier self expressed a truth by 'That there is gin and tonic is a reason Bernie has to take a sip'.[11] Even if one could somehow talk oneself into a combination of views like that, the case does not seem dialectically very powerful against what is, prima facie, a more natural view of the matter.

It may be helpful to take a step back and articulate two competing visions of what possessed-normative-reasons and motivating-reasons talk is all about. On a view that we reject but which is evidently compelling to Schroeder, this kind of reasons talk is primarily designed to latch onto considerations that agents weigh against one another. Motivating-reasons talk latches onto which considerations actually carried the day (with respect to action, doxastic state, or conative response). Meanwhile possessed-normative-reasons talk latches onto which considerations, normatively speaking, tell in favour of or against this or that response. In neither role is it important that the consideration is a true proposition and so, on this vision, there is no need for any factivity requirement on normative reasons. The consideration that actually drove Bernie to imbibe may have been that the glass contained gin and tonic even if it, in fact, contained gasoline. And there is obviously a perfectly good sense in which that consideration counted in favour of imbibing. Someone who loved gin and tonic and who treated that consideration as telling heavily in favour of having a drink would, generally speaking, earn our respect even if the glass, with no warning, contained gasoline. Let us call this cluster of phenomena the 'consideration profile' of an agent. (Of course it is an important further question whether there is an ordinary reading of questions like 'What ought an agent to believe?', 'How confident ought the agent be in such and such?', and so on, according to which the answer supervenes on the consideration profile—and so where facts about which considerations are known and which are not, as well as the dispositional issues alluded to in Section 3 are neither here nor there. Here is not the place to properly examine that issue.)

Even those who embrace our favoured framework cannot deny that these are all real phenomena. And regardless of how we think about reason talk, we have

---

[11] Hawthorne and Magidor (2018: 124) make the point that speeches along the lines of 'There is no reason for S to V but S has a reason to V' sound very strange. Note that Comesaña and McGrath (2014: 76) think that there are two readings of sentences of the form 'There is a reason for S to V, namely P', one factive, one not. While we don't like that view (for reasons already explained), it at least (as they point out) saves the inference from possessed-reasons constructions to the construction that is silent on possession (on one reading, at any rate).

language that gets at these phenomena. For example, we can ask questions of the form 'Which consideration drove S to V?' without requiring that the answer allude to a true proposition. Similarly we can ask 'How much weight should be given to that consideration?' in a setting where we abstract away from whether the relevant proposition is true. That said, according to the picture we are presenting, motivating- and possessed-reasons talk is not, in its primary use, a vehicle for capturing the consideration profile. It is, instead, in its primary use, a way of describing which facts in the world creatures are responding to with this or that action or attitude and which facts in the world that they are aware of tell in favour of or against some action or attitude. Let us call this cluster of phenomena 'the worldly interface'. On our picture, knowledge is the key relation that allows a person to respond in the sense of interest to a fact in the world. And this is the source of the knowledge constraint.

Now, quite obviously, there are some points of contact between the two projects. If a fact in the world motivates an agent, then the relevant true proposition will serve as a consideration that moves the agent. So the worldly interface will tell us something about the consideration profile. But one will not be able to read off the consideration profile from the worldly interface. In cases where the consideration does not correspond to a piece of knowledge, there will be no associated fact that motivates the agent in the sense of interest. Clearly, both the worldly-interface account of a situation and the consideration profile of a situation are of interest. Our main ideas are that (i) knowledge is crucial to understanding how the worldly interface works and (ii) the primary use (as opposed to fallback use) of the possessed-reasons ideology we have in natural language is crafted for displaying the worldly interface and is (on the default reading of the possessive) less well suited for limning the contours of the consideration profile. That said, the fallback use is a pretty good way of getting at the consideration profile. If we introduce the (non-factive) term of art 'c-reason', where p is a c-reason for S's v-ing just in case p is a consideration that motivated S to v, then we can say that p is a c-reason for S's v-ing just in case *in the fallback sense* (illustrated by the tropical-disease doctor and not the psychiatrist version of 3 above), one of S's reasons for v-ing was that they believed that p. By contrast, in the default sense (illustrated by the psychiatrist version of 3 above), the claim that one of S's reasons for v-ing was that they believed that p entails that the fact that they believed p both figure in the worldly interface as a motivating known fact and also that this psychological proposition served as a c-reason. Clearly various of the authors we have been discussing think 'reason' in English works like the non-factive 'c-reason'. We don't. But we don't want to pretend either that this semantic issue is *all that* exciting. Such ideas as that the knowledge relation is crucial to understanding the worldly interface and that dispositions rather than c-reasons are important to our ordinary conceptions of rationality (a theme of Section 3) are arguably more important to our worldview.

3. Rationality-Based Arguments

A central theme in Comesaña (2020) and Schroeder (2021) is that a factivity constraint on reasons breaks intuitive connections between reasons and rationality. The basic worry is that in 'bad cases' of faultless illusion, there is no loss of rationality, but factive views of reasons are under pressure to say otherwise, since reasons present in the 'good case' are absent in the bad case. Here, for example, is Comesaña:

> Suppose that you want to drink a Crush, and you know that you can do so by pushing the button labeled "Crush"—but not, of course, the one labeled "Coke." Due to a bizarre interaction between your brain and a nearby radiation source, your experience represents the buttons as having their labels interchanged—the button labeled "Crush" is represented as being labeled "Coke" and vice versa. About this case, I want to say two things: first, it is rational for you to push the button labeled "Coke" (which your experience represents, remember, as being labeled "Crush"); second..., it is rational for you to push that button only if you rationally believe that it is labeled "Crush." Therefore, your belief that the button is labeled "Crush" is rational. Factualists have to disagree. They have to disagree because your belief that the button is labeled "Crush" is false, and thus it doesn't amount to knowledge. So, Factualists must either deny that it is rational for you to push the button labeled "Coke," or they have to deny that rational action requires rational belief.
>
> (Comesaña 2020: 127)

Schroeder similarly consider a pair of possible cases C1 and C2 involving remarkably similar agents that differ only in that an agent (with phenomenally matching experiences) has a perceptual illusion in C2 but not C1. In C1, the agent knows some p by vision that is false in C2. Schroeder then worries that on the factive view:

> It seems to follow that your belief in C2 is not rational, even though your belief in C1 is—or at least this can happen in similar pairs of cases. But cases C_1 and C_2 differ in a way that is incredibly minimal. Not only are they the same in their internal, subjectively accessible features, they also shared exactly the same history up until just before the formation of this very belief.
>
> (Schroeder 2021: 64)[12]

He then complains that this vision problematically 'allows the rationality of belief to hinge on single-case differences in the veridicality of a single perceptual experience' (Schroeder 2021: 65).

---

[12] See also Comesaña and McGrath (2014: sect. 3.1) for a very similar argument.

Schroeder is aware, of course, that the proponent of our framework might try to account for the rationality of the belief in the illusion case by appeal to propositions that *are* known in that case (e.g. that *p* is probable, that it looks as if *p*, and so on). But he makes a reasonable case that this is challenging as a general strategy; for example, it may just not be the case that knowledge of probabilities, even if it was there, was motivating in the case at hand.

In response, we think it is important to understand that the relationship between rationality and reasons is quite complex. There are two important strands to our ordinary thinking about rationality. One kind of consideration that counts in favour of rationality ascriptions has to do with how well supported the relevant response is by reasons/evidence.[13] But another kind of consideration is more dispositional, driven by such questions as 'Is the agent doing what agents that are generally disposed to respond well to the evidence would do?' In his 'Ambiguous Rationality,' Williamson argues that we tend to oscillate between these two ideas in rationality ascriptions and that 'conflating the two ways of thinking about rational belief has had damaging effects in epistemology' (2017: 263).

Here is not the place to assess the extent of the damage. The main thing we want to suggest is that in many of the 'bad cases' of interest, the basis for talk of rationality will be dispositional rather than evidential.[14] Note that many paradigms of irrational belief in common parlance and psychology are naturally thought of as beliefs that arise from sinister dispositions rather than beliefs that are evidentially outweighed. Consider, for example, stock examples of beliefs to the effect that one is of no worth or that one needs the approval of others to have worth.[15] Even if one crafts the rest of one's belief system to fit nicely with such beliefs, we would naturally classify such beliefs as irrational.

Consider a simple case: Jones has a generally reliable memory. But stored in Jones's preservative memory is a belief that Smith was born in 1934. In fact, Smith was born in 1943. Jones used to know this, but there is occasional distortion of

---

[13] It's a good question what the relationship is between a reason to believe *p* and evidence for *p*. Schroeder suggests the following: '*Evidence as Reasons*: Evidence matters in epistemology because if something is evidence that P, it is a reason to believe that P' (Schroeder 2021: 16). In a footnote he recognizes that this is wildly at odds with a Bayesian conception of evidence, remarking 'I do not assume that everything that raises the prior probability that P must count as evidence that *p*' (Schroeder 2021: 16 n. 23) If *p* has a prior of 1/50, learning it has an objective chance of 1/3 is, in the Bayesian sense, evidence for *p*, since it raises the probability of *p*, but it is hardly a reason to believe that *p*. Those sympathetic to the Bayesian conception might instead consider: *Evidence as Reasons Mark II*: Evidence matters in epistemology because if something is evidence that *p*, it is a reason to increase one's credence in *p*.

[14] That is not to say that we wish to sign up to the precise details of Williamson's gloss on the dispositional construal. Indeed, for reasons we do not wish to go into here, we would not. For current purposes we will make do with a fairly rough and ready take on the dispositional phenomenon according to which, very roughly, beliefs pass the dispositional test just in case they manifest good epistemic dispositions.

[15] Sources such as the following are ubiquitous: https://transformationacademy.com/2020/08/the-3-irrational-beliefs-at-the-root-of-all-suffering-approval-judgment-and-comfort/, accessed 15 February 2024.

information over time in Jones's preservative memory, and this is one of those times. Jones gets the opportunity to wager a small sum on Smith's being born before the beginning of the Second World War. Jones does so and loses. It is natural to count Smith's bet as rational and, relatedly, natural to count Jones's belief that Smith was born in 1934 as rational. But it seems very much a stretch to say that Jones believes this for good reasons or that Jones believes that on the basis of good evidence. Rather, our sense of the rationality of Jones is in good part based on our sense that Jones is displaying good habits—typically, reliance on the deliverances of preservative memory taps into a healthy store of knowledge. (Perhaps in *some* versions of the case, one can argue that Jones does have excellent evidence for the belief—perhaps he knows that the belief is in preservative memory and knows that preservative memory tends to yield knowledge in his case. But even so, this will not make for a belief that is based on good reasons/evidence if such background knowledge is not what is motivating the retention of the belief. Even if it is not motivating, it is natural to count Jones as rational in this case.) It is thus important to the framework that we are advancing that we acknowledge ordinary notions of rationality that are not to be explained in terms of strength of reasons or evidence. This problematizes principles such as the following:

> If one is rational to do something, then one has reasons to do that thing and those reasons make it rational for one to do it.
> (McGrath and Comesaña 2014: 61)

If rationality—in one perfectly good sense—is dispositional along the lines explained, then rational belief or action may be present even though reasons are absent. Once this has been absorbed, the master arguments with which we began this section look rather less convincing. After all, in the one-off cases of illusion, the agents in question are manifesting laudable dispositions that typically yield knowledge. And so the agents in question will count as rational—there is no need to search for a reason or evidence that is present in the particular case.

It is very much in keeping with knowledge-first sensibilities to think of dispositional rationality in terms of dispositions to know (and Comesaña's critique of the dispositional approach is very much focused on this kind of construal; see Comesaña 2020: ch. 5). But it bears emphasis that the bifurcated approach to rationality does not depend on it. Suppose, for example, one subscribed to a 'belief is weak' doctrine according to which it is implausible that belief is somehow normed by knowledge (see Hawthorne, Rothschild, and Spectre 2015). Still, one could perfectly well think that there is both an evidential and a dispositional way of thinking about rational belief. The twin categories of (i) beliefs well supported by evidence and (ii) beliefs that manifest a disposition to form beliefs that, if not known, are at least well supported by evidence may well be important to thinking about rationality in this alternative setting. And in this alternative setting, a belief might be dispositionally rational even though it has, so to speak, no shot at being knowledge.[16]

Our package invokes a dispositional strand to our thinking about rationality. But our opponents might think to themselves that their preferred conception of reasons can save a clean connection between reasons and rationality. It might thus be seen as a cost of our preferred package that it has to make the relation between reasons and rationality much more complex than it needs to be.[17] But we don't think this critique is promising. Even our opponents will have a tough time maintaining a neat and tidy connection between reasons and rationality. To illustrate, we give two examples drawn from Schroeder and Comesaña's own work.

Example 1. Schroeder on Bayesianism

Schroeder (2021) takes seriously a Bayesian account of our cognitive architecture. Elsewhere in the book, he suggests that there are reasons pertaining to belief that are not evidence. (For example, he suggests that if we are aware that we will get decisive evidence regarding p soon, that may be reason to hold off believing p. But the fact that we will get decisive evidence soon regarding p need not itself be evidence for or against p.[18]) That said, he suspects that if the basic architecture is Bayesian then the basic doxastic state—credence—is one that only admits evidence as reasons:

> But if our psychologies are organized much like the classical Bayesian picture takes them to be, the *very same* view that I have been defending about the nature and source of right-kind reasons for attitudes predicts that only *evidence* should count as a right-kind reason pertaining to our only belief-like state, credence.
> (Schroeder 2021: 162)

With Schroeder, let us take seriously the idea that the fundamental architecture is Bayesian and that the only reasons for having a credence are evidence. What we

---

[16] Similar remarks apply to rational suspicions, which are not plausibly normed by knowledge and also to those who think that while one use of 'belief' picks out a state normed by knowledge, another does not. Note that even if belief is not normed by knowledge, that does not undermine the thesis that evidence is factive, the thesis that only knowledge can be evidence, or even the identification of one's evidence with one's knowledge.

[17] Note also that if we thought that rationality supervened on the considerations in play (which we don't), it would also be open to us to say that it is reasons in the fallback sense and not the primary sense that determine rationality. The basis of the critique would then presumably have to be that it is somehow problematic that the primary sense of 'one's reason' is one that fails to provide a proper basis for rationality talk. Since we don't think rationality in the ordinary sense is determined by the space of considerations available to one, we don't want to go down this track in any case.

[18] Of course, there are some cases where we are aware that we will get a decisive answer to a question only if the answer breaks in one direction.

now want to focus on is the rationality of priors. Consider a Bayesian baby with, as yet, no evidence to speak of. The baby, like any good Bayesian engine, will have priors. According to permissive conceptions of rationality, all sorts of priors are rational. According to more demanding conceptions, very few are rational. That debate need not concern us right now. What is important is that priors can be evaluated for rationality so that at least some are rational. And this is so even when no evidence has come in yet. In this situation, since there is no evidence, and assuming that Schroeder is right that reasons for credence are evidence, there will be no possessed reasons for prior credal states. But what that means is that the rationality of priors cannot be accounted for in terms of the reasons for which those credal states are held. And this observation does not require that we adopt a factive approach to reasons and evidence.[19, 20, 21]

Example 2. Comesaña on Evidence

Comesaña does not impose a factivity constraint on evidence: he allows that p can count as evidence for S even if p is false. That said, he does not want any old p that is believed to provide thereby the proposition believed as evidence. His preferred approach—'Experientialism'—holds that 'an empirically basic proposition gets to be part of your evidence provided that it is justified by an experience you are having' (Comesaña 2020: 119).

Comesaña also expresses some sympathy for 'time slice rationality', according to which synchronic duplicates match with respect to rationality. Consider now Swampchristina, who is a duplicate of Christina that recently came into being in a

---

[19] An interesting subtlety on updating: suppose S's total evidence is p, that S is unaware of that, but S still conditionalizes appropriately and, let us suppose, moves to .71 on q. That p is not a good reason to move to .71. What is a good reason to move to .71 is that p is one's totality of evidence. But S does not possess that reason. Is this a case of rationally moving to credence .71 without having a good reason for doing so?

[20] Note also that such ideology as 'tied evidence' (ideology that figures prominently in Schroeder 2021: ch. 6) is quite dangerous in a Bayesian setting (and may be somewhat problematic for related reasons in any case). What does it then mean for the evidence for and against to be tied? One might naturally think it means that the conjunction of evidence for raises the probability just as much as the evidence against lowers it. But, again because of interaction effects, the conjunction of evidence for and evidence against can do all sorts of things by way of total evidence. The ideology of reasons is shot through with analogies to a scale, and such analogies are completely unhelpful as a path to understanding the probabilistic impact of evidence in a Bayesian setting. Of course, one could simply define 'tied evidence' to be a matter of the total evidence being inert, but then—again because of interaction effects—that predicts nothing as to what the weights are of individual pieces of evidence. Thus, if one's total evidence is the conjunction of p and q and this conjunction is inert, it may be that both p and q individually raise, that both lower, that just one is inert, and so on.

[21] Note that a similar point can be made in a coarse-grained non-Bayesian setting for agents with no evidence yet and who as yet suspend belief. Suspension of belief is presumably rational for many propositions for such an agent. But insofar as reasons require doxastic commitment, an agent short on beliefs will be short on reasons for suspension. Here again, the rationality of suspension seems to break free of possessed reasons for suspension.

swamp by a fortuitous quantum event. Swampchristina performs some action on the basis of background beliefs that were coeval with her creation. Such beliefs are not justified by any experiences, past or present, that Swampchristina enjoyed. But if time slice rationality holds, the rationality of Swampchristina's beliefs are on a par with Christina's. Now it would be very strange to suppose that Christina's counterpart background beliefs are irrational—many such beliefs are knowledge generated by prior experience. So assuming time slice rationality, Swampchristina's corresponding background beliefs—including many not justified by her experiential history—are rational. But what that means is that, on a vision Comesaña is in effect very sympathetic to, Swampchristina has many rational beliefs that are not justified by her evidence. Barring a large stock of possessed reasons for belief that have a source that is non-evidential, we reach a picture according to which Swampchristina has a variety of rational beliefs for which she has no good reasons. Here again, we see an important gap between rationality and reasons, one which does not rely on the factivity assumptions that we favour.

In sum, rationality-based arguments against our favoured conception of reasons presume too tight a link between rationality and reasons. Once one realizes that our thinking about rationality has a dispositional strand that can't be assimilated to support-theoretic ideology, one should be hesitant to advance arguments to the effect that our favoured conception of reasons bring too much irrationality in their wake. Moreover, as we have seen, it would be far too quick to think that alternative approaches have the advantage of a clean and simple link between possessed reasons and rationality.

4. Factive Attitudes

Dietz (2018) defends an important link between factive emotive constructions like 'angry that p', 'regrets that p', on the one hand, and motivating-reason constructions on the other. The key link here is given by the following principle:

For factive emotional state ascriptions, if S v's that *p*, then one of S's motivating reasons for v-ing is that *p*.

(Dietz 2018: 1684)[22]

---

[22] Following Grice (2001), Dietz uses the label 'personal reasons' instead of 'motivating reasons'. We use the latter here, as it is more familiar to the contemporary reasons literature. She notes that the reverse conjecture is not right: supposing John's car has been stolen and one of his reasons for being angry is that it is brand new, it is still not right to say that John is angry that his car is brand new (see Dietz 2018: 1684–5, n. 11). Intuitively, for a reason to be of the right sort, the associated event or state has to be a focal point for the anger (the associated event or state—in this case the newness of the car—has to be an event John is angry about), though we are not sure how to develop this thought in a rigorous fashion.

The factivity of motivating-reasons constructions, in combination with the above principle, provides a nice explanation for factive emotional-state descriptions.

Comesaña and McGrath (2014) use the very same kind of argument that we considered in Section 3 as a weapon against the supposed factivity of constructions such as 'glad that' and so on. They then consider a case where a gin and tonic lover is given a glass that appears to contain gin and tonic but doesn't. The gin and tonic lover feels glad and it is easy to fill in the case so that they are intuitively rational. But now they observe:

> What is he glad about? Go through the factualist candidates: is he glad that he thinks the glass contains gin and tonic? Is he glad that it looks like it contains gin and tonic? He might be somewhat glad of these things, but not nearly as glad as he is in fact, and rationally so. If he is to be as glad as he is, and rationally so, he must be glad that the glass contains gin and tonic.
>
> (Comesaña and McGrath 2014: 70)

The key idea is that if one is to be rationally glad to a certain degree, there has to be some p such that one is glad that p and such that p warrants that degree of gladness. They conclude that we should relinquish factivity for emotive state constructions.

As the reader might anticipate, we reject the key idea. In light of the dispositional strand to our thinking about rationality, such principles are problematic (on at least one natural construal of 'rational'). When the subject is glad in this case, the subject is responding in ways that we would expect a flourishing agent to be disposed to respond in a case like this. The agent is showing themselves to be the kind of agent that typically has emotions for reasons, and nothing about the case shows them to be prone to being glad for odd reasons.[23] That there is no p in this one-off case such that one is glad that p and such that p makes the level of gladness fitting is neither here nor there.[24]

Many perceptual verbs—'perceive that', 'see that', and so on—are factive. In these cases, the factivity is not plausibly explained by the connection to reasons. Following French (2012) and Williamson (2000), Dietz maintains that these verbs are designed to capture a way of knowing. In short 'glad that p' describes an upshot of knowing p, whereas 'sees that p' conveys information about how knowledge that p was acquired. This points to an important contrast within the class of factive attitude verbs.

---

[23] Of course, if the agent was overwhelmingly glad at the sight of gin and tonic, that might be a sign of a drinking problem and the case might lead us to look contemptuously on their emotional response for that reason.

[24] For further discussion of the relevant aspects of unity and disunity, see Dietz (2018).

Schroeder (2021) does not challenge the factivity of 'sees that' but does challenge the idea that 'sees that' describes a way of knowing. In his framework, seeing that p can then provide a channel for reasons that is independent of knowing that p. We do not find his reasons for denying the sees-that to know-that link compelling. He essentially offers three arguments. The first is that 'perception represents many more things than we form beliefs about'(Schroeder 2021: 89). He gives the example of someone who sees that a certain door is open but is too busy thinking about Kant to bother forming the belief that the door is open. The second is that there is a time lag between seeing that p and forming the belief that p. The third is that in cases where you don't trust your vision, you may see that p without even forming a belief that p. (He gives the example of someone who thinks that they are wearing rose-coloured glasses but is not, sees that something is red, but does not believe that it is red because they think they are wearing glasses).

We suspect that the first worry trades at some level on too intellectualist an account of belief, one according to which beliefs are like little inner assertions.[25] Suppose someone is thinking about Kant and passes a door that juts out into the corridor. They surely know where the door is and that is why there is no risk of them colliding with the door. Assuming we want knowledge-to-belief entailment, they also have beliefs about where the door is. (And if we deny the knowledge-to-belief connection, the see-that to know-that connection will still remain intact.) If seeing-that describes a kind of process that includes knowledge as its culmination, then there is obviously no time lag between seeing that p and knowing that p (just as there is no time lag between when one finishes playing a sonata and finishes playing its last note). Schroeder's description of the third kind of example also seems rather tendentious. Suppose Jones is told by a normally reliable source that he is about to hallucinate a baseball. Someone throws a baseball at his child in full view, but he does not move—Jones believes himself to be hallucinating. The baseball hits his child on the head. There is no question that he sees the baseball. But it is not the concatenation of the noun phrase and the perceptual verb that is under discussion here. What seems far less clear is that Jones sees that a baseball is heading towards his child. Consider the following speeches:

26. Jones saw that the baseball was going to hit his child on the head but did nothing.

Jones could see that his child was about to get injured but did nothing.

---

[25] Dietz (2020) similarly complains that anti-cognitivist arguments against a belief requirement on emotions tend to over-intellectualize belief. She emphasizes that it is important not to conflate the act of of judging with the state of believing. (Some philosophers seem to want to describe judgings as 'occurrent beliefs,' though we think that this way of talking is apt to lead one to mischaracterize judgement as a subspecies of belief.)

For our part, we are not particularly comfortable with this speech. Relatedly the following combination does not sound so great:

27. Jones saw that the ball was heading towards his child's head but could not tell by looking that the ball was heading towards his child's head.

But it is not acceptable either to say that Jones could tell by looking that the ball was heading towards his child's head.

At one point, Schroeder evinces a slightly 'don't care' attitude about 'see that'.

> For even if 'sees that' expresses such a hybrid state, there are still purely perceptual relations to the world that underlie this state, and these perceptual relations happen only if the world is as they represent it to be. Such relations would be factive attitudes to the world, whether or not we have verbs for them in English.
> (Schroeder 2020: 89)

The idea seems to be that even if 'sees that' entails 'knows that', there are 'purely perceptual relations' to propositions that are not knowledge-involving and these are the kinds of relations that provide propositions as evidence. In response, we would like to draw attention to one theme in Schroeder's discussion that we believe slightly distorts the dialectical situation. Recall that when he pushed the rationality argument against a knowledge account of reasons (discussed in Section 3), he complained that, for Williamson and others, differences in rationality seemed to hinge on 'the veridicality of a single perceptual experience'. But it is important to emphasize that veridicality is by no means sufficient to do the work of perceptually accessing a fact. Suppose two trees look to be exactly the same height. And suppose it just so happens that they are exactly the same height. The perceptual experience is veridical in the relevant respect. But the perceiver cannot see that they are the same height. The perceiver is not that discriminating. Seeing-that involves the kinds of safety and margin-for-error requirements that we are familiar with for knowledge. Supposing that one agrees that bare veridicality is nothing like enough for seeing that on account of its sometimes involving a kind of luck incompatible with seeing that. And suppose we think that, to access facts about the world through vision in a way that makes them available to us as reasons, there needs to be a kind of connection that is apt to be described using the very same kind of ideology that we use to get at the conditions for knowledge. (We don't here want to fuss about the exact contours of that ideology). Then, perceptual relations that are not knowledge-like will no longer seem so plausible as the kind of thing that can provide worldly evidence.

Another theme in Schroeder (2021) raises a question about whether knowing a fact is *sufficient* to make it available as a motivating reason. One idea that he advances, albeit tentatively, is that for a proposition to count as possessed, it has to be the content of a factive state *that one appears to have*. According to this picture, for p to be possessed, it is not sufficient that one sees that p: if one sees that p, but it does not appear to one that one sees that p, then p is still not possessed. (See his discussion of the 'apparent factive attitude' view Schroeder 2020, 100–124, though he has some sympathy with the view that seeing that p is self-intimating in a way that guarantees its appearance. Of course, given his denial of factivity, he does not think either that a factive attitude is required for p to be a possessed reason; but that is not the issue just now.). This appearance requirement might naturally be applied to knowledge itself. The idea would be that even if one knows p, p is only possessed in the relevant sense if it appears to one that one knows p.

We do not find this idea compelling. It is true enough that, in order to do anything with a tool in one's garden, it has to appear to be there. But we should not think of knowledge along these lines. Suppose we know p and believe q– perhaps deductively—on that basis. It would be wrong, we think, to assume that, in order to deduce something from what we know, the knowledge has first to appear to us to be there. Inference can be rather more automated than that. And if we do believe q on this deductive basis, then it is surely right to think that p was our reason for believing q, whether or not it appears to us that we know p. And what goes for knowing that p goes for seeing that p—one version of this case might be one where we see that p and believe q for the reason that p. Here again, p can serve as a motivating reason whether or not it appears to us that we see that p.

5. Non-Factive Alternatives

Schroeder (2021) and Comesaña (2020) both offer alternative non-factive conceptions of reasons and evidence, where some false proposition p can function as one's reason for doing something and can also function as evidence. Those authors disagree somewhat about which false propositions can play this role. The main idea in Comesaña seems to be that it is propositions that get basic justification from experience. The main idea in Schroeder seems to be that any proposition believed can serve as a reason. He is trying to explain the presence or absence of justification in terms of reasons (that is part of his 'reasons first' project) and so does not want an independent justification filter on reasons. Rather the idea is that even if we are permissive about reasons, we will not let in too much, since competition between reasons will mean that the considerations provided by intuitively unjustified beliefs will get swamped by competing considerations.

One common thread to both of these views is that they allow for inconsistent evidence. (Note that even if one had a view according to which pairwise inconsistent propositions are never both 'basically justified', that would still not preclude a larger set of basically justified propositions forming an inconsistent set.) Williamson clearly thinks that this is a bad feature of such views, complaining that views according to which some truths are inconsistent with one's evidence are 'hardly attractive' (Williamson 2000: 92). In response, Schroeder complains that it is 'hard to call this an argument', since the bald assertion that the views in question are not attractive is 'straightforwardly question-begging' (Schroeder 2021: 78).

Schroeder is right that the passage in question from Williamson (2000) does not, taken in isolation, have much dialectical force against views like those of his and Comesaña. But it is helpful, we think, to situate those remarks in the context of Williamson's presentation of what he takes to be orthodox ideas about the functional role of evidence. In the chapter on evidence in Williamson (2000), he identifies at least three such roles: first is inference to the best explanation: 'We often choose between hypotheses by asking which of them best explains evidence'. Secondly, our evidence 'rules out some hypotheses by being inconsistent with them' (Williamson 2000: 196). Thirdly, our evidence is used to evaluate theories by probabilistic confirmation—we evaluate theories by inquiring how likely each is on the evidence. Where our evidence is *e*, the comparative merits of hypotheses *h1* and and *h2* are revealed by probing the conditional probability of *h1* on *e* and of *h2* on *e*.

It is important to notice that a set of inconsistent propositions is ill-suited to play these roles. If we count those propositions as evidence and take ourselves to have ruled out any proposition inconsistent with our evidence, then we have ruled out everything. Meanwhile, the conditional probability of any proposition on the conjunction of those propositions will not be defined, so the standard method of probabilistic confirmation will get us nowhere. Similarly, supposing the conjunction of the set is some contradiction C, we will get nowhere in the evaluation of theories by asking ourselves questions like 'Does that theory offer a nice explanation as to why C?' Now we don't want to get into whether these concerns are decisive. But it helps us to see why, set in the broader context, Williamson's complaint is not 'straightforwardly question-begging'. And it also let us see why, at least prima facie, it doesn't look as if an inconsistent set of propositions is well suited to play the roles traditionally assigned to evidence by epistemologists and philosophers of science.

It may be helpful to look at Comesaña's (2020) own elaboration of the 'ruling out' role. One central idea of his is that evidence constrains decision matrices—when we are making a decision, certain worlds are left out of the decision matrix entirely. So, for example, when deciding whether to go to the cinema, possible worlds where one gets abducted by aliens may simply not show up in the decision matrix. (For this reason he thinks that basically justified beliefs are highly important to decision theory). The mechanism seems to be one according to which worlds get eliminated from consideration by being inconsistent with one's evidence—one simply doesn't need to worry about them, so to speak, for the purposes of decision-making. It should be clear enough what the problem here is for his framework, insofar as it allows inconsistent propositions to play the role of evidence. If they do, then all worlds will be incompatible with the evidence. Thus, if basically justified beliefs are inconsistent, they are ill suited to play the decision-theoretic role that Comesaña has in mind for evidence (see Hawthorne 2023, for further discussion).

It should at least be clear by now that views of evidence that allow our evidence to be inconsistent have significant costs. There are familiar roles for evidence that can be wrought from a routine examination of philosophy of science, and inconsistent evidence is ill suited to play those roles. For his part, Comesaña (2020: 132) says that it is 'enough of a problem' for everyone that we can't generate conditional probabilities conditional on what we are basically justified in believing. But this doesn't seem like nearly so great a problem as the one we end up with if we suppose that our evidence consists of those propositions that are the contents of our basically justified beliefs.

All that said, there is something that Schroeder is right about and which is an important theme in his discussion. There is nothing in principle preventing there being a recipe that takes as input a set of inconsistent propositions and yields as output a recommended doxastic state (whether a set of outright beliefs or instead a set of credences). As a simple example (though not what he has in mind), one such recipe would first take each proposition p in the input set to the proposition that one believes p, and then apply a set of priors to conditionalize on the resultant (consistent) set of propositions to generate a credal distribution over a field of propositions.

Drawing on work by Horty (2012), Schroeder holds out hope for recipes that can give astute normative guidance even when the input set of 'considerations' forms a set of inconsistent propositions. This kind of framework raises a number of questions that we cannot fully address here, including: for someone following such a recipe, is it reasonable to think of all the considerations as playing a functional role that merits the label evidence? To what extent (if we recall its dispositional threads) can recipes of this sort usefully regiment ordinary concepts of rationality?

There are also larger questions about the usefulness of such recipes when it comes to providing sharp normative guidance about credences. Ordinary Bayesian models, while somewhat idealized, can, for example, provide very clean and precise models of how base-rate fallacies get people into trouble and can provide very helpful models of what it might be like to calibrate one's credences in a way that avoids base-rate fallacious thinking. Similarly, it provides very precise guidance as to how to bet on sequences of coin flips and dice rolls. Bayesian models have been of great use in many disciplines outside philosophy, in social science, fingerprint analysis, public health, computer science, and so on.[26]

---

[26] Within Bayesian modelling, it is, of course, a further decision to impose a knowledge-theoretic constraint on evidence. Normative guidance predicated on what we know rather than what considerations we are working with may be a little less followable, since it may be a bit harder to know what we

One would hope that the envisaged recipes that accommodate inconsistent inputs do not sacrifice all that illumination, precision, and fruitful application. It should be clear enough what our instincts are here. But we shall postpone a fuller discussion of these issues to another occasion.[27]

Bibliography

Alvarez, M. (2010), *Kinds of Reasons: An Essay on the Philosophy of Action* (Oxford: Oxford University Press).

Comesaña, J. (2020), *Being Rational and Being Right* (New York: Oxford University Press).

Comesaña, J. and McGrath, M. (2014), 'Having False Reasons', in C. Littlejohn and J. Turri (eds.), *Epistemic Norms* (New York: Oxford University Press), 59–79.

Dietz, C. (2016), 'Are All Reasons Causes', *Philosophical Studies* 173: 1179–90.

Dietz, C. (2018), 'Reasons and Factive Emotions', *Philosophical Studies* 175: 1681–91.

Dietz, C. (2020), Doxastic Cognitivism: An Anti-Intellectualist Theory of Emotion', *Philosophical Perspectives* 34: 27–52.

French, C. (2012), 'Does Propositional Seeing Entail Propositional Knowledge?', *Theoria* 78(2): 115–27.

Grice, H. P. (2001), *Aspects of Reason* (Oxford: Clarendon Press).

Hawthorne, J. (2023), 'Evidence, Experience and Decision', *Philosophical Studies* 180: 2491–502.

Hawthorne, J., and Magidor, O. (2018), 'Reflections on the Ideology of Reasons', in D. Star (ed.), *The Oxford Handbook of Reasons and Normativity* (New York: Oxford University Press), 113–42.

Hawthorne, J., Rothschild, D., and Spectre, L. (2015), 'Belief is Weak', *Philosophical Studies* 173: 1393–404.

Hornsby, J. (2007), 'Knowledge, Belief and Reasons for Acting,' in M. Penco, C. Beaney, and M. Vignolo (eds.), *Explaining the Mental* (Newcastle: Cambridge Scholars Publishing), 88–105.

Hornsby, J. (2008), 'A Disjunctive Conception of Acting for Reasons,' in A. Haddock and F. MacPherson (eds.), *Disjunctivism: Perception, Action and Knowledge* (New York: Oxford University Press), 244–61.

Horty, J. (2012), *Reasons as Defaults* (New York: Oxford University Press).

Hyman, J. (1999), 'How Knowledge Works', *Philosophical Quarterly* 49: 433–51.

---

do and don't know than what considerations we are working with. But any factive conception of evidence will carry similar costs regarding followability, unless it has an incredibly restrictive conception of which propositions can be evidence.

[27] We are grateful to the Juan Comesaña, the editors, and an anonymous referee for helpful feedback.

Hyman, J. (2011), 'Acting for Reasons: Reply to Dancy', *Frontiers of Philosophy in China* 6: 358–68.

Hyman, J. (2015), *Action, Knowledge, and Will* (Oxford: Oxford University Press).

Nebel, J. (2019), 'Normative Reasons as Reasons Why We Ought', *Mind* 128: 459–84.

Schroeder, M. (2021), *Reasons First* (New York: Oxford University Press).

Unger, P. K. (1975), *Ignorance: A Case for Scepticism* (Oxford: Clarendon Press).

Williamson, T. (2000), *Knowledge and Its Limits* (Oxford: Oxford University Press).

Williamson, T. (2017), 'Ambiguous Rationality', *Episteme* 14: 263–74.

Zeno Vendler, Z. (1972), *Res Cogitans: An Essay in Rational Psychology* (Ithaca: Cornell University Press).

12

Knowledge and Prizes

Clayton Littlejohn and Julien Dutant

1. Introduction

Many epistemologists endorse a broadly evidentialist approach to epistemic rationality.[1] They might say that a belief is rational iff it 'fits' the evidence or the evidence provides 'sufficient' support for that belief. These claims can seem truistic. Things get interesting when we try to say what fit or sufficiency amounts to.

In this chapter, we will evaluate two familiar theories of fit and offer a third. According to the first, beliefs 'fit' the evidence when the evidence provides sufficiently strong support for them (and fails to fit the evidence otherwise). Given plausible assumptions about the relationship between strength of evidential support and rational degrees of belief, this is a veritistic *strength-centred* view. It is similar to the Lockean view of rational belief (Dorst 2019; Easwaran 2016; Foley 2009; Sturgeon 2008). On this view, it's always rational to believe if the probability of the target proposition on the thinker's evidence is sufficiently high (High) and it's not rational to believe if the probability of that proposition is insufficiently high (Low).[2] According to the second, we should think of rational support in terms of explanation (McCain 2014, 2015; McCain and Moretti 2021).[3] On this *explanationist* view, it is rational for a thinker to believe at a time when that belief stands in the right explanatory relation to the evidence the thinker has at that time.

We think there are prima facie plausible arguments for the veritist's strength-centred view as well as the explanationist's view. If we're right that they disagree

---

[1] We use 'evidentialism' in the way that Conee and Feldman (2004) and McCain (2014) do. It is the view that a thinker's evidence entirely determines what is (*ex ante*) rational for her to believe. Sometimes 'evidentialism' is associated with the view that every epistemic reason should be thought of in terms of evidence. (See, for example, Shah 2006.) Some authors (e.g. Owens 2000) have argued that some epistemic reasons (e.g. the reasons a thinker has *not* to believe) are not pieces of evidence even if it's true that all epistemic reasons supervene upon a thinker's evidence. Nothing we say turns on whether evidentialism in this second sense is true.

[2] Appley and Stoutenburg (2017) assume something like High in their critical discussion of explanationism. We see rejecting High as a wise move for the explanationist, but there might be other strategies available to the explanationist.

[3] We focus on the work of McCain and Moretti (2021) for the most part for two reasons. First, they provide the most recent defences of explanationism. Secondly, we note that it's often unclear whether explanationists are interested in credence, confirmation, or outright belief. We're primarily interested in outright belief and the norms that govern this notion of belief. The same holds true for McCain and Moretti.

about a key case, this is a diplomatic way of stating that there are prima facie plausible *objections* to each of these views. We see our proposal as offering a way to build on these approaches. We incorporate aspects of the strength-centred theory and find a role for explanation in the theory of rational belief in a way that overcomes the difficulties that these two more familiar approaches face.

Just to put our cards on the table, we think that the difficulties that arise for these views have two sources. We think that our theories of rational belief should tell us something about epistemic *prizes* and something about the proper ways to *pursue* prizes. A theory of epistemic prizes tells us what features of our beliefs might make them objectively desirable or undesirable from the epistemic point of view. It further should tell us something about how desirable or undesirable happy or unhappy results might be. A theory of rational pursuit tells us which responses are rational, given our information and assumptions about prizes. When we find putative counterexamples to the Lockean view, the assumption that beliefs are objectively epistemically desirable iff accurate is usually not questioned. The first move is to find some relation between the evidence and truth that differs from the assumption proposal that it's rational to pursue these desirable states by forming those attitudes that are sufficiently likely to have the properties we desire. This is a move we shouldn't make. We should critically examine the veritistic assumptions about prizes.

2. Two Perspectives on Strength

In this section, we'll present two arguments. The first purports to show that we should reject High. The second supports High. We think it's important for anyone offering a theory of rational belief to say something in response to these arguments.

2.1. The Lottery Argument

Much has been made in the literature about claims like these:

Hearing: if someone tells you that p, you might, knowing little else, come to rationally believe that p.
Seeing: if it seems visually as if p, you might, knowing little else, come to rationally believe p.
Playing: if you hold a ticket for a fair lottery, you will not, knowing little else, come to rationally believe that it lost.[4]

---

[4] We said, 'little', not 'nothing'. On the explanationist view we consider, testimonial beliefs and experiential beliefs are rational because of an explanatory inference, and that might require more than just knowledge of how things sound or look, say. Intuitions about lottery-type cases have loomed large

Not everyone accepts these claims, of course, but we are satisfied with the things people have said in support of them. We will look for ways to explain Hearing, Seeing, and Playing rather than ways of trying to explain away the intuitions that underwrite them.

Getting the precise details of what's going on in hearing and seeing cases that confers rational support on your beliefs is tricky, but the idea is that testimony and sense experience can provide justification for beliefs when the kinds of grounds we have in a lottery case (when the only information we happen to have about the outcome is extracted from our knowledge of the set-up and we know the lottery to be fair) do not make it rational to believe outright (Harman 1968).

It's clear that this sort of contrast causes trouble for the veritist's strength-centred view. Consider three further claims:

Hearing+: if someone tells you that p, you might, knowing little else, come to rationally believe that p and rationally be very confident in p.

Seeing+: if it seems visually as if p, you might, knowing little else, come to rationally believe p and be rationally very confident in p.

Playing+: if you hold a ticket for a fair lottery, you will not, knowing little else, come to rationally believe that it lost but you will rationally be nearly certain that you lost.

Rationality attaches to the experientially grounded and testimonially supported beliefs but not to lottery beliefs, even when you should be more confident in the lottery belief than you should be in some of the rationally held beliefs based on testimony or experience.

It's difficult to make sense of these intuitions if we think of rational support in terms of strength.[5] The intuitions that underwrite these claims are an obvious threat to High. If we think of sufficient strength as allowing for justification in the testimony or sense experience case, this lets the lottery beliefs in. If we want to keep the lottery beliefs out and raise the bar accordingly, we have to concede that many of our testimonial and experiential beliefs are not rational.

If we reject the strength-centred theory that connects rational degrees of belief to rational belief on these grounds, we'll have to allow for this initially surprising possibility—that there might be pairs of propositions, p and q, where we should

---

in the arguments for knowledge-centred theories of rational belief. See Bird (2007); Hirvelä (2022); Ichikawa (2014); Kelp (2014); Dutant and Littlejohn (2021); Rosenkranz (2021); Sutton (2005); and Williamson (2000). Intuitions about the lottery seem to be relatively robust, as evidenced by the robust intuitions that people have about statistical-evidence cases in the law (Gardiner 2019; Littlejohn 2020; Moss 2018; Thomson 1986). We agree with Smith (2016) that it is awkward at best to say that jurors can rationally be convinced of a defendant's guilt on the basis of naked statistical evidence but shouldn't convict. Perhaps this is because, as Conee (2004) has suggested, a natural way of understanding justified or rational belief is in terms of a reasonable doubt standard.

[5] We say 'difficult', but not impossible. See below.

be more confident of the former but can only rationally believe the latter. This is the price we must willingly to pay to make sense of our intuitions that seem to vindicate Hearing, Seeing, Playing, and their strengthened counterparts.[6]

Nelkin (2000) and Smith (2016) note that there is this important difference between the testimonial and experiential cases and the lottery case. While we should expect more errors in the testimonial case and experiential case than in the lottery case, we don't respond the same way to the discovery of such errors. When we discover that the target proposition in the lottery case is false (and calm down a bit having discovered that we've just become very rich), we don't think that this calls for any sort of special explanation. When, however, we discover that the target proposition is wrong in the testimonial case or the experiential case, we do think that this calls for a kind of explanation. This seems to be an important contrast between the cases. When the grounds or evidence makes it rational to believe, it might not guarantee that the target proposition is true or show that it's more likely to be true than some lottery proposition, but there seems to be some sort of explanatory tie between evidence and belief as evidenced by the desire to explain the lack of connection when we discover that the target proposition is false.

Enter the explanationist theory of rational belief (McCain and Moretti 2021).[7] The explanationist proposes that explanatory connections between the evidence and a target proposition make it rational for a thinker to believe. This is what fit consists in. If it happens to be the case that some propositions aren't rational to believe, despite the fact that they're more likely to be true than some other propositions that are rational to believe, the explanationist will say that this is because high probability is not a sufficient condition for explanatory connection. We already know that, and the puzzling pattern of intuitions seems to be neatly accounted for.

We'll focus on this version of explanationism:

Believing p is justified for S at t if and only if at t: (1) S has total evidence, E; (2) either (i) p is the best (sufficiently good) explanation of e (where e is a subset of E),

---

[6] This point has convinced some that belief could not be understood in terms of high credence. See Jackson (2019) and Littlejohn (2015) for discussion. See Leitgeb (2014) for an interesting positive proposal about how belief and credence might be linked that delivers the same verdict about lottery cases.

[7] There is a long tradition of explanationist views in epistemology. An important discussion of inference to best explanation can be found in Russell's (1912: 22) discussion of scepticism. Many explanationists defend the view that inference to best explanation is fundamental in the sense that it's rational force should not be understood in other terms. See Lipton (2001), Lehrer (1970), Lutz (2020), and Poston (2011) for sympathetic discussion. More ambitious is the idea that explanatory inference is somehow fundamental to rational inference as such. In addition to McCain and Moretti (2021), see Lycan (1988). We focus on the most ambitious explanationist views because it seems only this most ambitious version of the view predicts that high probability wouldn't be sufficient for rational support in the absence of explanatory connection.

or (ii) *p* is an explanatory consequence of the best (sufficiently good) explanation of e (i.e., the relevant explanation of e would provide an explanation of *p*'s truth that is significantly better than the explanation it would provide of ~*p*'s truth); (3) it is not the case that *p* fails to satisfy (i) and (ii) with respect to e because of the additional evidence included in E.

(McCain and Moretti 2021: 86)[8]

Let's note a few things. First, while we understand why some authors would want to deny that rationality and justification really amount to the same thing, we do not distinguish them here. Those who do distinguish them should take our remarks as applying in the first instance to rationality. Secondly, McCain and Moretti take E to be constituted by some set of mental states. None of our objections targets this conception of evidence. Thirdly, we assume that better explanations are better because they are lovelier explanations and exhibit explanatory virtues better than rivals. Fourthly and finally, we take the explanationist view to be primarily a view about what makes it (*ex ante*) rational to believe. We set aside questions about the role that loveliness plays in the rational assignment of subjective probabilities.[9]

Here's the key to explaining Seeing, Hearing, and Playing in the explanationist framework:[10] given the setup of the lottery, neither the hypothesis that you'll lose nor the hypothesis that you'll win provides a better explanation of the evidence, but they would compete as explanations if offered. If neither does better than the other, neither explanation would be good enough. And if neither explanatory inference is good enough, neither the belief that the ticket lost nor the belief that it won would fit the evidence. Suspension would be the only remaining option.

2.2. The Expectationist Argument

The argument against High is case-driven. The argument for High is theory-driven. Consider two *veritist* theories. The first is a theory of epistemically desirable outcomes or prizes. It's inspired by some of William James's (2014: 17) woolly remarks about what matters to the would-be believer:

---

[8] As Dellsén (2021) observes, many explanationists see their view as a view about the processes by which rational thinkers assign (subjective) probabilities to hypotheses (e.g. Henderson 2014). Such views don't directly bear on questions about rational outright belief.

[9] For concerns about explanationist views that concern subjective probabilities, see Climenhaga (2017).

[10] We do not know what our explanationists think about the lottery case. It's not discussed in McCain (2014) or McCain and Moretti (2021), though the idea that the evidence that 'merely' makes it very probable that something is true is not sufficient to warrant outright belief has figured prominently in debates for thinking that something akin to an explanatory connection between evidence and belief is necessary for rationality (e.g. in (Harman 1968; Nelkin 2000; and Smith 2016).

Evaluative veritism: The most desirable outcome (epistemically speaking) is that our beliefs are accurate. The least desirable outcome is that our beliefs are inaccurate. It is more desirable to suspend than to believe falsehoods.

This gives us an ordering in terms of a kind of epistemic value that we can think of as *objective* epistemic value. As James (2014) rightly observed, the implications of this value theory for questions about what we should believe (if these are understood in some more *subjective* or *perspectival* way) are not straightforward. If we should attach some great disvalue to believing falsehoods, this will make it harder to find evidence that would make it rational to believe. If, however, we do not attach some great disvalue to believing falsehoods, rational belief might be easier to come by.

This way of thinking about the matter seems to rely implicitly on a kind of *expectationist* outlook. It seems to assume that a rational thinker's doxastic 'choices' between the options of belief, disbelief, and suspension will be sensitive to two things: the objective values that would be realized by the possible outcomes and the twin risks of believing falsehoods and failing to believe truths. The expectationist thinks that *if* we rationally should be guided by the evaluative considerations that figure in the veritist view, we should believe (suspend/disbelieve) when believing (suspending/disbelieving) does better in terms of expected veritistic value than the alternatives. While we can debate the merits of views on which the value that's realized by our attitudes depends upon practical factors, whether some epistemologists instincts reflect too much or too little aversion to believing falsehoods, etc., these can be seen as 'in-house' disagreements between people who accept High and Low. Given plausible weightings, it's not at all clear how we could end up rejecting High and embracing claims like Seeing, Hearing, and Playing.

Someone who accepts this sort of outlook might say that the explanationist view is mistaken if it tells us that we should refrain from believing in lottery cases. They might say something like this: explanatory inferences are fine and good as *instruments* for acquiring true beliefs or rooting out false ones, but the presence or absence of explanatory connections between evidence and belief only matters to the estimation of *prizes* if we happen to have the interests of someone who is curious about and desires beliefs about such explanatory connections. If, however, we remember that the perspective of the would-be believer is that of someone who desires to get hold of the truth and is averse to the acquisition of false beliefs, we have to remember that from *this* perspective the 'decision' to withhold or suspend when the probability of a target proposition is sufficiently high is not reasonable. To suspend in this instance would be to prefer one response (suspension) to another (belief), when it should be evident to the thinker that the favoured response does *worse* in terms of expected desirability.

If the explanationist concedes that high probability without the right explanatory connection is sufficient for rational belief, they might avoid this line of objection, but then they lose the support of the lottery argument.[11] If they wish to reject High, their options are more limited. They could deny that considerations of epistemic desirability and expected epistemic desirability matter to the 'choice' between options. Alternatively, they could say that evaluative considerations do matter but challenge the veritist theory of epistemic value on the grounds that it doesn't treat explanatory loveliness as part of what determines the value of epistemic prizes.

We see two potential problems with rejecting evaluative veritism on the grounds that it doesn't recognize explanatory loveliness as something that helps determine the value of epistemic prizes. Dialectically speaking, what the expectationist would need to say is something stronger than the claim that being part of the best explanation confers additional value upon a belief. Remember that responding to the lottery argument requires them to say that suspending does better in terms of expected epistemic value than believing in the lottery case in spite of the fact that the target proposition is nearly certain to be true. To explain why suspension would do better than belief in terms of expected epistemic value, they would have to say that it is *undesirable* to believe truths that lacked the right explanatory properties. This seems to us to be a difficult claim to sell.

Moreover, this position on epistemic desirability might actually be in tension with the explanationist view under consideration. Consider clause (ii) in McCain and Moretti's account. They use this to try to explain how things like the logical consequences of propositions justified by clause (i) would be justified. On the face of it, it seems that some such logical consequences would be *mere* consequences of the best explanations and not themselves things that get positive status by virtue of doing explanatory work. They are, nevertheless, things that the explanationist rightly regards as rationally believed. It thus seems unlikely that they would embrace the expectationist approach in linking rational belief to beliefs that maximize expected epistemic desirability whilst adopting this alternative value theory.

We don't know how the explanationist would respond to the expectationist argument. Nevertheless, we think that it has significant force, given certain background assumptions that strike us as plausible (i.e. that rational believers care about expected epistemic desirability and that the veritist theory is a plausible approach to thinking about the value of epistemic prizes). We'll see that there are cases where something akin to the expectationist approach will be needed to make sense of some intuitions about cases. We don't see how to make the

---

[11] This would not be the only problem that this would create for their view. They would also need to explain how probability connects to loveliness. See Lipton (2001). Would the idea be that an explanation is lovelier than a rival by virtue of its probability on the evidence or the other way around? The explanationist should not use comparative probability to determine comparative loveliness, but then it's not clear how they could argue that the hypothesis that a ticket loses provides a better explanation than the hypothesis that it won.

explanationist view say the things that the strength-centred view says whilst making sense of the intuitions that support Seeing, Hearing, and Playing, so we hope readers will agree that our view enjoys at least one advantage over the explanationist view.

3. Metacoherence and Rational Support

In this section, we'll argue that the explanationist view doesn't explain intuitions that a strength-centred theory explains straightforwardly. Before we present the cases, let's consider a challenge that arises for any theory of rational belief. This is the challenge of accounting for metacoherence constraints. These constraints can be thought of as rational constraints that hold between levels (i.e. constraints that reveal something about the support provided for attitudes concerning first-order propositions and higher-order propositions about these first-order attitudes and the support they receive). Here is a relatively uncontroversial constraint. It is a *local* constraint that concerns *accuracy*: it is not rationally co-tenable to believe p whilst believing that this belief is inaccurate or incorrect. If it were rational to hold the beliefs that violated this constraint, it could be rational, say, both to believe that it's raining and to believe that your belief about the rain is mistaken. This, in turn, is to hold beliefs that are inconsistent, and it's hard to see how both propositions might enjoy adequate support on the explanationist view. It is a credit to this view that it explains this constraint.[12]

The metacoherence constraints that we usually focus on are more interesting than this one. McCain and Moretti (2021: 133) argue that their explanationist view can vindicate additional local metacoherence constraints. They maintain that their view shows that the evidence cannot simultaneously support (a) believing p and (b) believing that the evidence doesn't support p. In turn, this suggests that they can explain why the evidence cannot simultaneously support (a) believing p and (b) believing that it's not rational to believe p. In both cases, they claim that insofar as p being true is part of the best explanation of the thinker's evidence, neither the lack of evidential support nor the irrationality of the attitude would also provide the best explanation of the thinker's evidence. If we wanted to generalize this to cover the case of knowledge, we might be able to argue that the evidence wouldn't support both (a) believing p and (b) believing p isn't known on the explanationist view. We struggle to think of a case in which p and the subject's failing to know p are both parts of the best explanation of something. We don't

---

[12] To see the inconsistency, we'll assume that the subject has self-knowledge so that she knows that her belief about the rain is the belief that it is raining. If she knows that she believes that it's raining and she believes this content is mistaken, she believes both that it's raining and that it's not true that it's raining.

know what line the explanationist wants to take on risk, but we might also consider whether the evidence can simultaneously support (a) believing p and (b) believing it's not likely that p. Intuitively, it seems hard to believe that it might be rational both to believe p and to believe it's unlikely that p. On the face of it, it's hard to imagine a case in which the (apparent) fact that it's unlikely that p and the (apparent) fact that p both figure in the best explanation of something.

The metacoherence constraints that McCain and Moretti discuss are *local* and concern *binary* attitudes. They are local because they concern particular attitudes. They concern binary attitudes like outright belief rather than, say, connections between belief and credence. We think it's important to consider less localized constraints and constraints that hold between beliefs and credences. Let's consider the contrast between two global constraints:

Local accuracy constraint: It is not rationally co-tenable to believe p and believe your belief about p is inaccurate.

Global accuracy constraint: It is not rationally co-tenable to believe what you do and believe that there is one belief you hold that is inaccurate.[13]

While we think that the local accuracy constraint is a genuine constraint on rationality, we don't think the global accuracy constraint is.

In terms of generality, there are general constraints that are neither local nor global:

Generalized accuracy constraint: It is not rationally co-tenable to hold your F-beliefs and believe there is an F-belief that is inaccurate.

We can pick out sets of beliefs in various ways. The 'F-beliefs' might be grouped by source (e.g. beliefs based on visual experience), content (e.g. beliefs about Dolly Parton's career), epistemic status (e.g. your rational beliefs), and so on. For the same reasons that we think the global accuracy constraint doesn't hold, we think that some generalized accuracy constraints won't hold.

In some cases, the failure of the generalized or global accuracy constraints will be connected to failures of generalized or global evidence constraints:

Local evidential constraint: It is not rationally co-tenable to believe p and believe your belief about p isn't supported by the evidence.

Global evidential constraint: It is not rationally co-tenable to believe what you do and believe there is something you believe that is not supported by the evidence.

---

[13] For defences of this constraint (under different names), see Evnine (1999); Leitgeb (2014); Pollock (1986); Ryan (1991); and Smith (2016). For arguments against accepting this constraint, see Easwaran (2016); Foley (2009); Littlejohn and Dutant (2020); Makinson (1965); Praolini (2019); and Worsnip (2016).

Generalized evidential constraint: It is not rationally co-tenable to hold your F-beliefs and believe there is an F-belief that is not supported by the evidence.

We'll consider some of the cases in a moment.

There should also be some metacoherence constraints that connect beliefs and credences. Consider the global accuracy constraint, the constraint that says that it's not rationally co-tenable to believe what you do while believing that there is something you believe that's false. Compare this with the constraint that says that it's not rationally co-tenable to believe what you do about whales, say, whilst being nearly certain that nearly everything you believe about whales is mistaken. We think that if the *outright* belief puts rational pressure on the thinker to suspend (to the extent that this belief is rational), the *credences* in light of which a thinker rationally expects widespread epistemic failure should also put pressure on the thinker to suspend.

Here is a generalized accuracy constraint that we think can pose trouble for the explanationist:

(*) It is not rationally co-tenable to hold your directly justified beliefs and believe that at least one of your directly justified beliefs is false.

This constraint uses some new jargon. The *directly* justified beliefs are those beliefs that, according to the explanationist, are justified by virtue of being parts of the best explanation of the thinker's evidence. (The indirectly justified ones are only justified by virtue of being explanatory consequences of such beliefs, and we'll set those aside.)

We can ask two questions about (*). Is (*) a genuine metacoherence constraint? Does the explanationist view predict that (*) is a genuine metacoherence constraint? We think that (*) is *not* a plausible metacoherence constraint, but we don't see how the explanationist can take a plausible line on constraints like (*). On the one hand, we think that a thinker can acquire evidence that makes it rational to believe she holds at least one directly justified belief that is false. On the other, we think the explanationist either gets this wrong or gets something very similar to (*) wrong. If they end up saying that (*) is a genuine constraint, their view predicts that evidence that shouldn't defeat threatens a large class of beliefs en masse.[14] If they dodge this result, they'll be committed to a view that treats evidence that *should* defeat as if it's rationally benign.

---

[14] In what follows, we assume that the beliefs contained in the aggregate are supported equally and are equally doubtful. We also assume that when there is rational pressure to suspend on the aggregate, there are not beliefs that constitute discernibly weak elements in the collection. For discussion of this assumption in preface cases, see Smith (2022).

Here's an initial case. Step one: imagine an author has written a large work of non-fiction that contains all and only her directly supported beliefs. At this stage, upon pain of scepticism, it must be possible that this book contains a great many of her beliefs about contingent matters of fact that she rationally believes, even though she's not maximally certain of any claim in the book. Step two: a panel of experts tells her that her book contains *precisely* one error. Step three: our author must decide whether to expand her book by adding this to her preface and whether to revise her book by removing some of its content.[15] Remember that the book should contain all and only her directly supported beliefs, so at this stage, we can ask this: can she have direct support for her belief that the book contains an error *and* (continued) direct support for each of the beliefs in her book?

The explanationist view tells us that a belief is directly justified iff it is part of the best explanation of the evidence and that a belief will cease to be directly justified if it ceases to be part of some best explanation of the evidence. Once we know or rationally believe that an explanation contains a falsehood, the beliefs contained in that explanation will cease to be directly justified, because no successful explanation contains falsehoods.[16] (Once it's certain that something isn't a successful explanation, it's no longer one of the best and good enough explanations.) The explanationist can either say that this information about the success of the explanations contained in the book (a) makes it the case that not each of the initially directly justified beliefs remains so or (b) each of the initially directly justified beliefs might remain so The explanationist either has to say that this information about the ratio of successful to unsuccessful explanations in the book (a) makes it the case that some of the initially directly justified beliefs are no longer justified or (b) that these beliefs remain justified despite this information.

Let's consider the (a) answer first. On this view, once the author learns that the book contained an error and learns that one explanation is unsuccessful, the

---

[15] This version of Makinson's (1965) case can be found in Littlejohn and Dutant (2020) and Praolini (2019). Ryan (1996) and Smith (2022) provide important discussions of the preface, including ones with the stipulations from above. We think that Smith's (2016) view is similar to explanationism in some respects, the main difference being that the explanationist isn't so clearly committed to the idea that our evidence always supports a set of propositions that's logically consistent. We provide further arguments against imposing this consistency requirement in Littlejohn and Dutant (forthcoming).

[16] In saying that the explanation contains a falsehood, we simply mean that the relevant purported explanation of the evidence consists of a falsehood or consists of more than one proposition where at least one is a falsehood. In writing this, we were intrigued by the question as to whether there is a significant difference between explaining something by citing p and citing q or by citing their conjunction. It was difficult to see these as competing explanations, so one view to consider is that the difference between ampersands and commas doesn't matter to the individuation of explanations. To avoid taking a stand on questions about the individuation of explanation, we wanted to be open to the idea that an explanation might consist of a series of claims that aren't conjoined and that a purported explanation might fail because at least one of these claims isn't true. One potential problem for the explanationist view that we don't consider here concerns the connection between the individuation of explanation and the rational support the evidence provides. Claims that individually we might take to be quite probable might constitute parts of a purported explanation. If the evidence justifies these claims only insofar as they are parts of an explanation and explanations are taken to be conjunctions of these claims, it might seem difficult to see how these individual claims might be rational since it might seem implausible that a highly improbable conjunction that contains them is true.

beliefs contained in one or more of the explanations cease to be justified. They can say either that some are lost or that each is lost. We'll suppose that each explanation antecedently seemed to be on an equal footing. Without any discernible weak link, it seems that the view that says that some remain justified and others do not is too externalist, in the sense that the support relation picks winners and losers on grounds that couldn't be discernible to the thinker. (Alternatively, we could think of this selection as arbitrary.) On the other hand, the view that doesn't choose between winners and losers is too sceptical. For reasons we'll sketch below, it seems that learning that one and only one mistake was made shouldn't lead to the widespread abandonment of beliefs that were adequately justified previously.

If this is right, then it seems the explanationist might opt for (b), the view that each of the beliefs that were directly justified remains so. We assume that the explanationist doesn't want to say that this is so because the author isn't justified in believing her work contains an error. It seems dogmatic to retain beliefs and refuse to believe a panel of experts when they tell you that you've made a mistake. If the explanationist says that the author can rationally believe that the book contains a mistake *and* retain belief in each of the parts of the original explanations, they can reject (*). We think that anyone who believes there can be rational but false beliefs should reject (*), but we worry that the explanationist who goes this route will struggle with related constraints like the following:

(**) It is not rationally co-tenable to hold your directly justified beliefs and believe that many/most/nearly every one of your directly justified beliefs are false.

We can imagine lining up increasingly error-ridden books similar to the author's where the number of errors is revealed by the panel. Once we arrive at those books where nearly every one of the directly justified beliefs is believed to be mistaken (where these higher-order beliefs are is based on the panel's testimony), we should find a case where the evidence *cannot* provide adequate support for each of the initial beliefs *and* the belief about the prevalence of errors and unsuccessful explanations.

How does the explanationist view make sense of the difference along this continuum (i.e. the difference between (*) and (**))? We can see how in a local case the (apparent) discovery that an explanation fails can defeat the justification to believe the claims contained in the explanation, but we cannot see how this information about the ratio of success to failure could bear on the particular explanations the author initially accepted. Suppose she initially believed something about octopuses, something about the First World War, something about the clarinet, something about whiskers on kittens, etc. by means of justification-conferring explanatory inferences only then to learn that most of these explanations were unsuccessful. We don't see how this bears on the loveliness of the various explanations for the evidence about octopuses in particular. We do think we see, however, that information about the ratio of success to failure matters to the rationality of this author's beliefs—when the risk of believing falsehoods is too great, it seems obviously irrational to believe even *if* that belief is contained in some seemingly lovely explanation.

It is no mystery why scale would matter on a strength-centred view. There are some risks that we rationally should tolerate and some we should not. Deciding which risk is which is, according to the strength-centred theorist, determined by the probability of undesirable outcomes and the values involved. It seems that the explanationist view offers us no rational basis for distinguishing (*) from (**), so perhaps they'll encourage us to bite the bullet and accept both (putative) constraints.

Is it really so bad to accept (*)? We think so. Our case is a version of Makinson's (1965) preface with a few twists.[17] It's important to our argument that readers agree that the preface differs from the lottery in that it's possible to have a preface-type case in which there's a set of beliefs that's known to be inconsistent and still be comprised entirely of rational beliefs.

One thing to note about the preface-type cases is that some preface-type cases seem to be paradigmatic cases of knowledge. In a preface case in which (say) a subject memorizes every entry in a phone book along with the claim that the phone book contains an error, the subject seems to acquire quite a lot of knowledge about phone numbers and knowledge of the fallibility of the source. In the admittedly odd case where an expert testifies the book contains one error out of n claims, we think, in principle, someone could come to believe each of the n claims and the true ones (i.e. n-1 claims) could be known. In the absence of discernible differences between the n-cases, it is very tempting to say that the beliefs will not differ in terms of their rational status. Paradigmatic cases of knowledge are plausible cases of rational belief. Cases in which it's nearly certain that someone will come to know are also plausible cases of rational belief. Denying knowledge in these cases leads us to something close to scepticism.

We can put further pressure on views that accept (*). When we accept (*) and try to avoid the apparent sceptical consequences of (*), we end up with very odd views about comparative epistemic preferability about sources or about responses. Contrast (*) with this:

(***) It is not rationally co-tenable to hold your directly justified beliefs and harbour small doubts about the accuracy of each of these beliefs.

Here's a toy case. Suppose we say that if a thinker has a credence of .95 or greater in *p*, this thinker's doubts about *p* are small. Now consider two questions about epistemic preferability, a question about preferable situations/sources and a

---

[17] We think that while Ryan (1991) is right that it might be rare that the book consists entirely of well-founded beliefs, we should be able to focus on the hypothetical case where this condition is met.

question about preferable responses. In our original case (Author 1), the author believed n claims (including the claim that n-1 claims were true). In our variant case (Author 2), the author is not told by a panel that she's made any mistakes. Instead, she believes n claims and is .95 confident in each. Let's suppose the number of claims here is 100. Notice that, in Author 2, the expected number of errors greatly exceeds the number of expected number of errors in Author 1. In Author 1, the expected number of errors matches the believed number of errors and actual number of errors: 1. In Author 2, the expected number of errors is 5. If we accept (*) and reject (***), we're saying that suspension is preferable to belief in (*) but not in (***). Why would we prefer believing in the case where the expected number of errors and failed explanations is *greater* than in the case where suspension is preferable to belief? This preference strikes us as odd.

Ask yourself which source you prefer. We cannot think of any reason why anyone would prefer the second author's work as a source to the first. It's true that nobody is yet *convinced* that the second source contains an error, but it's hard to believe that this difference between conviction and expectation matters much. If we told you (and you believed us) that out of 100 fireworks, one will be a dud and then asked you whether you would trade this for a box of 100 where the expected number of duds is 5, it's hard to believe that if you wanted to get a bang for your buck, you wouldn't trade the former for the latter.[18]

If the explanationist responds by saying that we should accept (***), we feel the game is up. If we cannot rationally believe when we harbour only these small doubts about accuracy, we're going to be forced towards the view on which none of our beliefs is rational unless it's completely certain that it is true. But this view, we think, is functionally indistinguishable from scepticism and impossible to reconcile with the generally optimistic outlook epistemologists take towards the prospect of acquiring knowledge from fallible sources like phone books, Wikipedia entries, and our flawed but knowledgeable friends.

4. Strength and Knowledge

We seem to be pulled in different directions by intuition. When we try to make sense of the intuitions that support Seeing, Hearing, and Playing, we might be tempted to embrace explanationism and reject High. When we try to make sense of intuitions like these, a strength-centred view might seem attractive:

---

[18] Assuming, that is, that you don't need for some reason to get 100 explosions. If you value each explosion equally and are disappointed by each dud equally, it's clear to us that when presented with a choice between a container of n items where it's certain that n-1 are desirable and a container where the expected number of undesirable items greatly exceeds 1, you should prefer the former.

Authoring: If an author carefully researches her large book and bases each claim on the right kind of evidence, she can rationally believe each of the claims in the book, including the claim that the book contains an error.

Authoring-: Even if the author carefully researches her book and bases each claim on the right kind of evidence, it can be irrational for her to retain belief if the expected number of errors is too great.

It's tempting to appeal to a strength-centred theory to explain Authoring and Authoring-, since the most obvious difference between the cases where it is rational for the author to believe and the cases in which it is not is precisely that the strength of support decreases as the number of expected errors increases.

We think that we can make the most progress in making sense of these intuitions by introducing a strength-centred view that explains Low and explains why we should reject High. Our view will be strength-centred by virtue of the fact that it incorporates expectationism. It differs from the most familiar strength-centred theories in that it doesn't combine expectationism with veritist assumptions. The key, we think, to making sense of these puzzling intuitions is to retain expectationism and combine that view with a better view of what's truly epistemically desirable.

Many theories of rational belief fail to predict or explain the intuitive difference between lottery-type cases and preface-type cases, but if we're right about Playing and Authoring, this is something that a theory of rational belief should be expected to do. Foley observed that there is at least one key difference between the cases:

> To be sure, there are important differences between the lottery and the preface. An especially noteworthy one is that in the preface you can have knowledge of the propositions that make up your book whereas in the lottery you do not know of any given ticket that it will lose.
>
> (Foley 2009: 44)

Unfortunately, he immediately added the remark that, "This difference, however, is to be explained by the prerequisites of knowledge, not those of rational belief" (Foley 2009: 44). We don't see why this difference should be irrelevant to the theory of rational belief if rational believers desire to *know* the truth and have an aversion to believing without knowing the truth.

Suppose that what's desirable from the epistemic point is acquiring knowledge and that it's undesirable to believe without thereby acquiring knowledge, so that we replace veritism with this theory of epistemic value:

Gnosticism: It is most epistemically desirable (objectively speaking) to acquire knowledge. The least desirable outcome is believing without knowing. Suspension is preferable to believing without knowing.

What happens if we opt for a strength-centred view that combines expectationism with gnosticism instead of veritism? We end up with this view:

Gnostic expectabilism: It is rational for a thinker to believe *p* iff (and because) it is rational for this thinker to be sufficiently confident that by believing *p*, she will know *p*.[19]

On the supposition that it would be worse to believe what's not known than it would be to fail to believe in a situation in which a belief would constitute knowledge, gnostic expectabilism tells us that it's rational to believe *p* outright only if it's more likely than not that by so believing one will come to know.

When it comes to Seeing, Hearing, and Playing, gnostic expectabilism and explanationism deliver the same verdicts. In the lottery case, it is very likely that the lottery proposition is true, but it is *certain* that the belief will not constitute knowledge. Given the certainty, it is surely not true that it's more likely than not that, by believing, a thinker will acquire knowledge, and so suspension does better than belief in terms of expected epistemic value. In mundane cases, however, we normally assume that the cases in which it's rational to believe on the basis of testimony, memory, or observation are cases in which it's not likely that we'll fail to acquire knowledge. When it comes to these intuitions, it seems that explanationism and gnostic expectabilism are both doing fine.

It should be noted that we now have on the table a strength-centred view (admittedly, an unorthodox one) that explains Low and explains why we should reject High. If it's rational to believe only if it's more likely than not that you know, it's rational to believe only if it's more likely than not that your belief is correct. (The probability of knowing will generally be exceeded by the probability of the truth of the target proposition.) We know that High fails on this view, because, however high the probability of the target proposition, the probability that this proposition could be known could be 0. At the very least, then, we can see that the lottery argument against strength-centred views only works against a subset of such views. It fails as an argument against all such views.

When it comes to Authoring and Authoring-, we think gnostic expectabilism delivers just the verdicts we want.[20] As the expected number of errors increases,

---

[19] In Dutant and Littlejohn (2021), we use this view to give a unified treatment of defeaters. On our view, defeaters are defeaters because they are 'indicators of ignorance' (i.e. evidence that lowers the probability that our beliefs meet the conditions necessary for knowledge). We provide further arguments for this approach in Littlejohn and Dutant (forthcoming).

[20] We should note that some might be concerned that unsophisticated agents (e.g. animals or children) might not have the cognitive tools to track their degrees of confidence. Is this a problem for our view? We think that if it is, it's a problem that arises for any expectationist view, including the Lockean view. The main difference between their proposal and ours is really about the desirable properties of belief. Of course, someone might think that this is to their advantage because (a) rationality is not a constitutive part of the property they take to be desirable (i.e. accuracy) and (b) rationality is a

our confidence that the beliefs that correspond to the claims in the book constitute knowledge will decrease. Even if it's a possibility that such beliefs turn out to be knowledge, belief might do worse than suspension in terms of expected epistemic value and when that happens, we can see why the scale matters and why we should take the view that there's a continuum of cases here. We should not take the view that a handful of errors is incompatible with rationality, since it's compatible with having most of the beliefs corresponding to claims in the book turn out to be knowledge. We should not take the view that widespread inaccuracy is rationally tolerable. We don't see how a view that dispenses with expectationism can explain the full range of cases here, so we think that our expectationist view does a better job with preface-type cases than the explanationist view can.

Gnostic expectabilism and explanationism take explanatory considerations to matter to rationality. We want to note some of the differences in the ways that we do that. It is supposed to be a platitude about knowledge that knowledge differs from mere true belief in that knowledge requires that it's not a mere coincidence that the belief in question is true.[21] If this is right, some explanatory connection between the facts that our beliefs concern and our beliefs must hold when those beliefs constitute knowledge. On our view, the presence of such an explanatory tie is a necessary condition for the realization of the fundamental epistemic good that rational believers hope to acquire (i.e. knowledge). It's absence, in turn, is a sufficient condition for the realization of the undesirable epistemic outcome that rational believers hope to avoid, believing without knowing.

Our view does not imply that rational belief requires that the explanatory connection between belief and fact obtains, only that the evidence makes it sufficiently likely that it does. The explanatory connections between belief and fact matter to rationality, we think, but they only matter *indirectly*. Thus, we can have large sets of beliefs where each belief is rationally held where there are some doubts that each belief in that set is connected to the facts in such a way that it isn't a coincidence that they are correct. Our view also might explain why inference to best explanation is itself a way of acquiring rational beliefs. If it's true that this form of inference is a reliable way of acquiring knowledge, it is not surprising that it is a way of forming rational beliefs. Doubts about whether *all* beliefs are

---

constitutive part of the property we take to be desirable (i.e. knowledge). We have a quick response to this. We deny that rationality is necessary for knowledge. The case of unsophisticated agents is helpful here. If I tell you Agnes knows that it's time for dinner, you might *think* she rationally believes this. If I tell you that she's an infant or a dog, you might agree with the knowledge attribution but feel funny about the attribution of rational belief. Once we think of knowledge as a kind of non-normative relation between an animal and a fact (Hyman (1999)), it's eligible to play the role we're assigning to it, that of the desirable property that bears an indirect relation to rationality. For defence of this non-normative notion of knowledge, see Kornblith (2002) and Sylvan (2018). Thanks to Artūrs Logins for raising some of these issues.

[21] For helpful discussions of the connection between knowledge and explanation, see Jenkins (2006) and Nelkin (2000).

made rational by virtue of some explanatory inference do not cast doubt on our view, since our view explains the rational force of explanatory inference in terms of the expectation that such inferences will expand our knowledge. Since we don't think it's wise to reject expectationism, we don't think that the explanationist is right to put explanation into their theory of how we ought rationally to pursue our epistemic ends if we want to acquire true belief or knowledge (and avoid false belief or ignorance). We also don't see why someone would want to treat loveliness of explanation as a kind of epistemic prize that supplants the role that we assign to knowledge. We think it makes more sense to think that things turn out well when we acquire knowledge and that things turning out well require a lovely explanation only in those cases where the explanatory inference was our means for coming to know. So, while we find some room for explanatory considerations in our theory of rational belief, it differs from the role that the explanationist assigns to it. We think this helps us see why we'd approach the lottery cases in similar ways and why our approach might have important virtues when it comes to metacoherence constraints and preface-type cases of the kind discussed above.

5. Prizes and Pursuits

We know that some readers might be sceptical of the gnostic value theory. We cannot offer a full defence of that here. We wanted to note, however, a few things in its support.

First, the theory fits with things that epistemologists often say in the course of trying to explain the value of truth. They often describe the desire for truth in terms of a desire for *having* the truth or a desire for being in touch with reality. This desire to be in touch with reality or having the truth is then identified with the desire for having true beliefs, but it's not at all clear that these come to the same thing.

Think, for example, of Nozick's (1974) experience machine. In the machine, we think that a subject is completely cut off from reality, and, as Lynch (2004) puts it, what we desire in desiring the truth is a kind of contact with reality that's missing from the life we'd live if trapped in the machine. Being in the machine seems to be incompatible with being in touch with external realities. What Nozick seems to be right about is that we think that being regularly in contact with certain external realities is necessary for attaining goods that we prize quite highly and, arguably, take to be necessary for living a life worth living. In the machine, we'll find no friendship or love and our projects come to nothing.

Here's a conjecture. If we're focusing on just beliefs about the world beyond appearances, the fundamental epistemic good that we seek is unattainable in the experience machine. We learn from Gettier that being trapped in the machine and having experiences produced by a machine that doesn't take account of what's happening in reality might trigger true beliefs (e.g. it might be a coincidence that the machine produces the experiences that convince you that your political party won the recent election right when your political party happens to win the recent election). When you come to believe that your party won, you believe the truth. Are you thereby in touch with the events taking place in the world that you correctly believe are happening because of this bizarre coincidence? No. Is this really what you want, this kind of mere match between fact and belief that could amount to a mere coincidence in which you are detached from reality? Maybe not. Maybe only knowledge gives us the connection we desire. That intuition favours gnosticism (Littlejohn 2013).

Our impression is that many philosophers think that something else must be able to give us this connection. For someone like McDowell (1995), we need some kind of contact with reality prior to and independent of knowledge in order to acquire knowledge. This is because, he thinks, knowledge requires the possession of reasons that guarantee that we can know. To be sure, they might say, mere true belief doesn't give us the connection we seek. The experience machine tells us that. It's striking, however, that in the experience machine we're also not in *perceptual* contact with our surroundings. Won't perceptual contact give us the connectedness to the world we seek?

We think not. Nozick's thought experiment suggests to some that there are *relational* goods, goods that we can enjoy only if we bear the right relation to things outside us, where this relation has some psychological or mental dimension. We don't think mere perceptual awareness gives us this connection for two reasons. First, such perceptual relations might not reveal the meaning or significance of these events for an individual. If it's perceptual contact rather than knowledge that explains why it matters that you are connected to some event of tremendous personal importance (e.g. a wedding or a funeral), remember that the perceptual relations you bear to these events will be similar to the ones that children and animals bear to these events. It matters how we conceive of the events we have before the mind, and we think that perceptual contact places too few constraints on how events are presented to do the requisite work.[22]

Secondly, perceptual relations are *neutral* on what's happening outside us. If someone is *upset* by something, seeing something upsetting isn't sufficient, not if you're agnostic about whether this event is happening. The realization of some relational goods requires *conviction* that is contained in belief but not contained in perceptual consciousness. Knowledge gives us conviction and connection. Perception, at best, gives us a kind of connection.

Things happening in the world which we're completely detached from might not harm or benefit us. This thought, we think, helps to explain why people find

---

[22] Obviously, this issue requires further discussion about the connection between perception and cognition. Some authors, particularly Silva (2020, 2022), have argued that we can be aware that p without knowing that p.

the prospect of life in the machine unpalatable. If knowledge is necessary for being related to these events so that they might be good or bad *for us*, we think that we'll make some progress towards explaining the value of knowledge and the connection between knowledge and belief. Belief's role, we think, includes that of putting us in contact with reality, so beliefs that fail to do that are, to that extent, undesirable. Our hypothesis is that beliefs that fail to constitute knowledge are undesirable for this reason. Once we're clear that there's a notion of objective epistemic desirability on which desirability involves more than a mere match between believed propositions and the world, it starts to make sense that more than mere high probability is necessary for rational belief. It also seems that the project of finding new and exotic connections between belief and truth is somewhat misguided if that doesn't ultimately appeal to the properties that beliefs need to be knowledge.

We think that epistemically loaded prizes (i.e. prizes that can only be completely and accurately described by reference to some thinker's epistemic state) have been largely overlooked in the literature on epistemic rationality. We also find this neglected in the literature on practical rationality. Once we start to think that *knowing* things about your surroundings or people you surround yourself with is necessary for realizing certain goods (e.g. being in a loving relationship, sharing meaningful projects, or developing true friendship), it makes sense that in some choice situations, information about what we might know or not know matters to choice.[23] Knowledge might matter to rational choice if, say, what we know determines in whole or part what evidence we have. Rational agents don't just want to change the world in certain ways without being informed of such changes. We think rational agents sometimes desire for the world to change in certain ways whilst enjoying awareness of these changes. If our preferences are sensitive to such epistemically loaded prizes, knowledge can matter to rational choice because of the role it plays in describing prizes and needn't play any role in the theory of how rational agents pursue the things they value.

6. Conclusion

We have proposed a theory of rational (full) belief that seemingly does the impossible. It reconciles our intuitions about lottery cases with a strength-centred theory of rational support. The key is to think about what a thinker's evidence has to say to her to convince her to take a stand on some matter. We don't think it's enough to produce conviction in addition to high credence that the evidence says, 'Hey, *p* is probably true!' If the evidence says *both* 'Hey, it's very likely that *p*'

---

[23] For arguments that knowledge is an essential part of certain emotional reactions and reactive attitudes, see Logins (2021) and Unger (1975).

and 'You'll never know whether p', we don't think that a rational thinker should thereby become convinced that p is true. If the evidence, however, says, 'Hey, it's nearly certain that you'll know the answer to the question whether p if you believe p', we think a rational thinker should settle the question whether p affirmatively. That's because we think such thinkers rationally aspire to know whether p and so desire to know and are averse to believing what's not known.

What the evidence must do to convince a rational thinker to commit is say that the risk of believing without knowing is sufficiently small. The evidence is sufficient for rational belief when it provides sufficiently strong support for the hypothesis that the thinker will come to know by believing. This view combines a not wildly unpopular value theory and a wildly popular way of thinking about the connection between rationality and desirability. While this might be sufficient to convince readers that our proposal is correct, we hope it will convince them to give our proposal consideration and think of whether there are alternative accounts that better make sense of the data.[24]

References

Appley, Bryan C., and Stoutenburg, Gregory. (2017). 'Two New Objections to Explanationism', *Synthese* 194(8), 3069–84. doi: 10.1007/s11229-016-1093-1.

Bird, Alexander. (2007). 'Justified Judging', *Philosophy and Phenomenological Research* 74(1), 81–110. doi: 10.1111/j.1933-1592.2007.00004.x.

Climenhaga, Nevin. (2017). 'Inference to the Best Explanation Made Incoherent', *Journal of Philosophy* 114(5), 251–73. doi: 10.5840/jphil2017114519.

Conee, Earl. (2004). 'Externalism, Internalism, and Skepticism', *Philosophical Issues* 14, 78–90.

Conee, Earl, and Feldman, Richard. (2004). *Evidentialism: Essays in Epistemology.* New York: Oxford University Press.

Dellsén, Finnur. (2021). 'Explanatory Consolidation: From "Best" to "Good Enough"', *Philosophy and Phenomenological Research* 103(1), 157–77. doi: 10.1111/phpr.12706.

Dorst, Kevin. (2019). Lockeans Maximize Expected Accuracy. *Mind* 128(509), 175–211. doi: 10.1093/mind/fzx028.

Dutant, Julien, and Littlejohn, Clayton. (2021). 'Defeaters as Indicators of Ignorance', in Mona Simion and Jessica Brown (eds.), *Reasons, Justification, and Defeat.* New York: Oxford University Press, 223–46.

Easwaran, Kenny. (2016). 'Dr. Truthlove or: How I Learned to Stop Worrying and Love Bayesian Probabilities', *Noûs* 50(4), 816–53. doi: 10.1111/nous.12099.

---

[24] We want to thank Artūrs Logins, Jacques-Henri Vollet, and an anonymous referee for very helpful comments on this chapter. We also want to thank Kevin McCain and Martin Smith for discussing the issues in this chapter.

Evnine, Simon J. (1999). 'Believing Conjunctions', *Synthese* 118(2), 201–27.

Foley, Richard. (2009). 'Beliefs, Degrees of Belief, and the Lockean Thesis', in Franz Huber and Christoph Schmidt-Petri (eds.), *Degrees of Belief*. New York: Springer, 37–47.

Gardiner, Georgi. (2019). 'The Reasonable and the Relevant: Legal Standards of Proof', *Philosophy and Public Affairs* 47(3), 288–318. doi: 10.1111/papa.12149.

Harman, Gilbert. (1968). 'Knowledge, Inference, and Explanation', *American Philosophical Quarterly* 5(3), 164–73.

Henderson, Leah. (2014). 'Bayesianism and Inference to the Best Explanation', *British Journal for the Philosophy of Science* 65(4), 687–715.

Hirvelä, Jaakko. (2022). 'Justification and the Knowledge-Connection', *Philosophical Studies* 179(6), 1973–95. doi: 10.1007/s11098-021-01741-x.

Hyman, John. (1999). 'How Knowledge Works', *Philosophical Quarterly* 49(197), 433–51.

Ichikawa, Jonathan Jenkins. (2014). 'Justification Is Potential Knowledge', *Canadian Journal of Philosophy* 44(2), 184–206.

Jackson, Elizabeth. (2019). 'Belief and Credence: Why the Attitude-Type Matters', *Philosophical Studies* 176(9), 2477–96.

James, William. (2014). *The Will to Believe: and Other Essays in Popular Philosophy*. Cambridge Cambridge University Press.

Jenkins, Carrie. (2006). 'Knowledge and Explanation', *Canadian Journal of Philosophy* 36(2), 137–64. doi: 10.1353/cjp.2006.0009.

Kelp, Christoph. (2014). 'Two for the Knowledge Goal of Inquiry', *American Philosophical Quarterly* 51(3), 227–32.

Kornblith, Hilary. (2002). *Knowledge and its Place in Nature*. Oxford: Clarendon Press.

Lehrer, Keith. (1970). 'Justification, Explanation, and Induction', in Marshall Swain (ed.), *Induction, Acceptance and Rational Belief*. Dordrecht: D. Reidel, 100–33. doi: 10.1007/978-94-010-3390-9_6.

Leitgeb, Hannes. (2014). 'The Stability Theory of Belief', *Philosophical Review* 123(2), 131–71.

Lipton, Peter. (2001). 'Is Explanation a Guide to Inference? A Reply to Wesley C. Salmon', In Giora Hon and Sam S. Rakover (eds.), *Explanation: Theoretical Approaches and Applications*. Dordrecht: D. Reidel, 93–120. doi: 10.1007/978-94-015-9731-9_4.

Littlejohn, Clayton. (2013). 'The Russellian Retreat', *Proceedings of the Aristotelian Society* 113, 293–320.

Littlejohn, Clayton. (2015). 'Who Cares What You Accurately Believe?' *Philosophical Perspectives* 29(1), 217–48.

Littlejohn, Clayton. (2020). 'Truth, Knowledge, and the Standard of Proof in Criminal Law', *Synthese* 197(12), 5253–86. doi: 10.1007/s11229-017-1608-4.

Littlejohn, Clayton, and Dutant, Julien. (2020). 'Justification, Knowledge, and Normality' *Philosophical Studies* 177(6), 1593–609.

Littlejohn, Clayton, and Dutant, Julien. (forthcoming). 'What is Rational Belief?' *Noûs*.

Logins, Artūrs. (2021). 'Persistent Burglars and Knocks on Doors: Causal Indispensability of Knowing Vindicated', *European Journal of Philosophy* 30(4), 1335–57.

Lutz, Matt. (2020). Explanationism Provides the Best Explanation of the Epistemic Significance of Peer Disagreement. *Philosophical Studies* 177(7): 1811–1828. doi: 10.1007/s11098-019-01286-0.

Lycan, William. (1988). *Judgement and Justification*. Cambridge: Cambridge University Press.

Lynch, Michael P. (2004). *True to Life: Why Truth Matters*. Cambridge, MA: MIT University Press.

McCain, Kevin. (2014). *Evidentialism and Epistemic Justification*. New York: Routledge.

McCain, Kevin, and Moretti, Luca. (2021). *Appearance and Explanation: Phenomenal Explanationism in Epistemology*. New York: Oxford University Press.

McDowell, John. (1995). 'Knowledge and the Internal', *Philosophy and Phenomenological Research* 55(4), 877–93.

Makinson, David C. (1965). 'The Paradox of the Preface', *Analysis* 25(6), 205.

Moss, Sarah. (2018). *Probabilistic Knowledge*. Oxford: Oxford University Press.

Nelkin, Dana K. (2000). 'The Lottery Paradox, Knowledge, and Rationality', *Philosophical Review* 109(3), 373–409.

Nozick, Robert. (1974). *Anarchy, State, and Utopia*. New York: Basic Books.

Owens, David. (2000). *Reason without Freedom: The Problem of Epistemic Normativity*. New York: Routledge.

Pollock, John L. (1986). 'The Paradox of the Preface', *Philosophy of Science* 53, 246–58.

Poston, Ted. (2011). 'Explanationist Plasticity and the Problem of the Criterion', *Philosophical Papers* 40(3), 395–419. doi: 10.1080/05568641.2011.634248.

Praolini, Francesco. (2019). 'No Justificatory Closure without Truth', *Australasian Journal of Philosophy* 97(4), 715–26. doi: 10.1080/00048402.2018.1564059.

Rosenkranz, Sven. (2021). *Justification as Ignorance: An Essay in Epistemology*. New York: Oxford University Press.

Russell, Bertrand. (1912). *The Problems of Philosophy*. Oxford: Oxford University Press.

Ryan, Sharon. (1991). 'The Preface Paradox', *Philosophical Studies* 64(3), 293–307.

Ryan, Sharon. (1996). 'The Epistemic Virtues of Consistency', *Synthese* 109(2), 121–41. doi: 10.1007/BF00413765.

Shah, Nishi. (2006). 'A New Argument for Evidentialism', *Philosophical Quarterly* 56(225), 481–98.

Silva, Paul. (2020). 'Possessing Reasons: Why the Awareness-First Approach is Better than the Knowledge-First Approach', *Synthese* 199(1–2), 2925–47. doi.org/10.1007/s11229-020-02916-5.

Silva, Paul. (2022). 'Basic Knowledge and the Normativity of Knowledge: The Awareness-First Solution', *Philosophy and Phenomenological Research* 104(3), 564–86. doi: 10.1111/phpr.12754.

Smith, Martin. (2016). *Between Probability and Certainty: What Justifies Belief.* Oxford: Oxford University Press.

Smith, Martin. (2022). 'The Hardest Paradox for Closure', *Erkenntnis* 87(4), 2003–28.

Sturgeon, Scott. (2008). Reason and the Grain of Belief. *Noûs*, 42(1), 139–165. doi: 10.1111/j.1468-0068.2007.00676.x.

Sutton, Jonathan. (2005). 'Stick to What You Know', *Noûs* 39(3), 359–96. doi: 10.1111/j.0029-4624.2005.00506.x.

Sylvan, Kurt. (2018). 'Knowledge as a Non-Normative Relation', *Philosophy and Phenomenological Research* 97(1), 190–222.

Thomson, Judith Jarvis. (1986). 'Liability and Individualized Evidence', *Law and Contemporary Problems* 49(3), 199–219. doi: 10.2307/1191633.

Unger, Peter K. (1975). *Ignorance: A Case for Scepticism* (369). Oxford: Clarendon Press.

Williamson, Timothy. (2000). *Knowledge and its Limits.* Oxford: Oxford University Press.

Worsnip, Alex. (2016). 'Belief, Credence, and the Preface Paradox', *Australasian Journal of Philosophy* 94(3), 549–62. doi: 10.1080/00048402.2015.1084343.

Clayton Littlejohn and Julien Dutant, *Knowledge and Prizes* In: *Putting Knowledge to Work: New Directions for Knowledge-First Epistemology.* Edited by: Artūrs Logins and Jacques-Henri Vollet, Oxford University Press.
© Clayton Littlejohn and Julien Dutant 2024. DOI: 10.1093/9780191976766.003.0012

13
Perceptual Knowledge and the 'Activity' of Belief

Johannes Roessler

> For as the Philosopher says, it is a weakness of intellect to search for reason in cases where we have sensation, since one should not search for a reason for the thing we possess that is more valuable (*dignius*) than reason.
>
> (Henry of Ghent 2002: 98)

1. Introduction

Recent work on the nature of our responsibility for what we believe is marked by a broad consensus on a basic question and a variety of opinions on how to develop the consensus view. It is widely agreed that since we can appropriately be held answerable for what we believe, there must be a sense in which we are 'active' in relation to our current beliefs. Believing something, according to the consensus view, involves an exercise of 'rational agency' or 'self-determination'. I will call this the Activity Thesis (AT). A multitude of different suggestions have been aired about how to understand the operative sense of 'activity' or 'self-determination'. For some, the essence of the matter lies in the relation between belief and active deliberation or in the 'deliberative stance' we are said to occupy vis-à-vis our own current beliefs (Moran 2001). Others focus on what they see as the central role of acts of judging in the formation of beliefs, with different accounts having been proposed of the nature of such acts (McDowell 1994, 1998a; McHugh 2013). Yet others suggest that there is a sense in which believing itself—a state, not an event or process—amounts to a rational activity (Boyle 2009a, 2011).

In what follows I want to connect the question of the sense (if any) in which believing may be said to be 'active' with a topic that has been conspicuous by its absence from recent discussions of that question: the relationship between belief and propositional knowledge. Two major contributions to the two areas—Timothy Williamson's *Knowledge and its Limits* and Richard Moran's *Authority and Estrangement*—were published within a year of each other (Williamson 2000; Moran 2001), but despite the temporal proximity, there has been little interaction between the debates generated by these works. One might find this surprising, simply insofar as both debates are concerned with the nature of belief. Still, it is a good question whether there are any substantive connections between the two debates. Might they simply be orthogonal to each other? I want to suggest that they are not. Current work on AT, I will try to show, is informed by a contentious conception of the relation between two kinds of questions: 'Why do you believe that p?' and 'How do you know that p?' Roughly speaking, the unspoken assumption in this work is that the former question enjoys a certain explanatory priority. Focusing on the case of perceptual knowledge/perceptual belief,[1] and drawing on work by Williamson, Alan Millar, and Barry Stroud, I will argue that the 'belief-first' approach taken for granted by proponents of AT distorts a central area of our ordinary practice of questioning and vindicating beliefs.

Friends of AT, I think, have always tended to feel some unease about perceptual beliefs. The way we come to believe, or the way we judge, that something is so when we non-inferentially perceive that it is so is not, intuitively, a shining example of our occupation of a 'deliberative stance' or of exercising the power of making up our minds about some question. If the argument of this chapter is on the right lines, the sense of unease is apt but has been widely misdiagnosed. The problem is not that perception yields reasons for belief that are so compelling as to make explicit deliberation superfluous or (differently) that perceptual beliefs are caused by non-rational mechanisms. Rather, the case of perceptual beliefs looks awkward because such beliefs are in a sense derivative or secondary. In the words of Henry of Ghent quoted at the head of this chapter, we ordinarily take it that, in the best cases, perceptual experience gives us something 'more valuable' (Henry of Ghent 2002: 98) than beliefs or even reasons for belief: it gives us (direct) knowledge. Of course, by giving us knowledge, perception *also* gives us belief. But the ground of such beliefs does not lie in our free responsiveness to reasons. It lies in our ability to perceive and thus know what objects around us are like.

The bulk of the chapter (Sections 3–5) is devoted to developing Henry's challenge (as I will call it) and examining two lines of response. I start with a brief review of the target of the challenge. I conclude by considering (all too briefly) where the challenge leaves us.

2. The Activity Thesis

David Owens writes: 'In the end, it is *the world* which determines what (and whether) I believe, not *me*. When I reach a conclusion by means of evidence, one external

---

[1] I think the case of perceptual knowledge and belief most clearly illustrates the issue I want to raise, but the issue may not be peculiar to that case. For example, beliefs and knowledge reflecting the operation of memory—and perhaps testimony—may raise analogous issues.

fact is convincing me of another... Where is *my* input at this final stage?' (Owens 2000: 12). It seems right that when 'one external fact is convincing me of another', there is a sense in which I submit to the force of the evidence and so might be said to be passive. Advocates of AT, I take it, will be happy to grant this.[2] They will acknowledge that if all goes well, it is indeed the world that determines what I believe. Their point is that the world does not, in such cases, act on its own, but jointly with my assessment or recognition of the probative value of the evidence. My coming to believe what I do reflects my *judgement* as to what I have reason to believe. This is so even in cases in which, as I recognize, my evidence is conclusive. And there is a sense—compatible with the element of passivity just alluded to—in which, in exercising my judgement, I myself determine what I believe. As Boyle puts it, a believer's 'condition is thus active or self-determined in an intelligible sense: its ground lies in her accepting the rational correctness of this very condition' (Boyle 2011: 22).

What is the relationship between the claim that there is this distinctive explanatory structure—that the 'grounds' of our beliefs lie in our appraisal of our reasons for belief—and the claim that beliefs are (sometimes? typically? potentially?) acquired by performing certain kinds of acts or carrying out certain activities? As indicated earlier, the literature presents a variety of perspectives on this question. For current purposes, we need not try to resolve the matter, but I would like to highlight two points which, I think, are common ground among most recent adherents of AT. One is that the sense of 'activity' germane to beliefs is to be distinguished from the notion of *voluntary* activity. A helpful framework for marking this is to draw a distinction between a genus and several species of the notion of activity. (See Boyle 2009a for this way of framing AT.) The sense in which we are active in relation to our beliefs is in some ways analogous to the case of voluntary activity, and reflection on the analogies enables us to see the two cases as instantiating a common genus. That is compatible, however, with acknowledging significant 'specific differences'. For example, it would be a mistake to characterize the genus by reference to the notion of the will or by reference to our responsiveness to practical reasons.[3] And perhaps we should allow that not all ways of being 'active' share the same temporal profile (for example, they may not always involve the occurrence of events or the unfolding of processes).

A second area of common ground concerns the rationale for AT. The most promising way to support the thesis, many would agree, develops not from

---

[2] See, for example, Gary Watson's discussion of Owens's view, in Watson (2004: 144).

[3] Advocates of AT have a tendency (in my view) to sail close to the wind by characterizing the 'activity' of belief in terms that have their home in the sphere of choice and voluntary control. For example, what we believe is said to be 'up to us', we are said to be able to 'take charge' (or 'control') of our beliefs, we are even said to enjoy 'discretion' over them. Possibly such phrases can be heard in a 'generic' sense, implying not decision or voluntary control but merely responsibility and rational self-determination. In any case, I take it their use is not mandatory.

introspective scrutiny of what tends to happen when we come to believe something, but from reflection on the way we engage with each other's beliefs in our ordinary dialectical practice.[4] The point is often put by saying that we are 'answerable' (or appropriately 'held answerable') for our beliefs. As I argue in the next section, just what this means is a less straightforward matter than is sometimes assumed. But the basic idea is highly intuitive. Beliefs are akin to intentional actions—and quite *unlike* sensations—in that they are familiar, intelligible targets of questions that have a distinctive normative import. 'What makes you think there are rabbits in the garden?' is not asking for a detached, neutral record of the aetiology of your belief. A good answer would show why you are *right* to believe what you do. If you can give no such answer (say, it turns out you mistook a squirrel for a rabbit), you would be expected to revise your first-order belief, demonstrating that the 'ground' of your belief lies in your normative judgement about its 'rational correctness'. The standard route to AT, then, consists of two moves. First, the observation that we hold each other answerable for our beliefs is spelled out in terms of the idea that we believe what we do for normative reasons as we see them. In turn, that kind of intelligibility is said to implicate a form of self-determination (hence, a species of 'activity'). To put it schematically:

Answerability → reasons → self-determination

McDowell puts the latter move as follows:

> We should make sense of the idea of believing for reasons, like the idea of acting for reasons, in the context of the idea of a subject who can take charge of her beliefs and actions—hence, a subject who can step back from candidate reasons and acknowledge or refuse to acknowledge their cogency.
>
> (McDowell 2001: 183)

One might object that 'stepping back' from a 'candidate reason' is not something we routinely do. Doing so is time-consuming and can divert attention from more pressing concerns.[5] We usually seem to respond to reasons without any such critical reflection. AT, to use the familiar ugly term, might be said to 'over-intellectualize' the way we ordinarily come to believe what we do. McDowell's response, I take it, would be that while we only 'freely' adopt a belief when we engage in the occurrent activity of 'making up our minds what to think',[6] our *capacity* to do so has a

---

[4] This has an obvious bearing on the status of AT. Typically, in contemporary work, the thesis is intended not as a (possibly revisionary) philosophical theory but as an articulation and affirmation of our pre-theoretical view of belief, as a state intelligible 'at the personal level'.

[5] It can also be hard. Compare Montaigne's observation that 'the principal effect of the power of custom is to seize and ensnare us in such a way that it is hardly within our power to get ourselves out of its grip and return into ourselves to reflect and reason about its ordinances' (Montaigne 2003: 100).

[6] '(J)udging, making up our minds what to think, is something for which we are, in principle, responsible—something we freely do as opposed to something that merely happens in our lives' (McDowell 1998a: 434). In other places McDowell seems to come close to the view elaborated by

wider significance. For believing something is an 'actualization of capacities of a kind...whose paradigmatic mode of actualization is in the exercise of freedom that judging is' (McDowell 1998a: 434). An alternative response would be to invoke Boyle's neo-Aristotelian account of 'activity'. We might insist that even when we exploit reasons unthinkingly and automatically, and indeed even just in *holding* a belief for a reason, we count as practising a form of self-determination, insofar as we exercise judgement, conceived as a *capacity* (the 'power of judgement') rather than as an act of judging that something is so (Boyle 2011).

Either way, adapting a well-known remark of Elizabeth Anscombe's, we might say that AT is not primarily a claim about 'mental processes' involved in acquiring beliefs; it is a claim about an 'order that is there' when we hold a belief for a reason.[7] My question is: do perceptual beliefs exhibit that order?

3. Henry's Challenge

To see why the question can look pressing, consider Austin's distinction between evidence and perception. When you believe that there is a pig around because you interpret various observable facts as evidence of the presence of a pig, your resulting belief looks like a good illustration of the idea of 'doxastic self-determination'. You hold a belief because you take it that there is a good reason for that belief. But suppose the pig emerges and now stands there right in front of you, 'plainly in view'. In that case, Austin insists, you have no need for evidence as to whether there is a pig around. You can 'just see' that there is a pig in front of you, so the question is 'settled' (Austin 1962: 115). Your belief seems to be determined by 'the world', in a stronger sense than when one fact convinces you of another. Since you are not drawing an inference (not even unthinkingly or automatically), your belief does not implicate your capacity to assess the probative force of reasons. It is not just that you don't exercise your capacity to 'step back' from a candidate reason. There is, on the face of it, nothing for you to step back from.

Defenders of AT tend to assume that if they face a problem here, it derives from the fact that, as Moran puts it, '(p)erceptual belief is a favored case for eliciting externalist intuitions' (Moran 2004: 459). In other words, those who doubt that we are 'active' in relation to perceptual beliefs must be attracted by the thought that such beliefs reflect the operation of the sort of non-rational 'belief-forming mechanism' familiar from purely reliabilist theories of perceptual knowledge. The question for friends of AT, on this construal of the challenge, is whether they should seek to *accommodate* such 'externalist intuitions' as may be elicited by

---

Boyle. Compare his remark that '(r)ationality, in the demanding sense,...can be operative in quite unreflective belief formation' (McDowell 2010: 8).

[7] See Anscombe (1957: 80).

perceptual beliefs (as does Moran) or *repudiate* them (as does McDowell). I will come back to these responses. But I first want to suggest that it is quite wrong to assume that the challenge must be fuelled by 'externalist intuitions'.

Consider Henry's dictum: 'it is a weakness of intellect to search for reason in cases where we have sensation' (Henry of Ghent 2002: 98). Or consider Barry Stroud's more recent claim that 'there is no need for something to serve as our reason for believing that there is a red apple on a brown table' in a situation in which we can non-inferentially see that there is a red apple on a brown table (Stroud 2015: 394). Neither Henry nor Stroud subscribes to a 'purely reliabilist' or any other kind of 'externalist' analysis of perceptual knowledge. If we need an 'ism' to refer to their outlook we could do worse than calling them 'primitivists'. They take it that the explanatory connection between perception and knowledge is basic: it is not to be analysed by reference to some underlying explanatory link between perception and *belief*, whether conceived along internalist or externalist lines. In other words, an account of how you know that there is a pig before you makes no reference to either a reason for belief or a non-rational cause of your belief. It makes no reference to your belief at all.[8] When you see a pig, you will, under favourable circumstances, be able to exercise relevant capacities for *visual knowledge* and, as a result, will come to see (and thus know) that there is a pig in front of you. Occasionally, of course, things do not go well, and you merely end up acquiring a perceptual belief. But that does not mean that even in a good case, perception yields, at least most immediately, mere beliefs, or that the way perception yields knowledge is to be understood by reference to its role in grounding beliefs.

On this analysis, if perceptual beliefs are troublesome for AT, this is not because they elicit 'externalist intuitions'. Then what *is* the problem? Much here depends on how the idea of a 'primitive' connection between perception and knowledge is to be developed. Does the idea really exclude the possibility that we have reasons for our perceptual beliefs? Is it committed to a view on which perceptual beliefs belong to the 'passive side' of the human mind? Does it deny that rational capacities are implicated when a rational thinker holds a perceptual belief? I want to set these complicated questions to one side for now. I want to start with a fairly straightforward way in which a primitivist view of perceptual knowledge puts pressure on AT. In a nutshell: the view challenges the conception of what it means to be answerable for our beliefs that underpins the case for AT.[9]

---

[8] For recent elaborations of this sort of view, see Stroud (2009, 2011); Millar (2008, 2010, 2011, 2019); Williamson (2009, esp. 357–63); Roessler (2009, 2019). On Henry's epistemology and its Aristotelian background, see Perler (2006, sects 4–5). On the role of the notion of 'evidentness' in medieval epistemology, see Pasnau (2017, esp. 31–35 and 188–197).

[9] This might make it sound as if a primitivist account challenges merely an *argument for* AT, rather than AT itself. However, the conception of the practice of 'answering for' our beliefs that is at issue here is arguably internal to AT—at least to those versions of AT that present themselves as articulations of our ordinary conception of belief.

As a particularly clear example of that conception, consider Pamela Hieronymi's use of what she sees as a basic parallel between our answerability for actions and beliefs. Hieronymi starts with a definition: 'One is *answerable* for an activity or a state of affairs just in case one can rightly be asked for the reasons, if any, for which one engaged (or engages) in the activity or brought about the state of affairs' (Hieronymi 2007: 359). She connects this notion with Anscombe's suggestion that intentional actions are actions that are open to the question 'Why are you ϕ-ing?', used as a request for your reason for ϕ-ing (Anscombe 1957). Hieronymi goes on to suggest that an analogous point holds for belief: 'whenever one believes that *p* (where *p* stands for a proposition, such as "The butler did it" or "It is going to rain"), one can rightly be asked, "Why do you believe *p*?"' (Hieronymi 2007: 359). On this picture, to be answerable for ϕ-ing or for believing that p *just is* to be open to a request for one's reason for ϕ-ing or believing that p.

The trouble with this account is that it builds into the definition of 'answerability' an assumption that is not only substantive but, arguably, dubious. Consider Austin's gloss on the question 'Why do you believe that p?' When we use this as a 'pointed question', we insinuate, or at least raise the possibility, that *you oughtn't* believe that p (Austin 1961: 78). We might put this by saying that the question invites an account of how you have come to believe that p that would simultaneously provide an effective defence of your believing that p or would show that it's OK for you to believe that p. We might also suggest an analogous gloss on the question 'Why are you ϕ-ing?' Armed with this broader definition, we can then ask how the request for (as we might put it) a vindicating explanation of your belief/action relates to the request for a *reason* for believing or acting. It seems clear that offering a good reason would amount to an effective vindicating explanation. Moreover, in the case of intentional actions there may well be no alternative to this sort of account. To ask, pointedly, 'Why are you ϕ-ing?' is to ask about the point or the good or the justification of your ϕ-ing, and the matter, it seems, inevitably turns on your reason for ϕ-ing. In the case of beliefs, however, there does seem to be an alternative to provision of your reason for belief: you may instead explain *how you know that p*. Since coming to know that p entails coming to believe that p, the account will shed light on the origin of your belief. And since there can be nothing wrong with believing that p if one knows that p, the account amounts to an effective defence or vindication of your belief. It is hard to think of a better 'vindicating explanation' of believing that p than an account of how one knows that p.

We can now begin to see how a primitivist account of perceptual knowledge would spell trouble for AT. The idea that AT articulates our ordinary conception of belief turns on the assumption that 'answerability' is inextricably connected with the demand for reasons; specifically, that our answerability for what we believe shows beliefs to be under the sway of our capacity to assess the force of reasons (hence to exercise a form of self-determination). Yet if the explanatory connection between perception and knowledge is primitive and immediate, we will be able effectively to 'answer for' a perceptual belief without invoking any reason for which we hold the belief. We could instead say things like 'I can just see that there is a pig in front of me' or 'I can tell a pig when I see one', where these statements should be taken to gesture towards an account of how seeing a pig, in concert with our visual-epistemic capacities, gives us knowledge that there is a pig in front of us—dispensing us from the task of exercising judgement as to the probative value of the evidence. This would mark a fundamental disanalogy between intentional action and belief. While exhibiting the point of an intentional action can only be a matter of setting out one's reason for it, one can establish the credentials of a belief that p by showing that—and how—one knows that p. Call this Henry's challenge.

How plausible is the primitivist picture that underwrites the challenge? At this stage, I just want to make three points that help to get the dialectical situation into focus.

First, a clarification. We should distinguish two projects: there is the project of articulating the way perception figures in our ordinary practice of explaining how we know what we know and (thereby) defending our claims to knowledge; and there is the project of constructing what philosophers may consider to be a satisfactory explanation of perceptual knowledge. Primitivism, as I understand it, is primarily a contribution to the first project. Accordingly, if appeal to perceptual-epistemic capacities is deemed to be question-begging relative to the philosophical problem of our knowledge of the external world, that will not necessarily be an objection to a primitivist analysis of our ordinary practice. Advocates of the latter may wish to grant that a solution to that problem would require an independent account of how perception warrants our beliefs about the objective world.[10] They just insist that we ordinarily understand our knowledge in a more simple-minded way.

Second, 'primitive' does not mean 'unintelligible'.[11] We can distinguish two sorts of factors that render our possession of perceptual knowledge intelligible, on a primitivist account. On the one hand, the subject needs to have certain standing abilities, such as the ability visually to tell a pig.[12] On the other hand, circumstances must be such as to permit the subject to exercise the relevant abilities. For example, to exercise the capacity visually to tell that an animal is a pig, the animal must, from the subject's point of view, *look like* a pig: the sorts of features

---

[10] Stroud's view might be interpreted in that way, with a further important ingredient, viz. scepticism about the prospects of achieving a philosophical understanding of perceptual knowledge. (See, for example, Stroud 2009.) The relationship between the two projects raises a number of complex questions that I cannot address here. For some preliminary discussion, see Roessler (2019).

[11] As Alan Millar puts it, a perceptual-recognitional capacity is not a mere disposition to acquire knowledge (we know not how) but an 'ability that has a certain structure' (Millar 2008: 336).

[12] Such abilities may be underpinned by a distinctive kind of knowledge: knowledge of what pigs (typically) look like.

that go into the (or a) characteristic visual appearance of a pig need to be sufficiently clearly visible.[13] What these various factors render intelligible is how seeing the pig reveals or discloses or makes it manifest to the subject that there is a pig in front of her. Note that these natural phrases all entail that she comes to *know* that there is a pig in front of her. The account makes no mention of her belief that there is a pig in front of her at all. But it is not clear why this should diminish its explanatory value.

Third, the case for a primitivist account of our ordinary practice may be organized around a dilemma facing the project of a 'belief-first' analysis. How are we supposed to understand the allegedly more basic explanatory connection between perception and beliefs (in virtue of which we are said to find perceptually grounded knowledge intelligible)? The options here seem to be limited. Perceptual beliefs may be explained by reference to reasons for which we hold them or by reference to non-rational 'belief-forming mechanisms'. The trouble is that neither option looks particularly promising as an account of our ordinary practice. Austin is surely right that we would often deem the request for evidence off-key when the objects of our knowledge are 'plainly in view' (or clearly audible or tangible) (Austin 1962: 115). It is not just that the request would be pedantic: we wouldn't really know how to answer it. If even our most basic perceptual beliefs were formed on the basis of reasons, we should be familiar with such requests. On the other hand, if perceptual beliefs are the effects of the operation of non-rational mechanisms, their aetiology will not be transparent to us. We should be expected simply to find ourselves believing such things as that there is a pig in front of us, with the question of why we have these sorts of belief being at best a matter of theoretical speculation. That does not seem quite right as a description of what it is like to find oneself confronted by a pig. Furthermore, it would make it hard to see why the request for evidence should be deemed off-key. That a belief is the effect of a non-rational cause is hardly a reason to regard evidence as irrelevant. If anything, the demand for evidence should be particularly to the fore in such cases.[14]

---

[13] That is not to say that one must be able to *describe* the features that go into the distinctive appearance of a pig. See Austin (1961: 84–5) and Millar (2010: 122). I am following Millar in insisting that we *exercise* (as distinct from *trying* to exercise) a perceptual-recognitional capacity only when it delivers what it is a capacity to acquire (viz. knowledge). On this, see Millar (2019: ch. 6).

[14] Moran aims to reconcile AT with our 'externalist intuitions' about perceptual beliefs by distinguishing two ways in which such beliefs may be held. He grants that 'perceptual presentations...normally compel belief in an automatic and unreflective manner' (Moran 2004: 459), yet insists that reflection brings perceptual beliefs under the control of reason. On reflection, I may either 'accede to the habit of belief', in the light of such considerations as that 'my senses are in good working order, nothing seems awry, what they appear to present to me does not conflict with anything else I believe or am attending to at the moment' or, in the presence of countervailing evidence, I may 'well not accede' to that habit. (Moran 2004: 459–60) One problem with this picture is that it would make reflective perceptual knowledge thoroughly inferential. That seems implausible. There is, in any case, familiar room for doubt as to whether the sorts of considerations Moran canvasses would provide us with adequate reasons for perceptual beliefs. But more to the point, it seems far-fetched to suggest that

In brief, while the first (broadly 'internalist') option is hard to square with the *immediacy* of perceptual knowledge, the second (broadly 'externalist') option is incompatible with the *intelligibility* of perceptual beliefs. A primitivist analysis promises to accommodate both. It does so by the simple expedient of reversing the direction of explanation that has been treated as sacrosanct in modern epistemology. In good cases, perception reveals to us (= gives us *knowledge* of) what the world is like, and it does so in a way that is typically intelligible to the perceiver herself. In such cases, the intelligibility of perceptual belief *follows* from that of perceptual knowledge. And the request for evidence is off-key precisely because perception, manifestly, gives us something better than evidence (let alone mere belief).

So much for my initial presentation of Henry's challenge. In essence, the idea is that the natural way to 'answer for' our perceptual beliefs is to explain how we know what we believe to be the case, undermining the assumption that we can only be 'answerable for' actions and attitudes that are open to a reason-giving explanation. In the following two sections I want to strengthen and develop the challenge by considering two lines of response. The first says we should resist the primitivist analysis, since the immediacy of perceptual knowledge can be accommodated by a version of internalism. The second line of response is more concessive. It grants the primitivist analysis of our ordinary practice but insists that on closer inspection AT is consistent with that analysis.

4. Non-Inferential Internalism

Many will have been itching for some time to protest that the quotation from Henry works with a false dichotomy. According to a widely held view in contemporary epistemology, perception gives us knowledge *by* giving us a distinctive sort of reason for belief. On that view, the reasons perception affords are surely as valuable as the knowledge they make possible. The view is not always framed in terms of reasons, but this may just be a terminological matter. Consider a series of claims McDowell makes in *Perception as a Capacity for Knowledge*: 'perceptual states warrant perceptual beliefs'; perceptual beliefs count 'as knowledgeable in virtue of being warranted in that way'; 'the grounds on which the belief counts as knowledgeable' in such cases are distinctive in being non-inferential (see McDowell 2011: 22–25). While our 'warrant' for perceptual beliefs (in virtue of which such beliefs 'count as knowledgeable') does not take the form of an inference, it is nevertheless 'accessible to the knower' (McDowell 2011: 17). Accordingly,

---

those considerations are *the reasons for which* ordinary perceivers, even on reflection, believe what they do about the world around them.

McDowell characterizes his view as 'internalist' (McDowell 2011: 17).[15] Connectedly, he often emphasizes that our responsiveness to the non-inferential sort of warrant afforded by 'perceptual states' constitutes an exercise of rationality.

This picture would stop Henry's challenge in its tracks. It would enable us to acknowledge the immediacy of perceptual knowledge Austin highlights without reversing the direction of explanation dear to traditional epistemology. Correlatively, if the case of perceptual belief *appears* to pose a challenge to AT, that could only reflect a confused reaction to the distinctive cogency of the reasons or 'warrant' we get from perception. The following passage elaborates this diagnosis:

> We might put this [that one does not choose to accept that p when one's experience plainly reveals to one that p] by saying there is a sense in which perceptual experience can compel belief. But because capacities for rational self-determination are at work in one's being subject to this compulsion, it does not detract from one's being in rational control of one's life. Compare the sense in which one can be compelled to accept the conclusion of a cogent argument whose premises one is unshakeably committed to. One does not sacrifice one's freedom if one acquiesces in the authority of what one recognizes as compelling reasons.
>
> (McDowell 2009: 139)

Suppose McDowell is right that being compelled to believe something by a conclusive argument is compatible with (indeed entails) the exercise of 'rational self-determination'. Does that point—or an analogue of it—apply to the case of *non-inferential* perceptual beliefs? Some critics have expressed misgivings or puzzlement about the suggestion that a belief can be rationally intelligible in the light of a perceptual experience. Barry Stroud has insisted that the content of one's experience can only provide one with a reason to believe something if one *accepts* the content (Stroud 2002: 89). Hannah Ginsborg has argued that McDowell's picture rests on a failure to distinguish between two senses of 'reason' (roughly: normative reasons vs mental states invoked in 'rationalizing explanations') (Ginsborg 2006). McDowell himself has been notably—almost ostentatiously—unconcerned about these worries, dismissing them as amounting to no more than a restatement—by 'Berkeley colleagues of Davidson's'—of Davidson's notorious insistence that 'nothing can count as a reason for holding a belief except another belief' (See McDowell 2009: 269 n. 19). To my mind, the 'Berkeley objection' is much more serious than McDowell allows (and it has no truck with Davidson's view of what counts as a reason for belief). But I think the force of the objection is best appreciated in the context of a wider question about McDowell's account that

---

[15] An interesting complication (exploration of which would take us too far afield) is that some of McDowell's remarks, in some of his writings, are naturally read as recommending a primitivist account. See, in particular, McDowell (1998b, 2009).

has not received the attention it deserves. We can distinguish two perspectives that are in play in McDowell's picture. Perceptual knowledge is supposed to be intelligible to two audiences, as it were: on the one hand, to philosophers; on the other hand, to reflective perceivers in general. The question that I think has been neglected is how the two kinds of intelligibility are related to each other, and whether they are mutually consistent.

McDowell's *philosophical* explanation of perceptual knowledge centres on his account of how 'perceptual states warrant perceptual beliefs', an account that is intended to enable us (philosophers) to see how it is that perceptual beliefs 'count as knowledge'. McDowell does not, of course, expect ordinary members of the public to make their knowledge intelligible (and to defend their claims to knowledge) by talking about 'warrant' or 'counting as knowledge' or 'perceptual states'. At the same time, it is a key commitment of McDowell's ('internalist') theory of perceptual warrant that perceptual knowledge *is* intelligible to reflective perceivers. How? What would a *reflective* explanation (as I shall call it) look like? What should an 'ordinary perceiver' be expected to say if we ask her: 'How do you know that p?'

Some terminology will be useful. Let's call the question 'How do you know that p?' HK and the question 'Why do you believe that p?' WB. And let's call an answer to HK that works *by* answering WB a *belief-centred* account of your knowledge. It seems clear enough that in the case of inferential knowledge a good answer to HK will be belief-centred in that sense. The premises of a good inference to the conclusion that p provide a reason for believing that p, and if someone comes to know that p by exploiting the inference, this means they must have been appropriately responsive to that reason. Thus 'Her car is in the drive' can be a good account of how you know your neighbour is at home. It explains your knowledge by stating the fact that constitutes your reason for believing she is at home. Call this a *reason-giving* account of your knowledge.

Does a reflective explanation of perceptual knowledge, as McDowell conceives it, take the form of a reason-giving account? For the moment let us assume the answer is 'yes'. This seems plausible, since perceptual beliefs are supposed to be open to 'rationalizing' explanations. We are supposed to make sense of such a belief by 'displaying [it] as a result of [an] operation of rationality' (McDowell 2009: 132). And a rationalizing explanation without a reason (or at least a putative reason) would surely be Hamlet without the Prince. Then what would a reason-giving account look like? Some of McDowell's readers have assumed that when perception yields non-inferential knowledge that p, one's reason for believing that p must be *that p* (a fact that is made 'available' to one, as it were, by the representational content of one's experience).[16] As we'll see in a moment,

---

[16] For accounts of perceptual knowledge that pursue this programme, see Brewer (1998) and Schnee (2016).

McDowell has rejected this reading, instead proposing that one's reason is 'I see that p.' So there are two possible answers to HK that might be thought to articulate a reason-giving account of one's perceptual knowledge that p:

(1) p.
(2) I see that p.

It is worth spelling out first why (1) can look like the natural candidate for a reflective explanation as McDowell conceives it, dovetailing with McDowell's philosophical explanation of perceptual knowledge. Consider this formulation of the philosophical explanation: '(w)hen one sees how things are...a warrant...for one's belief that things are that way is visibly *there* for one in the bit of reality that is within one's view' (McDowell 2002: 280). Add to this that the warrant in virtue of which perceptual beliefs count as knowledge is supposed to be 'accessible to the knower' (McDowell 2011: 17). Now suppose that, accessing that warrant, a knower tries to account for her belief (and in turn her knowledge) that p. It seems that (1) would be the obvious thing to say. What is labelled 'warrant' in McDowell's philosophical explanation, on this reading, is what ordinary knowers think of as a reason. As McDowell put it in *Mind and World*, perception makes it possible for the layout of reality to exert a rational influence over our thinking (McDowell 1994: 26). Thus, it seems natural to suggest, we should cite the relevant piece of reality as our reason for a perceptual belief.

Yet (1) does not ring true as a description of the way we ordinarily make our perceptual knowledge intelligible to ourselves and others. One problem is that it would fail to meet our expectations for a good answer to HK. First note that HK is routinely asked as a 'pointed question' in its own right. The possibility HK may bring into play is that you do *not* know that p but merely believe or conjecture it (Austin 1961: 78). When it is used in this way, the question invites reassurance that what you have—what your assertion that p would express—is indeed knowledge. A good answer is expected to explain your knowledge in a way that simultaneously validates your *claim* to knowledge. Now, the fact that p may well be (or even *have to* be) part of a reassuring explanation of how you know that p. Nevertheless, the bare affirmation that p seems unsatisfactory. (1) merely reiterates the claim to knowledge it is expected to make good. There is also another worry: it is not clear that in believing that p for the reason that p we could be seen to exercise our capacity for rational self-determination.[17]

Perhaps the relationship between the philosophical explanation (in terms of 'warrant') and the reflective explanation (invoking the subject's reason), then, is less close and less straightforward than that initial reading assumes. Even if the

---

[17] For discussion of this latter problem, see Roessler (2009); Giananti (2019).

warrant is provided by the perceived 'bit of reality', it is the *fact that we perceive the relevant bit of reality* that constitutes our reason for belief. That would appear to be McDowell's considered view. He writes: 'If my experience is a case of seeing how things are, the fact itself exerts a rational influence on me, but only by being experienced, and a sheer statement of the fact makes no sense as a specification of my reason for my belief' (McDowell 2006: 134).

Clearly the distinction between 'warrant' (featuring in the philosophical explanation) and 'reasons' (featuring in the reflective explanation) raises a number of questions. Here I just want to press one of them. Is a reflective explanation along the lines of (2) *compatible* with McDowell's philosophical explanation? One concern might be that (2) does not look like a *belief-centred* explanation of your knowledge. (2) simply tells us about the way in which you know that p (i.e. through vision), without so much as touching on the question of the basis of your belief that p. Thus construed, (2) would seem to be more hospitable to a primitivist analysis of our ordinary view of perceptual knowledge. But I want to set that concern to one side. McDowell protects his account from collapsing into primitivism by insisting that verbs of propositional perception express belief-independent 'perceptual states', rather than ways of knowing. 'S sees that p', on this view, does not entail that S knows or believes that p. It can therefore figure in a rationalizing explanation of why S believes that p and so provide a belief-centred account of her knowledge that p. Suppose McDowell is right about this. Even so, it is not clear that (2) expresses a reflective explanation that coheres with McDowell's philosophical explanation. If you take the fact that you see that p (in McDowell's sense) as a good reason for believing that p, you somehow need to recognize that that fact *counts in favour* of believing that p. How? The natural answer is: by recognizing that *S sees that p* entails *p*. So while (2) (on McDowell's construal) looks like a good candidate for a reason-giving explanation of your knowledge that p, that explanation will show your knowledge to be inferential, contrary to McDowell's protestations. Your understanding of the reason turns on your grasp of the soundness of a certain inference. Note that for the premise of that inference to be available to you, you not only need to *be* in a certain 'perceptual state'; you also need to have reflective *knowledge* that you are in that state.

This completes my version of the 'Berkeley objection' to non-inferential internalism. To summarize, there are two conditions a reflective explanation à la McDowell would need to satisfy: it would need (a) to cohere with McDowell's philosophical explanation and (b) to provide a credible articulation of the way ordinary knowers make their knowledge intelligible. (1) meets (a) but not (b). (2) looks promising in relation to (b) but not in relation to (a), insofar as it would make the account collapse into either primitivism or inferential internalism. Several lines of response would be worth considering. Might it be possible to rescue (2) by drawing a distinction between a reason and the 'mode' in which a reason is available to us? That is to say, could (2) be interpreted as an *indirect* indication of your reason, one that works by self-ascribing the attitude in virtue of which you are able to respond to the reason?[18] Alternatively, should we rethink the assumption that a rationalizing explanation without a reason (or presumed reason) would be Hamlet without the Prince? Could (2) count as a rationalizing explanation even if no reason for your belief is in the offing?

While I cannot pursue these questions here, I think it is clear that there are grounds for pessimism, at least insofar as the answer is supposed to help sustain AT. Since doxastic self-determination is a matter of being able to assess the probative force of our reasons for belief, perceptual beliefs will continue to look like counterexamples to AT so long as we cannot say what are the reasons for which we hold such beliefs. Furthermore, assessing the force of a reason involves reflecting on the reason. So the reason-giving fact, it seems, will not be properly 'available' to us, in the sense required for the exercise of self-determination, just in virtue of being the content of a perceptual experience. Only if you know or believe that p can you ponder the rational significance of the fact that p.

In the light of all this, it seems worth considering a more concessive response to Henry's challenge. Might AT be shown to be compatible with a primitivist view of perceptual knowledge?

5. Knowing That p as a Reason for Believing That p?

Let me start with a question. If the explanatory connection between perception and knowledge is basic and irreducible—if a good answer to 'How do you know?' will not, in the case of non-inferential perceptual knowledge, invoke any grounds for belief—what should be said about the request for a reason, in the case of a perceptual beliefs? Clearly, our reasons will not figure in the explanation of how we know what we know through perception. Furthermore, it will be possible to reverse the direction of explanation traditionally favoured by epistemologists: we will be able to shed light on why you believe that p simply by pointing out that (and how) you are able to know that p, without mentioning any reason for belief. Nevertheless, it's not clear that a request for a reason would be nonsensical or inappropriate. This observation might encourage an even more radical reversal of the traditional view. When you non-inferentially see that there is pig in front of you, you will normally be aware that you see there is a pig in front of you. Furthermore, the content of that awareness—'I can just see that there is a pig in front of me'—would be a good reason for believing that there is a pig in front of

---

[18] Compare the quote from McDowell given earlier: 'the fact itself exerts a rational influence on me, but only by being experienced' (McDowell 2006: 134). Compare also Jonathan Kvanvig's suggestion that our reason for a perceptual belief is a 'content under a certain modality', viz. 'the content-as-experienced' (as distinct from the 'content-as-believed') (Kvanvig 2009: 159).

you (since it entails the truth of that belief). Then why should you not cite that reason, were someone to pose a reason-seeking question such as 'What makes you think there is a pig in front of you?' We might go even further: why should the fact that you see and know that there is a pig in front of you not be *your reason for believing* that there is a pig in front of you?

These questions raise difficult issues. Among leading advocates of the primitivist view, opinion over them is divided. Alan Millar has proposed a view along the lines indicated by my questions. On his view, that you see and so know that p can be a reason that helps to 'sustain' your belief that p, even if it is not a consideration that leads you to *form* the belief that p.[19] (How could you rationally form the belief that p in the light of a consideration that manifestly entails that you believe that p?) By contrast, according to Stroud, when we can see or otherwise perceive things to be so, 'there is no need for something to serve as our reason for believing' them to be so; indeed, there is 'not even any room' for such a reason. (Stroud 2015: 394). Millar and Stroud are agreed, of course, that perceptual knowledge is not open to a reason-giving account. They disagree on how to deal with a reason-seeking question in cases where we have direct perceptual knowledge. For Millar, 'I can see that p' would deliver just what the question is asking for, your reason (albeit a merely 'sustaining' reason) for believing that p (though of course it would also, simultaneously, deliver a different explanation: an explanation of how you acquired the belief that p by reference, not to your reason for the belief, but to your exercising your capacity visually to tell whether p). For Stroud, the statement 'I can just see that p' would suggest that the reason-seeking question is off-key: it is simply the wrong question to ask if we are interested in your belief's credentials.

Fortunately, for my purposes here, there is no need to try to adjudicate the disagreement between Millar and Stroud. Let us suppose, for the sake of the argument, that the primitivist approach is best developed in the way Millar recommends. Suppose, in other words, that there is nothing incoherent or otherwise objectionable about the idea that the reason for which S believes that p may be the fact that S knows (more specifically, sees or hears or feels) that p. Would this enable us to reconcile primitivism about perceptual knowledge with the claim that we are active in relation to our non-inferential perceptual beliefs? I think it's true that Millar's picture would provide a *partial* response to Henry's challenge. As I presented the challenge, the idea was that the primitivist approach calls into question the connection between answerability and reasons on which the case for AT turns. In other words, primitivism was supposed to put pressure on the first arrow in my schematic representation of the route to AT:

Answerability → reasons → self-determination

---

[19] See Millar (2011: 332, 342).

If Millar's account of 'sustaining' reasons is correct, that concern turns out to be baseless. Perceptual beliefs are open to two different (yet complementary) explanations, corresponding to two different (yet complementary) ways of establishing their credentials: one invoking the exercise of perceptual-recognitional capacities, the other invoking the subject's reason for her belief. Reasons turn out, after all, to have an important part to play in our practice of holding each other answerable for perceptual beliefs.

The trouble is that if we interpret and reinstate the first arrow in this way, it becomes difficult to uphold the second arrow. Suppose you believe that p for the reason that you see and so know that p. In being responsive to that reason you are responsive to a consideration that certainly counts in favour of believing that p but also transparently implies that you do believe that p. It is not a consideration on the basis of which you could coherently make up your mind as to whether p. It displays a mind that is already made up. That is not to say that you could not (in a sense) subject that reason to critical scrutiny or that it must be wrong to think of it as a reason for which you believe that p. You could certainly 'step back' from it in the sense that you could ask whether it is in fact true that you see that p. If, on reflection, you judge that you are not able to see whether p after all, you may, as a result, discard your belief that p. Perhaps that helps to secure a sense in which your reason 'makes a difference' and so may count as a reason for which you believe that p. What you could not (coherently) do is *determine* what you believe about the question whether p on the basis of that sort of reason. To recognize that reason is to be aware of the fact that your view as to whether p has already been determined, by the operation of your visual-epistemic capacities. In the case of Millar's 'sustaining' reasons, therefore, the notion of doxastic self-determination gets no purchase. Such reasons cannot provide input to the activity of making up one's mind. They do not nourish but pre-empt deliberation.

The difficulty this creates for AT is not a phenomenological but a structural one. The point is not just that there is no experienced transition from reflecting 'I see that p' to forming the belief that p but that there can be no such transition at all, at least not a rational transition. If you are right—if you do see that p—then you already believe that p. If not, you at least take yourself to be in a state of mind that involves believing that p, so you could not coherently try to determine what you believe about p by 'acknowledging or refusing to acknowledge' the cogency of your reason. The ground of your belief is not your assessment of the probative force of your reasons for belief but your exercising relevant capacities for perceptual knowledge.

Appealing to 'sustaining' reasons, then, does not provide a fully successful answer to Henry's challenge. True, contra Henry, it would be acceptable (and not a 'weakness of intellect') to request a reason in cases in which perceptual experience reveals to us what objects are like. However, the reasons that would be relevant in such cases have a peculiar character. For one thing, our responsiveness to such reasons would not explain how we know what we know. (What gives us a reason is precisely our possession of perceptually grounded knowledge.) Connectedly, since 'sustaining' reasons entail that we have the belief they recommend, we could not coherently take our assessment of their force to determine what we believe.

6. Conclusion: Fractionating 'Activity'

Henry's challenge turns on a certain interpretation of the way in which we ordinarily make our perceptual knowledge intelligible to ourselves and others. On that interpretation, the distinctive immediacy of perceptual knowledge entails the explanatory priority of knowledge over belief: we routinely acquire beliefs about things around us *because* perception yields knowledge of what they are like (rather than because we take ourselves to have adequate reasons for them). I have considered, and presented grounds for dissatisfaction with, two ways in which defenders of AT may respond to this challenge. One argues that, contra Henry, the immediacy of perceptual knowledge is best understood as reflecting the distinctive way in which perceptual experience makes beliefs rationally intelligible. The other tries to highjack Henry's view by insisting that, even on a 'perceptual knowledge first' view, perceptual beliefs are held for reasons. Both lines of response would deserve more extended scrutiny, but I want to end by asking where the argument of this chapter leaves us.

One might wonder whether Henry's challenge really affects what advocates of AT most deeply care about. Recall Boyle's formulation quoted earlier: a person's believing something is a condition that is 'self-determined in an intelligible way: its ground lies in her accepting the rational correctness of this very condition' (Boyle 2011: 22). It might be said that this structure holds even in the case of perceptual beliefs as pictured by primitivists. Millar's account of 'sustaining reasons' might be read as a way of filling out what, in the perceptual case, 'accepting the rational correctness' of a belief comes to. Even on Stroud's view, the structure may be in place. For even if your seeing that p is not your reason for believing that p, it remains the case that if you didn't think you could see that p, you would (other things being equal) abandon your belief that p. The relevant counterfactuals may be all we need to substantiate the sense in which your understanding of your belief's credentials constitutes the 'ground' of your belief. Or at least: *a* ground. (The primary ground being your ability to perceive what is so.) The upshot of Henry's challenge may thus seem to be a relatively modest point: it is just that we should replace the definite with the indefinite article in our formulation of AT.

But I think that diagnosis is not quite right. What Henry's challenge enables us to see is that there are two distinguishable (and dissociable) things advocates of

AT care about: a stronger and a weaker thesis. The weaker thesis says that, in the case of rational believers, the subject's view about the credentials of a belief she holds plays a role in sustaining the belief. Roughly speaking, she wouldn't believe what she does if she didn't take her belief to be justified or well-founded or OK. Call this *Reflective Endorsement*. The stronger claim says that the subject's view of the merits of her belief consists of her assessment of the force of the reasons in the light of which she has made up her mind about the relevant question (or at least would be able to do so if she gave the matter some attention.) Call this *Self-determination*. We can see that advocates of AT care about the stronger claim by noting that it is *Self-determination*, not merely *Reflective Endorsement*, that is doing crucial work in two explanatory projects in which the 'activity' of belief has figured prominently in recent years. An influential suggestion that goes back to Hampshire and has been elaborated by Moran and others is that the way we *know* our current beliefs is intimately connected with our role in *determining* what we believe through the activity of deliberation or otherwise exercising capacities for doxastic self-determination.[20] Again, doxastic self-determination has been appealed to as a solution to a putative puzzle over the possibility of doxastic responsibility (how can we aptly be held responsible for attitudes that are not under our voluntary control?).[21]

While primitivism is certainly compatible with *Reflective Endorsement*, it arguably challenges *Self-determination*. It undermines the assumption that the credentials we are able to produce for our beliefs are invariably reasons our responsiveness to which is a matter of freely exercising our power of judgement. It suggests that our credentials may instead be provided by considerations that pre-empt deliberation. Where does this leave the project of articulating a generic notion of 'activity', of which intentional action and belief could be seen to represent different species? One option would be to define the generic notion in terms of the exercise of reflective endorsement rather than self-determination. Yet, it would be hard to motivate the claim that this is the only notion we need in thinking about what belongs to the 'active side' of the human mind. It seems no longer clear that there is a single line of partition between the 'active' and the 'passive'. There may be a variety of lines, corresponding to different notions of 'activity'. We may distinguish between conditions that do or do not involve the exercise of reflective endorsement, that do or do not implicate a form of self-determination, and (it seems natural to add) that are or are not voluntary. And there may be further such distinctions to draw. The blanket contrast between activity and passivity

---

[20] See Hampshire (1965); Moran (2001); Boyle (2009b). For a response to this approach that is congenial to Henry's challenge, compare Jane Heal's observation (in her comments on Moran's *Authority and Estrangement*) that 'in many cases reflecting on my view of the world takes the form of my asking myself what I know, not what I believe' (Heal 2004: 429). See also Campbell (2018) for critical discussion of the 'agentialist' approach.

[21] See, for example, Hieronymi (2008); Moran (2012); McHugh (2013).

fractionates. The lesson I would draw from Henry's challenge, then, is that the geography of the human mind is more complex than has generally been allowed by philosophers engaged in the project of partitioning the mind into active and passive sides.[22] It may be more illuminating to distinguish between different senses in which a given sort of mental condition may involve activity or passivity. For example, seeing that there is a pig in front of one may involve reflectively endorsed belief, but not an exercise of self-determination; and while it is not a voluntary activity, it is typically *informed* by the voluntary activity of paying selective attention to the pig. Perceptual belief, as so many other psychological states, may involve a characteristic mix of activity and passivity, in various senses.[23]

References

Anscombe, E. (1957), *Intention* (Oxford: Blackwells).

Austin, J. L. (1961), 'Other Minds', in *Philosophical Papers* (Oxford: Clarendon Press), 76–116.

Austin, J. L (1962), *Sense and Sensibilia* (Oxford: Oxford University Press).

Boyle, M. (2009a), 'Active Belief', in D. Hunter (ed.), *Belief and Agency* (Calgary: University of Calgary Press), 119–147.

Boyle, M. (2009b), 'Two Kinds of Self-Knowledge', *Philosophy and Phenomenological Research* 78/1: 133–64.

Boyle, M. (2011), "Making Up Your Mind' and the Activity of Reason', *Philosophers' Imprint* 11/17: 1–24.

Brewer, B. (1998), *Perception and Reason* (Oxford: Oxford University Press).

Campbell, L. (2018), 'Self-Knowledge, Belief, Ability (and Agency?)', *Philosophical Explorations* 21.3: 333–49.

Eilan, N. (1998), 'Perceptual Intentionality, Attention and Consciousness', in A. O'Hear (ed.), *Current Issues in Philosophy of Mind* (Cambridge: Cambridge University Press), 181–202.

---

[22] It is a good question how to understand Kant's place in that tradition. Advocates of AT sometimes invoke him as something of a founding father, and there are certainly passages that encourage this reading. Compare his reference to the 'freedom to think, without which reason does not exist' (Kant 1923: 14). Yet, as so often, his view turns out to be nuanced to the point of making it hard to place. Consideration of this issue would need to start from two relevant Kantian distinctions: between the understanding and theoretical reason; and between theoretical and practical reason. Exercises of all these faculties have some kind of claim to belong to the 'active side' of the human mind. What is less obvious is that the same notion of 'activity' is used in substantiating these claims. For one thing, Kant holds that theoretical reason shows a 'purer spontaneity' than the understanding, bound as the latter is by the deliverances of sensibility. For another, it is only 'the causality of our own will' (or *practical* reason—not theoretical reason, let alone the understanding) that we 'cannot think otherwise than under the idea of freedom' (Kant 1997: 57).

[23] I borrow this formulation from Eilan (1998). For illuminating comments on previous drafts and helpful suggestions for improvements, I am grateful to Lucy Campbell, Naomi Eilan, Alexander Greenberg, Jennifer Hornsby, Michael Kremer, Guy Longworth, Alan Millar, and an anonymous referee. Special thanks to the editors for their encouragement (and flexibility).

Giananti, A. (2019), 'The Weight of Facts: A Puzzle about Perception, Reasons and Deliberation', *Ratio* 32/2: 104–13.

Ginsborg, H. (2006), 'Reasons for Belief', *Philosophy and Phenomenological Research* 72/2: 286–318.

Hampshire, S. (1965), *Freedom of the Individual* (London: Chatto and Windus).

Heal, J. (2004), 'Moran's *Authority and Estrangement*', *Philosophy and Phenomenological Research* 19/2: 427–32.

Henry of Ghent (2002), '*Summae questionum ordinariarum* (art. 1)', in R. Pasnau (ed.), *The Cambridge Translations of Medieval Philosophical Texts*, iii: *Mind and Knowledge* (Cambridge: Cambridge University Press), 94–108.

Hieronymi, P. (2008), 'Responsibility for Believing', *Synthese* 161/3: 357–73.

Kant, I. (1923), 'Rezension von Schulz' "Versuch einer Anleitung zur Sittenlehre für alle Menschen, ohne Unterschied der Religion, nebst einem Anhange von den Todesstrafen"', *Akademie-Ausgabe* 8: 10–14.

Kant, I. (1997), *Groundwork of the Metaphysics of Morals*, trans. M. Gregor (Cambridge: Cambridge University Press).

Kvanvig, J. (2009), 'Assertion, Knowledge and Lotteries', in P. Greenough and D. Pritchard (eds.), *Williamson on Knowledge* (Oxford: Oxford University Press), 140–60.

McDowell, J. (1994), *Mind and World* (Cambridge, MA: Harvard University Press).

McDowell, J. (1998a), 'Having the World in View: Sellars, Kant and Intentionality. Lecture I: Sellars on Perceptual Experience', *Journal of Philosophy* 95: 431–50.

McDowell, J. (1998b), 'Knowledge by Hearsay', in *Meaning, Knowledge and Reality* (Cambridge, MA: Harvard University Press), 414–443.

McDowell, J. (2001), 'Comments on Richard Schantz, "The Given Regained"', *Philosophy and Phenomenological Research* 62/1: 181–84.

McDowell, J. (2002), 'Responses', in N. Smith (ed.), *Reading McDowell* (London and New York: Routledge), 269–305.

McDowell, J. (2006), 'Response to Jonathan Dancy', in C. Macdonald and G. Macdonald (eds.) *McDowell and his Critics* (Oxford: Blackwell), 134–41.

McDowell, J. (2009), 'Avoiding the Myth of the Given', in *Having the World in View* (Cambridge, MA: Harvard University Press), 256–72.

McDowell, J. (2010), 'Autonomy and its Burdens', *Harvard Review of Philosophy* 17: 4–15.

McDowell, J. (2011), *Perception as a Capacity for Knowledge* (Milwaukee, WI: Marquette University Press).

McHugh, C. (2013), 'Epistemic Responsibility and Doxastic Agency', *Philosophical Issues* 23: 132–57.

Millar, A. (2008), 'Perceptual-Recognitional Abilities and Perceptual Knowledge', in A. Haddock, and F. E. Macpherson (eds.), *Disjunctivism: Perception, Action, Knowledge* (Oxford: Clarendon Press), 330–47.

Millar, A. (2010), 'Knowledge and Recognition', in D. Prichard, A. Millar, and A. Haddock, *The Nature and Value of Knowledge* (Oxford: Oxford University Press), 91–188.

Millar, A. (2011), 'How Visual Perception Yields Reasons for Belief', *Philosophical Issues* 21/1: 332–51.

Millar, A. (2019), *Knowing by Perceiving* (Oxford: Oxford University Press).

Montaigne, M. de (2003), *The Complete Works*, trans. D. Frame (London: Everyman Library).

Moran, R. (2001), *Authority and Estrangement* (Princeton, NJ: Princeton University Press).

Moran, R. (2004), 'Replies to Heal, Reginster, Wilson, and Lear', *Philosophy and Phenomenological Research* 69/2: 455–72.

Moran, R. (2012), 'Self-Knowledge, 'Transparency', and the Forms of Activity', in D. Smithies and D. Stoljar (eds.), *Introspection and* Consciousness (Oxford: Oxford University Press), 211–36.

Owens, D. (2000), *Reason without Freedom* (Abingdon: Routledge).

Pasnau, R. (2017), *After Certainty* (Oxford: Oxford University Press).

Perler, D. (2006), *Zweifel und Gewissheit: Skeptische Debatten im Mittelalter* (Frankfurt am Main: Vittorio Klostermann).

Roessler, J. (2009), 'Perceptual Experience and Perceptual Knowledge', *Mind* 118/472: 1013–41.

Roessler, J. (2019), 'The Manifest and the Philosophical Image of Perceptual Knowledge', F. Stadler and C. Limbeck-Lilienau (eds.), *The Philosophy of Perception and Observation: Proceedings of the 40th International Wittgenstein Symposium* (Berlin: de Gruyter), 275–302.

Schnee, I. (2016), 'Basic Factive Perceptual Reasons', *Philosophical Studies* 173/4: 1103–18.

Stroud, B. (2002), 'Sense-Experience and the Grounding of Thought', in N. Smith (ed.), *Reading McDowell* (London and New York: Routledge), 79–91.

Stroud, B. (2009), 'Scepticism and the Senses', *European Journal of Philosophy* 17/4: 559–70.

Stroud, B. (2011), 'Seeing What Is So', in J. Roessler, H. Lerman, and N. Eilan (eds.), *Perception, Causation, and Objectivity* (Oxford: Oxford University Press), 92–102.

Stroud, B. (2015), 'Perceptual Knowledge and the Primacy of Judgement', *Journal of the American Philosophical Association* 1/3: 385–95.

Watson, G. (2004), 'The Work of the Will', in *Agency and Answerability* (Oxford: Oxford University Press), 123–57.

Williamson, T. (2000), *Knowledge and its Limits* (Oxford: Oxford University Press).

Williamson, T. (2009), 'Replies to Critics', in P. Greenough and D. Pritchard (eds.), *Williamson on Knowledge* (Oxford: Oxford University Press), 281–384.

Index

Since the index has been created to work across multiple formats, indexed terms for which a page range is given (e.g., 52–53, 66–70, etc.) may occasionally appear only on some, but not all of the pages within the range.

ability/skill 6, 12, 39, 45, 55, 60, 145–52, 157–9, 164–5, 171–2, 175, 177, 224–5, 309, 315–16, 325
action 1, 4, 7–12, 30–1, 34, 43, 45–6, 50–6, 93–4, 99, 129–42, 145–54, 156, 158–9, 163–5, 179, 181–95, 207, 209, 225, 237–8, 241, 248, 251–2, 268–9, 272, 274–5, 310–11, 314–15, 317, 326–7
analysis 2, 22, 25–6, 39, 42, 58–9, 61, 77–8, 104, 131–2, 140–1, 156, 210, 221–2, 229–30, 313, 315–17, 321
Anscombe E. 30–1, 147–8, 152, 312, 314
anti-luminosity 2–3, 38, 47–8, 62, 121–2
artificial intelligence 9–10, 39–40, 183–4, 187–8
assertion 1, 7–9, 12, 30, 37, 39, 121–2, 129–30, 203–4, 212–17, 237, 277, 279–80, 320
Auriol P. 71–2, 81, 83–6
Austin J. L. 312, 314, 316, 318, 320
Aveling F. 71–2, 77, 79–81
Ayer A. J. 26–7

belief 26, 28, 30–5, 40–5, 47, 49–64, 71, 77, 79–81, 93–5, 100, 106, 111–12, 129–31, 133–5, 139–42, 145, 148–9, 158–61, 163–4, 171, 178–9, 181–2, 184–5, 188–9, 195–6, 201–2, 205–7, 209–12, 221–7, 231, 233–4, 237–44, 246–55, 261–3, 266–7, 270–5, 277, 279–81, 284–304, 308–27

Comesaña J. 260, 262–5, 268, 270, 272–6, 279–81

Dubray C. A. 71–2, 77–9, 81, 88
Duhem-Quine thesis 12–13, 222, 230–1
Dummett M. 36–8
Duns Scotus J. 10–11, 71–2, 81
disposition 6–8, 55, 60–2, 77, 86, 93–4, 100, 157–8, 210–11, 268–9, 271–3, 275–81, 315–16

E = K thesis 4–6, 222, 227–8, 231–2, 239
Edgington D. 37–8

emotion 46, 129–30, 133–7, 140–3, 245–6, 275–6
epistemic injustice 9–10, 13, 216–17
Evans G. 33, 36
evidence 1, 4–8, 12–14, 24–5, 36, 38–40, 47–8, 54, 57, 59–62, 75, 79–81, 84, 93, 97–8, 109–10, 114, 116–19, 122, 129, 132–3, 137, 139–41, 146–7, 150–1, 153, 156, 158–60, 162, 221–2, 226–34, 239–40, 246–7, 249–52, 254–5, 271–4, 278–81, 284–5, 287–9, 291–6, 298, 300–1, 303–4, 309–10, 312, 316–17
excuse 7–8, 60–1, 237–8, 241–2, 252–4
explanation 4–5, 8, 11–14, 26, 34–5, 40, 77–8, 122, 131, 133–5, 138–41, 149–50, 153, 156–7, 193, 202, 211, 214, 227–8, 248–65, 276, 280, 284–5, 287–97, 299–301, 314–15, 317–24
externalism/internalism 10, 13, 30, 32–5, 40, 60, 239–41, 250, 252–5, 317, 321–2

factivity 2–4, 8, 11–12, 25–6, 35, 42, 46, 63, 93–6, 111–12, 116, 119, 129, 134–5, 141–2, 145–9, 151–4, 157–8, 165, 171–2, 184–5, 187–8, 238, 240–1, 250–1, 253, 255, 260–3, 265–6, 268–70, 272–9
fallibilism/infallibilism 12, 57–9, 97–106, 111, 208–9, 211, 216, 297
Fricker M. 9–10, 204–5, 216–17, 243–5, 248
Fricker E. 8, 212–13, 238–9

Gettier 2, 11, 22, 39, 41–2, 49, 58, 93, 142, 158–64, 222–3, 301–2

Henry of Ghent 308–9, 313

inquiry 9, 49, 180–205, 207, 229
intention 11–12, 30–1, 35, 50–1, 55–6, 84–6, 106–8, 130–1, 134, 139–41, 145–59, 164–5, 310–11, 314–15, 326–7

justification 1, 4–9, 13, 22, 25–6, 39, 59–60, 63, 93, 184–5, 226–7, 237–8, 240–3, 246–51, 253, 279, 286, 288, 295–6, 314

know-how 12, 147–51, 154–9, 161–5
knowledge-first 1–13, 21–3, 30–1, 38–40, 46–9, 51–2, 54–6, 59–60, 88–9, 112, 141, 147, 149–51, 171–2, 221–3, 225–9, 231–4, 237–42, 247, 249, 252–6, 272–3
Kraemer's puzzle 154–5, 157–8
Kripke S. 28, 56

McDowell J. 24–5, 33, 36, 302, 308, 311–13, 317–22
McGrath M. 260, 262–5, 268, 270, 272, 276
mental state 2–4, 8, 11, 21–2, 34–5, 40, 42–5, 53, 71, 77–8, 80–1, 86–9, 93–6, 111–12, 116, 129–32, 134–6, 139, 145–9, 151–4, 157–9, 165, 171–2, 178–9, 183–5, 187–9, 225, 240–1, 254, 288, 318–19
mindreading 4, 10, 12, 40, 42, 44–7, 49, 54, 130–1, 145–7, 151–4, 158, 165

new evil demon 240
norm 1, 6–8, 10, 12, 30, 37, 39, 51–3, 55, 59–63, 134, 138–9, 203–4, 212–17, 231, 237, 254–5, 272–3, 284
Nozick R. 301–2
Nyāya 11, 93–9, 101–4, 106–8, 110–14, 117–18, 120–1

Ockham G. 10–72, 81, 86–7

perception 9, 14, 24–5, 34, 43, 46, 48–9, 59, 74, 81–5, 95, 100, 114–15, 130–2, 135, 142–3, 160–1, 205–6, 227–9, 232, 244, 246, 277–302, 309, 312–23, 325
practical knowledge 147–9, 151–3
presence/presentiality 10–11, 62, 71–2, 76, 81–6, 88–9, 113, 116, 118, 120–1, 186
probability 1, 4–5, 8, 13–14, 38, 48–9, 57, 60, 186–208, 271, 273–4, 280, 284, 287, 289–90, 296, 299, 302–3
progress (scientific) 12–13, 221–3, 225–6, 232, 234

rationality 1, 7–8, 13–14, 30, 45–6, 54, 59, 61–2, 116–17, 227–8, 237, 244, 246–7, 250–6, 269–76, 278, 281, 284, 286, 288, 291–2, 295–6, 299–301, 303–4, 317–20
realism/antirealism 10, 12–13, 23, 36–8, 72–3, 86, 107–8, 135, 221–3, 226–31, 233–4
reason 4–9, 13–14, 39–43, 45–7, 52–5, 78–80, 82–3, 96, 110, 115–16, 130–5, 139–40, 238, 241, 243, 247–56, 260–82, 284, 302, 308–27
reasoning 50, 52–5, 93–4, 101–2, 109–10, 117–18, 131, 205, 208–9
responsibility 145–6, 165, 251–2, 255–6, 308–10, 325–6
Russell B. 26–7, 163, 165, 287

safety 2–3, 40, 51–2, 160–1, 179, 209–11, 278
skepticism 4–6, 8, 88, 119, 165, 245, 287, 294, 296–7, 315
Schroeder M. 208, 260, 265–8, 270–1, 273–4, 277–81
science 12–13, 22, 39–40, 56–9, 72, 80, 133–5, 221–34, 280–2
Searle 7–8
Sellars 24
shared world 10–11, 44–8, 54, 134–8, 140–1
Śrīharṣa 11, 94–9, 101–23
Stroud B. 1, 5–6, 308–9, 313, 315, 318–19, 323, 325

truth 8, 22, 27–8, 31, 36–40, 42, 45, 49, 53, 56, 59, 63, 71, 79–80, 87–8, 93, 95–6, 116, 129, 139–40, 142, 149–50, 172, 181–2, 187–9, 206, 208, 210, 213, 221–3, 226, 232, 238, 260–2, 268, 279–80, 285, 287–90, 298–9, 301–3, 322–3

Udayana 94–5, 97–102, 104–6, 111–12
Unger P. 4–5, 39, 262

vagueness 38
value 13–14, 39, 54, 87, 133–4, 175, 177–8, 181–3, 185–9, 208, 211, 216–17, 224, 284, 289–91, 296–304, 309–10, 314–16

Wilson C. 23–5, 30, 36, 80
Wodehouse H. 71–7, 79, 81